Be Ye Transformed

by

Chuck & Nancy Missler

KHW

The King's *High* Way Ministries, Inc.

Be Ye Transformed

© Copyright 1996 by Nancy Missler

Eighth printing, August 2004

Published by The King's High Way Ministries, Inc.
P.O. Box 3111
Coeur d'Alene ID 83816
www.kingshighway.org

ISBN: 0-9753593-2-0

All Scripture quotations are from the King James Version of the Holy Bible.

Cover design by David Clemons, Coeur d'Alene, Idaho

PRINTED IN THE UNITED STATES OF AMERICA.

Dedication

This book is dedicated to the hurting members of the Body of Christ.

It is our prayer that God will use this book "to heal the broken-hearted, to preach deliverance to the captives, recovering of sight to the blind, and to set at liberty them that are bruised...."

Luke 4:18

A Special Thanks

To our precious Savior, Friend, Counselor, Comforter and Lord, who is experientially teaching us all these principles; and in the process, setting us free to walk in His *Love* and *Truth*.

"I have not hid Thy righteousness within my heart; I have declared Thy faithfulness and Thy salvation: I have not concealed Thy *Lovingkindness* and Thy *Truth* from the great congregation." (Psalm 40:10)

Table of Contents

Introduction (By Chuck Missler) 9

Section One: Renewed Like the Eagle 23
    Chapter One: How Do Our Lives Become Transformed? 25
    Chapter Two: Mind Renewal.. 41

Section Two: Light on Top of a Candle 61
    Chapter Three: What Is Our Mind?.. 63
    Chapter Four: Satan's Ways to Keep Us Double-minded 85

Section Three: Seven-fold Spirit of God 99
    Chapter Five: The Mind of Christ (Part 1) 101
    Chapter Six: The Mind of Christ (Part 2).............................. 117
    Chapter Seven: The Mind of Christ (Part 3) 139

Section Four: The Temple of God... 159
    Chapter Eight: Blueprint of a Believer................................ 161
    Chapter Nine: New Spirit, Heart and Will 173
    Chapter Ten: Soul and Body.. 189

Section Five: Searching the Hidden Chambers.......................... 207
    Chapter Eleven: The Hidden Chambers (Part 1)..................... 209
    Chapter Twelve: The Hidden Chambers (Part 2) 233
    Chapter Thirteen: How God's Mind Works In Us 249

Section Six: Setting the Prisoners Free 291
    Chapter Fourteen: How Do We Renew Our Minds?.................... 293
    Chapter Fifteen: Inner Court Ritual.................................... 309
    Chapter Sixteen: Results of a Renewed Mind......................... 337

Section Seven: Appendices 351
    History of the Subconscious.. 353
    Greek Words for Mind.. 357
    Hidden Chambers 361
    Knowing God Loves Me 363
    Bibliography... 365
    Glossary.. 369

"I beseech you therefore, brethren, by the mercies of God, that ye present your bodies a living sacrifice, holy, acceptable unto God, which is your reasonable service.

And be not conformed to this world: but *be ye transformed* by the renewing of your mind, that ye may prove what is that good, and acceptable, and perfect, will of God."

Romans 12:1-2

Introduction
(By Chuck Missler)

Nancy and I have been labeled "psychoheretics." From the bitter controversies which erupted from the first printing of this book, we clearly have struck some very sensitive nerves! Because of the surprisingly unscholarly (and unChristian) attacks, I felt compelled to add this tutorial introduction for this subsequent printing. Not surprisingly, at the root of these difficulties lies a controversy of major proportions.

Fortunately, we are deeply indebted to the encouraging ground swell of supporting letters from our readers, the continued flood of case histories of repaired marriages and healed lives, as well as the scholastic confirmations from Biblical authorities, for their validation and their continuing encouragement. Clearly, there continues to be much personal pain among Christian believers. Part of this tragedy is that much of it endures because *we do not appropriate the resources that God has given us*.

Two Extremes Among Christians

Compounding all this is much well-intentioned advice which condemns the unfortunate recipient into one of two extremes, each of which leave them without an effective remedy. On the one hand, many orthodox Christians believe and teach that all we need to do in order to deal with our hurts, fears, and painful past experiences, is to simply appropriate the fact that Christ died for our sins and has risen from the dead to live His Life out in us. They teach that all we are supposed to do is just forgive and love others because of God's Love and forgiveness to us. Unfortunately, these can be just superficial platitudes which often fail to appropriate, in practical day-to-day, moment-by-moment operational terms, the remedies which God has provided and thus they deny the realities of our personal architecture. Some feel that the idea of "hidden chambers" or a "secret place" where we hide and bury our hurts, fears and insecurities is a purely Freudian idea and therefore must be discarded.

At the other extreme, we encounter Christian psychologists and psychiatrists—more specifically, psychotherapists—who believe and teach that the only way we can deal with our hurts, past experiences and fears is by going through years of in-depth therapy, inner healing, visualization, healing of the memories, etc. The spiritual bankruptcy of these secular nostrums deny the real root causes of our problems. They attempt to deal with the symptoms, denying the real source of our difficulties which is *sin*.

Freud's Deceptive Legacy

Freud's controversial ideas have had vast implications far beyond the field of psychiatry and psychotherapy. His ideas have had a major impact in our art, entertainment, education, and political conduct—and in shaping the dominant world view which is so pervasive in our modern society. He is one of David Breese's "Seven Men Who Rule the World from Their Graves."[1] The prevalence of some of his ideas among "Christian counselors" has also led to tragic consequences within the Body of Christ.

Sigmund Freud was born on May 6, 1856. As a creative physician specializing in treating the mentally ill, he developed a comprehensive theory concerning the psychological structure and functioning of the human mind. One can't deal with any model of the human personality without putting into perspective the impact of Freud upon our prevailing conceptions and even on our common vocabulary. We speak of being "egocentric," or that someone is an "egomaniac;" and we often experience the "Freudian slip," attributing to a slip-of-the-tongue some hidden, subconscious agenda.

The Subconscious

Freud recognized, as did many before him, that the complex of mental activities within an individual precede without his conscious awareness. He believed his own complicated set of early memories were decisive in determining many of his later decisions.[2] Often, hidden experiences seemed to influence subsequent behavior, defying conscious, deliberate, rational intent. Freud distinguished among different levels of consciousness. Behind a person's immediate field of awareness there seemed to lay deeper levels of preconscious and subconscious activity.[3]

In his early practice, Freud became convinced that aberrant behavior in the present could be traced to experiences in the past, even as a very young child. It appeared, at first, that behind the apparent neuroses of a patient was some kind of aberrant sexual practice. It was later that even Freud began to have doubts about what his patients had said.[4] He began to realize that most of the seductions his patients had reported had, in fact, never taken place. He concluded that they were simply attributing their symptoms to imaginary traumata which they themselves had created in fantasies.[5] (It is interesting that these notions continue to dominate some of the destructive psychological fads of today, such as "repressed memory syndrome," and others.)[6]

It was Freud's explorations and conjectures that led to many of the present concepts of psychoanalysis. The attribution of the origin of neurotic symptoms to conflicts that have been removed from consciousness through a process called repression is now a major tenet of psychoanalytic theory derived from Freud and his followers.

Freud's Model of the Self

As Freud continued to develop his ideas, he saw the human personality as consisting of three somewhat overlapping components: the *id*, the *ego*, and the *superego*.

The id, to Freud, was the repository of the dark, elemental components of the human personality—a caldron of seething emotions—the passions, irrationalities, and, primitive elements of human nature.

Superimposed upon the id was the ego—the entity through which the id interacted with the outside world. It formulated the personality, selectively accepting and rejecting the emergent emanations from the id.

Above these components was the superego—something like, but not quite, the conscience. In a somewhat judgmental sense, the superego brought into consciousness the ideas of guilt or approval. The ego then reacts to the moral dictates of the superego, rebelling against them or submitting to them. Behind these entities were a pair of instincts—the life instinct and the death instinct—that produce the energies accumulated in the id. For Freud, the libido was the great reality: the life force, broadly associated with the sexual instinct. He saw this as the universal motivation for all things.

This was the Freudian picture of the human inner being that moved into the consciousness and table talk of our present world. We all have found ourselves alluding to his concepts and vocabulary at one time or another.

Freud created these arbitrary delineations in his own mind and then superimposed them on the personalities attributed to his patients. Although his data came from unconfirmed and unconfirmable testimony of privately interviewed patients, fascination with his ideas spread throughout his world and has continued into ours.

However, the professional class, even then, was less convinced and analyzed him to the point of repudiation. Although the outside world was captured by his titillating theories, his contemporaries, including Eugene Bleuler, Carl G. Jung, Alfred Adler, and others broke away from him.

Even to this day, recent articles have continued to cast serious doubts on the efficacy of psychoanalysis and its related arts.[7]

Social Implications

With all of its confusing contradictions, the influences of Freud have had a profound and subversive effect on the thinking of our present age. He changed man's view of himself and his nature. Perhaps the most critical influence Freud has had upon society was his invention of a new determinism by which man does what he does and becomes what he becomes. He saw the libido as the prime mover. This legacy has dragged sex into the streets, our homes, into every nook and cranny of our lives—and has also filled our psychiatrists' couches. Sexual determinism, however, is a fascinating, titillating *lie*.

"Even the ancient Greeks recognized that *Eros* was prone to uncontrollable excess, destructiveness and violence. *Eros* was the blaze that burned Troy and left its plains strewn with corpses, the flame kindled by Paris and Helen's illicit passion. The Greeks understood that cultural and social controls were necessary to limit the force of sex and harness its energies. Sexual taboos, institutions like marriage, emotions like guilt and shame, even reason itself were all devices for clipping *Eros'* wings. Philosophers and tragedians may have debated whether these devices ultimately could work, but no one seriously believed that *Eros* could be "liberated" from social checks and limits and left to the individual alone."[8]

Then, with an assist from Freud, we liberated *Eros*. We dismissed traditional social restraints as repressive impediments and puritanical inhibitions which stifled the expression of our authentic selves. Guilt and shame were discarded as hurtful and hypocritical; no-fault divorce reduced marriage to a lifestyle choice as changeable as a car or a job; reason was dismissed as the instrument of repression and neurosis.

The results of this novel experiment? We have poured our youthful energies into the sinking sands of time. The combination of Darwinism, values relativism, and the physiological determinism of Freud has plunged our society into moral free fall.[9] Venereal plagues, illegitimacy, weakening of the family, debasement of women, vulgarization of sex in popular culture, chronic dissatisfaction with sexual identities—all testify to the costs of failing to restrain *Eros'* dark power.

Political Implications

Freud's notions have also been picked up in an ominous way by totalitarian society. Paul Johnson notes, "The notion of regarding dissent as a form of mental sickness, suitable for compulsory hospitalization, was to blossom in the Soviet Union into a new form of political repression."[10]

It is terrifying to see the same signs on our own domestic horizon with enforced insanity of "political correctness." It is frightening to note that those who harbor dissenting views of independence, traditional family values, and other Biblically based attitudes are now being labeled as "extremist nuts," "kooks," and the like.

David Breese suggests, "In giving us the determinism of libido, Freud did at least two things. First, he caused the world to concentrate on libido to the point of addiction. Second, he legitimized the creation of determinisms, thereby opening the door for the invention of the plethora of other determinisms that are being concocted in the minds of the would-be pied pipers of our time."[11]

The Fallacies

What is the determinism that really makes man what he is? The most significant force moving through history is not Darwin's natural selection, Marx's economic determinism, or Freud's libido. It is the *Will of God*. There is nothing else of significance in life except that: God and His perfect Will for man. The Apostle Paul points out, "We can do nothing against the truth, but for the truth."[12]

The key to all reality is the intelligent human will responding affirmatively to the Will of God. One of the primary insights is given to us by God Himself:

And God said, 'Let us make man in our image, after our likeness; and let them have dominion over the fish of the sea, and over the fowl of the air, and over the cattle, and over all the earth, and over every creeping thing that creepeth on the earth.' So God created man in His own image, in the image of God created He them; male and female created He them.

Genesis 1:26-27

Profound beyond description is the assertion that we are images of the Creator of the Universe. Man is not merely a collection of psychological forces. Neither are we a subspecies of the animals. Freud was one of the great deceivers, confusing millions as to the nature of man and ignoring the nature of God. One of the productive discoveries is that the architecture of man is the Temple designed for the worship of, and fellowship with, God. (This will be explored in Chapter Eight.)

Freud concentrated on himself to the exclusion of the Being by whose creative power and present grace we are able to continue our existence. God Himself has given us His map of our inner being in the architecture of the Temple. This was introduced in *The Way of the Agape*, the first book in this series. *Be Ye Transformed* will explore the practical implications of this architecture.

The believing Christian avoids the deceits and conceits of Freud. He recognizes that the soul of man grows out of the interaction between the body and spirit and is the means by which man communicates to the outside world. Through faith in Jesus Christ, the believer possesses the indwelling source of God's life from whom he is possessed with joy, fulfillment, and victory.

Psychology's Frustration

The field of psychology is ultimately doomed to frustration since it cannot penetrate beyond the psyche (soul).[13] It is impossible to infer the inner structure of man from only observing his external behavior. This is just as futile as attempting to ascertain, from its external behavior, the internal architecture of software running on a computer since it is also a self-modifying entity operating inside an infinite state machine.[14]

Furthermore, while psychology recognizes the destructive and corrosive role of guilt in the human psyche, it can only address the symptoms, not the cause. The root problem is *sin*. Values relativism denies sin's existence. Psychology ignores its reality.

Only God can deal with sin—and He already has. That is the core issue in the entire Biblical drama: His redemption of a fallen race through the ultimate love affair; with a comprehensive reprieve, written in blood on a wooden cross erected in Judea almost two thousand years ago. Have you availed yourself of its healing and its liberation from bondage in your life? This is what this book is hopefully intended to facilitate.

The Controversy over the Subconscious

In their zeal to distance ourselves from the deceits of Freud, many people are confused both about the existence of what is commonly called the subconscious[15] and its role. Many Christians, driven by their concern about the preoccupation of psychologists with the subconscious, mistakenly deny its existence, ignore its Biblical basis, and thus fail to avail themselves of an essential cleansing.

Because the writings of Sigmund Freud have had much influence on our daily vocabulary and familiar idioms, many erroneously assume that the subconscious itself is also a Freudian concept. While we in no way accept Freud's peculiar views and obsessions with the subconscious, we do believe that our memory does work below the conscious level. In their rejection of the deceptions of Freudianism, many Christians assume that the concept of the "subconscious," or "unconscious" is also fallacious. However, the recognition of the subconscious pre-dates Freud by over 1500 years! (A brief history of the subconscious has been included as an Appendix.)

Personal Experience

How often have you attempted to recall a once-familiar name, and yet have been frustrated by it's remaining just beyond your direct recall? And then, a short time later, you find it suddenly emerge in your conscious memory? This common phenomenon simply demonstrates that there is a portion—apparently the major portion—of our memory which operates below the conscious level.

Most people, especially those who have devoted themselves to creative en-terprises and problem solving, have also discovered an astonishingly effective technique to resolve an unusually difficult or illusive problem. After reviewing all of the relevant facts and factors impacting some troubling dilemma, they then deliberately abandon the direct attack, and subsequently indulge in some alterna-tive, absorbing, diversion: a sports activity, a hobby, or more commonly, a good night's sleep, only to have the difficulty clearly resolved upon waking. Clearly, there are powerful information processing resources at work below our direct, conscious level. We usually call this region of "memory," the subconscious, the unconscious, or hidden memory. (These terms will be used interchangeably in this book.)

Biblical Basis

The Bible, of course, is the ultimate validation of any truth. The Bible alludes many times to parts of our memory and experience that are not directly accessible to our conscious mind.

In Psalm 19:12-13, David asks God, "Who can understand his errors? Cleanse Thou me from secret [covered up, closed up, hidden] faults...let them not have dominion over me...." From whom are these faults secret? God? I think not. Ourselves? Yes, this is what David is imploring God to do; to show him and cleanse him from his *secret* faults. These are things that we have hidden away either out of our ignorance or our simply not wanting to deal with them. Only God, by His Spirit, can show us and cleanse us from them.

The Amplified Bible calls these faults "hidden and *unconscious*." Its publishers state in their foreword, "...amplification helps the English reader comprehend what the Hebrew and Greek listener understood as a matter of course."[16]

Psalm 139:23-24 follows this same line of expression, "Search me, O God, and know my heart; try me, and know my thoughts; and see if there be any *wicked way in me*...." Again David is asking God to expose any "secret, unknown faults" in him, so he can confess and repent of them. And Psalm 51:6 states, "Behold, Thou desirest truth in the inward parts; and in the *hidden part* Thou shalt make me know wisdom." Here, David refers not only to "inward parts," but also to "hidden parts" of our internal architecture. What is he referring to, if there really is no *hidden place* or *secret place*?

And in 2 Corinthians 10:3-6, what are the "strongholds" that Paul is talking about? Are these strongholds simply conscious attitudes and physical behaviors that we have? Or, could these also be the secret, hidden faults that David asks God to cleanse him of in Psalm 19:12? The writer of the Epistle to the Hebrews also refers to a "root of bitterness" (Hebrews 12:15). We understand that a "root" is something hidden or covered up. Often we are not even aware that a "root of bitterness" has sprung up in us, until God, by His Spirit, points it out.

Then, of course, there is the undeniably clear Scripture in Jeremiah 17:9 which tells us that not only is our human heart "deceitful above all things, and desperately [incurably] wicked," but, "who can know it?" No one but God can understand the wickedness of our hearts. In other words, there are things in our hearts that are hidden and secret, *even to us*!

Daniel 2:30, Psalm 44:21 and 1 Corinthians 14:25 also present this same line of expression. God is the only One who "knoweth the secrets of our hearts" because He is the only One who can see, search and try our hearts.[17]

Among other Scriptures that hint at covered, closed and hidden things that we are not even aware of are Deuteronomy 7:20, Acts 8:21-23, Psalm 16:7 and Ezekiel 14:1-6.

The Hidden Chambers

The actual word "subconscious" or "unconscious" is not used in our translations. The Hebrew word found in Scripture is "*cheder*," which means the innermost part, the hidden chambers, the inward part or the secret place. Of the over 38 Scriptures that use the word *cheder*, over half refer to a secret, hidden, innermost chamber or parlour. Here are a few examples.

Proverbs 20:27, "The spirit of man is the candle of the Lord, searching all the *inward parts* (*cheder*) of the belly." (Why would the spirit search our inward parts, if not to reveal hidden sin in us, to us?);

Proverbs 18:8, "The words of a talebearer are as wounds, and they go down into the *innermost parts* (*cheder*) of the belly." (If there is no "secret place" or "hidden chambers," where is this "innermost part"? This is also quoted in Proverbs 26:22).

Proverbs 20:30, "The blueness of a wound cleanseth away evil; so do stripes the *inward parts (cheder)* of the belly." (What does God mean, if we don't really have an innermost part or hidden chambers where evil can hide?).

And, Proverbs 24:4, Only "by [intimate] knowledge *(daath)* shall the chambers (*cheder*) be filled with all precious and pleasant riches." (Intimate knowledge of God happens internally—in our soul. How then, can these "chambers" be filled with "all precious and pleasant riches," if there really is not an "innermost part"?)

Psalm 51:6 seems to follow this same line of thinking. David declares "...in the *hidden part* Thou shalt make me to know wisdom." (God wants this hidden part—this secret place—cleansed of "secret faults" and then filled with all precious and pleasant riches, i.e., God's Wisdom.)

Among other provocative Scriptures that use the word *cheder* are Ezekiel 8:12, Deuteronomy 32:25, Proverbs 7:27 and 2 Chronicles 18:24.

Destructive Roots Must Be Dealt With

Jesus, of course, must be at the center of any true healing.[18] Yet if we deny the reality of our "hidden chambers," and don't allow Him to expose and deal with the *root causes* of our problems (because we deny their existence, and simply concern ourselves with the *symptoms*), then those symptoms will return again and again.

(We are *not* saying that everything we think and feel has a hidden, root cause, but we *do* believe that much of what makes us bitter and angry and fearful, does.)

As a result of seeing our symptoms return, we end up discouraged, depressed and convinced that God doesn't love us, because He hasn't answered our prayers— He hasn't taken these things from us. And of course, Satan rejoices!

Similar results can occur with the Christian psychologist's or psychiatrist's viewpoint. Many of these "Christian" counselors and doctors do <u>not</u> put Jesus in the center as the only true Healer of our souls, but rather the therapy itself. All they are doing in their counseling sessions then, is re-programming those same negative hurts, fears and insecurities right back into our hidden chambers where they become even more tenacious strongholds for the enemy. As a result, we again end up discouraged, depressed and convinced that God doesn't love us, because he hasn't answered our prayers—He hasn't taken these things away from us. And once again, Satan rejoices!

In order to genuinely *walk in the Truth*, we must also experience truth *inwardly*. "Behold, Thou desirest truth in the inward parts, and in the hidden part Thou shalt make me know wisdom." (Psalm 51:6)

Thoughts and feelings in our life that are "not of faith" and that we don't immediately "deal with" and give over to God, automatically get pushed down into our *hidden chambers* (the secret recesses of our soul) and eventually become a *hidden* motivation for our actions. All of our fears, insecurities, memories, etc., that we bury, thinking "no one will see and no one will know," can ultimately end up controlling and directing our lives and forcing us to *live a lie*.

As God begins to teach us how to "take every thought captive," we'll see that we can get free of, not only our *conscious* negative thoughts and emotions, but also all the *hidden, secret* doubts, fears and insecurities that we have buried deep within our souls and that have motivated us for most of our lives.

By His Mind operating in us, God can penetrate deep within these hidden chambers of our souls and not only expose, cleanse and heal these areas, but also root out the strongholds of the enemy. God wants "truth in the inward parts." He wants us freed and unencumbered to serve Him.

This book is dedicated to exploring the authority and power of God that He has *already* given us to literally "free us" from anything that "is not of faith," so that we <u>can</u> walk in God's Love and Truth.

The Solution

We need to understand how to allow the Spirit of God to work in our *whole person*, not only in the conscious part of us where we experience many of the "symptoms" of our problems, but also in the "hidden, secret part" of us where many of the roots of our problems lie. If we don't allow the Spirit of God to point out the roots, many of our symptoms will return again and again (as in the two above ways of thinking).

What is needed in the Christian body is first, *to put Jesus in the center as our only true healer.* Because only Jesus can see our hearts; only He can show us the real "root causes" of our problems; only He can remove them "as far as the east is from the west"; only He can align our feelings with our choices and make us genuine; and only He can give us the Love we need to go on as if nothing has happened.[19]

And second, *to allow Jesus, by His Spirit to expose, cleanse and heal our hidden and secret faults*, so that God can completely remove these roots from us and we can truly be healed.

At this point, we <u>will</u> be able to let *Christ live His Life out* through us and we <u>will</u> be able to *genuinely love and forgive others* as Christ would have us do. We needn't wait, by the way, until *all* our problems and hurts are dealt with before God can live His Life out through us. If we can choose to give over to God, any root of bitterness, unforgiveness, unbelief, fear, (whatever God shows us), then His Life and His Love will flow through us in a new and powerful way. As a result, we'll experience an intimacy with Him that we haven't known before—experiencing more of His Love not only for ourselves, but "unconditionally" for others.

So, as Christians we don't have to work at cleaning up our *past* as psychology teaches, but simply giving God permission to expose, in the *present*, the whole man—not only our conscious sins, but also our secret faults. Once He brings up the roots and they are dealt with as He would have us to do, then He will remove them "as far as the east is from the west" and we truly will be healed.

Be Ye Transformed

Romans 12:1-2 is the key: "I beseech you brethren, by the mercies of God, that ye present your bodies a living sacrifice, holy, acceptable unto God, which is your reasonable service. And be not conformed to this world, but *be ye transformed* by the renewing of your mind, [so] that ye may prove what is that good, and acceptable, and perfect will of God." (emphasis added)

The question becomes, *how* do we do this? How are we transformed into God's Image? Again, Romans 12:2 gives us the answer. It says the only way we can be *transformed* is by the constant *renewing of our minds*.

Only by learning how to *put off* the limitations and presuppositions (the garbage) in our own thinking and *put on* the Mind of Christ can we experience the freedom to drop our masks and facades, be transparent in sharing our needs and genuinely show forth Christ.

Jesus promises in John 8:32, "You shall know the truth and the truth shall make [set] you free." God knows how desperately we Christians need to be "set free:" set free, first of all, from ourselves, from our circumstances, from others' responses, and from Satan's deceptions. Only by renewing our minds—putting off the garbage in our thinking and putting on the Mind of Christ—will we ever enjoy this freedom in our lives. The incredible ability to throw away our self-protective defenses and just be who God created us to be in the first place.

Overview

The first book in the King's High Way Series, *The Way of Agape,* explored what God's Love is and how it differs from human love; what it means to love God; and, how we are to love others.

Be Ye Transformed explores what God's Truth is and how we can be "set free" to live it, what the Mind of Christ is, and what it means to renew our minds so that we *can* be transformed into God's Image.

Remember, Acts 17:11: Be like the Bereans, and "receive the Word of God with all openness of mind, yet search the Scriptures daily to prove whether those things are so." Also,

"Prove all things; hold fast that which is good."

1 Thessalonians 5:21

It is our earnest prayer that this book will prove of practical help in *your own* Christian walk.

This is really Nan's book; just as we did in *The Way of Agape*, let's let her tell it her own way.

In His Name!
Chuck Missler,
Beneficiary at large

Endnotes:

1. Dave Breese, *Seven Men Who Rule the World from the Grave*, Moody Press, Chicago IL, 1990. This is "must read" book from one of the towering Christian communicators of our time and a dear personal friend.

2. Early Background: Sigmund Freud was born on May 6, 1856, in Freiberg, Moravia. From his father's previous marriage, he had two older brothers as old as his mother. Among his younger brothers and sisters was a younger Julius who died in infancy, leaving Sigmund with guilt feelings (having harbored evil thoughts toward him as a rival for his mother's love). He later viewed the death as a fulfillment of his evil thoughts, thereby beginning a life-long tendency to self-reproach. Years later he wrote that he had been sexually aroused by seeing his mother naked, an event to reverberate years afterward in Three Essays on the Theory of Sexuality. On another occasion he recollected having deliberately urinated in his parent's bedroom at the age of seven, prompting his father to remark: "That boy will never amount to anything." Beginning at an early age, allusions to this scene, accompanied by demonstrations of "accomplishments and successes," constantly occurred in his dreams. Anti-Semitism also played a part. A powerful memory destined to haunt Freud was based on his father's account of a Gentile who had knocked his new fur cap into the gutter one day and shouted: "Jew, get off the pavement." When the 12-year-old boy inquired of his father how he reacted to such treatment, he replied: "I stepped into the gutter and picked up my cap." The remark permanently damaged the father's image in the boy's eyes.

3. Freud first published systematic statements about the unconscious in the *Proceedings of the London Society of Psychical Research* in 1912; also, in *Zeitschrift*, Vol III, 1915. Freud wasn't the first to recognize this: cf. Karl von Hartmann, *The Philosophy of the Unconscious*, 1893.

4. He recounted four factors which began to undermine his own confidence in these theories: His continued unsuccessful attempts to bring his analysis to a conclusion; the impossibility of believing that so many fathers were sexual perverts; the definite realization that there is no "indication of reality" in the subconscious; and the absence of memories of sexual assault in serious mental illness when the personality was invaded by the subconscious. Gérard Lauzun, *Sigmund Freud: The Man and His Theories*, Fawcett, Greenwich CT, 1962, p. 49 (as quoted in Breese).

5. *Freud, The History of Psycho-analytic Movement, ibid.,* p. 50.

6. Paul Gray, "Lies of the Mind," *Time*, 11/29/93, pp.52-59.

7. Paul Gray, "The Assault on Freud," *Time*, 11/29/93, pp.47-51; Eric E. Goode w/Betsy Wagner, "Does Psychotherapy Work?" *U.S. News & World Report*, 5/24/93, pp. 56-65.

8. Bruce Thornton, "When Cupid Aims, You'd Better Duck," *L.A. Times*, February 14, 1997.

9. Review Alan Bloom's *The Closing of the American Mind,* and Robert Bork's *Slouching to Gomorrah* for an excellent (secular) review of our present predicament.

10. Paul Johnson, *Modern Times*, Harper & Row, NY, 1983, p.6.

11. Breese, p.146.

12. 2 Corinthians 13:8.

13. Hebrews 4:12.

14. A full discussion appears in the briefing package, *The Architecture of Man*, published by Koinonia House or the book, *The Way of Agape*, published by the King's High Way, Ministries, Inc.

15. We use the words, subconscious, unconscious and memory as synonyms.

16. *The Amplified Bible*, Zondervan Publishing House, Grand Rapids, Michigan, 1970, page 265.

17. Luke 9:47; Proverbs 21:1-2; Hebrews 4:12; Psalm 139:23; 1 Chronicles 29:17; Jeremiah 11:20; 17:10; 20:12 and many more.

18. Isaiah 53:5; 1 Peter 2:24; Isaiah 61:1; Luke 4:18-19.

19. Proverbs 20:27; Psalm 19:12; Psalm 103:12; 1 Corinthians 13:4-7.

Section One:
Renewed Like the Eagle

"Bless the Lord, O my soul, and forget not all His benefits:
Who forgiveth all thine iniquities;
Who healeth all thy diseases;
Who redeemeth thy life from destruction;
Who crowneth thee with loving-kindness and tender mercies;
Who satisfieth thy mouth with good things;
So that *thy youth is renewed like the eagle's.*"

Psalm 103:2-5

Chapter One
How Do Our Lives Become Transformed?

In the Old Testament, God speaks to the Israelites rather harshly and warns them of some "heavy" things to come. In Hosea 4:1, he warns, "Hear the word of the Lord...for the Lord hath a controversy [a contention] with the inhabitants of the land, because *there is no truth, nor mercy [love], nor knowledge of God in the land.*"[1]

The very same thing can be said of today. *The Way of Agape* addresses how, in the end times "the Love [*Agape*] of many shall grow cold."[2] This book will address how many, again in the end times, will not *walk in the truth.*

First of all, we must understand what "truth" is. Truth is where our *words* and our *deeds* match and become one. *Jesus, of course, is the Truth.* He is the Word who became the Deed. He also "lived the truth." His Words (promises) always matched His Deeds and His Life actions.

In 3 John 3, the apostle John comments on how important it is that we "live the truth." He states, "I have no greater joy than to hear that my children *walk in truth.*"

Why does seeing his "children walk in truth" bring him so much joy? John says this brings him joy because it shows that they were genuine and authentic Christians (whose words and deeds matched). There were no "masks" or "facades." They were truly showing forth God's Life in their actions and thus, the Gospel could be passed on.

Clearly, "walking in truth" is God's Will for every one of us. And I believe God's heart must be grieved as He sees this not occurring in the Christian body today. I think this is also one of the main reasons why so many non-believers do not want to come to the Lord. They see so many *phony* Christians whose deeds don't match their words and they want no part of it. Why should they want something that doesn't seem to work for us?

An Example: Tolstoy

Leo Tolstoy wrote the famous Russian novels *War and Peace* and *Anna Karinna.* I recently picked up his autobiography, *Confession,* because I had heard that he eventually became a Christian.

Tolstoy is probably one of the most renown writers of all time and yet, he says in this book, that when he reached the prime of life, after all the fame, fortune, prestige and power he had attained, he came to the conclusion that life was meaningless. So he set out on a personal quest to find life's meaning and purpose.

He studied everything there was to learn about philosophy, science and every avenue of knowledge. When he exhausted these subjects, he came to the conclusion that they had no answers either and that faith alone, had to be the only anchor that provides mankind with reasons to live.

So, he decided to investigate "religion." He quickly ruled out Islam and Judaism and zeroed in on Christianity. First, he turned to his peers—all the Christian believers in his own circle, the learned, the aristocrats and the theologians.

But, he quickly saw that their lives were no different than his own. They feared poverty, suffering and death, just as he did. They seemed to live only to satisfy themselves, just like everyone else. So, he concluded that they really didn't have the answers to life either, and that they were only deceiving themselves.

Tolstoy finally found "true faith" in the lives of the Christian peasants of his day. He said these people genuinely lived their faith. They weren't afraid of poverty, sickness or dying. They truly *lived the truth* and their lives were full of peace and joy.

Tolstoy grew to love these people very much. After many years befriending them, Tolstoy chose to leave his position, his wealth and his family and live among these Christian peasants for the remainder of his life.

Tragically, his wife never accepted his new beliefs. She remained with his children on his estate, and ended up inheriting all his money and prestige. Tolstoy, however, had found the true meaning of life (Jesus Christ) and he also had learned to live the truth!

Loving in Deed and Truth

I think this story is fascinating because this is exactly what God is trying to teach each one of us as Christians. How to make the words of our mouth (where we say, "Jesus is the answer to all my problems; He is my life; I trust Him in everything," match and become one with our actions.

In reality, is Jesus the answer to all of our problems? Is He really our life? Do our actions portray that we trust Him in everything? 1 John 3:18 says, "My little children, let us not love in word, neither in tongue; but [love] in deed and in truth."

Years ago when my daughter was away at a Christian camp, she often would write home and tell us of the tremendous changes that were going on in her life. In her letters, she made very specific promises as to how she was going to behave in the future. She always qualified her statements, however, by saying, "Mom and Dad, I know these are just words now, but I'll show you in my actions when I come home that they're true."

I had to smile, because she was just parroting back to us what we'd taught her ever since she was a little girl. "What you *say* with your words, must match what you *do* in your actions, in order for it to be the truth!" "Truth," I would tell her, "is where the words of your mouth match and become one with the deeds of your life."

After meditating on her letter for a while, I began to realize that that's exactly what God is trying to do in each of our lives—teaching each of us how to "live the truth."

Living the Truth

Our words are so very easy, but to act out those words in our lives is a completely different thing. This is the area that I believe God is most concerned with in all of our lives. He wants what we say and what we do to be one, so that we can be genuine representatives of Him and we can live the truth.

"...If we say [with our words] that we have fellowship with Him, and [yet] walk in darkness, we lie and do not the truth." (1 John 1:5-6)

God is saying here in 1 John, that He wants the supernatural Life that He has already placed in our hearts (if we are believers), not just to remain in our hearts (and be *words* only), but to be shown forth out in our lives. He wants us to genuinely walk in His Love and Truth, not just talk about it. Then others will see God's Life in us and want what we have. "By this shall all men know that ye are My disciples, if ye have Love one to another." (John 13:35)

Abundant Life

John 10:10 tells us that the purpose of our being called as Christians is so that we might have life and have it more abundantly.

Whose "life" is John talking about here? Does he mean our own natural, human life? Is this what we are supposed to live abundantly? I don't think so. It's not our own *human* love, wisdom and power that God wants us to show forth, but **His** supernatural Life.

In order to clarify, let's establish some definitions. When I say "God's super-natural Life," I mean His supernatural Love (*Agape*), His supernatural Thoughts and His supernatural Power to perform these in our lives.[3] When I say our natural life, our human life or our *self-life*, I mean our own human thoughts, emotions and desires (that are usually contrary to God's) performed in our lives by our own human abilities. Sometimes this is called *the flesh*.

[Please refer to Glossary at the end of this book to understand and help clarify the thoughts that lie behind the important words and phrases that I use throughout this study.]

Originally Adam had abundant life. He experienced God's supernatural Life in and through him. But, when he fell, God's supernatural Love and Wisdom became "...hid from the eyes of all living..." as Job 28:20-21 tells us. Jesus came expressly for the purpose of restoring that *sight* and that wholeness to all of us. When we ask Jesus to be our Savior and we become *born again*, God comes into our hearts and, once again, restores that supernatural Life.

However, God doesn't want this supernatural Life to remain in our hearts. He wants His abundant Life to be shown forth out in our lives (our souls) so that all can see it and desire it. He wants us to be those open vessels living His Life, not just talking about His Life. He wants us to be *Life Imparters*.

The Exchanged Life

Constantly, we are to relinquish our *self-life* to Him, so that His Life from our hearts can freely come forth into our souls. This is what Galatians 2:20 means when the apostle Paul declares, "I am crucified with Christ; nevertheless I live; yet not I, but Christ liveth in me: and the life which I now live in the flesh I live by the faith of the Son of God, who loved me, and gave Himself for me." And also, what Paul means in Philippians 1:21 when he states "For me to live is Christ."[4]

This is Christ's Life through us. We are to moment by moment set aside our life, so that God's Life can come forth. It's sometimes called the *exchanged life*. We give God our life—He gives us His.

John 12:24 supports this interpretation, "Verily, verily, I say unto you, Except a corn of wheat fall into the ground and die, it abideth alone: but if it die, it bringeth forth much fruit."

This Scripture exhorts us to become "emptied of self," so that we can be "filled with Him." Now being emptied of self does not mean becoming some sort of mindless robot, or a non-entity with no personality or individuality of our own. Quite the contrary, when we surrender ourselves to God, He takes our own unique personality, our own individual temperament, our own make-up and then fills it with His Love, His Thoughts and His Power.

How Are We Able To Do This?

The next question becomes, "Okay, that sounds great. I want to live Christ's Life. I want to live the truth. I want my words and my deeds to match. But how on earth do I do this? *How* am I emptied of self-life and filled with God's Life? *How* does Christ become my very life itself?"

The answer is Romans 12:1-2, "I beseech you therefore, brethren, by the mercies of God, that ye present your bodies a living sacrifice, holy, acceptable unto God, which is your reasonable service. And be not conformed to this world; but *be ye transformed* [how?] *by the renewing of your mind*, that ye may prove [in your actions] what is that good, and acceptable, and perfect will of God." (emphasis added)

This Scripture tells us that a renewed mind is the "key" to our transformation. *Transformation simply means an exchange of life. It means taking off self and putting on God.* A renewed mind is the "bridge" or the "link" between our being emptied of self and being filled with God. In other words, it's the mechanism or instrument by which *Christ's supernatural Life* in our hearts can become *our life* in our souls.

Ephesians 4:22-24 explains what a renewed mind does: "That ye *put off* concerning the former conversation the old man, which is corrupt according to the deceitful lusts; and *be renewed in the spirit of your mind*; and that ye *put on* the new man, which after God is created in righteousness and true holiness." (emphasis added)

Goal and Purpose of Being a Christian

Being transformed into Christ's Image is the basic goal and purpose for each of our lives as Christians. God wants us to show forth and reflect His Life in our souls and not our own. This, to me, is what Romans 8:28-29 means when it says, we are to be *conformed into the image of Christ.*

When we allow God to do this, then we'll be able to live the truth and our words and our deeds <u>will</u> match and the Gospel <u>will</u> have a chance to be passed on.

So, a renewed mind is the *key* to our transformation and our living the truth. You talk about important subjects, this one is critical.

A renewed mind takes God's Life that is already resident in our hearts if we are born-again and sees to it, that that Life doesn't just remain in our hearts, but is manifested in our day-to-day living. Only then will we have the freedom to drop our masks and facades, be real and transparent and yet, still reflect Christ.

When we don't choose to renew our minds, however, either because we don't know how or because of hurts, fears and insecurities that we have chosen to hang on to, then we quench God's Spirit in our hearts and block His Life from coming forth. Consequently, the life that is shown forth in our souls is not going to be God's Life as it should be, but self-life. And this is what causes us to be those phony and hypocritical Christians, saying one thing with our words and yet, doing something else in our lives.

Satan's Schemes - "Conformed to World's Image"

Satan, of course, is dedicated to preventing our transformation into Christ's Image in any way he can. He knows that if he can just keep us *ignorant* as to how to renew our minds and what the Mind of Christ is, then we'll go on depending upon our own self-centered thoughts and emotions and end up *being conformed to the world's image* and not Christ's, as God desires.

This is why it's so important to pray each time you pick up this book. *Satan does not want you to learn these things.* He wants to keep you ignorant and blinded as to the *real freedom* that's in Christ. And he will do that by simply keeping you in bondage to your own habitual and emotional way of thinking. That's the *key.*

Hidden Chambers

When we don't know how to renew our minds or how to put off the "junk" in our thinking, then we not only give Satan handles to grab hold of in our conscious thinking, but we also allow him to establish strongholds in our *hidden chambers* or our innermost part as Scripture calls it.

In this book, we are going to talk a lot about the things in our lives that we don't deal with, either out of *ignorance* or *disobedience*, but simply push down into the secret recesses of our souls. These are the things that eventually can become the hidden motivation for much of what we do.

As God begins to teach us how to renew our minds, we'll see that we <u>can</u> be set free, not only from our conscious negative thoughts and emotions—which are often only the *symptoms* of our problems—but also all the *secret, hidden* faults within us—the doubts, fears and insecurities, that are often the real *root causes* of our problems.

Psalm 19:12-13 speaks to this, "Who can understand his errors? [his mistakes, his strayings, his wanderings] Cleanse thou me from *secret faults* [hidden, covered, not discerned]...let them not have dominion over me."

Satan, of course, is dedicated to preventing this renewal in our lives in any way he can.

An Example: Confusion and Distraction

Here's an example of the extremes that Satan will go to keep us from hearing how to renew our minds.

Three or four years ago, I was invited to do a *Be Ye Transformed* seminar up in the mountains of Southern California. The women were absolutely precious and so very hungry to hear what God had for them. Of all the seminars that I have done, however, this weekend was probably one of the most *spooky*.

I had previously gone over the details and plans for the seminar with the leaders before the first session began (where to set up the screen, where to put the overhead projector, the chairs, etc.). Everything seemed to be understood and in order.

However, the first session turned out to be a nightmare. When all the women arrived, for some reason the screen and projector were at the wrong end of the room and the chairs were facing backwards. I don't understand why someone would have thought to do that, but nevertheless, I had to postpone starting the session until everyone had picked up her chair and turned them around to face the screen. It seemed like such a strange beginning!

After taking 10 minutes or so to rearrange the chairs, we began again. Right in the middle of an important point that I was making, the woman video-taping the seminar stood directly in front of my line of vision towards the audience. Now, again, I thought we had covered all of this in our preplanning meeting. However, since she was causing such a distraction not only to me, but to everyone in the audience, I stopped lecturing again and politely asked her to move.

I began again. About 15 minutes into the presentation, the entire wall of decorations in the back of the room collapsed. The leaders of the group had strung up a clothesline to hold all their handmade decorated items for the weekend. The clothesline mysteriously broke and everything fell to the floor. We stopped the lecture and everyone helped clean up the mess.

I have never experienced such confusion and such distraction in all of my teaching days. We all laughed, and once again, I began to teach. Not two minutes later, a woman in the front row bolted out of the room holding her mouth as if she was going to vomit. One of her friends immediately followed her. We stopped the lecture and all of us prayed for her.

The final thing that alerted us as to what was really going on, was that an entire shelf on one side of the room displaying antique cups and dishes (again, a part of the girls' decorations) came crashing to the floor. All the cups and plates broke into a million pieces. The shelf, as it careened to the floor, hit several of the ladies sitting close by. None of them were seriously hurt, but the class was in total chaos!

At this point, we all realized who was behind these blatant attacks. Satan was trying to keep these precious women from hearing how to renew their minds so their lives could be transformed. Immediately, we went to battle in prayer. "For though we walk in the flesh, we do not war after the flesh: for the weapons of our warfare are not carnal, but mighty through God to the pulling down of strong holds." (2 Corinthians 10:3-4)

After that prayer time, the seminar went smoothly. Many of the women came to know the Lord in a deeper and more intimate way. Many were freed from "baggage" (hurts, bitterness, resentment, etc.) they had carried around for years; and many began to understand how to, moment-by-moment, renew their minds. God blessed us abundantly with His Presence.

So, we must all be aware of Satan's schemes. He does not want us to learn this material and he will stop at nothing to confuse us, disarm us and discourage us. Always remember, however, "...greater is He that is in [us], than he that is in the world." (1 John 4:4)

We All Have The Mind of Christ

1 Corinthians 2 tells us that as Christians we *all* possess the Mind of Christ in order to get God's Life from our hearts out into our lives. "Now we have received, not the spirit of the world, but the Spirit which is of God; [why?] that we might *know* the things that are freely given to us of God." (verse 12) "...For who hath known the mind of the Lord, that he may instruct him? But *we* have the Mind of Christ." (verse 16)

Even as believers, most of us have been completely ignorant, not only as to what the Mind of Christ is, but also what it does and how it works. And because of this ignorance, we have not been able to use this incredible gift that God has given us. As a result, we've gone on depending upon our own thoughts and our own emotions, again playing right into the enemy's hands.

This is exactly what happened to me for the first 20 years of my Christian walk. I desperately wanted to show forth God's Life and live the truth. But I just didn't know how. One day I would be *up* and living the Christian life because I felt great, my circumstances were good and others were being sweet to me; but, the next day, I would be *down* in the dumps and completely miserable because these three things were intolerable. So, my life was a continual emotional roller coaster. I call it the Christian Yo-Yo Syndrome—constantly dependent upon our emotions, other's responses and our circumstances.

Friends would tell me, "Nancy, just read the Bible more." I did and still there was no change. They would tell me, "Just pray more." I did and still nothing changed my life. They would tell me, "Go to church more." I did and still nothing. "Go to this seminar." "Go to that seminar." But, still, there was never any lasting life transformation until I learned how to daily, moment by moment, renew my mind—put off the junk and put on Christ.

It's very much like those fad diets we so often go on. With each diet, we lost weight, but over time, we always seem to gain that weight back and sometimes, even more. The reason is that our basic eating habits have not been changed. And, it's the same thing with our spiritual lives. *If our basic thinking patterns are not changed, then our lives will not change either, no matter what we do.*

Isaiah 59:10 graphically describes this, "We grope for the wall like the blind, and we grope as if we had no *eyes*; we stumble at noon day as in the night; we are in desolate places as dead men." *Eye* in Scripture is often referred to as our mental vision or our mind. And it's true; we do *grope for the wall as if we had no eyes* because we don't know how to put off our old thinking and put on the Mind of Christ...our new *"eyes."*

So, maturity in Christ is not knowing a bunch of Scriptures, going to church regularly, attending prayer meetings, leading Bible studies, writing books or even being on T.V., but simply knowing how, moment by moment, to make the proper faith choices to renew our minds, so that God's Life from our hearts can continue to flow.

Reasons Why We Depend Upon Our Own Thinking

Now, besides *ignorance* there are a couple more reasons why many of us, even as Christians, are not using this incredible gift that God has given us (the Mind of Christ), but instead are continuing to depend upon our own emotional way of thinking.

One of the most common reasons why we tend to see things through our own understanding and not the Mind of Christ is that many of us are not even aware that our own thinking is any different from God's.

Even though Isaiah 55:8-9 plainly tells us, "For My thoughts are not your thoughts, neither are your ways My ways, saith the Lord. For as the heavens are higher than the earth, so are My ways higher than your ways, and My thoughts than your thoughts," even as Christians, we still continue to depend upon our own way of thinking.

Isaiah tells us here that our own natural thinking is not only different from God's, but usually completely opposite from God's.[5] Haven't you found this to be true? You will have just figured out in your own mind how God is going to work out your circumstances. Then He accomplishes His Will in a totally different way than what you thought.

We must realize that just because we're Christians does not mean we automatically have God's Thoughts in our lives. We don't. Just as God's Love can be blocked and quenched in our hearts by our own emotional choices, so God's Thoughts can also be withheld.

So, it's critical to realize that our own natural thinking is completely different than God's thinking, and that His Mind, just like His Love, can operate through us, only when we are open and cleansed vessels.

Proverbs 3:5 declares, "Trust in the Lord with all thine heart, and lean not unto thine own understanding. In all thy ways acknowledge Him, and He shall direct thy paths."

Take Every Thought Captive

Another reason why many of us continue to depend upon our own thinking rather than God's, is that we seldom "...take every thought captive to the obedience of Christ," as 2 Corinthians 10:5 exhorts us to do.

How many of you do this? Most of us, even after we're Christians, just react naturally. Very few of us stop to think before we respond.

Now, when God says *take every thought captive*, He doesn't mean examine every single thought that we have. He means stop and take a good, hard look at the anxious thoughts, the hurtful ones, the doubtful ones, the frustrations, the anger, the pride, and all the other "emotional" and self-centered thoughts that take away our peace. Lack of peace is a good barometer for us to see which thoughts God wants us to deal with. Romans 14:23 teaches, "...whatever is not of faith is sin." So, any thought that is *not of faith* and takes away our peace is a thought that we need to deal with.

Chain Reaction

The reason our thoughts are so important to God is that our thoughts are the *first* to be triggered in the chain reaction of our souls. Our *thoughts* stir up our *emotions*; our emotions then cause our *desires*; and our desires produce our *actions*. This is why our thoughts are so critical. If we can catch our negative thoughts when they first occur, then we'll stop the whole chain reaction of our souls before it even begins. And, we might even be able to prevent some of the sin before it occurs in our lives.

What happens, however, when we don't take every thought captive, is that we end up being carried on by the tide of emotion (that chain reaction), quenching God's Spirit, and His Life in our hearts is not able to come forth.

So, yes, as Christians we all have the Mind of Christ, but we won't be able to use this incredible gift, unless we recognize, first of all, that our own emotional way of thinking is totally opposite from God's and recognize the importance of taking every thought captive.

Conclusion

What I pray the Holy Spirit will continually remind us of throughout this book is the critical importance of setting aside our own natural, emotional way of thinking and beginning to think with the Mind of Christ. If we can learn to do this, Romans 12:2 tells us we will be *transformed into God's Image.*[6]

Transformation is God's Will and His goal for all of us. He wants us constantly taking off *our self* and putting on *Himself.* He wants us living the Truth and walking in His Love. The only way this is possible, however, is by the constant renewing of our minds.

"Therefore, I beseech you brethren, by the mercies of God, that ye present your bodies a living sacrifice, holy, acceptable unto God, which is your reasonable service. And, *be not conformed to this world*; but *be ye transformed* [how?] *by the renewing of your mind*, [so] that ye may prove what is that good, and acceptable, and perfect will of God." (Romans 12:1-2, emphasis added)

Endnotes:

1. Isaiah 59:14; 2 Timothy 4:4; Amos 8:11; Jeremiah 7:28

2. Matthew 24:12

3. Romans 5:5; Hebrews 8:10; and Galatians 4:6 (the *dunamis power* of God means "power to reproduce itself")

4. Colossians 3:4

5. Job 28:20-21; Jeremiah 10:23; Isaiah 40:28

6. 2 Corinthians 3:18

Scriptural References:

Chapter One

Loving in Deed and Truth
A. Our words and our deeds must match
1. We must learn to "live the truth" (John 3:21; 3 John 3; 1 John 3:18)
2. God wants His Life to show forth in our lives (John 13:35; Romans 15:18), not our self-life (1 John 1:5-6)
B. Definition of the truth
1. Truth occurs when the Word matches and becomes one with the Deed (1 John 3:18; Jeremiah 1:12; 23:20; Isaiah 34:16; Ezekiel 12:25; Nu. 30:2)
     a. Jesus is the Truth (John 14:6)
     b. He is the Word that became the Deed (John 1:14)
2. God's Word (John 17:17) and His Spirit (John 16:13) are Truth because they always confirm and validate each other (Isaiah 11:4; 46:11c; Ephesians 6: 17; 1 Corinthians 1:24; John 6:63; Romans 1:16; Jeremiah 10:12; Matthew 3:16-17; Genesis 1:3; Hebrews 1:3; 2 Corinthians 6:7)
3. Truth means *faithfulness*, trustworthiness, reliability, *covenant loyalty* (Acts 13:22d)

Abundant Life
A. We are to live "abundant lives" (John 10:10)—God's Life in place of our own
1. *Self-life* is: our own thoughts, emotions and desires that are contrary to God's
2. *God's Life* is: His supernatural Love (*Agape*) (Romans 5:5; 8:39; John 17: 26); His supernatural Thoughts (*Logos*) (Luke 4:4; Hebrews 8:10); and, His supernatural Power (*Dunamis*) (1 Corinthians 1:24; 2 Corinthians 4:7; Luke 4:14, 36; 5:17)
     a. This is "Christ in us, our hope of Glory" (Colossians 1:27)
     b. God wants His Life to be manifested out in our lives (Galatians 2:20)
     c. We are to be "life-imparters"
B. Adam was originally created in "perfect knowledge of God"— He had God's Life (Genesis 1:27-30)
1. He walked in truth (Genesis 1:27)
2. When he fell, God's Life was hidden from the "eyes of all living" (Job 28: 20-21). Jesus came to restore that "sight"—that wholeness (John 1:14, 17; 10:10; 14:6)
3. Jesus came, not only to save us, but also to give us His abundant Life (John 10:10; Colossians 2:3)

The Exchanged Life
A. We are to surrender our lives to God. In exchange, He gives us His (John 12: 24-25; Galatians 2:20; Ephesians 3:16-19)
B. Jesus wants to be our very Life itself (Philippians 1:21; Colossians 1:27; 3:4)

How do We Exchange Lives?
A. How are we emptied of self-life and filled with God's Life? How are we transformed?
1. Scripture says, the way we are transformed is by "the renewing of our minds" (Romans 12:1-2; Ephesians 4:22-24)
2. A renewed mind is the "key" to our *walking in the truth* (Romans 7:25)

B.   Only as we renew our minds, can God fill our lives with His Love, Wisdom and Power

Basic Goal and Purpose of Being A Christian (1 Timothy 1:5; 1 John 4:16; John 13:35; Romans 8:29; 12:1-2; Ephesians 1:4; 5:17-18; 2 Corinthians 3:18; Galatians 1: 16; Ecclesiastes 12:13)
   A.   Being conformed into Christ's Image (Romans 8:29; Galatians 4:19; 5:14; 1 John 4:12-17; 1 Peter 4:8; Colossians 3:14; Micah 6:8; John 15:16; 17:11, 23)
      1.   Being emptied of self-life and filled with God's (2 Corinthians 4:10-11; John 3:30; 12:24-25), and then:
      2.   Being filled with God's Life (Ephesians 3:17-19) Knowing His Life as our own (Philippians 1:21; Galatians 2:20; John 5:11; Colossians 3:4; Deuter-onomy 30:20; 1 John 4:9; Psalm 73: 25-26)
   B.   Walking in God's Love and Truth - bearing witness of the Truth (John 13:35; 18:37; 14:6; 1 John 1:5-7; 2:6; 3:18; Colossians 2:6; Galatians 5:25; Ephesians 5:2a, 8; 2 John 6; 3 John 4)
   C.   Showing forth God's Life, not our own (2 Corinthians 4:10-11; John 1:4, 8; 17: 3; Philippians 1:21; Galatians 2:20; 1 John 4:9; Deuteronomy 30:20; Colossians 3:4, 17; Jeremiah 9:23-24; Matthew 5:16; Luke 11:33; John 7:18)
   D.   Proving what is the "good, acceptable and perfect Will of God" (Romans 12: 1-2; 1 John 2:12-14; Matthew 13:8)
      1.   What is God's Will? (Ephesians 5:17-18, "Be filled with the Spirit")
         a.   God's *good* Will is bearing fruit "thirty-fold" (as children) (Matthew 13:8; 1 John 2:12)
         b.   God's *acceptable* Will is bearing fruit "sixty-fold" (as men) (Matthew 13:8; 1 John 2:13b; Ephesians 5:9)
         c.   God's *Perfect* Will is bearing fruit "a hundred-fold" (as fathers) (Mat-thew 13:8; 1 John 2:13a; Mark 10:37; Hebrews 5:14; 13:21)
      2.   Walking in *Love* is proof we are doing God's Will (2 Corinthians 2:8-9; 1 John 4:12, 17)
      3.   Walking in *Truth* is proof we are doing God's Will (2 John 4; 3 John 3-4)
   E.   Others seeing Jesus in us (1 John 4:12; Psalm 90:17; Judges 5:31b; Mark 4:21)

Satan Will Do Anything To Prevent Our Transformation (2 Corinthians 10: 3-5)
   A.   When we don't know how *to renew our minds*, we give Satan many holes to attack (Luke 11:24-26)
   B.   We are ignorant of things in the *hidden part* of our soul. We must allow God to expose our "whole" man (Psalm 19:12-13)
   C.   Our warfare is mighty to the "pulling down strongholds" (1 John 4:4; 2 Corin-thians 10:3-4; Ephesians 6:10-19)

Our Mind is the *Link* to this Transformation
   A.   A *renewed* mind is the only way we can be transformed into Christ's Image (Romans 12:1-2; Ephesians 4:22-24)
      1.   The natural mind is hostile to God (Romans 3:11; 8:7; Job 28:20-21; Isaiah 40:28)
      2.   The natural man doesn't receive the things of God (1 Corinthians 2:14)
   B.   Our mind is the connection between God's Life in our hearts and its expression in our lives (Romans 7:25; Ephesians 2:2-4)
      1.   God's Life does no good if it's blocked in our hearts (Psalm 119:70)
      2.   This causes us to *live a lie* in our souls—showing forth self-life (1 John 1: 6)

We all have the Mind of Christ

A. The Mind of Christ helps to get God's Life from our hearts out into our lives (1 Corinthians 2:16; Proverbs 3:5; Romans 7:25)

B. As Christians, however, many of us still depend upon our own thinking, rather than God's (Proverbs 3:5; 30:12; Jeremiah 10:23; Philippians 2:21)

C. And we end up *groping for the wall like the blind* (Isaiah 59:10)

Reasons We Depend upon our own Thinking, and not God's

A. We are not aware that our own thinking is any different than God's (Isaiah 55: 8; 40:28; Job 28:20-21; Psalm 94:11)
   1. We walk after our own thoughts and feelings (Proverbs 12:15a;14:12; 30: 12; James 4:4; 2 Timothy 3:1-4; Isaiah 65:2)
   2. We are ignorant, not only of Mind of Christ, but also of Satan's schemes (2 Corinthians 11:3; 1 Corinthians 14:33)

B. We don't take the time to take every thought captive (2 Corinthians 10:5; Romans 14:23c)
   1. We are carried on by "tide of emotion"- *chain reaction* of our souls
      a. Thoughts - feelings - desires - actions (James 1:14-15)
      b. Even as Christians, we naturally respond this way
   2. We become *double-minded*, serving the law of sin (Romans 6:16; 7:23; 25b; James 1:8)
   3. We don't "live the truth" (Isaiah 59:15a; 1 John 1:6)

C. We don't know how to "perform that which is good" (Romans 7:18b)

D. We are not prepared or equipped to stand in the battle against Satan (Psalm 11: 3; Matthew 24:44; Luke 21:34-36)

Chapter Two
Mind Renewal

What Is Mind Renewal?

Romans 12:2 tells us we are *transformed* into God's Image by the renewing of our minds—transformed by "putting off" the garbage in our own thinking and by "putting on" the Mind of Christ. Ephesians 4:22-24 explains it further, we are to *put off* concerning the former conversation [behavior] the old man [old self], which is corrupt according to the deceitful lusts; and *be renewed in the spirit of your mind*; and...*put on* the new man [the new self], which after God is created in righteousness and true holiness." (emphasis added)

A *renewed mind* then, is one that has done *two* things: it has *put off* any sin (any thought, any emotion or any desire "that is not of faith")[1] and has *put on* the Mind of Christ.

Renewing our minds is not simply changing our thoughts, but actually *putting off* our old, negative thoughts, as well as *putting on* God's Thoughts. In other words, we can't just say to God, "Lord, give me Your Thoughts," and expect Him to automatically give us His Mind. It doesn't work that way. We must *first* put off our own self-centered thinking by *confessing it, repenting of it,* and *giving it to God;*[2] then, at this point, we can put on the Mind of Christ. (We will explain this procedure in detail in Chapter Fifteen.)

Hal Lindsey points out that to renew something means *to exchange one thing for another*. In other words, when we renew our minds, we're exchanging our own thinking for God's thinking. In Chapters Five, Six and Seven, we'll talk specifically about the seven-fold process of thinking by the Holy Spirit that makes up the Mind of Christ. God's Holy Spirit gives us His Wisdom, His Understanding, His Counsel, His Strength, His Knowledge, and helps us to walk in the Fear of the Lord. These are the incredible gifts we receive when we put on the Mind of Christ.

Why Is Mind Renewal So Important?

Now, there are many reasons why mind renewal is so very important. I'd like to cover a few critical ones here:

One of the most important reasons for continually renewing our minds is because <u>God wants us to have His viewpoint, His perspective (His Mind) in every situation</u> we find ourselves in.

God wants us to be able to discern everything that happens to us from His vantage point or His perspective and not be weighed down by how we feel or by what *we* perceive to be happening. If we can truly discern our situation from God's point of view, then, we'll be able to soar above our circumstances and our problems without getting emotionally buried under them.

A Perfect Example: "Ye thought evil against me"

Joseph, of the Old Testament, is a perfect example of one who was able to see all that happened to him from God's perspective.

The story goes like this: Joseph was the most beloved of all the sons of Jacob. When he was young, he made the mistake of telling his brothers about a dream he had in which they bowed down to him. His brothers, already jealous of him because he was their father's favorite, became irate and determined to get rid of him any way they could.[3]

They tied Joseph up, put him in a pit and sold him to the Midianites, who were sojourners going down to Egypt. The Midianites, in turn, sold Joseph to Potiphar, an officer of Pharaoh's army and captain of the guard. Potiphar's wife was smitten with Joseph and tried many times to seduce him. When Joseph spurned her advances, however, she got her revenge by making it look like he was the one who had tried to seduce her and consequently, Joseph was sent to prison.[4]

While in prison, Joseph met the king's baker and butler and did them a great favor by interpreting their dreams. He begged them to remember him when they were released from jail. However, when it came time for the chief butler to be released, he forgot all about Joseph.[5]

Two more years went by, then Pharaoh dreamed a dream. The chief butler then remembered Joseph in prison and how he had interpreted his own dreams. He told Pharaoh about Joseph and they released him from prison. Joseph interpreted Pharaoh's dream and, eventually, through a series of events, became the Prime Minister of Egypt.[6]

Joseph was only 17 years old when his brothers threw him in the pit and he was well over 30 years old, when Pharaoh finally released him from prison. Joseph had been *in bondage* for over 13 years!

You know Joseph must have struggled with "justified" hurts, resentments and bitterness. He was not a super saint, but someone just like you and me. Scripture tells us, however, that all who saw Joseph "knew God was with him."[7] In spite of all the horrendous circumstances and all the natural emotions Joseph must have had, his countenance and his life actions still showed forth his love for God.

The only way Joseph could possibly have made this impression, was by constantly putting off his own natural bitterness and resentment and putting on God's Wisdom and God's Understanding, thereby enabling him to see all that was happening to him, not from his own viewpoint, but from God's.

This interpretation is supported by Joseph's declaration in Genesis 50:20 when he says (after finally meeting up with his brothers again), "...ye thought evil against me; but God meant it unto good, to bring to pass, as it is this day, to save much people alive."

Do We "See" All Things This Way?

This response is so incredible and certainly *not* the natural reaction many of us would have had. Humanly speaking, I'm sure Joseph would have liked to have had his revenge, but that's not how he acted. He was able to surrender his hurts and anger to God and trust that somehow God would use all of these things for His ultimate purposes.

How hard it is for us to *see* things in this way, especially when we are going through hard trials—trials that, perhaps, we don't see God's hand in, let alone as being used for our good. In the middle of these circumstances, it's so difficult for us to see how God could be orchestrating things for our best. Romans 8:28, however, tells us that if we are truly *loving Him,*[8] truly giving ourselves over to Him, He will use all things in our life for good and for His eternal purposes.

An Example: Beloved Pastor

A perfect example: Joe, the husband of a dear friend of mine, was taken seriously ill about two years ago. He is a beloved associate pastor of a well-known church in Southern California. We were all heartsick and grieved when it was announced that he had had a stroke and was not expected to live. The terrible news spread quickly throughout the Christian community. We couldn't understand why God had allowed this horrible thing to happen right at the height of Joe's ministry.

God, however, had His own plans. That precious pastor was in the hospital for about six weeks and as I recall, Joe led over 17 people to the Lord, gave out numerous Bibles and continually witnessed to all the intensive care nurses, doctors and even the janitors. After a few weeks, he regained the feeling on one side of his body, and after a few more weeks, Joe was able to walk again. It's been over a year now, and this wonderful man is fully back to normal and continuing to bless hundreds of people with his ministry of love and caring.

God's ways are <u>not</u> our ways, and He knows "best" how to orchestrate people and circumstances to fit His perfect Will and purposes. We don't always see or understand what He is doing at the time, and often the in-between times seem so dark and bewildering.

Now, when everything around me crashes down in confusion, I often remember Joseph and Pastor Joe's story and I am, once again, encouraged and filled with hope. Jeremiah 29:11 explains, "For I know the thoughts that I think toward you, saith the Lord, thoughts of peace, and not of evil, to give you an expected end."

If Only I Could Have

Twenty years ago when Chuck and I were going through all our own marital trials, had I only known how to renew my mind, so that I could have seen my circumstances from God's perspective, I might have been a better witness of Christ *going through the trials*, just like Joseph and my pastor friend. But, because I didn't know how to renew my mind and I didn't know how to *put off* my hurts, I wasn't able to see from God's perspective and instead, I was buried in my own self-centered emotional way of thinking. Thus, God's Life in me became quenched; I wasn't able to *live the truth* and the Gospel wasn't passed on.

Of course, this quenching is exactly what Satan wants! He revels in our bondage to our emotions. He wants us totally immersed and consumed in our own problems and our circumstances, bound by our hurts, fears, pain and wounds (our "chains of sin"[9]), so that we'll be conformed to the world's image and others won't be able to see Jesus in us.

Remember, the witness that others see in us, is *not* just what we *say*; the witness people seem to notice and relate to the most, is our *life actions* in the middle of our trials. Do we still show forth God's Life? Does *Christ in us* still work for us then—even in the hard times?[10]

Isaiah 40:31, "But they that wait upon the Lord shall renew their strength; they shall mount up with wings as eagles; they shall run, and not be weary; and they shall walk, and not faint."

The Eagle - Symbol of Our Renewal

Scripture often refers to the eagle as a symbol of this *renewal process*. Psalm 103:5 tells us that "...[our] youth is renewed like the eagle's." *Youth* here, I believe, refers to the original image or original character[11] that God created us to have from the very beginning. As we allow God to renew our minds, we <u>will</u> be transformed into God's Image, which was the original image or the original character that God created us to bear.

One of the reasons God uses the eagle as a symbol of this transformation process, is because the eagle's entire physical strength is literally renewed after each molting season.[12] In other words, only after the eagle has *put off* his old feathers, so to speak, does he actually receive "new" physical strength to soar above his enemies. And it's the same with us. When we *put off* the old and *put on* the new, we too, receive God's supernatural strength to soar above our enemies.

Another reason why God uses the eagle as a symbol of our renewal and transformation, is because the eagle has *telescopic sight*, a kind of "zoom-in focus" lens. An eagle literally can search out objects miles away (indistinguishable to the human eye). Eagles can see a quarter from over 200 yards away and a rabbit from over a mile away. This lens, of course, increases their ability to judge and discern the *real* situation. And, it's the same with us. When renewed by God's Spirit, our minds have the same supernatural ability. We are able to judge and discern things that the natural eye (natural mind) would never be able to see or understand. In other words, we are given the supernatural ability to discern the true situation because we'll be seeing it from God's perspective.

Isaiah 11:2-4 promises, "And the Spirit of the Lord shall rest upon him...and shall make him of quick understanding in the fear of the Lord. And he shall not judge after the sight of his [own] eyes, neither reprove after the hearing of his [own] ears, but with righteousness shall he judge...."

Whoever Directs Our Thinking Will Direct Our Lives

A further reason mind renewal is so critical is because <u>whoever directs and controls our thinking is ultimately the one who will direct and control our lives</u>.[13] Remember the chain reaction of our souls: what we think affects how we feel; how we feel influences our desires; and our desires are what produce our actions.

Well, if Satan can influence our thinking by simply keeping us immersed in our own natural, emotional way of responding, then he's got us and he doesn't have to do another thing. We've played right into his hands—he is directing our lives at that moment.

An Example: Humiliation

For many years, Evelyn, a friend of mine back East, had trouble with her next door neighbor. After much prayer, she felt lead to go to her neighbor, apologize, and make things right. However, for some reason the neighbor would not accept her apology, but instead, ridiculed and humiliated her.

Evelyn carried this rejection and humiliation buried tight in her own heart for seven months, constantly mulling it over and letting it totally consume her. By worldly standards, she was completely justified in being hurt and angry, but by God's standards, because Evelyn chose to hang onto her hurt feelings rather than release them to God, she quenched His Spirit in her heart. As a result, she wasn't able to *show forth Christ Life* or *live the truth*.

Thoughts of rejection and humiliation not only consumed her, but they also began to motivate her actions. Every time she passed by her neighbor's house, she would find herself angry for no apparent reason. Every time she pulled into her own driveway and glanced over and saw her neighbor's dog, feelings of humiliation and resentment would again overwhelm her.

This hurt and anger continued for seven long months, until an incident occurred between the two families that somewhat alleviated her hurt feelings. (She never told me exactly what it was.) But, had Evelyn been able that very first night, to *renew her mind*—to take her thoughts captive, to give her hurts to God, and by faith, put on the Mind of Christ—she might have been able to show forth God's Life and perhaps, been a better witness of Him in the middle of the trial.

So, you see how Satan revels in our bondage to our own self-centered thoughts and emotions? When this occurs, he <u>is</u> able to direct our lives and our actions through our flesh.

We must understand that our hurts, resentments and bitternesses won't go away on their own. Those "secret faults" that Psalm 19:12 warns us about, will only accumulate, grow stronger and eventually become strongholds of the enemy. Scripture tells us, only God can take these negative things away from us and truly heal us.

Without a renewed mind—without the Mind of Christ in operation—God will never really be able to hold the reins of our lives. This is why Satan battles so hard for our minds. If he can control our thinking, ultimately he will control our lives.

Therefore, *our efforts to change should not be focused on our wrong actions, but on our wrong thinking. If we can change our thinking, then our life actions will follow.*

No Mind Change, No Life Change

A third reason why mind renewal is so important is that if there is no mind change, then there will be no life change either.

In other words, without a renewed or changed mind, our lives will remain the same as they've always been, no matter what we do or what we try. No matter how many Bible studies we attend, no matter how many Scriptures we read, no matter how often we go to church, no matter how much we pray, *if we don't have a mind change, our lives will still have the same problems, the same failures, and the same defeats as they always have.*

Jeremiah 48:11 is a fascinating Scripture that clearly illustrates this point, "Moab hath been at ease from his youth, and he hath settled on his lees, and hath not been emptied from vessel to vessel, neither hath he gone into captivity; therefore, *his taste remained in him, and his scent is not changed."* (emphasis added)

The Moabites were a people who were bent on *self-preservation* at all costs. This is what "settled on his lees" means.[14] These people had never been broken or emptied of self-life. They were out to protect themselves at all costs and would never allow themselves to *go into captivity* or be *cornered* for the purpose of exposing their sin and secret faults. And because of this, their "taste (which I see as their *thinking*) remained the same," and their "scent (which I see as their *lives*) never changed."[15]

In like manner, if we have not been broken or emptied of our self-life, and we are "bent on preserving that self at all costs" (loving ourselves, holding on to ourselves just as the Moabites did), then our thinking will never be renewed and there certainly will be no life transformation.

What this means is that unless we learn to "deal" with each pain, each hurt, each insecurity, each instance of pride and unbelief as it occurs (and begin to allow God to cleanse the *junk* that we have already programmed in), we'll just continue to act out of these negative things, no matter what we do or try. And, the same crumbling that has occurred all along in our lives, will just continue to happen no matter what we do. Therefore, a *mind change* is essential, if there is *ever* to be any *life change* in us at all![16]

If we can allow God to expose, root out and change our old ways of thinking, then we can be assured that a transformed life will follow.

Discerning the True from the False

The fourth reason for daily renewing our minds, is <u>so that we might be able to discern the "true" from the "false."</u>

The Mind of Christ not only renews our thinking *inside* by setting us free from ourselves, from other's responses, and from our circumstances, but it also gives us the discernment and the wisdom we need on the *outside* to walk circum-spectly—aware of Satan's deceptions.

In these last times there are so many false teachings, even within the Christian Body. 2 Corinthians 11:13-15 warns us, "For such are false apostles, deceitful workers, transforming themselves into the apostles of Christ. And no marvel; for Satan himself is transformed into an angel of light. Therefore, it is no great thing if his ministers can also be transformed as the ministers of righteousness; whose end shall be according to their works."

Christ warns us in Mark 13:22 that in the end times "...false prophets shall rise, and shall show signs and wonders, to seduce, if it were possible, even the elect." What is so scary, is that these deceivers or false prophets are going to masquerade as *ministers of Christ* and people will believe them and follow them, becoming ensnared.

How can we tell what is true and what is false? How can we avoid getting caught up in false teaching as we see so many of our brothers and sisters doing? Isaiah 11:3-4 gives us the answer: We are not to judge or discern by the sight of our own eyes or by the hearing of our own ears, but with Christ's righteous discernment (the Mind of Christ) we are to judge.

Satan's time is short, and he's going to use every deception, every hole—inside and out—that he can find, to keep us from wholeheartedly and single-mindedly following God. The Mind of Christ is the only thing that will give us the wisdom and the keenness that we need in order to walk prudently and enduringly in these end times.

Psalm 32:8 promises us, "I will instruct thee and teach thee in the way which thou shalt go: I will guide thee with Mine eye."

Our Weapons are Mighty

2 Corinthians 10:3-4 tells us that even "...though we walk in the flesh, we do not war after the flesh. (For the weapons of our warfare are not carnal, but mighty through God to the pulling down of strongholds.)"

"Pulling down of strongholds" here, means literally wiping them out, demolishing them and destroying them. As we begin to "take every thought captive," we'll learn that we <u>can</u> get rid of, not only our *conscious* negative thoughts and feelings, but also, all the *hidden, secret* doubts, fears and insecurities that all of our lives we have buried deep within our souls.

By His Mind in us, God can penetrate deep into the uncharted areas of our soul and not only expose, cleanse and heal us from all our ungodly thoughts, but also root out any strongholds of the enemy there. As God promises, He wants us to know "truth in the inward parts."[17] He wants us set free—free from ourselves, free from other's responses and free from our circumstances. And, most of all, He wants us free from Satan's schemes.

My Dream

A few years ago, I had a dream. In the middle of the night, God had me sit up and write something down on a pad of paper that I keep by my bed for just such occasions. Now, I didn't know what I had written until the next morning. There on my paper was: *"If you will give Me your thinking, I will give you My Life."*

If you don't remember anything else from this book, if you can simply recall this statement—"If you will give Me your thinking, I will give you My Life"— I believe, it's enough to change your life.

This is why God says it's so critical to "bring every thought into captivity"—to capture it, to expose it and to examine it. (2 Corinthians 10:5) We must see where our thoughts are coming from and see if they reveal God's voice, Satan's voice or self's voice. (In Chapter Fourteen, we explore this discernment in depth.)

Then, as the rest of 2 Corinthians 10:4-6 says, we must begin to "Cast down...every *high thing*—every *stronghold*, and every *imagination*—that exalteth itself against the knowledge of God...And have a readiness to revenge all disobedience,..." (Again, in Chapters Fourteen and Fifteen we'll explore what it really means to *practically* "revenge all disobedience."[18])

How Does God Bring About this Renewal?

God is constantly nudging us to quit our own way of thinking and go in a 180-degree opposite direction. Unfortunately, we don't always *hear* Him, and often we *don't want* to hear Him, because we'd rather stay in control ourselves and do what we want.

However, because God loves us so much and because He wants us to have *abundant life* here and now, He often allows circumstances into our lives that will force us to see for ourselves our wrong priorities and our wrong dependencies. He pushes us into a *corner* where we'll see ourselves as we truly really are. And, we see that, we too, even as Christians, have been doing just what the Moabites did—"preserving ourselves at all costs" and "out to protect self" above everything else.

God knows that one of the surest ways for our self-life to be exposed, is for us to trip, fall and be broken. God loves us so much that He is willing to do whatever is necessary to bring about our mind renewal and life transformation.[19]

An Example: "Mine eye seeth Thee"

The book of Job is a good example of the benefits of brokenness. Job was a good man—a righteous man—and he loved God with all his heart, but he was woefully ignorant of the true state of his own soul.

In Job 42:5, after all of his trials and tribulations, Job finally confesses, "I have heard of thee by the hearing of the ear [he only had intellectual knowledge of God); *but now mine eye seeth thee* (because of his trials, he began to know God intimately]." (emphasis added)

Because of his totally broken state, Job not only began to see himself in the proper light ("I have sinned," and "I abhor myself and repent in dust and ashes,"[20] but he also saw God for who He was ("with Him is wisdom and strength, He hath counsel and understanding."[21]   As a result of brokenness, Job realized his need to trust God even when everything in his life contradicted it. "Though He slay me, yet will I trust in Him." (Job 13:15)

Job thought he knew God before, indeed, he had taught others about God,[22] but everything he had believed in had been disproven by his own experiences. In other words, he was totally broken by what God had allowed in his life and he didn't understand at all why he had to suffer so. However, through his brokenness, he not only came to see the truth about God and who He was, but he also saw the truth about himself and his need for repentance:"...I uttered things I understood not; things I knew not"[23] "... [They were] words without knowledge."[24]

Brokenness: The Emptying Out Process

To be broken simply means to have our *self-life* (all our own thoughts, emotions and desires that are contrary to God's) uncovered, exposed, brought into captivity, and weeded out. Jeremiah 1:10 instructs, "See, I have this day set thee over the nations and over the kingdoms, to root out, to pull down, to destroy, and to throw down, [but then] to build and to plant."

God allows us to be broken through our trials and through our storms so that we will see the need for mind renewal. In Job 37:13, God states that He uses the storms either for correction or for mercy. Of special note, in Job 37:9, He tells us that these storms often come from the *south*. The word *south* is the Hebrew word *cheder* which the Bible also uses to describe the hidden chambers or the innermost part of our minds.

In other words, He allows the storms to come from these inward chambers, either in His merciful Love to free us from Satan's strongholds, or in His discipline Love to force us to deal with our sin. Then, the evil that's encamped there will be exposed, cleansed and expelled. Proverbs 20:30 helps explain this a little more clearly. "The blueness of a wound cleanseth away evil: so do stripes the inward parts [*cheder*] of the belly."

(Again, we will spend several chapters in Section Six exploring these "hidden chambers" and their important implications.)

An Example: Why Can't I Stay In Control?

I had lunch with a dear friend of mine not too long ago and when she heard about all the trials that Chuck and I continue to go through, she said, "Nan, I'm afraid to let go completely. Look at you! Look what happens when you let go! It's scary! Why do I have to relinquish everything to God? Why can't I just stay in control myself?"

"Marcia," I asked her, "do you love God? Totally giving yourself over to Him, moment-by-moment, is really what it means to love Him. The word *agapao* (to love) is not a natural feeling or an emotional love, but a love where we relinquish everything to God—where we put His Will and His desires above our own.

That's exactly what Matthew 16:24 and John 12:24-25 mean where Jesus instructs us to deny ourselves and follow Him. If we do this, then we will bear much fruit. *Brokenness is simply God's way of exposing our self-life. Brokenness removes every hindrance in our lives that keeps us from being fully surrendered and from bearing much fruit."*

I went on to share with Marcia that God loves us so much, He wants us to see, through our trials and through our brokenness, that there is *life* from no other source, but Christ and His Spirit in us. For me to live, must be Christ. (Philippians 1:21)[25] I told her, as far as Chuck and I were concerned, the trials that God has allowed in our lives is a very small price to pay for the freedom from self and the intimate knowledge of Him that we are now experiencing. And, we would both genuinely say, "It is good for [us] to have been afflicted; [so] that [we] might learn Thy statues." (Psalm 119:71)

Suffering's Lessons

The Gospel is not *health and wealth* in this life, but a call to follow in Jesus Christ's footsteps. He left us an incredible example to follow. He willingly suffered, was rejected, and crucified. "The Son of man must *suffer* many things, and be rejected of the elders and chief priests and scribes, and be slain, and be raised the third day." (Luke 9:22) *To suffer* means to bar ourselves from sin. When we endure, refuse and *bar ourselves from following* any lust, sin or evil affection, it will cause us suffering.[26]

Remember, however, the most glorious news of all, is that resurrection always follows suffering and crucifixion. "I am crucified with Christ: nevertheless I live; yet not I, but Christ liveth in me; and *the life which I now live* in the flesh I live by the faith of the Son of God, who loved me and gave Himself for me." (Galatians 2:20, emphasis added) So, crucifixion or death to self always leads us to life.

Watchman Nee in his book *The Normal Christian Life*[27] teaches that, "No one can be a true servant of God without knowing the principle of death and the principle of resurrection." And, 1 Peter 2:21 supports this view, "For even hereunto were ye called, because Christ also suffered for us, leaving us an example, that ye should follow His steps."

Is Brokenness a Must?

Many years ago, a couple of young gals came up to me after a seminar and said, "Oh Nan, does it always have to be through trials that we learn to walk as Jesus walked? Isn't there any other way that we can do it?" These two young women had beautiful, young families and much happiness in their lives and they were scared to death as to what God might do if they totally relinquished themselves to Him.

"First of all, remember that God loves you and He won't allow anything in your life that's not *Father filtered*," I explained. Then, fully understanding what they were feeling, I added, "You know, I really do believe we could all learn to walk as Jesus walked, without any trials in our lives, if we would just be willing to totally give ourselves over to Him. If we could do this freely, there wouldn't be any need for 'cornering' in our lives."

The truth is, of course, none of us would voluntarily make this relinquishment—our human nature is to *preserve self* and to *hold on to self* at all costs. In fact, our human nature screams to get its own way. That's the battle we are in. And unless we are *cornered* by God, *out of His Love*, we would just continue going our own way. *Brokenness, therefore, is God's way of letting us see the need for a change of thinking.*

Mind Battle

So, we are in a *mind battle* because whoever directs or controls our thinking, ultimately is going to direct and control our lives. If Satan can direct our minds without our even being aware of it, by our simply choosing to go along with the *tide of emotion*, then he will also control our behavior.

This is why it's so very critical that we learn what mind renewal is—how to allow the Holy Spirit and the Mind of Christ to be in full control of our minds. Then, we can be assured it will be God's Life coming forth and not our own.

God wants us freed. He wants us freed from ourselves, freed from others' responses, freed from our circumstances and freed from Satan's deceptions. That freedom allows us first to be transformed, then for others to see Jesus in us and, finally, for the Gospel to be passed on.

Consequently, our efforts to change should not be focused on our wrong actions, but on our wrong thinking.

"I beseech you therefore, brethren, by the mercies of God, that ye present your bodies a living sacrifice, holy, acceptable unto God, which is your reasonable service. And be not conformed to this world: but *be ye transformed* [how?] by the renewing of your mind, that ye may prove what is that good and acceptable, and perfect will of God." (Rom.12:1-2)[28]

Endnotes:

1.   2 Corinthians 10:5

2.   See Chapter Fifteen for details

3.   Genesis 37

4.   Genesis 39

5.   Genesis 40

6.   Genesis 41

7.   Genesis 39:3

8.   The Greek word *agapao* means what we "totally give ourselves over to." We can *agapao* God, man or things of the world.

9.   Proverbs 5:22

10.   See Chapter Seven, "Book of Remembrance."

11.   Romans 8:29

12.   *The Eagle Story*, Institute in Basic Youth Conflicts, Inc., Rand McNally and Company, 1982

13.   For clarification: If we are Christians, then the Holy Spirit is the source, the origin and the beginning of our minds. However, if Satan can sever, quench or thwart God's control, by simply causing us to choose to follow our own emotional way of thinking, rather than what God has prompted, then Satan will end up directing our lives through the "flesh."

14.   "Lees" is *shamar* in the Hebrew (8104) which means: to protect, preserve and keep self.

15.   2 Corinthians 2:14-16

16.   Ephesians 4:22-32

17.   Psalm 51:6

18.   1 Peter 5:8-9; James 4:7

19.   James 1:2-4

20.   Job 7:20; 42:6

21.   Job 12:13

22.   Job 4:3

23. Job 42:3

24. Job 38:2

25. Deuteronomy 30:20

26. To "bar ourselves from following" is one of the definitions of the Greek word *anechomai*. Lust, sin or "evil affection" comes from the Greek word *epithumia* "Suffering" comes from the Greek words *pathema, pathos* and *pascho*.

27. Page 165, 167, *The Normal Christian Life* by Watchman Nee, Christian Literature Crusade, Fort Washington, Pennsylvania 19034, 1970

28. Ephesians 5:10

Scriptural References:

Chapter Two

What is Mind Renewal? (Romans 12:1-2)
- A.   A *renewed mind* is: putting off the *old* and putting on the *new*; it's exchanging one thing for another
  1.   It's *putting off* the garbage of our thinking (the "old self") (Ephesians 4: 22-24; 2 Corinthians 10:5; Romans 6:6-12; 13:12; James 1:21; Colossians 2:11; 3:5,9)
  2.   As well as, *putting on* the Mind of Christ (Ephesians 4:22-24; Isaiah 11:3) (the "new" self—Christ in us, our hope of Glory) (Colossians 3:8-10, 12-14; Galatians 3:27; 5:22-25; Romans 7:25; 13:12, 14; Ephesians 6:11-20)
  3.   A *renewed mind* is one in which the Mind of Christ is operating fully; it's being single-minded (John 17:11) and serving the "law of God" (Romans 7:25)

Why is Mind Renewal so Important?
- A.   God wants us to have His Mind in everything; He wants us to see all things that happen to us from His perspective (Genesis 50:20; Romans 8:28; John 11:14-15; Philippians 2:5-9; 3:8-15)
  1.   God thinks only good things about us (Jeremiah 29:11)
  2.   When we renew our thinking, we won't be bound by our "chains of sin" (Proverbs 5:22)
  3.   We will be *renewed like the eagle* (Isaiah 40:31; Psalm 103:5)
    - a.   The eagle is a symbol of the renewal process (Psalm 103:5)
      - .   The eagle has telescopic sight
      - .   After molting, the eagle's physical strength is renewed
    - b.   Our youth is renewed like the eagles when we are conformed into Christ's Image (Psalm 71:20b; Job 33:25)
      - .   *Youth* is the original image that God created us to have (Romans 8:29)
      - .   When our minds are renewed, we will have God's Life (Isaiah 11: 2-4; 40:31; 59:19)
    - c.   We will be brought back from darkness to light (John 3:20-21)
    - d.   We will have the ability to *see*—judge and discern things—from God's perspective (1 Corinthians 2:14-16; Hebrews 11:13; Deuteronomy 32: 11-12) and not get buried in our own emotions
- B.   Whoever directs our thinking will direct our lives
  1.   Whoever controls our minds, will be the one controlling our lives (Proverbs 23:7; Matthew 6:23; 1 John 1:5-7)
  2.   If Satan can direct our thinking by keeping us immersed in our own emotional reactions, he's got us and he doesn't have to do anything else
  3.   We will be "conformed to the world's image," not God's (Romans 12:2)
- C.   If there is no mind change, there will be no life change either (Jeremiah 48:11; James 1:22-24)
  1.   We must constantly have our *self-life exposed and rooted out* so that our souls <u>can be</u> transformed (Isaiah 1:19)
  2.   Without a renewed mind, our thinking will remain the same and our life will not change (2 Corinthians 2:14-16; Romans 12:2)
    - a.   Our lives will have the same crumbling as before (Isaiah 59:10; Zephaniah 1:12-13)
    - b.   Our wounds are incurable (Jeremiah 30:12)
    - c.   We won't be able to do God's Will (Philippians 2:13)

3. We'll be "conformed to the world," not transformed out of it (James 1:22-24; Ephesians 4:22-23)
    a. Because there is much disobedience in the Body of Christ today (Hosea 4:1)
       . Many are ignorant as to *how to* renew their minds (Isaiah 59:10)
       . However, others refuse to change or renew their thinking
    b. If our thinking process is not renewed, there will be no change of life in our souls no matter what we try
    c. We can't serve God from woundedness (Proverbs 18:14)
       . God's answer to woundedness is for us to renew our minds (Ephesians 4:23)
       . And to receive a transformed life (Romans 12:1-2)
D. Without a renewed mind, we're unable to discern the true from the false (Isaiah 11:3-4)
    1. Even as Christians, we can be deceived (1 John 2:26; 2 Corinthians 11:3,13-14; 1 Timothy 4:1; John 8:44; Ephesians 2:2)
    2. The Mind of Christ gives us the ability to discern the truth inside, as well as on the outside (2 Corinthians 11:13-15; Mark 13:22; 2 Timothy 3:8-15; Titus 1:13-16; Matthew 7:15-16a; 10:16; 24:14-15, 24; Proverbs 2:11-12)
    3. We need God's instructions (Psalm 32:8; Isaiah 11:3-4)
E. The Mind of Christ is what will "set the captives free" (Luke 4:18; Isaiah 61:1)
F. Only with a renewed mind, can we serve the law of God (Romans 7:25b; 12:2)

How Does God Bring Mind Renewal About?

A. If we continue on in our own way of thinking, we'll end up quenching God's Spirit (Proverbs 14:12; Judges 17:6; 21:25)
    1. This blocks God's Life in our hearts
      a. Nothing separates us from His Love in our hearts (Romans 8:35-39; 1 Corinthians 13:8; John 17:26; Colossians 1:27)
      b. However, when we make choices that are "not of faith"; we quench God's Life in our hearts— it can't flow out into our souls (Isaiah 59:2; Psalm 17:10; 119:70, our hearts are "fat as grease")
    2. All unrighteousness is sin (1 John 5:17). Whatsoever is "not of faith is sin" (Romans 14:23; James 4:17)
B. In His Love, God allows situations into our lives that force us to choose one way or another (Ezekiel 20:43; Job 16:12-14; 42:5-6; 2 Corinthians 1:9; 4:7-9; 7:10; Acts 14:22; James 1:2-4; 2 Timothy 4:5; Isaiah 45:7; John 9:3; 15:2)
    1. God wants us to see our <u>true</u> spiritual condition (Psalm 38:17-18; Matthew 15:7-8; 23:3)
    2. He wants us to see our wrong dependencies (Job 17:11; 19:8-10; 2 Corinthians 4:7-9) and learn to trust only in Him (Philippians 4:19; Job 13:15)
    3. He wants us to see the truth
      a. About God (Job 42:5; 12:13)
      b. About *ourselves* (Job 7:20; 42:3, 6; 38:2; Psalm 51:6; Isaiah 59:14-15)
        . He wants us to see that *self* is still in control (1 Samuel 12:17; 2 Samuel 12:13; Job 42:5-6; Ezekiel 20:43)
        . He wants to bring about a death to our self-life (Mark 8:34-35; 1 Peter 4:1; 2:20-24; Matthew 16:24; Job 41:25) so that we can be filled with His Life (John 15:2; 2 Corinthians 4:11)
    4. He allows brokenness in order to expose truth (Job 16:12-13; 17:11; 19:8-10; 37:13; Jeremiah 31:28; Psalm 38:17-18; Luke 1:51; James 4:7-10)
      a. He wants us to see the lies and untruths that come from within us (Job 37:9)

        b.   Some of the storms come out of the south, our "hidden chambers" (Job 37:9)

    5.   God wounds us in order to heal us (Job 5:17-18; 37:11-13; 42:5-6; Psalm 51:7-10; 71:20-21; 107:25-30; 119:71, 75; Jeremiah 30:14-17; John 12:24; Deuteronomy 8:16; 2 Corinthians 4:7-10; Acts 14:22; Hebrews 12:10)

        a.   He allows the trial, and then uses that trial for our good (Romans 8:28; James 1:2-4, 13; Job 16:12, 14; Hebrews 12:6-11; Isaiah 45:7; 53:10)

        b.   God allows these circumstances for His ultimate plans and purposes. He is our *Life* (Matthew 10:39; 16:25; Job 42:5; Leviticus 26:19)

Brokenness

   A.   Brokenness is the emptying out process (Jeremiah 1:10; 48:11-12; Zephaniah 1: 12-13; Matthew 23:26; Hosea 10:12 "breaking up the fallow ground")

    1.   Denying ourselves is learning to "set ourselves aside" (John 12:24-25; Matthew 16:24)

    2.   God wants us to see there is *life* from no other source—He must be our very Life itself (Matthew 10:39; 16:25; Philippians 1:21; 2 Corinthians 3:5; 5: 15; 12:10; Psalm 119:67, 71; Deuteronomy 30:20)

    3.   He wants us to depend totally upon Him (Psalm 34:4, 17, 19, 22; Matthew 10:37-39; 6:24-25; Proverbs 3:5-6; Jeremiah 9:23-24; 2 Corinthians 3:5b; John 12:25: Job 13:15)

   B.   So we might reach our *goal* of being "conformed into His Image" (John 3:30; 17:3; Job 42:5-6; Philippians 1:21; 3:10; 2 Corinthians 4:8-11; 12:9a; 13:4; Zechariah 4:6; John 12:24)

Suffering

   A.   Suffering is not an end in itself, but a by-product of being "conformed into His Image" (Romans 8:29; 1 Peter 5:10; John 3:30; 17:3; Job 42:5-6; Philippians 1: 21; 3:10; Hebrews 2:10; 2 Corinthians 4:8-10; 7:10; 12:9; 13:4; Zechariah 4:6; James 1:2-4)

    1.   Suffering causes pain and results in "death to self" (Matthew 16:24; Mark 8:34-35)

    2.   After, we have suffered, we will cease from sin (1 Peter 4:1)

   B.   Jesus gave us His example (Hebrews 5:8; 6:15; 1 Peter 2:21; Luke 9:22). He was made *perfect* through suffering (Hebrew 2:10)

   C.   This is the way God has laid out for us also (Hebrews 6:13-15; 1 Peter 4:1; 2 Timothy 2:11-12a; Romans 8:17)

    1.   We must "deny self, take up our cross, and *follow Jesus*" (Luke 9:23)

    2.   We must rejoice in tribulation knowing it brings forth patience (Romans 3: 3-5)

    3.   We must let the trial have it's perfect result (James 1:2-4; 1 Peter 5:10; 1 Corinthians 13:11; 2 Corinthians 4:8-11)

Resurrection

   A.   Resurrection always follows crucifixion (Galatians 2:20)

   B.   Letting go of what *we* think, feel and want, and obeying God no matter what (Matthew 10:32-35; Mark 8:32-35; Luke 17:32-33; John 12:24-26)

   C.   God's Life will then show forth

Is Brokenness a Must?

   A.   God wants us to reflect Him in all circumstances (2 Corinthians 12:9a; 13:4; Zechariah 4:6)

B. If we would surrender ourselves voluntarily, trials would not be necessary (James 1:2-4)
C. Jesus promises us, if we will resign ourselves completely to Him, He will give us His Life (2 Corinthians 4:8-11; 10:5-6)

Our Weapons are Mighty (2 Corinthians 10:3-4)

A. We wrestle not against flesh and blood (Ephesians 6:12)
B. God exhorts us to pull down (demolish) all the strongholds of the enemy (2 Corinthians 10:3-6)
    1. We must give God all our ungodly *conscious* thoughts and emotions
    2. We must also give Him all the *hidden things*, so the enemy will not have a handle in us anymore (Psalm 19:12-13)
C. We must be "wise as serpents," yet "gentle as doves" (Matthew 10:16)
D. Only by the Mind of Christ in us will we be cleansed, healed and then freed from every high thing that exalts itself against the knowledge of God" (2 Corinthians 10:5; Isaiah 59:19; 61:1; Luke 4:18; John 8:32, 36)
E. This is the only way we can "resist the devil" (James 4:7; 1 Peter 5:8-9)

It's a Mind Battle

A. Whoever directs our thinking will ultimately direct our lives (Luke 11:34a; Matthew 6:23; Proverbs 12:15a; 23:7a)
B. Only when our minds are renewed, can we serve the law of God (Romans 7:25b; 12:2; Ephesians 5:10)

Are you willing to see the truth about yourself? Are you willing to be broken of self, so that you can *know* Christ as your life itself?

Section Two:
Light on Top of a Candle

"No man, when he hath lighted a candle, putteth it in a secret place, neither under a bushel, but *on a candlestick*, that they which come in may see the light.

The light of the body is the *eye*; therefore when thine eye is single, thy whole body also is full of light; but when thine eye is evil, thy body also is full of darkness.

Take heed therefore that the light which is in thee be not darkness."

Luke 11:33-35

Chapter Three
What Is Our Mind?

Introduction

Before we can study exactly *how* to renew our minds, we must first understand exactly what our minds are. We can't renew them if we don't really know what they are.

Confusion abounds, not only secularly, but also in the Christian body, as to the definition of our *minds*. Are our minds just our conscious thoughts, our intellect, our reason? Do our minds include our will and our actions? Are our minds somehow different than our brains?

Dr. Hugh Ross, a renowned scientist in California, noted in one of his lectures that our minds are much more than our intellect or our conscious thoughts. He then sited examples of comatose people who seem to know exactly what's going on around them. He said it's been proven that some of these unconscious people, even though they are physically unable to function, do hear and do understand.

Another scientist, the late Dr. Wilder Penfield, made the statement: "It is possible to be unconscious—and unable to think—and yet accomplish complex tasks." Then, he cited the story of an epileptic train motorman who blacked out while driving a train. While unconscious, this man took his train from the 125th Street Station right into Grand Central Station in New York City. Along the way, he followed all the correct red and green lights. Penfield went on to state, "Mind would then have to be something quite different than simple brain activity."

These are some of the ideas we want to explore from Scripture to see what God tells us.

Confusion

Much of the confusion over the word *mind*, certainly in Christian circles, is caused by the liberal translation of the words "heart," "mind" and "soul" throughout the Bible. Because these words are often used interchangeably, they can cause major misunderstandings. For example, Proverbs 23:7 states, "For as [a man] thinketh in his heart, so is he."

Now, if you trace the word *heart* here back to its original Hebrew, you'll find the word is not really heart, but *soul (nephesh)*. Had the translators translated it "soul," we would have avoided the confusion.

Moreover, in the New Testament, there are 11 different Greek words simply translated *mind.*[1] Now, all these words relate to *a part of* our mind in some way or other, yet, each one of them has its own unique meaning. For instance, in the First Commandment (Matthew 22:37), Jesus teaches us to "...love the Lord, thy God, with all thy heart, and with all thy soul, and with all thy *mind....*" *Mind* here is the Greek word *dianoia. Dianoia* more precisely translated means our will and the power to perform our will. It's our willpower or our volition and yet, it is simply translated *mind.* Thus, it is often confused with all the other 11 different words rendered *mind.*

Because of the confusion, many of us have become fuzzy in our thinking as to what the real meaning of our *mind* is. And, of course, you know who again thrives on this confusion. Satan revels in it, because he knows having a *renewed mind* is the "key" to our transformation and our being able to live the truth.

"And be not conformed to this world, but *be ye transformed* [how?] *by the renewing of your mind,* so that ye may prove what is that good, and acceptable, and perfect, will of God." (Romans 12:2 emphasis added)

Satan knows that if he can just keep us *ignorant* as to what our minds are and *how to* renew them, then we'll continue to depend upon our own thinking, our own feelings and own desires (our self-life) and be guaranteed to be "conformed to this world."

Why Aren't Christians More Noticeable?

Listen to some provocative observations a Messianic Jewish believer wrote me about the overwhelming ignorance that she has observed in the body of Christ, since she has begun to learn what it means to renew her mind.

"The thing that staggers me the most is that the Church doesn't really know that they must choose to give up every scrap of self-protective justified hurt, and that we cannot feel anything (negative) for anyone, but Christ's Love. It seems to me that most of the Church is living "half" a Christian life. *I always wondered why Christians were not more noticeable in the world."*

She is right. Most of the Church <u>is</u> living "half of a Christian life." And the reason is, we have not been taught that "all these things within us"—justified or not—will not only keep us half a Christian, but will also guarantee our not being noticed in this world. And, you know why? We'll be being conformed to the world and not transformed out of it!

As you begin to learn the different words for heart, mind and soul, I would suggest that you put their real Hebrew and Greek meanings alongside the Scriptures in the margins of your Bibles. Then when you read a specific passage, you'll be assured that the word is *heart*, and not mind or vice versa.

I would also suggest getting a Strong's Concordance. You can even get a smaller paperback one that is much easier to use. You'll absolutely fall in love with the treasure house of God's Word and it will dynamically affect your walk with God. Both *The Way of Agape* and *Be Ye Transformed* began as a result of personal word studies in the margins of my Bible.

What is Our Mind?

The Greek word used for mind is *nous* (Strong's #3563). This is the Greek word used in Romans 12:2 ("renewing of our minds") and also in 1 Corinthians 2:16 ("the Mind of Christ"). *Nous* is the one Greek word you should remember for our study here. Strong's defines *nous* as "the intellect, the mind in thought, feeling or will; the understanding." Now, because this is such a general definition, it doesn't really give us too much help.

Fortunately, the Old Testament comes to our rescue. In the Old Testament, the word *mind* was translated from three Hebrew words that give us a very *graphic* picture of the importance and significance of our minds. Those words are: *reins, kidneys* and *spirit*.

Reins

What do reins do? Reins control, lead and direct action. Reins guide and make a horse do what the rider wants. Without reins, the horse will go where he pleases.

Years ago, when I was learning to ride with my girls, our trainer put us on a horse that had no reins at all, just a wire around his neck. The horse literally went in circles. He didn't know what I wanted him to do or where I wanted him to go. So, he just went in circles.

Well, our minds are just like *reins*: They can guide and direct our lives (our souls) in a straight and godly manner, if we have made the right choices. Conversely, if we have quenched God's Spirit by making emotional choices, then our minds will guide our lives in a crooked and ungodly manner.

Scripture speaks of "reins [cords, bands] of love" (Hosea 11:4) and also "reins [cords, bands] of sin." (Proverbs 5:22) God continually tries to lead and guide our lives through His *reins of love*; i.e., the Mind of Christ, whereas, if we thwart God's leading, then we give the enemy an opportunity to direct our lives through his *chains of sin*; i.e., the flesh.[2]

Psalm 32:9 seems to show this, "Be not as the horse, or as the mule, which have no understanding: whose mouth must be held in with bit and bridle...."

God wants us to be so yielded, so open and so pliable to His Holy Spirit, that as Psalm 32:8 says, He can easily "guide us with [His] eye."

Kidneys

The second Old Testament word that helps us understand a little more clearly what our minds really are, is the word *kidneys*. Kidneys have two vital functions: First, they filter out and eliminate all the debris, wastes and filth from our blood; and second, they control and regulate the amount of bloodflow into our bodies.[3]

It's the same analogy with our minds. If we are believers, then our minds filter out the debris and the filth in our lives, our hurts, resentments, unforgivenesses, etc., and our minds regulate and control whose life (whose blood) will be lived in our souls—God's or our own.

We can also note that there are two kidneys and two reins. This could be symbolic of God's *Spirit* and His *Word* that always work *hand in hand* giving us the Mind of Christ.

Spirit

The third word used in Scripture to describe our mind is the word *spirit*. This, to me, is the most significant and descriptive of the three words because our spirit and our mind are so closely related.

In the Old Testament, the words *mind* and *spirit* were often interchanged. They meant almost the same thing. Our spirit, which resides at the core of our being, creates the thoughts of our hearts and then takes those thoughts and produces them as actions out in our lives (souls). Our minds serve almost the same function. They are *the instruments or the channels* through which or by which our spirit creates our thoughts and produces our actions.

Eye and Fountain

Two other words that Scripture uses to describe our minds, are *eye* and *fountain*.

The Hebrew word for eye is *ayin* and the Greek word is *opthalmos*. Listen to a provocative Scripture about our eyes: "The light of the body is the eye: therefore when thine eye is single, thy whole body also is full of light; but when thine eye is evil, thy body also is full of darkness. Take heed therefore, that the light which is in thee be not darkness. " (Luke 11:34-35)

We have said before that *eye* stands for *mental vision* or *sight*. Now, two things are required for vision or for sight: the *light* that actually lets us "see," and the physical eye itself. This, to me, describes exactly what our minds are. Our minds are not the *Light*, God is. Our minds are simply the instrument through which or by which that *Light* comes. In other words, we see clearly, spiritually speaking, but only by the *Light* that beams through our eyes (or our minds).

Fountain

Another word used in Scripture for our minds, is the word *fountain*. Again, the Hebrew word is *ayin*, the same word for *eye*, and the Greek word is *pege*.

Ayin and *pege* denote a *fount*, a *well* or a *supply of water*, but not necessarily the original *source* of water. This again helps to explain the unique relationship between our mind and our spirit. Spiritually speaking, the *source* of the water in us is the spirit that resides at the core of our being. Our minds are simply the well or the fountain through which that water flows. (Note, if that well is not kept clean, then that water can become polluted, and eventually stopped up. Read James 3:11-12.)

A Whole Conceptual Process

Our minds, therefore, are not just our brain, our thoughts, our intellect or our reason, but a whole conceptual process that *begins* with the spirit that resides at the core of our being, and *ends* with the life actions that are produced in our souls. In other words, our minds not only include the *conception* or the creation of an idea in our hearts, but also its *fulfillment* in action in our lives.

So from now on, when you think of *mind*, don't just limit yourself to your thoughts, your intellect, or your reason. Our minds are much more than these things. Our minds not only initiate an idea in our hearts, but they also implement that idea in our souls.

In the New Testament, the proper Greek word for this total conceptual process of thinking is again *nous*.   So, from now on, whenever I speak of *mind,* either a renewed mind or the Mind of Christ,[4] I will always mean the Greek word *nous*—our total conceptual process, from spirit inception to spirit execution.

Let's get a visual picture of how this works.

Turn to **CHART 1** (on next page).

Our conceptual process of thinking, our mind, begins with the *spirit* that re-sides at the core of our being. Our spirit is the *power source* or the energy source of life source of our lives. Our spirit then creates the *thoughts* of our hearts. These thoughts are then produced out in our lives (our souls) as life *actions*. So remember: the spirit creates the thoughts and the thoughts produce the actions. This whole process is called our *mind*.

Three Types of Minds

There are three types of *minds*:

Turn to **CHART 2** (on page 70).

Mind in the natural man, i.e. an unbeliever, with no influence from God, is going to be a natural, self-centered conceptual process. This process begins when his human spirit, residing at the core of his being, creates self-centered thoughts in his heart and it ends when self-centered life actions are eventually produced in his soul.

Now, this person has no other choice because he has no other spirit, no other power source or life source within him, to produce something different from what his human spirit is telling him to think and to do.[5]

What is our Mind?

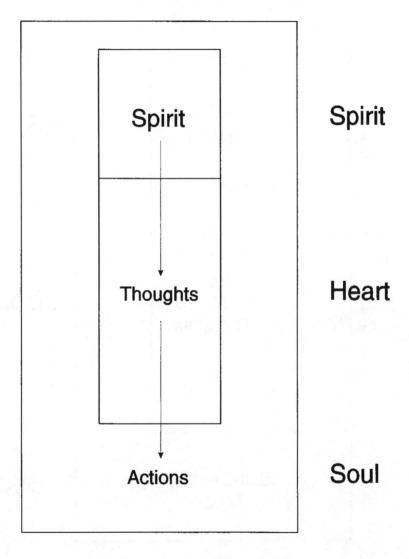

Chart 1

Unbeliever's Mind

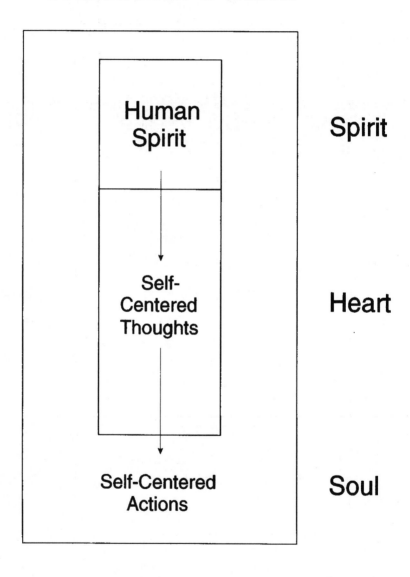

Chart 2

Turn to **CHART 3** (on next page).

Mind in a *believer,* someone who has asked Jesus into his heart, however, *should be* a God-centered conceptual process, because God's Spirit now dwells at the core of this person's being (i.e., a new supernatural power source or life source). God's Spirit creates God-centered thoughts in this person's heart, which *should* then produce God-centered life actions in his soul. This is God's ideal—His perfect Will.

This is called *single-mindedness* or being "one-souled" because there is only one life being lived here. God's Life (His Thoughts) from this person's heart is freely coming forth and producing godly life actions. This person is "living the truth" because his words and deeds match.

An Example: Joseph

A Scriptural example of someone who is *single-minded* would again be Joseph in Genesis 39. As we mentioned in Chapter Two, Joseph was assigned to work in the household of Potiphar, an officer of Pharaoh and captain of the guard. Potiphar chose Joseph to be an overseer of his house because he trusted him completely. Potiphar committed everything into Joseph's hands and God blessed Potiphar because of this.

Potiphar's wife, however, was not as trustworthy, as we said before. When Potiphar was gone, she enticed Joseph to lay with her. Refusing her offer, Joseph responded with, "how could I do that to Potiphar, when he has entrusted everything to me? And besides, how could I sin against God?" Potiphar's wife wouldn't take no for an answer and day after day, kept persisting.

One day, when Joseph went into the house, she physically caught hold of him. As he tried to flee, she ripped off his garment and kept it as evidence against him. She lied to the servants and to her husband that evening by saying that Joseph had attacked her. Potiphar was grieved, but he had no other choice but to put Joseph in prison.

The Lord adds a footnote to this story in Genesis 39:21. He says, "But the Lord was with Joseph, and showed him mercy and gave him favor...." It also goes on to say that all who saw Joseph knew God was with him.

Joseph, to me, is a perfect example of a person who is single-minded. Even though he was repeatedly tempted, he kept on choosing to give God his own self-centered thoughts so that God's Life could still freely come forth.

Believer's Mind

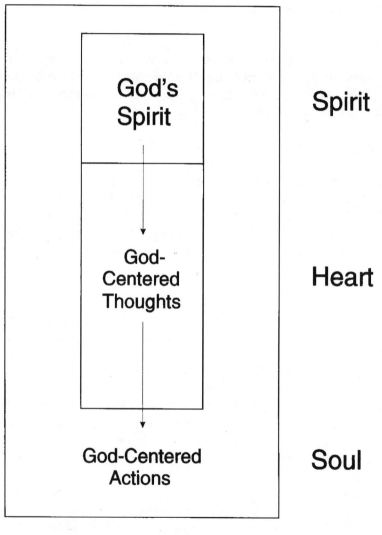

Chart 3

And, because of his single-mindedness, Joseph truly *lived the truth,* his words and his deeds matched, and everyone knew that God was with him.

Turn to **CHART 4** (on next page).

Unfortunately, there is a second type of mind in a believer and where many of us live. This is called *double-mindedness* or being "twice-souled," because two lives are being lived.

This is a believer who has God's Love and His Thoughts in his heart (one Life), but because he has chosen to follow his own lusts, hurts, frustration, anger (justified or not), guilt, etc., God's thoughts are blocked[6] from coming forth and instead, self-centered life actions are produced.

Therefore, we can be a Christian all of our lives, with God's Life in our hearts, and yet because we continue to make emotional choices to follow what we think, feel and desire <u>over</u> what God is prompting us to do, God's Life in us will be quenched. Thus, no one will ever see the difference between our life and that of our neighbors who don't even know God.

This double-mindedness makes us a hypocrite or a phony. Titus 1:16 states, "They profess that they know God [intimately], but in works [actions] they deny Him...." This is a Christian who is being conformed to the world and thus, "living a lie"[7] (his words and deeds don't match).

Double-mindedness, therefore, is the enemy's *game plan.* He will do everything he can to get us to act upon what we are feeling, what we are thinking and what others are telling us, rather than making faith choices to obey and trust God. Satan knows that double-mindedness will immediately quench God's Life in us so the Gospel won't be passed on.

Luke 11:17 explains, "...Every kingdom divided against itself is brought to desolation; and a house divided against a house falleth." [8]

An Example: David

A Scriptural example of double-mindedness is David in 2 Samuel 11. If you remember, David was on the roof of his house when he saw a beautiful woman bathing next door. Rather than catch those lustful thoughts when they first occurred, as Joseph had, David allowed those thoughts to stir up his emotions, feed his desires and finally influence his actions.

Believer's Mind

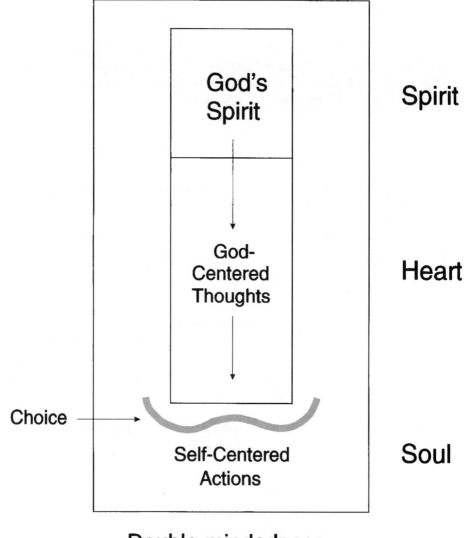

Spirit

Heart

Soul

Double-mindedness

Chart 4

David sent his servants to inquire after the woman. They came back and reported that she was Bathsheba, the wife of Uriah. That, however, didn't stop David. He chose to *act* upon his own desires, sent for Bathsheba and laid with her.

When David learned that Bathsheba was pregnant, he called Uriah home. However, in deference to his men on the front lines of the war, Uriah didn't sleep with his wife, but rested on the porch of his house.

When David found out that his coverup had not worked, he commanded that Uriah be put at the front lines of the battle and that the troops be pulled back from him. Just as David had hoped, Uriah was killed. David then took Bathsheba as his wife.

The Lord adds a footnote to this story and in 2 Samuel 11:27 He says, "...the thing that David had done displeased the Lord" and it also caused "...the enemies of the Lord to blaspheme." (2 Samuel 12:14)

David's behavior presents a perfect example of a double-minded man. Even though he had God's Life in his heart,[9] he nevertheless chose to follow the lusts of his own flesh over what God was prompting him to do.

James 1:14-15 is provocative in light of David's story. "But every man is tempted, when he is drawn away [from making the right faith choice] of his own lust [a strong desire], and enticed [captured by it]. Then when lust hath conceived [they have made the choice to follow it], it brings forth sin; and sin, when it is finished, brings forth death [separation from God]."

So, for this period of time, David lived a lie. His words *I love God* and his actions obviously did not match. People could no longer see God in him. He totally had given himself over to his own will and desires, and God's Life was blocked in his heart.

How Satan revels in our double-mindedness! He knows that double-mindedness not only keeps us bound to him by our hurts and wounds, but also, because of our actions, causes the enemies of God to blaspheme. *Double-mindedness, therefore, is Satan's game plan for each of us.*

Simplicity in Christ

In 2 Corinthians 11:3 Paul warns us about double-mindedness. He says, "I fear lest by any means as the serpent beguiled Eve through his subtilty, so your minds (*noema*) should be corrupted from the *simplicity* that is in Christ!"

Simplicity here, does not mean ignorance, or naiveté or being unschooled in the things of God. The Greek word for simplicity is *haplous* which means "singleness of mind." It means something that is folded together, braided together or intertwined. Simplicity in Christ means having our thinking folded together with and focused on Christ. It's the same thing as *single-mindedness*—having on the Mind of Christ.

Paul is saying here that just as Satan deceived, seduced and tricked Eve in her thinking by deceit and trickery, so he fears that our own thinking can easily be corrupted from the simplicity or the single-mindedness that is in Christ. He's right. Because so many of us have not understood the power and authority we possess because of the Mind of Christ in us, we've not been equipped or prepared to stand in the battle against Satan, and we've ended up falling even before we've begun.

You can see this defeat happening in the Body of Christ now. Many of us, because of *ignorance*, have become double-minded. We've not only been ignorant as to what the Mind of Christ is, but we've also been ignorant as to how, moment-by-moment, we renew our minds.

We haven't understood that it's only by constantly renewing our minds, that we can be "set free" from our fears, hurts, doubts, lusts, memories, unforgiveness and all the other negative thoughts and emotions that block God's Life in our hearts. And that God will replace these negative things with His Life: His Wisdom, His Counsel, His Strength and His Knowledge.

An Example: A Precious Sister

Let me give you an incredible example of a Christian sister who, in the worst of situations, recognized Satan's attempts to keep her double-minded, and by faith constantly chose to renew her mind.

I started corresponding with Sara only a few years ago. It was only by learning how to constantly renew her mind, that she was set free from an incredible three and a half year ordeal. Her two small children, a four month old baby son and a four year old daughter, were kidnapped by her former husband and missing for three and a half years!

Sara was in the process of divorcing this man, because of extreme physical abuse to her and her children. He had even threatened their lives. After their separation, however, he wouldn't leave her alone, but followed her and the children everywhere. One day, he literally stole the children out from under her at a day-care center. The police became involved, but they said that legally their hands were tied because there were no final custody papers.

Three Things Sara Had To Deal With

One of the first things that Sara said she had to deal with was *doubt*. She had been certain that God had told her to leave this emotionally unstable man and get the children away. "Why now, had this man won?" As she would "take those thoughts captive" and release that doubt to God, however, He would minister to her and give her peace. Repeatedly God gave her Psalm 71, which promises that He would restore her life and put to confusion those who wanted to harm her.

Next, she said, she had to deal with *unforgiveness*. By faith—not feeling like it at all—Sara choose to unconditionally forgive her ex-husband over and over again. Soon, she said, she found herself praying for his salvation and all the hate and bitterness just seemed to fade away.

Finally, there was the *fear*. Continually, she found herself in torment as she would think about her children, "Do my children have a place to sleep tonight? Are they eating right? Are they well?" Again, as she would give these things over to God, His voice would always come back, "Don't you think I love your children more than you do? Don't you think I can take care of them?"

She told me that she had to give her fears, doubts and unforgiveness over to God about 50 times a day and choose to trust and believe that God would be faithful to do what He had promised.

As she made faith choices, God always changed her negative feelings, giving her the strength to go on. Her continual promise from God was that "...all things work together for good to them that love God [to those who totally give themselves over to Him]...." (Romans 8:28)

After three-and-a-half years, a miracle happened. Through a series of events, Sara was able to locate her ex-husband and her children. At this point, the police took an active involvement in the case and the ex-husband was arrested. He went to prison, not only for kidnapping but also for many other charges as well.

Beautiful Sara is now married to a wonderful pastor back East and has an incredible ministry of her own to abused women. Her children have grown into healthy, godly children who love Jesus and who are learning to forgive, love and pray for their biological father.

If Sara can be set free of her fears, doubts and unforgivenesses, and learn to walk single-mindedly, reflecting God's Life in the midst of this situation, I believe any of us can! Sara is not a *super saint*, she's just like you and me. She has learned however, that single-mindedness is the only thing that will free us from ourselves, our circumstances and Satan's schemes.

Again, it's a mind battle. If Satan can just direct our thinking without us even being aware of it, by our continuing in our own natural emotional responses, then he has us and he doesn't need to do anything else!

Be a Light

Luke 11:33-36 describes both of the above two ways of thinking—single-mindedness and double-mindedness. "No man, when he hath lighted a candle, putteth it in a secret place, neither under a bushel, but on a candlestick, that they which come in may see the light. The light of the body is the eye: therefore when thine eye is single [*single-minded*], thy whole body also is full of light; but when thine eye is evil [*double-minded*], thy body also is full of darkness. Take heed therefore, that the light which is in thee be not darkness [covered over]. If thy whole body therefore be full of light, having no part dark, the whole shall be full of light, as when the bright shining of a candle doth give thee light."

Jesus' Life is the Light that Luke is talking about here.[10] Our goal and purpose as Christians should not only be to be filled with that Light, but also to let that Light out to others. We are not to *hide that light under a bushel* (under a wall of hurts, doubts and fears), but to *put it on a lampstand so all can see it*. In other words, be a genuine witness of Christ[11]—show forth His Life.

Turn back to **CHART 3** (page 72).

This passage in Luke says that when we are *single-minded* we will have a *body full of light* (i.e., Jesus' Life will exude from us like a flashlight). His Life will be on a lampstand where all can see it. This pictures a person living the truth, his words and deeds match.[12]

However, turn back to **CHART 4** (page 74).

You can see that when we are *double-minded,* we'll have a *body full of darkness.* We have chosen to hold on to and not deal with hurts, resentments, bitterness, anger, etc., thus, these things have blocked and quenched God's Life in our hearts.

Psalm 119:70 tells us that when we make emotional choices that quench God's Life in our hearts, our heart becomes "fat as grease." This grease then, not only clogs, chokes out and quenches any personal communication and leading from God, but it also causes us to become insensitive and unfeeling towards others.

This demonstrates how we put Jesus' Life—His Light—under a bushel (we cover it with hurts, bitternesses, etc. This then, is what forces us to *live a lie*—we say we are Christians, but our actions disprove it. This is why we then wear masks and facades—we can't let others see that Christ's Life is not working for us.

As Isaiah 59:10 describes this state, "We grope for the wall like the blind, and we grope as if we had no *eyes...*"

This is also why Christians so often get "tired"—we're *playing* Christ. We're working so hard at living His Life for Him, rather than simply relinquishing our own life, so that he can live His through us.

How the enemy revels in our *double-mindedness.* You can see by **Chart 4** how *double-mindedness* immediately blocks and quenches ("greases over") God's Life in our hearts.

Therefore, my sisters and brothers, "...be not conformed to this world, but be ye transformed [how?] by the renewing of your mind, so that ye may prove what is that good, and acceptable, and perfect, will of God [the truth]." (Romans 12:2)

Endnotes:

1. *Nous, Dianoia, Ennoia, Noema, Gnome, Phronema* and sometimes, *Katanoeo, Dianoema, Pronoeo, Noutheteo, Nouthesia* and a few more. See Appendix for "Overview of Greek Words for Mind."

2. See Chapter Ten, "Power of Sin."

3. Kidneys in the Old Testament were considered to be the choicest portion and the "life" of the animal was always considered to be "in the blood." (Leviticus 17:11)

4. Romans 12:1-2; 1 Corinthians 2:16

5. 1 Corinthians 2:14

6. Psalm 119:70

7. John 5:31

8. James 1:8

9.   Acts 13:22

10.   John 8:12

11.   Matthew 25 talks about those who are ready and prepared with their lamps trimmed. These are the ones able to go in and be with the Lord.

12.   Luke 12:35

Scriptural References:

Chapter Three

Confusion Over the Word *Mind*

    A.   There is much confusion, not only over secular word *mind*, but also concerning the Scriptural meaning of word

    B.   There are 11 different Greek words that are simply translated *mind* (see endnote #1 and "Overview of Greek Words for Mind" in the Appendix)

    C.   This confusion has caused major misunderstanding

Why aren't Christians More Noticeable in the World?

    A.   Christians are *not noticeable* because we are being "conformed to the world," not transformed out of it (1 John 3:18)

    B.   We have become under-cover Christians—no one knows that we are one because we don't know how to renew our minds (John 13:35)

What Is Our Mind? (*Nous*) (Romans 12:1-2; Ephesians 4:23)

    A.   *Mind* in the Old Testament is translated *spirit, reins* and *kidneys* (Psalms 7:9; 16: 7; 26:2; 139:13a; Jeremiah 11:20; 17:10; Job 16:13; Lamentations 3:13)

        1.   Reins

            a.   Control, lead and guide a horse (Psalm 32:9)

            b.   There are two types of horses: "hard-mouthed" and "soft-mouthed" (Psalm 32:9)

            c.   Our minds are like reins—they control, lead and guide our lives (Psalm 16:7; Revelation 2:23). Our minds are the reins between our inner man and our outer man, i.e., our *life-line*

               .   Our minds (reins) can lead and guide our lives in a crooked and ungodly manner (Satan directing) through "cords (reins) of sin" (Proverbs 5:22; Ephesians 4:18; Isaiah 5:18: Psalm 73:6)

               .   Or, our minds (reins) can lead and guide our lives in a straight and godly manner (God directing) through "cords (reins) of Love" (Hosea 11:4)

        2.   Kidneys

            a.   Have two functions:

               .   To filter out and eliminate all the debris (Leviticus 17:11)

               .   To control and regulate the amount of blood flow (Leviticus 4:9; 7:4)

            b.   When our minds are renewed, they filter out the debris of our lives and regulate whose *life* (blood) will be lived in our souls (Leviticus 17: 11)

        3.   Spirit (Ezekiel 11:5; 20:32; Daniel 5:20; Habakkuk 1:11)

            a.   In the Old Testament, spirit was often translated *mind* (Genesis 26:35; Proverbs 29:11; Ezekiel 11:5; 20:31-32; 1 Chronicles 28:9; Daniel 5: 10; Habakkuk 1:11)

               .   Our spirit creates the *thoughts of our heart* and then produces them as actions in our lives

               .   Our minds are the *instrument or channel* through which our spirit creates our thoughts and produces our actions

            b.   Our spirit is the *power source* (energy source or life source) of our lives

            c.   In an unbeliever, that "power source" is going to be the *human spirit* (Job 32:8; Zechariah 12:1); but in a believer, that "power source" is going to be the *Holy Spirit* (1 Corinthians 6:17)

    d.   The spirit of a man is the *candle of the Lord* (Proverbs 20:27; Psalm 18:28; Luke 11:35)
        .   In order for our spirit to be united (at one with) God's Holy Spirit, our candle must be lit (Psalm 18:28; 1 Corinthians 6:17; John 1: 9; 3:3; 2 Corinthians 4:6; Romans 8:16 ("beareth" means *union with*))
        .   Then, God's Spirit will be the *energy source* of our lives

B.   Another word helpful in understanding what our minds are, is *eye* (*ayin*) (Luke 11:34-35)
    1.   *Eye* stands for mental vision (Matthew 13:15; John 12:40)
    2.   We need two things for vision: the physical eye and the Light itself
    3.   This describes the function of our minds: it's not the Light itself, but the instrument through which that Light flows

C.   The word *fountain* is also useful in describing our minds *(*John 4:14; Psalm 36: 9; Jeremiah 2:13; 17:13; Proverbs 14:27)
    1.   It means a fount, a well or a supply of water (John 4:14)
    2.   Again, it's not the actual *source* of the water, but only the channel through which the water flows. The *Source* of water is God (Jeremiah 17:13; Psalm 36:9; Revelation 7:17)
    3.   That well of water, however, can become polluted, blocked up and poisonous (Jeremiah 2:13; James 3:11)

Mind (*nous*) is a Whole Conceptual Process   (CHART 1)

A.   Mind is not simply our thoughts, our intellect, or our brain, but a total conceptual process that includes not only the *conception* of an idea, but also it's *fulfillment* in our lives. (Romans 12:1-2; 1 Corinthians 2:16) It's spirit inception and also, spirit execution
    1.   This process begins with the *spirit* that resides at the core of our being which creates the *thoughts* of our hearts and then, produces those thoughts as *actions* in our lives
    2.   This process is made up of seven different stages or functions; each one builds upon the last

B.   This whole process is called *mind*

Three Types of Minds   (CHARTS 2, 3, 4)

A.   Mind in the *natural man* is a natural, self-centered process of thinking (Jeremiah 12:2). The human spirit creates natural, self-centered thoughts in our hearts, which produces natural, self-centered life actions in our souls (Matthew 12:35b; Ephesians 4:17-19)
    1.   These people cannot receive the "things of God" (Ephesians 4:17-19; 1 Corinthians 2:14)
    2.   Nor, can they "know" Him (Job 28:20-21; Romans 3:11)

B.   Mind in a believer <u>should be</u> a God-centered process of thinking. God's Spirit creates God's Thoughts in our hearts, which then become Godly actions in our lives (Matthew 12:35a; Luke 24:45)
    1.   This is called *single-mindedness* or being single-souled (Luke 11:34a; Genesis 39; 1 John 1:7; Romans 8:6) because only one Life is being lived—God's
        a.   Jesus' Life is the *light* (John 1:4, 8-9; 1 John 1:5; Isaiah 42:6) and His Life is what is shinning forth (Matthew 5:14-16; Ephesians 5:8; Isaiah 62:1; 1 John 1:5)
        b.   Be a "flashlight" (Luke 12:35; Matthew 6:22-25; Philippians 2:5)

      c.   When our *eye* (mind) is *single*, we will have a "body full of light" (Psalm 36:9b; Ephesians 5:8; John 8:12)

      d.   Salvation becomes apparent to all when that *Light* encompasses every part of the body (Psalm 96:2; Isaiah 62:1)

      e.   God's *fountain of living water* is then able to flow freely (John 7:38; Isaiah 41:18)

C.   However, a *believer* who has quenched God's Spirit (Psalm 119:70), will be *double-minded* or twice-souled (Luke 11:34b; 2 Samuel 11; Romans 8:6a; 1 John 1:6; Psalm 12:1-2) because two lives are being lived—God's and my our own (James 1:14-15)

    1.   This quenches God's Light and puts it "under a bushel" (Luke 11:33-34; Job 18:5-6; Isaiah 59:10)

      a.   This causes the enemies of God to blaspheme (2 Samuel 12:14)

      b.   This displeases God (2 Samuel 11:27)

      c.   We become hypocrites—our words and deeds don't match (John 5:31; Titus 1:16)

      d.   We are "conformed to the world" (Numbers 22:12-22) and living a lie because our words and deeds don't match (John 5:31)

      e.   We become unstable in all our ways (James 1:8; Luke 11:17)

      f.   We will have quenched God's fountain of living water (Jeremiah 2:13; 17:13; James 3:10-12; 2 Peter 2:17)

    2.   When our *eye* (mind) is evil (double-minded), we'll have a "body full of darkness" (Luke 11:34; Ephesians 2:3; 4:18; Matthew 13:15-16; 15:19-20; Romans 8:7; Colossians 2:18; Isaiah 32:6; 65:2)

    3.   We'll be doing what we *feel*, rather than what God's Word says (Genesis 3:3-6)

      a.   We'll be depending upon ourselves (Jeremiah 48:26, 29; Hosea 11:7; Ephesians 5:29; 2 Timothy 3:2)

      b.   Not trusting in or relying upon God

    4.   If we are not careful, we can lose our light, our savor and our saltiness (Luke 11:33-35; 14:34-35; Revelation 2:5; Matthew 25:1-13; Mark 9:50; Psalm 38:10; Job 18:5-6)

Chapter Four
Satan's Ways to Keep Us Double-minded

God's plan for our lives is that we might exhibit *single-mindedness.* As we show forth His Light (His Life), we will walk in the truth and the Gospel will be passed on. This only occurs, however, when we, moment-by-moment, renew our minds. Satan, therefore, will do anything he can to get us to follow our own thoughts and emotions, rather than taking every thought captive and putting off the junk. Satan's goal for us is double-mindedness, at any cost.

Double-mindedness will: 1) "keep us unstable in all our ways" (James 1:8); 2) quench the "light of the knowledge" of Jesus in our lives (Luke 11:34); and finally, 3) cause us to fall (Luke 11:17).

Disobedience, Doubt and Pride

The three primary ways Satan uses to keep us double-minded are: *disobedience, doubt* and *pride.* Notice the same three kinds of behavior in the following Scriptures

- These were the three responses that brought guilt upon the children of Israel. "This evil people which *refuse to hear My Words* (disobedient to God's Word), which *walk in the imagination of their heart* (doubt God's provision), and *walk after other gods* (follow and exalt other things besides God)...." (Jeremiah 13:10, emphasis added)

- These are also the same three things that Satan used to tempt Eve in the Garden of Eden: *Disobey* God's Word, *doubt* what He has provided and *do what you want.* (Genesis 3:1-7)

- Also, these are the same three tactics that show up in Matthew 4 when Satan tempts Jesus in the wilderness: Disobey God's Word, trust Satan (not God), and totally give yourself over to Satan (not God).

- Finally, these are the same three temptations that 1 John 2:16 warns us about. "For all that is in the world, the *lust[1] of the flesh* (to draw us away from His Word), the *lust of the eyes* (to doubt His provisions) and the *pride of life* (making idols of other things besides God), is not of the Father, but is of the world."

Let us explore these three strategies of Satan and see what personal application we can make. Perhaps if we can be a little more aware of the snares and pitfalls of the enemy ahead of time, we can avoid falling into some of them.

Disobedience

The first way Satan keeps us double-minded is by trying to make us <u>disobedient to God's Word.</u>[2]   God's Word says we are to "...bring into captivity every thought to the obedience of Christ; and having in a readiness to revenge all disobedience...." In other words, we are to constantly *put off* (revenge or deal with any disobedience) and *put on* the Mind of Christ. (2 Corinthians 10:5-6)

The enemy is determined to keep us consumed in and dependent upon our own negative thoughts, hurts, fears, doubts, guilt, lusts, memories, worry, judging, self-pity, bitterness, unforgiveness, criticalness, etc. If he can do this, then we'll just go along with the "tide of emotion" and end up confused, discouraged and hardened to doing God's Word at all.

Constantly, Satan whispers in our ear, "Go by how you feel. Do what you think is best. Don't listen to God. He doesn't care. He doesn't love you." ("...ye shall not surely die..." Genesis 3:4) Satan wants us to see everything that happens to us from our own emotional and horizontal viewpoint, certainly not God's.

An Example: "Only When They Come to Me First!"

I knew a young Christian girl many years ago, who was completely unwilling to forgive her friends for the unkind things they had done to her. Megan used to explain to me, "Only when they come to me first and ask my forgiveness, will I ever forgive them. And not until then!"

She was angry not only at her friends, but also at God for allowing these hurts to have happened. Now, what these young people had done to Megan *was* wrong and she *was* "justified" by worldly standards to be very hurt and angry. But God's Word tells us that we must be willing to unconditionally forgive whatever that other party has done to us, regardless if they ever ask our forgiveness or not. In other words, unconditional forgiveness is commanded in Scripture and is really the only thing that releases God to begin to work not only on us, but also on the others involved. When we don't forgive, we are not only being disobedient to God's Word,[3] but we are also opening ourselves up for the enemy.

As far as I know Megan is still unwilling to forgive her friends and still waiting for them to come to her. The last time I saw her, she had turned into a bitter, "old" woman. And, the sad part is, she's only 30! Even physically, we reflect the baggage that we carry around with us.

Can you see how the enemy reveled in my friend's "bondage" of unforgiveness? Her friends weren't his prisoners, she was! She was bound to him by her own "justified" hurts, unforgiveness and root of bitterness[4], because she refused to do what God's Word told her to do—take every thought captive, revenge all disobedience, renew her mind and allow God to love and forgive her friends through her.

Satan is the *father of lies* and his goal is to keep us disobedient to God's Word and consumed in our own negative thoughts and emotions. This, he knows, will lead us to double-mindedness.

Doubt

A second way the enemy tries to keep us double-minded is to get us to <u>doubt God's Power to perform His Word</u> in our lives. We can define "doubt" (unbelief) as simply not trusting God to keep His promises (or to do what He says), but looking to ourselves, others or things of the world to meet our needs.

First the enemy tries to get us to disobey God's Word and not take every thought captive. If that doesn't work, then he tries to get us to doubt God's faithfulness to perform His Word in our lives. The enemy loves to eat away at our confidence in God. He's a master at doing this and he knows all our holes and weaknesses.

Our Basic Needs

This doubt in the trustworthiness of God is one of the main reasons why so many Christian marriages are breaking up today. Many of us are looking *horizontally* (to each other) to have *all* our needs met, rather than looking *vertically* to God alone to provide for them.

This is exactly what Chuck and I did 20 years ago when our marriage was breaking up. We weren't looking to or trusting in God to meet our needs; therefore, we began to *strangle-hold* each other for the love, the security and the fulfillment that we each so desperately needed. And when we didn't get it from each other, our marriage began to crumble.[5]

I was talking to a woman on the phone not too long ago who made a similar comment. She said, "If I was only married to a godly man, then I would be happy and content and be a good Christian." I told her, "No, you've got the cart before the horse!"

There's no way in the world we can ever meet each other's basic needs, no matter what superman or superwoman we are married to. Only God can do that for us. And it's only when we get our eyes back on Him and trust Him to meet all our needs, that we will be happy and contented Christians.[6]

God promises us in His Word that if we "take every thought captive" and if we give Him all our fears, hurts, disappointments, anxieties, confusion, insecurities, etc., then He <u>will</u> remove them from us "as far as the east is from the west," align our feelings with our choices and meet all our needs.

Philippians 4:19 promises, "...my God shall supply *all* your need according to His riches in glory by Christ Jesus." This is His promise and He will be faithful to do this in our lives, if we simply trust Him to. Doubt quenches His Spirit and blocks what He wants to do.

An Example: "Oh, I Don't Doubt God"

Here's an example of someone who did this very thing.

Jay called me several years ago and shared how she and her husband were going through some very terrifying financial trials. She was absolutely frantic because she didn't think there would be enough money to put bread on the table.

At this particular time, Chuck and I were also experiencing financial problems, so we were not able to help them out. All I could do for her was pray and keep exhorting her to look to God because He promises to meet <u>all</u> our needs.

I kept telling Jay, "Dear friend, don't doubt God! He <u>will</u> come through." Her response, however, was one that I know grieves God's heart and quenches His Spirit. "Oh," she said, "Nancy, I don't doubt God, I just don't expect Him to meet this need."

Now, I ask you, how can God answer her prayers if she doesn't even expect Him to? James 1:6-7 declares, "But let him ask in faith, nothing wavering: for he that wavereth is like a wave of the sea driven with the wind and tossed. For let not that man think that he shall receive anything of the Lord." And Romans 14:23, "He that doubteth is damned...for whatsoever is not of faith is sin."[7]

If Satan can somehow make us think that God really can't meet all our needs, then we'll not only doubt God, but we'll also run to someone or something else that we think <u>can</u> meet our needs. And, in the case of my friend, it was *money*—money would be the answer to all her problems.

An Example: "Fully Persuaded"

During the last five years, God has given me certain and wonderful promises and has told me to "be fully persuaded that what He has promised me, He will perform" in His timing and in His way. When I look at these promises with the natural mind, these promises make no sense to me at all. And when I dwell on this, I begin to doubt that I ever really heard God to begin with—which then casts a shadow on God's faithfulness and that affects everything I do.

"If the foundations be destroyed, what can the righteous do?" (Psalm 11:3)

Our confidence and our trust must be in what God says in His Word He will do, and not in what our fears, our hurts or our doubts are telling us. God tells us that we are to have no confidence in the flesh (Philippians 3:3), but rely, trust and have confidence only in Him, regardless of how we feel or what we can see happening. Romans 4:20-21 tells us, "He (Abraham) staggered not at the promise of God through unbelief; but was strong in faith, giving glory to God; and being *fully persuaded, that what He had promised, He was able also to perform.*"[8] (emphasis added)

Shield of Faith

In Ephesians 6, God speaks about the "shield of faith" that we are to *put on* daily, in order to quench all the fiery darts of the evil one. We only put on this shield when we choose to believe what God has promised us He will do, regardless if we never see it, understand it or feel it.[9]

When we stop trusting and believing God, we let down our shield. Then, Satan comes in with all his arrows. His plan is to get us to act upon what we are *feeling*, what we are *seeing* and *what others are telling us*, rather than what God promises us He will do in His Word.

Pride

The last way that Satan tries to keep us double-minded is pride. Pride is one of his most deadly strategies, because pride affects so many other people.

Pride is simply giving ourselves over to and following what we think, feel and desire, rather than totally giving ourselves over to God. Pride is loving (*agapao*) ourselves, and not God. It's "I" before God.

William Law in his book *The Power of the Spirit* says, "Men are dead to God because they are living to self. Self-love, self-esteem and self-seeking are the essence and the life of pride; and the devil, the father of pride, is never absent from these passions, nor without an influence in them. Without a death to self, there is no escape from Satan's power over us."[10] (No wonder we have such huge problems in the Christian body today.)

The essence of pride is the declaration, "I will." Remember, Lucifer in the Old Testament who had a big problem with the "I will." Read Isaiah 14:12-15 and hear about Satan's five "I wills."

Some of our own personal thoughts of pride might be: "I don't deserve this." "I'm tired of being hurt by this person." "Why should I love him?" "I don't care anymore." "I can do it myself." "I have a right to my own thoughts." "I have a right to live my own life." "I don't need God's help."

What we are essentially saying here is that "my" own happiness (my self) is more important than what God wants. Whether we realize it or not, what we are doing here is putting ourselves above God and saying, "I am all that counts and there is none else."(Isaiah 14:14)[11]

Now, as Christians we would never consciously put ourselves before God. But, like it or not, every time we choose to follow our own thoughts and our own ways over what God is prompting, we are committing the sin of pride—and Satan rejoices.

Pride is not only disobeying God's Word and doubting His power to perform that Word, but it's being completely unwilling to follow God at all. *Pride is being so hardened in our own way of thinking that we refuse to be corrected or to change at all.*

An Example: "Neglected"

Over the last several months, I have learned of several pastor's wives who have walked out of their marriages. In each case, there was no other person involved, only the feeling of being unloved and neglected.

In each case, tremendous effort was made to counsel, coach and exhort these women that *changes could be made* and the marriage *could be reconciled*. But each woman was so hardened in her own hurts and bitterness, that she wouldn't hear. Now, I totally understand the feeling of loneliness and neglect that a pastor's wife experiences. My Chuck travels at least two weeks out of every month and when he is home, he runs the ministry, so he is gone or at least pre-occupied most of the time.[12] So, I do understand the lack of personal attention these wives experience, but what I <u>can't</u> understand is their jeopardizing their children's lives and the congregation's future by leaving.

"...I endure all things for the elect's sake, that they may also obtain the salvation which is in Christ Jesus with eternal glory." (2 Timothy 2:10)

What kind of an example are we showing to the church body at large, let alone nonbelievers? If marriage doesn't work for the pastor and his wife, how can we expect that it should work for them? If God is not the *answer* in our own lives, then how can we expect to teach others that?

It breaks my heart to see what happens to these dear pastors as a result. They are in the only profession that when your wife leaves you, you not only lose your family and friends, you also lose your job. Both pastors have been destroyed—materially, mentally, emotionally and spiritually.

For all parties involved here, I believe the problem goes back to the basic principle of having our *security* and *identity* in Christ and not in our spouses, our kids or our jobs. Then, if one of these supports is taken from us or the other person is not all that we expected him to be, we will neither crash ourselves nor affect so many other people.

Humility

Pride, then, is just the opposite of humility. Humility is putting God and what He wants above ourselves no matter how we feel, what we think, or what our circumstances are. The essence of humility is "Thy Will," rather than pride's "I will."

One of the reasons God hates pride so much[13] is because it automatically quenches God's Life from being shown forth in our souls and it causes us to *live a lie*—our words and deeds don't match. The end result is that the Gospel will not be passed on.[14] And, of course, that's just exactly what Satan wants.

Our Choice

Satan is after our faith itself. And since our faith is built upon the faithfulness of God, if Satan can just get us to be *disobedient to God's Word, doubt God's Power to perform His Word in our lives*, and be *pridefully unwilling to follow God* at all, then our faith will crumble and God's Life in us will cease flowing.

Please see **CHART 5** on the facing page.

So, it will be our continual choice which way we will choose to go:

1) We can choose to follow our *own* will ("self") by *disobeying, doubting and following after other things besides God.* Thus, ending up double-minded and living a lie; OR,

2) We can choose to follow God's Will by *obeying His Word, trusting His Spirit to perform His Word and following God,* no matter what He asks us to do. Thus, ending up single-minded and living the truth.

Notice, by the way, for those of you who are familiar with *The Way of Agape*, these three tactics of Satan to keep us double-minded (disobedience, doubt and pride), are the *exact* opposite of the three steps of what it means to love (*agapao*) God.[15]

To love God means to *obey His Word, trust His Spirit to perform His Word* and then *be willing to constantly follow Him* (worshiping and serving Him only)[16] no matter what we think or feel. When we do this, what we are saying is, "God is all who counts and there is no other." (Isaiah 44:6)[17]

Conclusion

So, again it is a *mind battle* that we are in. Whoever controls our thinking, will ultimately control our lives. When we don't understand how to renew our minds or how to put on the Mind of Christ, then we become double-minded, conformed to the world and we fall before we even get started.

If we can learn to *put off* the garbage, however, and put on Christ (even if we don't feel like it or think it will work), then we'll have a chance to become single-minded, transformed into Christ's Image and be able to stand against the enemy of our souls.

Therefore again, our efforts to change should not be focused on our wrong actions, but on our wrong thinking. Single-mindedness is the only thing that will free us from Satan's schemes. Only by constantly "taking every thought captive," putting off the debris and putting on the Mind of Christ, will we ever win the battle against the enemy of our souls and be able to walk the victorious Christian life.[18]

"I beseech you therefore, brethren, by the mercies of God, that ye present your bodies a living sacrifice, holy, acceptable unto God, which is your reasonable service. And, be not conformed to this world: but *be ye transformed* [how?] by the renewing of your mind, that ye may prove what is that good, and acceptable, and perfect, will of God." (Romans 12:1-2, emphasis added)

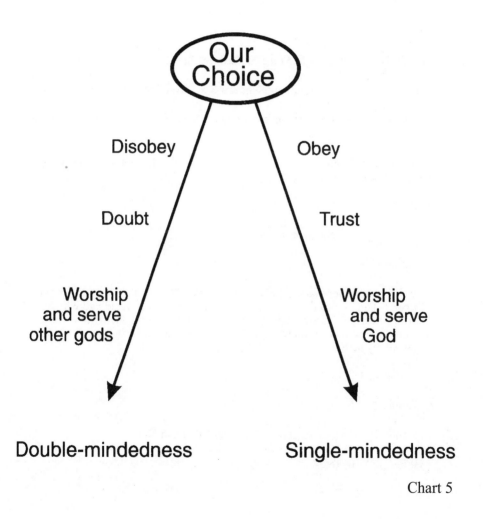

Chart 5

Endnotes:

1. The word "lust" (*epithumia,* Strong's # 1939), which means a longing for something forbidden, to covet or desire, comes from the power of sin (which we explore in detail in Chapter Ten). The whole purpose of the "power of sin" is to cause us to veer off course and miss the mark—that of being conformed into the Image of Christ.

2. Genesis 3:1

3. Jesus tells us in Matthew 6:14-15 and other places, that we are to unconditionally forgive others.

4. Proverbs 5:22

5. See our book, *Why Should I Be The First to Change?*

6. See *The Way of Agape* textbook, Chapter Six, "True Identity and Security."

7. I like this as a definition of sin: any choice that we make that is not of faith, is sin.

8. *Fully Persuaded* will be the name of my next book when God finishes what He has promised to do in my life.

9. Isaiah 59:19

10. William Law, *The Power of the Spirit,* 1761

11. Jeremiah 13:9-10

12. Does this sound familiar? Read our first book, *Why Should I be the First to Change?* This is exactly what Chuck did in the business world and why our marriage nearly fell apart. History has a way of repeating itself! This time around, I know what to do with my hurts, fears and insecurities so they don't motivate my actions. Praise God!

13. Proverbs 8:13

14. 2 Samuel 12:14

15. See *The Way of Agape* textbook, Chapters Eight and Nine

16. Matthew 4:4-10; 16:24

17. Isaiah 45:5, 21-22; 46:9

18. Luke 10:19

Scriptural References:
Chapter Four

Satan's Plan for us is Double-mindedness
A. Double-mindedness stops our *transformation* (2 Timothy 3:1-5; James 1:8; 3: 16; Job 10:15; Romans 8:6a; 1 John 1:6; 2 Corinthians 11:3; 1 Kings 18:21; Revelation 3:15-16)
   1. God's light will be quenched (Luke 11:34; Romans 7:14-18; 25c).
   2. "We grope for the wall like the blind" (Isaiah 59:10)
   3. We will be unstable in all our ways (James 1:8; Psalm 11:3; Matthew 6: 24)
   4. "A house divided against itself will fall" (Luke 11:17)
   5. Satan will be able to build stronger *strongholds* (Ezekiel 8:12; Ephesians 2: 2; Amos 3:11)
      a. He can continue to insert lies, doubts and temptations (John 8:44; Hosea 7:1)
      b. He can keep us his pawns (Proverbs 12:15; 16:2a, 25; 21:2a; Romans 6:16)
   6. We will end up "conformed to the world" and not transformed out of it (Numbers 22:12-22; 24:1; 2 Corinthians 4:4)
   7. We will be ignorant of the Mind of Christ and the power and authority we possess because of it (2 Corinthians 11:3)
   8. We will end up serving the law of sin and not the law of God (Romans 7: 23-25b)

Three Ways Satan Tries to Keep us Double-minded (Jeremiah 13:9-10; Genesis 3:1-7; 1 John 2:16; Matthew 4:1-11)
A. Disobedience to God's Word (Genesis 3:1-4)
   1. God's Word says we are to "take every thought captive" and have "readiness to revenge all disobedience" (2 Corinthians 10:5-6)
   2. Satan wants us to be consumed in our own negative thoughts (Genesis 3:4; James 3:16; Job 10:15; 2 Timothy 3:1-9; 4:3-4) and seeing everything that happens to us from our own perspective
      a. "Chains of sin" (Proverbs 5:22; Isaiah 5:18)
      b. Bondage of unforgiveness (Matthew 6:14-15)
   3. These things immediately quench God's Spirit (Psalm 119:70)
B. Doubt God's Power to perform His Word (Genesis 3:4-5)
   1. *Doubt* is not trusting God, but trusting in self, others or things of the world
   2. God promises, if we will give Him our negative thoughts, He will take them "as far as the east is from the west" and meet <u>all</u> our needs (Philippians 4: 19; 1 Timothy 2:8; Psalm 103:12)
      a. We must ask *in faith* (James 1:5-6)
      b. We are to have no confidence in the flesh (Philippians 3:3)
   3. Satan wants us to doubt God's provision, and listen to our own hurts and fears (James 1:6-7; Hebrews 3:12, 19; Ephesians 2:2-3; Psalm 11:3)
   4. Satan wants us to look to others, things, positions, etc. for the love and fulfilment that we so desperately need (Matthew 6:32; 2 Kings 18:21; Jeremiah 17:5-6)
      a. Our basic needs can only be fulfilled by Jesus (Psalm 73:25; Philippians 3:3; 4:19: 1 Corinthians 3:11)
      b. If we give Him our sin, He will cleanse us and meet *all* our needs (Psalm 103:12; Philippians 4:19)
      c. We must keep our eyes only upon Him (Psalm 4:8)

5. Trusting God (not doubting) is our *shield of faith* (Ephesians 6:16; Psalm 91:4)
   a. Must put on our shield daily (Isaiah 59:19)
   b. When we stop trusting God, we let our shield down
   c. We must remember that "anything that is not of faith is sin" (Romans 14:25)
   d. When we choose to believe, we are "more than conquerors" (Romans 8:37)
   e. We must be "fully persuaded" that God <u>will</u> do what He promises (Romans 4:20-21)
   f. If we doubt, our foundations will crack (Psalm 11:3) and then, we won't be equipped to stand in the battle against the enemy (Matthew 25:1-13; Luke 21:34-36)
C. Pridefully following what we think and feel (Genesis 3:6)
   1. Pride is "totally giving ourselves over to" ourselves—loving ourselves (Jeremiah 48:26, 29; Hosea 11:7; 13:6; Deuteronomy 8:10; Ephesians 5: 29a; Zephaniah 2:10; 2 Timothy 3:1-7)
      a. It's "I" before God (Isaiah 14:14). It's "I am all that counts and there is none else" (Jeremiah 13:9-10, 15-17; Isaiah 14:12-14; Ezekiel 28: 2-6). It's "I will," not "Thy Will" (Isaiah 14:12-15)
      b. It's "trusting in our own beauty," not God's (Ezekiel 16:15)
   2. Satan wants us to give in to and follow our own hurts, unforgivenesses, bitternesses, etc., so that our self-life shows and not God's Life (Jeremiah 48:26, 29; Hosea 11:7; Deuteronomy 8:11; Ephesians 5:29; 2 Kings 18: 29-30; 2 Timothy 3:1-7)
      a. This immediately *blocks* God's Life in our hearts (2 Peter 2:15; Daniel 5:20; Psalm 73:7; Ephesians 4:18)
      b. This causes us to *live a lie* and the Gospel will not be passed on
         . We become hardened to doing God's Word at all (Proverbs 16: 18)
         . We refuse to be corrected or to change at all (Daniel 5:20)
      c. This causes others to blaspheme God (2 Samuel 12:14)
   3. God hates pride (Proverbs 8:13). Pride and unbelief are two root causes of our sin (Deuteronomy 8:12-14, 17, 19; Daniel 5:20; Proverbs 3:7; 26:5b, 12; Isaiah 5:21; Psalm 73:6; 1 Timothy 6:4)
      a. God's rebuttal to pride is *death of self* (John 12:24-25)
      b. He wants us to *totally give ourselves over to* Him (not self), so we will show forth His Life (John 12:24-26; 2 Timothy 3:1-7; 2 Corinthians 4: 10-12)

God Continually Gives Us a Choice (CHART 5) (Deuteronomy 30:15-18; Joshua 24:15) either to:
A. Love self (Ephesians 5:29) which leads to *double-mindedness*
B. Love God (Matthew 4:4-10; 16:24) which leads to *single-mindedness* or,
   1. God wants us to love Him, by obeying His Word, trusting His Spirit to perform His Word and by totally giving ourselves over to Him
      a. If we do this, what we are saying is, "God is all that counts; there is none else" (Isaiah 44:6; 45:5, 21-22; 46:8-9)
      b. The only way we can do this is by constantly "renewing of our minds" (Romans 12:1-2)
   2. Single-mindedness is the only response that will free us from Satan's schemes (Luke 10:19)

G.D. Watson, a Wesleyan Methodist minister wrote a piece in the 1800s that has blessed many followers of Christ:

Others May, *You* Cannot

"If God has called you to be really like Jesus, He will draw you to a life of crucifixion and humility, and put upon you such demands of obedience that you will not be able to follow other people, or measure yourself by other Christians, and in many ways, He will seem to let other good people do things which He will not let you do.

Other Christians and ministers who seem very religious and useful may push themselves, pull wires, and work schemes to carry out their plans, but you cannot do it; and it you attempt it, you will meet with such failure and rebuke from the Lord as to make you sorely penitent.

Others may boast of themselves, of their work, of their success, of their writings, but the Holy Spirit will not allow you to do any such thing, and if you begin it, He will lead you into some deep mortification that will make you despise yourself and all your good works.

Others may be allowed to succeed in making money, or may have a legacy left to them, but it is likely God will keep you poor, because He wants you to have something far better than gold, namely, a helpless dependence on Him, that He may have the privilege of supplying your needs day by day out of an unseen treasury.

The Lord may let others be honored and put forward, and keep you hidden in obscurity, because He wants you to produce some choice, fragrant fruit for His coming glory, which can only be produced in the shade. He may let others do a work for Him and get the credit for it, but He will make you work and toil on without knowing how much you are doing, and then to make your work still more precious, He may let others get the credit for the work which you have done, and thus make your reward ten times greater when Jesus comes.

The Holy Spirit will put a strict watch over you, with a jealous love, and will rebuke you for little words and feelings or for wasting your time, which other Christians never seem distressed over. So make up your mind that God is an infinite sovereign and has a right to do as He pleases with His own.

He may not explain to you a thousand things which puzzle your reason in His dealings with you. But if you absolutely sell yourself to be His...slave, He will wrap you up in a jealous love, and bestow upon you many blessings which come only to those who are in the inner circle.

Settle it forever, then, that you are to deal directly with the Holy Spirit and that He is to have the privilege of tying your tongue, or chaining your hand, or closing your eyes, in ways that He does not seem to use with others. Now when you are so possessed with the living God that you are, in your secret heart, pleased and delighted over this peculiar, personal, private, jealous guardianship and management of the Holy Spirit over your life, you will have found the *vestibule* [entrance] to heaven."

Section Three:
Seven-fold Spirit of God

"And there shall come forth a rod out of the stem of Jesse, and a Branch shall grow out of His roots:

And the Spirit of the Lord shall rest upon Him, the Spirit of Wisdom and Understanding, the Spirit of Counsel and Might, the Spirit of Knowledge and of the Fear of the Lord;

And shall make Him of quick understanding in the Fear of the Lord: and He shall not judge after the sight of His eyes, neither reprove after the hearing of His ears:

But with righteousness shall He judge the poor...."

Isaiah 11:1-4

Seven Fold Spirit of God
That Gives Us
The Mind of Christ
(Isaiah 11:2)

Spirit of the Lord is the supernatural *power source* that creates God's Thoughts in our hearts

Spirit of Wisdom is all of God's *supernatural Thoughts* themselves

Spirit of Understanding is God's *personal illumination* of those Thoughts

Spirit of Counsel is God's *personal instructions* for Godly choices

Spirit of Strength is God's *supernatural ability* to perform those Thoughts in our lives

Spirit of Knowledge is *experiencing God's Life* (His Thoughts) in place of our own

Fear of the Lord is *walking in God's Love and Truth*, fleeing anything that would quench His Spirit

Chart 6

Chapter Five
The Mind of Christ
(Part 1)

As we said in Chapter Three, our *mind* (*nous*) is not just our conscious thoughts, reason or intellect but a whole conceptual process. On **Chart 1** (page 69) we showed that our *mind* begins with the *spirit* that resides at the core of our being. That spirit then creates the *thoughts* of our hearts, and, in turn, produces the *actions* of our lives.

The Mind of Christ is the very same conceptual process, only it's a "divine" process of thinking. *God's Holy Spirit* creates *God's supernatural Thoughts* in our hearts[1] and then, His Holy Spirit produces those Thoughts as *godly actions* in our lives. (Review **Chart 3**, page 72.)

An easy way to remember what the Mind of Christ is, is that it's God's supernatural Thoughts (or His Word) performed in our lives by His supernatural Power (or His Spirit). Here we have God's Word and His Spirit again working together to give us God's Mind.[2]

Now, there are seven stages or functions that form this conceptual process called the Mind of Christ and each stage depends upon the last.

My understanding for this seven-fold process of thinking comes from Isaiah 11:1-2,[3] "And there shall come forth a rod out of the stem of Jesse, and a Branch shall grow out of his roots [this is Jesus, of course]: and the *Spirit of the Lord* shall rest upon Him, [that is] the *Spirit of Wisdom and Understanding, the Spirit of Counsel and Might, the Spirit of Knowledge and the Fear of the Lord...*"[4] (emphasis added)

This passage offers us a clear understanding as to what the Mind of Christ is:

1) The Spirit of the Lord
2) The Spirit of Wisdom
3) The Spirit of Understanding
4) The Spirit of Counsel
5) The Spirit of Might
6) The Spirit of Knowledge
7) The Fear of the Lord

Divine Seven-fold Process of Thinking by the Holy Spirit

Let's visually take a look at this process. Turn to **CHART 6** (on page 100).

The divine seven-fold process of thinking called the Mind of Christ begins with the *Spirit of the Lord* (at the core of our being), who desires to impart to us, not only all of God's supernatural Thoughts (His *Wisdom*); but also *understanding* of those Thoughts; *counsel* as to which of those Thoughts are appropriate for our own situation; supernatural *strength* to implement those Thoughts in our lives; personal experiential *knowledge* of seeing those Thoughts manifested in our life actions; and lastly, the ability to walk in the *Fear of the Lord* (and not the fear of man), by fleeing anything that would quench His Spirit in us.

It helps me to think of the seven-fold Spirit of God that creates the Mind of Christ in us like a Jewish Menorah.

Turn to **CHART 7** (on facing page).

The *Spirit of the Lord* is the trunk or the center core of the lampstand, and then all the other six functions (capabilities, attributes) branch out from it—the *Spirit of Wisdom*, the *Spirit of Understanding*, the *Spirit of Counsel*, the *Spirit of Might*, the *Spirit of Knowledge* and the *Fear of the Lord*. So yes, the Spirit is all one (because it's the Holy Spirit), but with six different capabilities or functions or attributes. "...behold a candlestick all of gold, ...and his seven lamps thereon,..." (Zechariah 4:2)

So, it's the Holy Spirit's mission—with our consent—to produce this *mind* in us, so that we <u>can</u> "live the truth" and so that the Gospel <u>can</u> be passed on to others.

Something important to understand is that this *divine* conceptual process called the Mind of Christ does not automatically occur in our lives. Only as we "renew our minds" by putting off the garbage in our thinking, are we able to receive from the Holy Spirit, not only God's Agape Love, but also His Mind. Should we choose not to renew our minds, then we'll quench God's Spirit in our hearts, and His Love and His Mind will be blocked and prevented from coming forth.

Purpose of the Mind of Christ

This phenomenal gift of the Holy Spirit called the Mind of Christ was not just given to Jesus Christ and a few chosen men in the Bible, but 1 Corinthians 2 tells us that it was bestowed upon each of us the moment we believe and accept

Christ into our hearts. This Scripture also tells us that the whole purpose of the Mind of Christ in us, is that we might *know*—intimately experience—the things freely given to us by God.

"Now we have received, not the spirit of the world, but the Spirit which is of God; that we might *know* the things that are freely given to us of God. Which things also we speak, not in the words which man's wisdom teacheth, but which the Holy Spirit teacheth; comparing spiritual things with spiritual. But the natural man receiveth not the things of the Spirit of God: for they are foolishness unto him: neither can he know them, because they are spiritually discerned. But he that is spiritual judgeth all things, yet he himself is judged of no man. For who hath known the mind of the Lord, that he may instruct him? But *we have the Mind of Christ*." (1 Corinthians 2: 12-16, emphasis added)[5]

God wants us to *intimately know* these truths because He wants us to be able to judge everything that happens to us, <u>not</u> through our own *eyes* (our own mind), but through His Mind, through His Wisdom, His Counsel and His Knowledge, etc.

Again, throughout the Bible, the Spirit of the Lord is often referred to as "the eyes [or the mind] of the Lord." Psalm 32:8 supports this view, "I will instruct thee and teach thee in the way which thou shalt go: I will guide thee with Mine eye." And, Revelation 5:6 corroborates, "And I beheld, and, lo, in the midst of the throne and of the four beasts, and in the midst of the elders, stood a Lamb as it had been slain, having seven horns and *seven eyes, which are the seven Spirits of God* sent forth into all the earth."

Isaiah 11:3-4 also validates this: "He shall make him of quick understanding [renewed thinking] in the fear of the Lord. And he shall not judge after the sight of his [own] eyes, neither reprove after the hearing of his [own] ears: but with righteousness [Mind of Christ] shall he judge...."

Functions of the Mind of Christ

So, let's learn what the phenomenal capabilities are that we receive through the Mind of Christ, so we can implement them in our lives. Again, we can't use these incredible gifts if we don't really understand what they are.

The Spirit Of The Lord

1) THE SPIRIT OF THE LORD (Hebrew is *Ruwach* - Greek is *Pneuma*)

In this chapter, we will only touch upon the awesome subject of the Spirit of the Lord. I am not an authority or a theologian; I'm just a sister in the Lord. You have the same Teacher as I do and also the same Instruction Manual. So, be as the Bereans, check out everything that I share. (Acts 17:11) Here, we will just give an overview of the Spirit of the Lord which is the foundation of the Mind of Christ in us and His Spirit of Wisdom. The remaining five functions of the Mind of Christ will be covered in the next two chapters.

First of all, we cannot possess the Mind of Christ at all unless we have the Spirit of God in our hearts. Unless we have asked Jesus Christ into our hearts and have become, as John 3:3 says, "born again" (one Spirit with Him), this message will not work.

1 Corinthians 6:17 states, "...He that is joined unto the Lord is one spirit [with Him]." We are warned, however, in Romans 8:9 that "...if any man have not the Spirit of Christ, he is none of His."

The Bible tells us that "the spirit of a man is the candle of the Lord...." (Proverbs 20:27) Scripture goes on to say that in order for our spirit or our candle to be *united with God's Spirit*, it must be lit. And, Psalm 18:28 tells us that God is the only One who lights our candle.

So, the Spirit of the Lord is the energy source, the power source or the light source of our lives. Without God's Spirit in our hearts, we will have neither the *Agape* Love of God nor the Mind of Christ.

2 Corinthians 4:6 supports this, "For God, who commanded *the light* to shine out of darkness, hath shined in our hearts, to give [us] the *light of the knowledge* of the glory of God...."

So, the Mind of Christ is not the Light itself, God is, but simply the instrument through which God's Spirit gives us Light. Salvation occurs when the Lord "lights our candle" (when His Spirit becomes united with our human spirit); but we only "see" clearly when that Light (God) fully encompasses every part of our body.

The goal of our instruction then, as God sees it, is not more learning or more head knowledge, but simply showing forth more of Christ's Life (His Light). "Now the end of the commandment is Love [Christ's Life] out of a pure heart, and of a good conscience, and of faith unfeigned...." (1 Timothy 1:5)

The Ministry of the Holy Spirit

Let's review very briefly the various ways the Holy Spirit ministers to us. It's important that we understand how the Spirit *works with us, comes in us* and *comes upon us*, before we can understand how He daily *fills us* and manifests His Love and His Mind through us.

1) Before we belong to God, before we ask Him into our hearts, the Spirit of the Lord comes along side of us and works **with** us (*para*), leading and guiding us to Christ. He convicts us of sin and reveals Christ as the "answer."

2) The moment we ask Jesus Christ to be our Savior, the Holy Spirit then comes "IN" (*en*) to our hearts to dwell permanently. This is the time that God's Spirit becomes the indwelling power source, energy source or light source of our lives.

3) After the Spirit of God indwells us, there needs to be an *initial time* when the Spirit is released from our hearts, to come out **upon** (*epi*) our lives (our souls) for the sake of empowering us. In Acts 2, it speaks about God's Spirit coming "upon" them, so they might have power to become genuine witnesses of Him.

I believe God intended these last two ministries of the Holy Spirit, the *indwelling* of the Spirit (where He comes **in** us) and the *empowering* of the Spirit (where He comes **upon** us) to happen simultaneously. However, for many of us, this was not the case; the empowering occurred many years later.

If we are born again but not sure that God's Spirit has come *upon us*, we simply need to ask God by faith for this empowering in our lives. Scripture promises us, "how much more shall [your] heavenly Father give the Holy Spirit to them that ask him?" (Luke 11:13).

The visible *sign* that we <u>have</u> been empowered by the Spirit is not necessarily tongues, but God's *Agape* Love overflowing our lives. No one should ever need to ask us if we are "spirit-filled" or not. Our life actions should be so loving and so full of wisdom and power that they don't have to ask. They can just see. God tells us *to be* a witness with our lives, not just witness with our mouths.

"The fruit of the Spirit is Love, joy, peace, long-suffering, gentleness, goodness, faith, meekness, self-control: against such there is no law. And they that are Christ's have crucified the flesh with the affections and lusts. If we live in the Spirit, let us also walk in the Spirit." (Galatians 5:22-25)

4) Finally, once the Spirit has been released out upon our souls, there should be a constant, ***re-filling*** (*pleroo*) of the Spirit every day, all day long. The Greek word *pleroo* means to fill up a hollow or to be made complete. God's Holy Spirit desires to continually re-fill us as cleansed and empty vessels, thereby making us complete. Ephesians 5:18 tells us that we are to, "...be (being continuously) filled with the Spirit." In other words, it's a continual on-going process.

Now, this *indwelling* of the Spirit and the *empowering* by the Spirit are gifts from God and are free for the asking. However, this continual *re-filling* in our souls by the Holy Spirit depends upon our <u>own</u> moment-by-moment choices. In other words, it's our own responsibility to remain that open, cleansed and yielded vessel so that God's Spirit from our hearts can continually fill us up.

Confusion

The indwelling, empowering and re-filling by the Holy Spirit has become a very confusing and divisive subject for many Christians.

Much confusion occurs because of a misunderstanding in terminology. So, in review, God, the Holy Spirit:

Works ***with us*** (*para*) to lead us to Christ.
Comes ***in us*** (*en*) to indwell us permanently.
Comes ***upon us*** (*epi*) for a supernatural empowering to be His witnesses.
Continually ***re-fills us*** (*pleroo*) so that God's Life can continue to flow from our hearts into our lives

Therefore, the terms:

Born again means receiving the Spirit of God in our hearts—it's the indwelling of the Spirit.

Baptism of the Spirit means the initial, in-filling of our souls with the Spirit of God for empowering in order that we might be true witnesses of Christ.

Re-filling means the daily filling of our cleansed souls with God's Life from our hearts: His Love, His Wisdom and His Power. This is the "fulness of Christ"—experiencing His Life in place of our own.

Anointing means a special outpouring of the Holy Spirit for a specific task.

Fountain of Water

To help explain this continual re-filling of the Holy Spirit a little more clearly, let me give you an analogy. In Scripture, the Spirit of God is often spoken of as an eternal "fountain (or well) of water springing up from within us." Now, this *living water* begins in the deepest part of our hearts, the core of our being, where God's Spirit now resides, and wells up within us to overflowing.

Speaking of the Spirit, in John 4:14 Jesus says, "...the water that I shall give him shall be in him a well of water springing up into everlasting life."

Now, a well of water does not fill up from the "outside" inward, (like filling a glass of water), but a well of water fills up from the "inside," where the source is, upward and outward to overflowing. So, the way we are daily filled with God's Spirit is from the inside, where God's Spirit now dwells, upward and outward. (This is very different than the way many Christians teach that we are filled.)

As we learn to set our *self-life* aside, all our thoughts, emotions and desires that are contrary to God's, God's Spirit can freely come forth from the innermost part of our being and fill our souls to overflowing. This is what Ephesians 3:19 means when it instructs us to be, "...filled with all the fulness of God."

And, it's this "fulness of God" that we are talking about here with the Mind of Christ. It's a continual re-filling and overflowing of God's Spirit in a cleansed and empty vessel.

The Spirit of Wisdom

2) THE SPIRIT OF WISDOM (Hebrew is *Chockmah* - Greek is *Sophia*)

The first function or operation of the Mind of Christ in us (produced by the Spirit of the Lord), is the Spirit of Wisdom. The Spirit of Wisdom is simply all of God's supernatural Thoughts that He has already placed in our hearts at our new birth. Scripture tells us that God's Word—His Wisdom—is inscribed, engrafted and burned into our hearts the moment we believe in Him.[6]

God's Wisdom is His supernatural intelligence—His secret knowledge. It's like a *hidden mystery* that can only be revealed by God's Spirit.[7]

"That their hearts might be comforted, being knit together in Love, and unto all riches of the full assurance of understanding, to the acknowledgment of the *mystery of God*, and of the Father, and of Christ; *in whom are hid all the treasures of wisdom and knowledge.*" (Colossians 2:2-3)

God's Wisdom is not a wisdom of the world, because it can't be bought, studied for, or earned. That's why it seems that God so very often does use the "foolish things of the world" to confound the wise. God uses, not necessarily the intelligent ones, but the yielded ones. For example, Moses and David in the Old Testament and Peter in the New Testament. God does use the foolish things. Praise God, because that means He can use me!

There are many highly intelligent men who have exhaustive knowledge of the world's wisdom but are completely ignorant of God's wisdom, His thoughts and His Word. Recently we purchased Britannica's *Great Books*, which includes all the writings of the great minds of history, Plato, Aristotle, Virgil, Dante, Chaucer, Shakespeare, Descartes, Spinoza, Newton, Kant, Hegel, Darwin, Marx, Tolstoy, Freud, etc.. As I browsed through to see what these men thought our *mind* was, I was saddened, because even though these men were so gifted in so many areas with human knowledge, very few of them comprehended the truth.

As Job declares, "Great men are not always wise...." (Job 32:9) And, 1 Corinthians 1:19, "For it is written, I will destroy the wisdom of the wise, and will bring to nothing the understanding of the prudent."

Wisdom in Our Hearts

God's Wisdom is our blueprint for living. His Wisdom is going to tell us *how to come in, how to come out* and *how to judge between good and bad.*[8] How desperately we all need all three of these things. Wisdom truly is the "key."[9]

"I, wisdom, dwell with prudence, and find out knowledge of witty inventions. The fear of the Lord is to hate evil; pride, and arrogancy, and the evil way, and the perverse mouth, do I hate. Counsel is mine, and sound wisdom. I am understanding; I have strength." "Blessed is the man that heareth me, watching daily at my gates, waiting at the posts of my doors. For *whosoever findeth me findeth life*, and shall obtain favor of the Lord." (Proverbs 8:12-14, 34-35, emphasis added)

So, God's Wisdom is the *foundation* of our lives and the basis upon which the rest of our spiritual house will be built. Proverbs 24:3 validates this when it says, "through wisdom a house is built..." So, whether we realize it or not, God's Word—His Wisdom must be our sustenance, our nourishment, our food, our life's bread.

An Example: "Man shall not live by bread alone"

A few years ago, while having my coffee and toast and reading my morning newspaper, God spoke to my heart and said, "you give the best part of your day to your toast and the newspaper, what about Me?" Then, He brought to mind Matthew 4:4 which says, "Man shall not live by bread alone, but by every word that proceedeth out of the mouth of God."

As a result of this, I did a study of what it means to *live by God's Word* and I found that we are not to just dabble in and taste His Word, but we are to literally exist by it. In other words, only as we allow the Word of God to go down into our innermost part and begin to change and transform our lives, will we ever truly experience what Scripture means when it says we are to, "eat His Word." (Jeremiah 15:16)

In these end times, we can't afford to just *taste* the Word of God because, then we won't be able to stand against the wiles of the enemy or withstand the trials that God allows into our lives. I truly believe that we'll only grow in proportion to the daily diet of God's Word that we are "eating."

I know personally that my day-to-day actions are largely determined by the amount of time I've spent in the Word of God that day. Only in reading and eating His Word, will I be reminded to put off the garbage in my thinking and put on the Mind of Christ. Then, I'll be ready and prepared for whatever God might allow in my life.

An Example: "I don't have time to read"

Down the street from a house where we used to live, there were several tennis courts. Some of my Christian sisters who had told me, "I just don't have time to read the Word daily. I'm so busy," were out there on those courts at least two to three hours every day.

Now, please don't get the wrong impression. It's not that I object to exercise. I used to ride horseback and, I too, used to spend two to three hours a day riding, and I loved it. But, it was only <u>after</u> I had spent those same two to three hours seeking the Lord in His Word!

1 Timothy 4:8 is appropriate for horse back riders and tennis players, "For bodily exercise profiteth little: but godliness is profitable unto all things, having promise of the life that now is, and of that which is to come."

I think of God's written Word as a translation of the inscribed Word (Jesus) that's already in my heart. The more I understand God's written Word, the more I will understand the *living* Word who lives in my heart.

"If Any Lack Wisdom"

If you are having trouble disciplining yourself to read and hear from God, I would suggest getting a good daily Bible reading plan. There are many excellent ones available at any Christian bookstore.

Before you begin to read, pray and ask God to show you what He specifically wants you to see and understand from His Word at that particular time. If you don't find anything right away, keep on reading until you come away with something especially for you—even if it's only one verse.

"If any of you lack wisdom, let him ask of God, that giveth to all men liberally, and upbraideth not, and it shall be given him. But let him ask in faith, nothing wavering: for he that wavereth is like a wave of the sea driven with the wind and tossed. For let not that man think that he shall receive anything of the Lord." (James 1:5-7)

Another suggestion: read at least three chapters in the Bible a day—one from the Old Testament, one from the New Testament and one from Psalm or Proverbs. Then as you are seeking God and His Wisdom for your particular situation, you can watch for *His* answers in your daily reading.

Also, take any subject that you are interested in and do a word study on it. For example: if you are having marital difficulties, then do a Bible study on marriage, love, divorce, etc.. Do a study on children, husbands, jobs, careers, goals, purposes, money, etc. This is exactly how *The Way of Agape* and this particular book began.

It's critical to keep on investigating new and different ways to be excited about God's Word. Remember, we must eat His Word daily. "Unless thy law

[His Word] had been my delight, I should then have perished in mine affliction."
(Psalm 119:92)[10] We must have a daily diet of His Word.

An Example: Only Enough for a Day

Years ago, a dear friend of mine helped me proof-read all the Scriptures for
The Way of Agape. She painstakingly looked up over 1000 Scriptures. It was an
incredibly time-consuming job, so her house work and other pressing duties in
her own life were just put "on hold."

When she finished, she thought she would be able to coast for awhile, because
she'd had such a massive dose of God's Word. But, within 24 hours, she began
to falter and slip. And within a couple of days, she found herself at one of her
lowest points. God later revealed to her the critical necessity of "eating God's
Word" daily.

A massive dose of God's Word in one day won't carry us over like we might
think. Just like the Israelites had to go and get the manna (the bread from heaven)
daily, so we too, must read (and eat) God's Word daily. "...I will rain bread from
heaven for you; and the people shall go out and gather a certain rate *every day*, that
I may prove them, whether they will walk in My law, or no." (Exodus 16:4)

"...Faith cometh [how?] by hearing, and hearing by the Word of God." (Romans 10:17)

Hiding God's Word in Our Hearts

It's also very important to memorize Scripture and to literally "...hide His
Word in our hearts." (Psalm 119:11) In these end times, I'm convinced we are
going to need it.

It's always been very difficult for me to retain verses I've memorized over
a long period of time. I've had good intentions and done several memorization
plans, but I never seemed to be able to stick with any of them. Lately, the Holy
Spirit has given me a simple, but effective approach. I try to memorize and "eat"
(make my own) just one Scripture a week.

I take a particular verse that has especially ministered to me that week, write
it on a 3x5 card, look up and study the Greek or Hebrew meanings of the words,
keep that card with me at all times, and repeat the Scripture over and over again, as
I experience it and live it in my daily life. By the end of the week, that Scripture
has not only been *hidden in my heart*, it has become a part of my life.

Conclusion

A man recently wrote me, "there is an old Jewish saying that 'a wise man has no choice.' A wise man has no choice? Who in history had no choice? The obvious and immediate answer is Jesus who clearly chose the Father's Will, instead of His own. One who so loved His Father that He sacrificed His Life to His Father's Will. One so wise as to love His Father beyond all else. One that loves so much that He could not choose any other course of action. I pray that God makes me so wise as to have no choice. So wise as to always put His Will first."[11]

So, the entire Bible is God's written Wisdom and it's something I totally believe in and receive into my heart. However, I don't always understand, perceive or grasp some of the Scripture's full meaning.

As Proverbs 1:21 notes, wisdom is just the *entrance* to the city (the opening of the gates). In other words, wisdom is just the first step...to understanding...and then to knowledge....

Endnotes:

1.   Romans 8:27; 11:34

2.   1 Corinthians 1:24

3.   Revelation 1:4

4.   Proverbs 2:1-5

5.   Ephesians 3:17-19

6.   Hebrews 8:10; Psalm 40:8

7.   1 Corinthians 2:6-11

8.   1 Kings 3:7, 9

9.   Proverbs 4:7

10. Psalms 119:9-16, 33-40, 41-48, 98; Jeremiah 15:16

11. David Moore, 71233.2357@compuserve.com

Scriptural References:
Chapter Five

What is the Mind of Christ? (Isaiah 11:2-3; Revelation 5:6)
A. The Mind of Christ is a process by which the Word of God in our hearts becomes a living reality in our lives (Zechariah 4:2, 10-12)
    1. God's Word and His Spirit always work together (1 Thessalonians 1:5a; Ephesians 6:17; Psalm 23:4; John 6:63) giving us the Mind of Christ
    2. God performs His Word by His Spirit (Jeremiah 1:12; Isaiah 34:16; Psalm 33:9)
    3. Together, God's Spirit and His Word are called *truth* (1 Corinthians 1:24; Psalm 23:4c "Thy rod and Thy staff"; Isaiah 11:4c)
B. The Mind of Christ is God's supernatural *Thoughts* and His supernatural *Power* to perform them in our lives (Romans 11:34; 1 Corinthians 1:24)
C. The Mind of Christ is a divine conceptual process (Isaiah 11:2-3; Job 12:13) by which we might intimately know the things freely given to us by God (1 Corinthians 2:12-16; 2 Corinthians 4:6; Ephesians 1:17; Psalm 36:9; Psalm 139:13a; 2 Peter 1:3)
    1. Only the Spirit of God knows the *things of God* (1 Corinthians 2:12, 14)
    2. This is why He has been given to us (2 Peter 1:3)
D. The Holy Spirit creates godly thoughts in our hearts and then through a process, produces these thoughts as godly actions out in our lives (Psalm 32:8; Daniel 5: 11-12; Exodus 35:31)
E. The Mind of Christ is a seven-fold process by the Holy Spirit (Isaiah 11:1-3; Revelation 1:4): The Spirit of the Lord; the Spirit of Wisdom; the Spirit of Understanding; the Spirit of Counsel; the Spirit of Might; the Spirit of Knowledge; and, the Fear of the Lord (Proverbs 2:1-5; Daniel 5:11-12)
    1. The Mind of Christ is not the *Light* or the *Source* itself, God is (1 John 1:5; James 1:17; Matthew 4:16; John 1:4, 9; Psalm 27:1)
    2. The Mind of Christ is simply the instrument through which God's Spirit gives us Light. We *see* only through the eyes (Mind) of God (Psalm 32:8; Job 29:3; Isaiah 11:3).

The Purpose of the Mind of Christ
A. To intimately know (*oida*) the things freely given to us by God (1 Corinthians 2:12-16; Proverbs 3:5; 4:11; 20:24)
    1. The Holy Spirit through the Mind of Christ desires to teach us all things (1 John 2:20-27; John 14:26; Psalm 32:8; Ephesians 1:18; Luke 1:79; Job 12:13)
    2. The Holy Spirit through the Mind of Christ desires to give us all of God's Thoughts (1 Corinthians 2:12-16; John 16:13-15; 1 John 2:27)
    3. The Holy Spirit through the Mind of Christ desires to lead and guide us (Psalm 32:8; Job 29:3)
B. To be filled with the *fulness of God* (Ephesians 3:17-19)
C. To intimately *know* God (2 Corinthians 4:6; Ephesians 1:17)
D. To show forth Christ's Life through us, not our own (1 Timothy 1:5)
E. So, we won't judge by our own thinking, but by God's (Isaiah 11:3-4)
    1. The Mind of Christ helps us to judge all our circumstances from God's perspective and not our own (Isaiah 11:3-4; Romans 2:2a; John 5:30; 7: 24; 1 Corinthians 2:15; 2 Chronicles 19:6; Genesis 39:7-9; 50:20; Psalm 32:8)

    2.   Form a new spiritually-minded attitude (Philippians 2:5-9; 3:8-15)

F.   To fill us with knowledge of God's Will in all things (Colossians 1:9b; Luke 24:45; Proverbs 1:23; 8:8-9; Romans 8:27; Ephesians 5:17) and help us to serve the law of the Spirit (Romans 7:25a; 8:1-2, 4)

G.   All believers have the Mind of Christ (1 Corinthians 2:9-16; John 15:15; Psalm 32:8; Romans 8:15-16) in order to help them walk in the *Fear of God* (Isaiah 11:2-5) and not in the fear of man

H.   To give us *freedom* from ourselves, our circumstances, other's reactions and Satan's deceptions (Luke 4:18; Psalm 146:7-8)

I.   To help us *escape the corruption that is in the world* (2 Peter 1:4; Galatians 1: 4)

The Seven-fold Spirit of God is often called: (CHART 6)

A.   A Jewish Menorah (Zechariah 4:2)

B.   "Lamps of Fire" (Daniel 10:6; Revelation 4:5)

C.   The "candle of the Lord" (Proverbs 20:27; Luke 8:16; 12:35; Psalm 18:28)

D.   "Eyes of the Lord" (Isaiah 11:3-4; Psalm 32:8; Zechariah 4:10; Numbers 10:31c; Revelation 4:5) "Seven eyes" = seven Spirits of God (Isaiah 11:2; Revelation 1:4; 4:5; 5:6)

The Spirit of the Lord (*ruwach - pneuma*) (CHART 7)

A.   The Spirit of the Lord is the *energy source* or the life-giving power source that is now united with our spirit (1 Corinthians 6:17; 15:45; John 6:63; Romans 5:5; 8:16; Galatians 4:6)

    1.   The Spirit of the Lord is the power source that will create new Life in our hearts (Ezekiel 36:26; Isaiah 32:15; Joel 2:28-29; Romans 5:5; John 1:16; 2 Peter 1:3; Acts 1:8)

    2.   Without the Spirit of the Lord in our hearts, this message will not work. We must be *born again* in order to have God's Spirit as our new power source (John 5:3; Romans 8:9; 1 Corinthians 6:17; Galatians 4:6)

B.   The ministry of the Spirit

    1.   First, the Spirit of the Lord works *with* (para) us (Acts 19:4)

    2.   Then, the Spirit of the Lord comes *in* (*en*) us. (Acts 19:5; John 20: 22) This is where God lights the candle of our spirit (Psalm 18:28; 2 Corinthians 4:6)

    3.   Next, the Spirit of the Lord comes *upon* (*epi*) us (Acts 19:6; 1:8)

        a.   For empowering us to live the Christian life

        b.   Without this empowering, we will be lifeless, with a *form of godliness*, but denying the power (2 Timothy 3:5)

        c.   The sign that we have been empowered or filled with God's Spirit is *God's Love* (Galatians 5:22-25)

    4.   Finally, there needs to be a daily *refilling* (*pleroo*) of the Spirit all day, every day (Ephesians 5:18)

C.   The Spirit of the Lord is like a *fountain of water* that leaps up within us (John 4:10-11, 14; 7:38; Proverbs 5:15; Revelation 21:6; Jeremiah 17:13). God fills us from the *inside* (where the *Source* is) *outward* (Joel 3:18; Zechariah 14:8; Revelation 22:1; Psalm 46:4)

D.   Experiencing the *fulness of God* means continually setting aside our self-life, and allowing God's Spirit to re-fill us (Ephesians 3:19; John 4:14)

The Spirit of Wisdom (*chockmah - sophia*)
- A. The first function of the Mind of Christ produced by the Holy Spirit is the Spirit of Wisdom
  1. This wisdom is all of God's *Thoughts* that He inscribes in our hearts the moment we believe (Hebrews 8:10; Proverbs 4:4, 20-21)
  2. God's Wisdom is God's supernatural intelligence (Colossians 3:16; 1 Corinthians 2:7a; Psalm 40:8; Deuteronomy 4:5-6; Job 38:36)—His secret knowledge (1 Corinthians 2:6-11; Colossians 2:2-3)
     a. Wisdom is the ability to discern between good and evil (1 Kings 3:9, 28) and to understand our way (Proverbs 14:8)
     b. God's Wisdom is not a wisdom of this world, but a hidden wisdom (Job 28:12-21; Ecclesiastes 7:23; 1 Corinthians 1:19; 2:7-9; Ephesians 1:17)
     c. Great men don't always have God's wisdom (Job 32:9; 1 Corinthians 1:19)
- B. The Spirit of Wisdom is our *blueprint* for living (Matthew 7:24; Proverbs 4:7; 9:1; 14:8; Psalm 119:74-104)
  1. God's Wisdom tells us "how to come in" and "how to judge between good and bad" (1 Kings 3:7-9)
  2. Wisdom is the *key* (Proverbs 2:1-5; 4:7). It's the *principle* thing. Whoever finds Wisdom, finds *life* (Proverbs 3:18, 22; 4:10, 12-13, 21; 8: 12- 14, 34-35; Ecclesiastes 7:12c). It's a *tree of life*
  3. Only God's Word (His Wisdom) will bring peace and happiness (Proverbs 3:2, 13, 18; 8:11; 16:16; James 3:17)
  4. God's Wisdom is always available to us (James 1:5-6; Proverbs 7:3)
- C. God's Wisdom is the foundation of our house (Proverbs 24:3). It's our life (1 John 1:1; Deuteronomy 32:46-47; Ecclesiastes 7:12; Proverbs 4:22; John 12: 50)
  1. God's Wisdom is our bread of life (Matthew 4:4). We must *eat* of it every day (1 Timothy 4:13-16; 2 Timothy 2:15; Isaiah 34:16; Proverbs 8:34)
     a. If we only *taste* His Word, and never partake of it, our lives will never change (Jeremiah 48:11)
     b. God wants us to *eat* His Word (Jeremiah 15:16; Psalm 119:9-16, 33-40, 41-48, 92, 98)
  2. God's Word is our life (Philippians 2:16; 1 John 1:1; Deuteronomy 32: 46-47; Ecclesiastes 7:12; Proverbs 4:22; John 12:50)
  3. If we lack Wisdom, we must read God's Word (Exodus 16:19-20)
     a. Keep asking God for His answers, without wavering (James 1:5-7)
     b. Create new and exciting ways to make Bible study interesting
  4. Faith comes by hearing, and hearing by the Word of God (Romans 10:17)
- D. We must *hide God's Word in our hearts* (Psalm 119:11; Joshua 1:8; Psalm 1:2)
  1. Memorize Scripture
  2. Put on 3x5 cards
  3. Keep with you at all times
- E. Wisdom is just *the entrance* to the city" (Proverbs 1:20-21)

Chapter Six
The Mind of Christ
(Part 2)

The Spirit of Understanding

3) THE SPIRIT OF UNDERSTANDING (Hebrew is *Binah* - Greek is *Sunesis*)

The next function or operation produced by the Spirit of God giving us the Mind of Christ, is the Spirit of Understanding. Now, just because we have God's Wisdom written and inscribed in our hearts, does <u>not</u> necessarily mean that we'll have understanding of that Wisdom. This is a whole other step. A Scriptural example might be Revelation 13:18 which says, "Herein is wisdom [in other words, these are God's thoughts]; let him who has understanding [a totally new function] count the number of the beast...666."

Now, I know that the above Scripture refers to God's Wisdom, but I have no understanding of its meaning yet. It's the Spirit of Understanding that's going to open our eyes and give us the supernatural revelation we need. Proverbs 4: 7 says, "Wisdom is the principal thing; *therefore* get wisdom; [but] with all thy getting get understanding."

The Spirit of Understanding is simply God's supernatural revelations—His secret insights to His Word. Understanding means a *putting together*, a comprehending or a grasping of His Word. Again, the Spirit of God illuminates our hearts and gives us understanding of His Wisdom. In other words, He's the One who *turns on the lights* for us. Psalm 119:130 states, "The entrance of thy words giveth light; it giveth understanding unto the simple."

An Example: Written in the sand

Often in preparing for my classes over the last 20 years, I would come across something that I had no supernatural understanding of at all. As I would pray for God's enlightenment, eventually—in God's timing and in His way—the "lights" would go on.

On one occasion, when I was out riding my horse in the hills above our home, the insight (the understanding) to something that I had been struggling with for a long time, just clicked in and the "lights went on" for me.

Past history has taught me, however, that unless I immediately write down what the Lord is showing me, I won't remember it. See, I know it's not I who has turned on the lights at that moment, but God's Spirit of Understanding. And, since the insight is a supernatural revelation from God, it's <u>not</u> something that is registered in my own mind yet.

On this particular occasion, I knew I had to write down what God was showing me or I would lose it. When I ride horseback, however, I ride "English style," with britches that obviously have no pockets or any place to carry pencil or paper. So, I stopped my horse, got off, cleared a place in the sand and dirt, and scribbled with a stick what God was saying to me. Later, feeling rather silly, I drove my four-wheel drive jeep back up the hill and copied my notes.

This is a true story! God does use the "foolish things of the world...."

The point is: What good is God's Wisdom without our being able to understand it, so we can apply it to our lives? As Psalm 119:27 says, "Make me to understand the way of thy precepts: so shall I talk of Thy wondrous works."

Another Example: "Dripping wet"

Often when I'm in the shower, supernatural revelations and answers to questions that I've asked God about for months seem to pop into my mind. I don't know what it is about running water, but it seems that that's when God often opens my understanding to one of His mysteries. Again, so I won't forget it, I'll get out of the shower, tippy-toe to where I can find a pencil and paper and write down what God has shown me. Again, I know that I have not "turned on the lights" at that moment, but God's Spirit of Understanding.

So, God's Understanding comes to us in God's timing and in God's way, not our own.

Reading God's Word

The Spirit of God works along side of His Word, not only helping us understand a little more clearly the *things of God*, but also, helping us *understand ourselves better*—helping us to see our own true motivations and our own true feelings, etc.

Hebrews 4:12 declares this, "For the Word of God is quick, and powerful, and sharper than any two-edged sword, piercing even to the dividing asunder of the soul and spirit, and of the joints and marrow, and is a discerner of the thoughts and intents of the heart."

We have shared that one of the reasons why so many Christians are stumbling and falling today is because of *ignorance*. Not only ignorance about what the Word of God says and requires of us, but also ignorance about ourselves, our own attitudes, wrong dependencies and misconceived priorities. Hosea 4:14 warns us "...a people that do not understand shall fall."

All of us have God's written Wisdom lying in our laps, but many of us, because of busyness, distractions, unbelief, pride, and other self-centered thoughts and emotions, choose to depend upon how we feel, what our circumstances are and what others are telling us, rather than what God's Word says. Consequently, we not only don't understand what God desires of us, but also we don't understand why we feel and act the way we do. Then, of course, Satan comes along with another one of his subtle schemes, and total confusion sets in.

Proverbs 24:3 declares that only by understanding can a house be established. Understanding God's Wisdom is crucial to a victorious walk in the Spirit!

The Spirit of Counsel

4) SPIRIT OF COUNSEL (Hebrew is *Esa* - Greek is *Boule*)

The next function, operation or capability of the Mind of Christ in us, is the Spirit of Counsel. The Spirit of Counsel is supernatural knowledge of God's Will for our own individual lives. In other words, it's God's personal instructions, His directions, to help us make the godly choices![1] How many of you need this? I certainly do, continually.

The Spirit of Counsel becomes our personal advisor, our helper, our guide. He tells us what we should and what we shouldn't do. Philippians 2:13 promises that God is in us "...*to will* His good pleasure." This means God is in us to let us know what His Will is for our own particular situation.

The Old Testament word for counsel is *esa*. Esa means *steerage* or *not letting us veer off course* (i.e., not letting us miss the *mark*—being conformed into His Image). Naturally, only God can keep us *on course*, because only He knows our *true* course. Only He knows how to accomplish His perfect Will in our life.

Romans 8:27 instructs, "He that searches the hearts, knoweth what is the Mind of the Spirit, because He makes intercession for the saints according to the will of God."

An Example: "Lean not to thine own understanding"

Years ago, we knew a precious Christian family who lived down the street from us in Newport Beach, California. Their son was critically injured in a diving accident, similar to Joni Erekeson Tada's who broke her back and was paralyzed from the neck down. He, too, broke his back and was paralyzed.

The first week after an accident like this is always very critical. Many life and death decisions must be made. All the doctors had advised the family that if they wanted their son to survive, he must have a bone fusion operation immediately. This operation was going to be a very dangerous, especially because of the boy's already precarious physical condition.

All the doctors had concurred that the operation was the best course of action to take and everything had been done to prepare for it. The mom decided to go and be alone with God, pray and seek His Counsel. She told God that she didn't have the slightest clue as to what the best course of action was for her son. But, she acknowledged that God was in control of their lives and she asked Him that if this operation was the wrong decision, that He would intervene.

Proverbs 3:5-6 states, "Trust in the Lord with all thine heart; and lean not unto thine own understanding. In all thy ways acknowledge Him, and He shall direct thy paths."

Just as the boy was about ready to be wheeled into the operating room, an uncle who was also a neuro-surgeon on the East Coast called and told the family definitely not to have the operation. I've forgotten all the medical reasons he gave them, but the family felt God was intervening, so they chose to postpone the operation.

I'm sure the doctors were completely baffled at the family's decision, but they nevertheless conceded. Less than two hours after that phone call, the son came down with a serious respiratory problem and had he been in the middle of that operation, he never would have survived.

That operation was scheduled three more times. But in each case, God supernaturally intervened and managed to stop it. One time while the son was receiving a transfusion in preparation for the operation, he developed an allergic reaction and burst out with hives. Once again, the operation was postponed. The last I heard, the boy never had that operation, but had survived the ordeal and was doing quite well.

Waiting On God

"God's Ways are not our ways." This is why we so desperately need His Spirit of Counsel to help direct our ways, so they <u>will be</u> His ways and not our own.

God can be very creative in the ways He leads, guides and counsels us, if we allow and trust Him to and don't take matters into our own hands. The *secret* is, of course, that often we have to *wait* for His Counsel, His Advice, His Guidance as to what His Will is. In the Hebrew *to wait* means *to bind together by twisting*.

"They that wait upon the Lord, shall renew their strength; they shall mount up with wings as eagles; they shall run, and not be weary; and they shall walk, and not faint." (Isaiah 40:31)

Often, however, the waiting is the hardest part. Waiting and seeking God takes time and most of us are in too much of a hurry to do that.[2] So, rather than wait and listen for God's Counsel or His answer to our problems, we run to a friend, a pastor, a counselor or a psychologist because we feel they can give us the answers we need *right now*.

Something to remember, if our hearts are not cleansed, then we <u>won't</u> be able to hear God clearly. Psalm 66:18 acknowledges this, "If I regard iniquity in my heart, the Lord will not hear me."[3] This is often why we find it easier to talk to a pastor, a friend, or a counselor, because our hearts don't have to be cleansed, we can tell them our own side of the story and then be told what we should do.

Now, the truth is, of course, only God knows our true situation, the real, un-biased facts. Only He knows our hearts and all the debris (bitterness, resentment and unforgiveness, etc.,) that has covered them. Men can't see these things and even the best of them will still only be guessing as to what the *real cause* of our problems might be and what to do about them.

Psalm 108:12-13 makes it plain that, "...Vain is the help of man, [but] through God we shall do valiantly."

I am not saying don't ever go to counselors, because I do believe God uses them along the way. But be sure, however, that your counselor is a true, practicing believer, someone who is *living the truth*. Now, he doesn't have to be *perfect*—none of us is—but at least his life should reflect what he says. (I have known some of the *kookiest* counselors whose private lives were a mess, and yet, they still continued to tell others how to live.) If you can find someone who is living the truth, then you can be assured, as he leads you to Christ to help you renew your mind, God's Spirit of Counsel will be operating. And God will be faithful, not only to take your sins away "as far as the east is from the west," but also to speak to you and to show you what to do.

Please, and I stress this, if you are a Christian, don't go to secular, worldly counselors.[4] The reason is, you will get secular, worldly advice, which Scripture tells us is not only different from God's Wisdom and His Counsel, but is completely opposite. (Isaiah 55:8-9)

"But the natural man receiveth not the things of the Spirit of God: for they are foolishness unto him, neither can he know them, because they are spiritually discerned." (1 Corinthians 2:14)

An Example: "No one will ever dig these up again"

There was a Christian woman in one of my seminars back East, who had been going to a secular psychiatrist for years. Now, her psychiatrist helped her to see and understand some of the horrible things that had happened to her in the past. Her mother had tried to kill her by drowning her and throwing her down the stairs; she had been molested as a child; and raped as an adult, etc., but no matter how hard he tried, he could <u>not</u> take these wounds and memories away from her. In other words, He could not *heal* her.

Without Christ at the center of our counseling sessions, literally taking away our sins and renewing our minds, all we will be doing is *re-programming* those same hurts, wounds and memories right back down in the secret places (hidden chambers) making the strongholds even stronger.

Now, my friend *saw* these painful things of her past, but when her psychiatrist couldn't get rid of them for her, she had no other option but to bury them. At the time she didn't know how to give it to God. She couldn't retain them in her consciousness, because they were too painful. So, this time when she buried them, she put them under a ton of self-protective walls, vowing that *no one* would <u>ever</u> dig them up again.

This precious sister came to our seminar seeking God, but when she heard that God wanted to expose some of the things that were down in her hidden chambers, she froze, determined to leave the class at once. Three of the ladies she had come with, loved her and wouldn't let her go, however. Over a period of several days and nights, her precious friends stayed with her and ministered to her. Finally, because of God's Love through them, she felt the acceptance and the freedom to make faith choices needed to release, one more time, all of the hidden debris. Only this time she gave all the hidden things to the only One who could remove them completely.

My friend didn't have to *live through* those experiences again, but simply confess them, repent of them and give them to God. She wrote me a few weeks later and said that she was finally free and felt like a *new person*. She said she had never gone back to her old therapist, because as she puts it, she now has the "Master psychiatrist" and "He does a much better job."

So, worldly counselors can help us locate and identify our problems, but no matter how hard they try, they *cannot* take the root cause of those problems away. Without Christ in the center of our counseling session, guiding, healing and literally taking away our painful memories and wounds, we often will end up worse off than when we began.

Isaiah 30:1 declares, "Woe to the rebellious children, saith the Lord, that take counsel, but not of Me; and that cover with a covering, but not of My Spirit, that they may add sin to sin."

Another Example: "What about me?"

Many years ago, I attended a secular meeting for parents of troubled children (drug abuse, sexual promiscuity, alcohol, etc.). During this meeting of about 300 people, I was absolutely overwhelmed with the *hopelessness* that is in the world without Christ.

Parents stood up and pathetically shared how they had spent thousands upon thousands of dollars trying every way they knew of to heal their children—psychiatrists, care units, hospitals, prison schools. You name it, they had tried it.

One dad stood up and pathetically cried out, "What about me?" He said his wife had just recently left him because of the ordeal and he had spent his life savings trying to cure his daughter. The part that made him angry, he said, was that he felt his daughter was worse off now, than when she first began all the treatments.

Unanimously these poor people shared how their kids were more *hardened in their own ways*—more rebellious and more willful—now, than when they had begun the various cures. Rather than see their children healed and changed as they all had so desperately hoped for, these parents had watched as their children became even more messed up than ever before.

Why? Why were these kids worse off after these treatments, than when they began? I believe it goes back to Jeremiah 48:11—without a mind change, there will never be any life change.

The basic problem with these kids and the reason they weren't healed, is because most of them didn't have God's Spirit within them to produce a true mind change and thus, a life change. God's Spirit is the only thing that can change us from the inside out, and assure us that we <u>can</u> have lasting and permanent change.

So, no matter how hard these kids tried and no matter what secular form of therapy was administered to them, they could never have a permanent life change, because they didn't have another power source (another spirit) within them to produce something different than what they naturally thought, felt and desired. So, rather than seeing their self-life broken, as these parents desired, it was only strengthened and hardened,[5] "...adding sin to sin." (Isaiah 30:1)

Having Christ (the Spirit of God in us) is the only thing that gives us the authority to make faith choices, non-feeling choices, to change certain behaviors of ours, and know that God, by His Spirit, will produce those changes in our life actions. Thus, our only hope for consistent life change, is by constantly renewing our minds. We choose, by faith, *to put off the old*; God then, not only *puts on the new* for us, but also lives this new Life out through us.

Only God Can Be Our Healer

Even the best Christian counselors and pastors will still be unable to take away the real *root cause* of our problems. Again, they can help reveal the problems to us, but no matter how good they are as counselors, they can't cure us—they can't take these problems away for us. Only our Lord can do that. Only He is our healer.[6]

"For thus saith the Lord, Thy bruise is incurable, and thy wound is grievous. There is none to plead thy cause, that thou mayest be bound up; thou hast no healing medicines." (Jeremiah 30:12-13) But, *"...I will restore health unto thee, and I will heal thee of thy wounds, saith the Lord...."* (Jeremiah 30:17)[7] Now, this Scripture has a primary meaning for that particular time in history, but I also believe a spiritual application can be made for our lives also.

Only Jesus can see our hearts; only He can show us the real root causes of our problems; only He can take these things away from us "as far as the east is from the west"; and, only He can give us the Love we need in order to go on as if nothing has ever happened.

If more Christians could learn *how*, moment-by-moment, to renew their minds, how to put off the garbage in their thinking and how to put on the Mind of Christ, we wouldn't need the massive counseling industry that we have now. If we would just give God the opportunity to expose not only our conscious sins (the faults we are aware of), but also the hidden, root causes of these things, then more people would be genuinely and permanently healed.

Trials

God has such far-reaching purposes for the trials and the circumstances that He has allowed into each of our lives. No counselor, psychiatrist or therapist can really see, know or understand God's plans. And often in their compassion for us, they try to get us out of the *fire* before we are completely broken of self and before we have seen our self-life in it's proper light.

As a result, God, in His Love for us, must use another one of our *own* situations in order to teach us the very same lesson all over again.

So, as James 1:2-4 says, we should go to the end of our trials, so that they can have that *perfect* result that God is after—that transformation from self-life to His Life. Don't stop half-way through. Hear all of God's Counsel and let Him guide us right through to the end. In each of our situations, don't let the lessons be wasted.

During David's trials, he continually inquired of the Lord for His Counsel. David expected God to answer and God was always faithful to do so. We, too, must wait for God's Counsel and His Will, as long as it takes, we must wait.

Acts 9:6 is one of my favorites: "...Lord, what wilt Thou have me to do?" And God replies, "...It shall be told thee what thou must do."

An Example: "Don't wrap her head!"

Years ago, a nurse came up and told me an incredible story about the above Scripture.

During World War II, she was stationed on board an aircraft carrier that was being shelled. One of her fellow nurses was hit in the eye with shrapnel. As everyone rushed to her aid, God kept telling my friend "don't let them bandage her head."

The natural and most prudent medical thing to do in a case like this, is to wrap the wounded person's head to stop the profuse bleeding. And yet, over and over again in my friend's mind was, "Don't wrap her head! Wait!"

She was so convinced that it was God's voice, that against all her medical training, she obeyed His Counsel and didn't let the medics wrap her friend's head. When they got the woman to the hospital, the emergency doctors found a long sliver of shrapnel, like a needle, piercing directly into the nurse's brain. It couldn't be seen from the outside. Had they bandaged her head tightly, the sliver would have been pushed into her brain and she would have died instantly.

God's supernatural Counsel is available to all of us, when we're listening and waiting upon Him.

How Do We Know God's Will?

Now it's wonderful when we can *hear* God's voice in an emergency situation like the one above, but often, in our day-to-day living, God's Voice comes from reading His Word. This is where I am the most comfortable and where I am assured that it is, indeed, God's voice and not just my *own* thoughts.

I keep a pad and pencil in my Bible and, as I read His Word, I write down my questions to God. Now I'm careful to only ask Him one question at a time so that when He does answer me, I know which question He is answering. Then, in my daily reading, I expect God to talk to me. Now, it might take a day, or a week or even a month to get a specific answer to a particular question that I've asked Him, but He is always faithful to answer me in His timing and in His way.

As I read, if I find a Scripture that pertains to my question, I write it down and put a question mark beside it. When God confirms that Scripture at least two more times, then I know it's from Him and that He will give me the power I need to perform that particular thing in my life.

So, it's through God's Word that He speaks to us. This again, is another reason to be in the Word daily. Remember, *His Word will always confirm and validate what His Spirit is personally telling you, and vice versa.* As a rule, don't trust other "voices" you hear. Satan loves to play with our minds. I've been so deceived in the past by voices *I thought* were of God. When we receive something from God's Word and He confirms it over and over again, either by other Scriptures, counsel from intimate friends or life's circumstances, then we can be assured that it is from Him.

An Example: "Am I to cancel her party?"

Here's a classic example of how God's Word validates what His Spirit tells us:

On Michelle's twelfth birthday, we had planned a super birthday party. Everyone had already been invited, the place had already been reserved, the cake had already been ordered, and the food already bought. Michelle's attitude towards me that week, however, had been appalling.

After praying about it, I kept telling her that if her bad attitude kept up, I would have to cancel her party. Her behavior not only continued, but it even got worse. I threw myself upon the Lord and asked, "Am I really to cancel her party, Lord? Because it will be such a humiliating and public punishment." I wrote in my journal that day. "Lord, am I to cancel her birthday party?"

The next morning in my "daily devotional," I was in Amos 1. Now, how many times a year are we in Amos 1 for our daily reading? Certainly, not very often!

Five times in Amos 1, it says, "Do not turn the punishment away." Coincidence right? Well, I canceled her party and after "the explosion," Michelle was adorable and understood completely why I had to do it. Her behavior then began to improve dramatically.

So, God's Counsel to us can be very specific, if we are asking and if we are listening.

Another Example: Goeth out from Bethel

A dear Christian friend of mine complained that she had too many things going on in her life and was really stressed out about it. So she made of list of all the things that she was involved in, prayed and asked God to show her which commitments she was to quit. Her list read: Bethel Ballet, Bible Studies, pro-life groups, wife, mother, etc.

In her daily reading the next day, she got Joshua 16:2. "Goeth out from Bethel." Coincidence right? She also received several other confirmations in the

Word that it *was* God speaking and that He *did* want her to drop out of her ballet classes. Her husband concurred, so she did stop her classes and immediately her peace returned.

If You Have To Move Quickly

Waiting for God's answers is probably one of the hardest things we must do; but, it's also one of the most important things to do. If we can single-mindedly[8] *wrap ourselves around Jesus* while we wait, then He'll give us the peace we need, even in that waiting period.

If you have to move quickly, however, and you just don't have the time to *wait* for God's Counsel, I suggest this approach: First, pray and acknowledge that God is in control of your life; then, tell Him that you're not sure what His Will is in this particular situation, but that you have to move. He knows it already. Tell Him what you are about to do and then, ask Him to block it, if it's not His Will. Finally, walk confidently, knowing that God is great at slamming doors. You've done your part. The ball is now in His court and it's His responsibility to show you exactly what His Will is.

Proverbs 3:5-6 instructs, "Trust in the Lord with all thine heart; and lean not unto thine own understanding. In all thy ways acknowledge Him, and He shall direct thy paths." This is God's promise.

And also, Psalm 32:8 teaches, "I will instruct thee and teach thee in the way which thou shalt go: I will guide thee with mine eye (Mind of Christ)."

The Spirit of Strength

5) THE SPIRIT OF STRENGTH (*Gibbor - Kratos*)

The fifth function of the Mind of Christ is the Spirit of Strength or the Spirit of Might. This capability goes hand in hand with God's supernatural Counsel. Philippians 2:13 validates this, "for it is God which worketh in you, both *to will* [counseling us as to what His Will is] and *to do* [giving us His Power and ability to perform that Will in our lives]...."

What good is it to know what God's Will is for our lives, if we don't have the strength or the power to carry it out? The Spirit of Strength is God's supernatural ability to take what He has counseled us, and then, bring it forth (or perform it) in our lives.[9]

Why is it so important that God does both the *counseling* and the *performing*? It's critical because, if God does both, *He*, then, is the one who will get the glory. Jeremiah 9:23-24 declares, "Thus saith the Lord, Let not the wise man glory in his wisdom, neither let the mighty man glory in his might, let not the rich man glory in his riches: but let him that glorieth glory in this, that he understandeth and knoweth Me, that I am the Lord which exercise loving-kindness, judgment and righteousness, in the earth: for in these things I delight, saith the Lord."[10]

God doesn't need any of our own natural abilities or strengths in order to help Him out. Even though we might have great capabilities and assets of our own, He still wants us to set those aside and trust Him completely in everything. He tells us, "without Me, ye can do nothing."[11] In other words, everything we do on our own, apart from Him, is going to chalk up to nothingness or worthlessness.

An Example: Teaching

One time, I went to teach a class feeling particularly good about myself. God had given me the material I needed for the class, and I was excited about it and *confident*—always a warning signal—that I could present it well. I was really "up" for speaking that day.

However, when I got up to teach, I immediately recognized *I* was the one doing the performing and not God! I had quenched His Spirit by my self-confidence. I panicked and wanted to run because I know better—I can teach nothing in my own power and strength.

My dressing well, my being "put together" emotionally and mentally, and my knowing the material well didn't help a bit. God still must be *the One who does it all.* You had better believe I was frantically going through the steps of giving my pride over to God, even while I was up there teaching.

So, all self-confidence or dependence upon self-life has to be confessed, put aside and replaced with God-confidence. As Scripture says, "I can do all things [only] through Christ who strengthens me." (Philippians 4:13) All self-esteem (*I like what I do* and what I am) must be set aside for God-esteem (*I like what God does through me* and what He makes of me). We must always remember, it's not what *we* can do for God, but *what God will do through us*.

Yieldedness

Zechariah 4:6 points this out very clearly. It isn't "...by might [our own], nor by power [our own], *but by My Spirit*, says the Lord of Hosts." (emphasis added)

So, without God, in and of ourselves, we have no supernatural power—no inherent strength—at all. God's divine strength exists in us only when we are open and yielded vessels, freely allowing God's Life from our hearts, to flow through us.[12]

"And He said unto me, My grace is sufficient for thee; for My strength is made perfect in weakness. Most gladly therefore, will I rather glory in my infirmities, that the power of Christ may rest upon me." (2 Corinthians 12:9)

Now, *weakness* in the above Scripture does <u>not</u> mean feebleness or inability, but rather a person who is totally relinquished to God. Paul uses this word *weakness* in 2 Corinthians 13:4 when he explains, "...Jesus was crucified through weakness." Certainly, Jesus was not a weak person, but a totally yielded and surrendered Son whom God could use in whatever way He desired.

Yieldedness then, is <u>not</u> an attitude of "I give up" or "I don't care anymore." This way of thinking is really a self-centered defense mechanism and a way of protecting oneself from further hurts. This is <u>not</u> the attitude that we are speaking about here.

The Christian yieldedness that God is referring to in 2 Corinthians, is a kind of *neutral gear* that I used to talk about in my early classes on *The Way of Agape*. This type of surrendering, yielding or relinquishing is that of being a cleansed and prepared vessel—ready, willing and waiting to do whatever God asks. It's simply willing obedience, where we say, "Lord, I'm ready, cleansed and willing, use me in any way You want."

Self-Control

God's Spirit of Strength in the Greek means *power to rein in*, mastery over self, self-control, or better yet, *Spirit-control*. The Greek word *kratria* literally means to *rein in*. And this is exactly what God's Spirit of Strength does. It reins in (brings into captivity) our self-life, so that God's Life can come forth. Luke 21:19 even says, "In your patience possess [or rein in] your souls."

When we are going through hurtful times and we make faith choices not to go by what we feel, what we think and what we want, but to go God's Way, God will then give us His supernatural Strength to be able to set aside our own wild feelings, uncontrolled thoughts, and self-centered desires so that we <u>can</u> act out of His Life and not our own.

A Perfect Example: "I feel betrayed"

Years ago, Chuck and I had come to a mutual understanding on a very controversial Biblical issue and I had told several people how "we" felt on this subject. One Monday night, Chuck was going to be addressing this particular issue at his Bible Study. So, I told the interested people, mostly men, to come and hear Chuck expound on "our" position.

Much to my shock and amazement, my precious Chuck proceeded to present the exact opposite viewpoint from what we had earlier discussed privately and also from what I had told these gentlemen we believed. I was totally humiliated. These men had come to Chuck's Bible Study expecting to hear one viewpoint, and now they were hearing just the opposite from my own Chuck. I felt betrayed, embarrassed and close to tears. Had it not been my own husband's Bible Study, I'm sure I would have run out of that auditorium crying.

Luckily we had come in two separate cars, so I had 15 minutes after the study was over before I would see Chuck at home. I desperately needed to make some faith choices and get my negative thoughts and feelings *reined in.*

My car became my prayer closet. It's so critical to *deal with* our hurts and emotions immediately, before they cause us to choose our own ways. One of the first steps to dealing with our sin is letting our real feelings out and not burying them. If we can handle our emotions in the proper way by giving them to God, then Satan won't have a *place* in us.[13] (In Chapter Fourteen, we'll go into detail as to *how* we give things over to God.) But, basically, this is what I did:

1) I *recognized* my negative thoughts and feelings. I named all the feelings I was experiencing. "I feel betrayed, humiliated and embarrassed." "How could he do this to me?" "I am angry and resentful," etc.

I let God probe my inner thoughts and prayed He would show me any "secret, hidden faults." I asked Him what was the root of my wild emotions. What's really going on inside of me? God is always so faithful and He showed me that the real cause of my anger was *pride*. Chuck hadn't said what I wanted him to say and he made me look bad in front of those men! My humiliation revealed my pride.

2) I *confessed* that everything I was feeling was obviously *not of faith*, and therefore, I needed to turn around (i.e., *repent*) from following them. I, then, unconditionally chose to *forgive* Chuck (still not knowing why he said what he did. But, I needed to get clean, before I could find out).

3) I *gave all the thoughts and emotions* that God had showed me and that I was experiencing over to God and I asked Him to purge these things from me "as far as the east is from the west."

4) Finally, out loud I quoted a few of my *memorized Scriptures* so that truth could be put back in the hidden chambers where the lies had been.

By the time I got home, I experienced the most marvelous miracle. My wild negative thoughts and emotions that had been so out of control the previous 15 minutes were now completely reined in and set aside. When I encountered Chuck a few minutes later, I was able to genuinely act out of God's Love and Wisdom, and not out of my own emotions.

When I told Chuck what had happened and how I felt, he said, "Oh Honey, I didn't understand that was the position you expected me to take, I wouldn't have hurt you for the world!"

As it turns out, Chuck *never* heard me the night before when we discussed this issue, and so, he was just giving a position he felt comfortable with. When he explained this, my heart was immediately set at rest and I understood exactly what had happened. Chuck often *does* come home so totally preoccupied with business worries that if I'm at all insensitive to God's timing, whatever I share with him will go in one ear and out the other. Evidently, this was exactly what had happened the night before.

After Chuck shared his heart and I had a chance to share mine, we were able to come to a mutual agreement over the controversial issue and we called those men back and explained exactly what had happened.

Had it not been for God's Spirit of Strength to rein in my emotions, however, I don't believe we ever would have gotten as far as the truth. That misunderstanding would have turned into a *battleground* of emotions and hurts that probably would have lasted for weeks!

This is just a little example of how God can diffuse even the most volatile emotions through yieldedness and openness, even just on one side. If only one of us can simply renew our mind and deal with our emotions, then we will act out of God's Love. The other person will sense our unconditional acceptance; respond from his heart, not his defenses; truth will be revealed; and, the situation will have a chance to be righted.

If however, if we don't *deal with* our negative thoughts, but simply "go with the tide" and confront that other person out of our emotions, then, that other person will immediately sense our judgmental attitude, respond out of his defenses and not his heart. The truth will be hidden, and the situation will probably get worse.

So, just remember if we're *not* willing to take every thought captive and we're *not* willing to deal with our negative thoughts and emotions as they occur, then don't expect God's Spirit of Strength to *rein in* our self-life. He won't—He can't! We've already quenched His Spirit in our hearts.

Preparation

God's Spirit of Counsel and Strength is simply God's authority and God's Power to *put off* the habits of the flesh and to *put on* Christ. It's faith, not only to *choose* God's Will as revealed by His Counsel, but also faith that God will *perform* that Will in our lives by His Strength.

This is the victory that overcomes the world. 1 John 5:4 tells us, "For whatsoever is born of God overcometh the world; and this is the victory that overcometh the world, even our faith."

I have found that faith simply comes in the form of a constant choice.

In the Old Testament, the word for *might* (strength) is *gibbor*, which means *to overcome*. Overcomers are those who willingly, no matter what they see or feel, choose God's Will, and then, by faith, choose to trust God's Might—His ability—to work out that Will in their lives.

Overcoming means freedom from self, freedom from our circumstances, freedom from other's responses and freedom from the enemy. Revelation 12:11 tells us, "They overcame him [the enemy] by the *blood of the Lamb*, and by the *word of their testimony*, and they *loved not their lives* unto the death." Having a renewed mind, putting off our own negative thoughts and putting on the Mind of Christ is the only way that overcoming is made possible.

This is the *preparation* (the equipping, the cleansing) that each of us must do daily. It's our <u>own</u> responsibility to *put off* the old and to *put on* the new.[14] We already possess Christ's Life in our hearts, we simply must make sure that that's what's showing forth in our souls.[15] This is what will gird us for the battle ahead.[16]

I call God's Spirit of Counsel and Might, God's supernatural *willpower*, for it's God's Will and then His Power to perform it.

Endnotes:

1.   Ephesians 1:11

2.   Psalm 106:13

3.   Lamentations 3:44

4.   Psalm 1:1

5.   Psalm 81:12-13; 106:13-15

6.   Isaiah 53:5 (1 Peter 2:24); Isaiah 61:1 (Luke 4:18-19)

7.   Hosea 6:1

8.   See Chapter Three, "Simplicity in Christ."

9.   Isaiah 37:3

10. 1 Peter 4:11

11. John 15:5

12. Ephesians 6:10; Isaiah 40:29-31

13. Ephesians 4:27

14. Ephesians 4:22-24

15. Matthew 24:42, 44, 46; Luke 21:36

16. Ephesians 6:16

Scriptural References:

Chapter Six

The Spirit of Understanding (binah — *sunesis*)

A. The Spirit of Understanding is God's supernatural revelations, His insights, His illumination of His Word (Psalm 119:27, 73, 105, 130; Luke 24:31-32, 45; Ephesians 1:17-19; 3:3; Revelation 3:18; Job 32:8-9; 38:36; Psalm 36:9)
   1. Supernatural understanding is a gift from God (Proverbs 2:6; Ephesians 1:17; Luke 24:45)
   2. We are not to depend upon our own understanding (Proverbs 3:5)
B. God's Spirit of Understanding sheds light not only upon what God's Word says, but also upon what our own hidden motives are (1 Corinthians 2:14; Hebrews 4:12). God's Understanding *opens our eyes*
C. Without *understanding* we will fall (Hosea 4:14; Proverbs 2:1-5; 24:30-31). *Ignorance* is a major cause for God's "light" being quenched (Jeremiah 25: 8-11)
D. Understanding is *life* to our soul (Proverbs 3:21-22; 4:7-13, 22; Psalm 119: 144b; Nehemiah 8:8)
E. Only by understanding can a house be built (Proverbs 3:19)

The Spirit of Counsel (*esa* — *boule*)

A. The Spirit of Counsel is God's personal instruction for our individual lives (Psalm 33:11; Jeremiah 42:3; Hebrews 6:17; Ephesians 1:11b; Romans 8:27; Philippians 2:12; Acts 22:14; Isaiah 9:6). God's Spirit is our *legal advisor*
   1. Supernatural counsel is knowledge of God's Will (Romans 8:27)
   2. God's Counsel helps us make wise choices (Ephesians 1:1, 9; Proverbs 12:15; 19:20-21; Jeremiah 42:3; Romans 11:34; Isaiah 25:1)
B. *Esa* means *steerage*, not letting us veer off course or miss the *mark* (Psalm 32: 8; 89:21)
   1. The *mark* is being conformed into the image of Christ (Isaiah 30:21; Amos 7:7; Proverbs 20:18)
   2. Hearing God's Counsel helps us to be assured of *hitting the mark* (Isaiah 30:21; Amos 7:7; Proverbs 20:18; Colossians 2:7)
   3. God's Counsel *establishes* us and prepares us, so we can stand (2 Chronicles 27:6; Proverbs 25:5; Numbers 9:18)
C. We must *wait* for God's Counsel. Only He has the answers we need (Isaiah 1: 18-19; 40:13-14; Proverbs 12:15; 19:27; Habakkuk 2:1; 1 Chronicles 14:10, 14; Psalm 37:7, 9, 34; 108:12; Ephesians 1:11)
   1. God is in us *to will* (Philippians 2:13)
   2. If we don't *wait* to hear His Will (His Counsel), we will lose strength, become weary and fall (Isaiah 40:31; Psalm 106:13-14)
      a. Then, we'll become more hardened *in our own ways* (Psalm 81:12-13; 106:13-15)
      b. Our steps will be *narrowed* and we'll stumble (Job 18:7; Proverbs 1: 30-31; 11:14; Isaiah 30:1)
      c. Men (counselors) cannot help us, because they can't see our hearts (Psalm 108:12; 1 Corinthians 2:11; Proverbs 21:2)
      d. Secular counselors will give us *secular* advice, which is totally opposite from God's (Isaiah 55:8-9; Psalm 1:1; 1 Corinthians 2:14)
      e. We'll end up "adding sin to sin" (Isaiah 30:1)
      f. If sin *covers* our hearts, then we won't hear His Voice at all (Psalm 66:18; 119:70; Lamentations 3:40-44; John 9:31)

      3.   We must expect God to answer us (Acts 9:6; Hebrews 10:35-36; Proverbs 3:5; Job 12:13; Matthew 7:7-8; 1 Samuel 30:8)

D. Only God can be our healer (Psalm 147:3; Isaiah 30:26; 2 Corinthians 2:11; Isaiah 53:5; 1 Peter 2:24; Isaiah 61:1; Luke 4:18; Jeremiah 30:17)

      1.   Men cannot see or know the *root causes* of our problems—they can't see our hearts

      2.   Our wounds are incurable (Jeremiah 30:11-13; Hosea 6:1; Micah 1:9; Psalm 147:3)

      3.   Psychology teaches us to love ourselves, whereas God wants to use our *wounds* to bring us to Himself and to trusting Him more (2 Corinthians 4: 10-11)

      4.   We must "go to the end of our trials" and let them have their "perfect result" (James 1:2-4). God will continue to counsel us as to what to do (Acts 9:6)

E. How do we know God's Will?

      1.   God's Will is found by reading His Word (Psalms 32:8; 119:9, 105, 130; Proverbs 8:34-35)

           a.   Have a daily reading plan

           b.   Write out your questions to Him (one at a time) (James 1:5-6)

           c.   God will answer you through Scripture (Psalm 119:42b)

           d.   It may take a while, but wait and expect Him to answer (Ephesians 5: 17)

           e.   God will confirm His Word with other Scriptures, circumstances and godly counsel

      2.   If you have to move quickly, and you can't wait for His counsel

           a.   Pray and acknowledge God is in control

           b.   Tell Him you are not sure what His Will is, but you have to move

           c.   Tell Him what you are going to do

           d.   And ask Him to block it, if it is not His Will (Proverbs 3:5-6; Psalm 32:8)

The Spirit of Might (*gibbor — kratos*)

A. The Spirit of Might is God's supernatural ability to perform His Will in our lives (Philippians 2:13; Ephesians 3:16; 2 Samuel 22:33; Ezekiel 12:25; 1 Peter 4:11b)

B. God's Spirit of Counsel goes hand in hand with His Spirit of Might. God not only *counsels* us as to what His Will is, but He also *performs* His Will in our lives by His Might (Philippians 2:13; Jeremiah 1:12; 23:20; Isaiah 37:3; 46: 10-11; Ephesians 1:9-11; Psalm 18:32; 89:21; 2 Corinthians 8:11)

      1.   God must do both the *willing* and the *doing*, so He is the One who gets the glory (Jeremiah 9:23-24; 1 Peter 4:11)

      2.   Apart from Him, we can do nothing (John 5:19, 30; 8:28; Philippians 4: 13)

C. Yieldedness

      1.   "Not by my power, but by God's" (Zechariah 4:6)

      2.   We must be cleansed and yielded in order to have God's Power (Ephesians 6:10; 2 Corinthians 12:10; Isaiah 40:29-31)

           a.   "When we are weak, then He can be strong" (2 Corinthians 12:9-10; 4: 7; 13:9; John 5:30; Zechariah 4:6; Isaiah 40:29-31; 2 Chronicles 16:9; Ephesians 6:10; Psalm 138:3; Hebrews 11:34b; Proverbs 8:14; Leviticus 26:19-20)

           b.   He, then, will be glorified (1 Peter 4:11; Jeremiah 9:23-24; 1 Chronicles 29:11; Matthew 5:16; Romans 9:17; 1 Corinthians 1:29)

      c.   We should *boast* only in our infirmities (2 Corinthians 11:30; Galatians 6:14) and that we *know* God (Jeremiah 9:24; 1 Corinthians 1:31)

      d.   God's purpose is to show *His Power* through us (Exodus 9:16). We will be *witnesses* of Him only by His Power (Acts 1:18)

   3. Yieldedness means *totally relinquished* (in neutral gear) (2 Corinthians 12: 10; 13:4)

D. Self-control

   1. God's Spirit of Might means "mastery over self," "power to rein in," or "spirit control" (1 Corinthians 7:37; Galatians 5:16; Luke 21:19). It means *power to put off* the deeds of the flesh (Matthew 26:41; Psalm 138:3)

   2. *Kratos* means *rein*

E. Preparation

   1. God's Spirit of Counsel and Strength is God's authority and power to put off the habits of the flesh and to put on Christ. These are the true *overcomers* (Revelation 2:17)

   2. Old Testament word for might is *gibbor* which means to *overcome*

      a.   Faith is the "victory that overcomes" (1 John 5:4; Revelation 2:17, 26; 3:5, 21; Ephesians 2:8; 1 Peter 1:5, 9; Romans 4:20-21; Isaiah 34:16; Joshua 23:14)

      .   Faith to choose God's Counsel

      .   Faith that He will perform His Will in our lives by His Might

      b.   These two choices are our own responsibility (Ephesians 4:22-24)

      c.   *Overcoming* simply means "freedom from self" (John 8:31-32, 34-36), freedom from power of sin (Revelation 3:12; Romans 6:7; Galatians 1: 4) and freedom from the enemy (Revelation 12:11)

   3. Only the *exchanged life* will equip us for battle (Luke 21:36; Ephesians 6: 6; Matthew 24:42, 44, 46)

F. God's Spirit of Counsel and Might is God's Willpower—knowing His Will and then, having His Power to carry it out (Philippians 2:13)

Chapter Seven
The Mind of Christ
(Part 3)

Free Choice

Let me digress for a moment from exploring the supernatural functions of the Mind of Christ, and let's examine what it means to have a *free choice*. We have the free choice to follow what God has counseled us, His Spirit of Counsel, and to trust His Spirit of Strength to perform His Will in our lives, or we have the free choice to follow what we think, feel and desire (our own will) and perform it in our lives by our own strength. Our free choice is the critical *crossroads* of our lives because what we choose, moment by moment, determines whose *life* will be lived in our souls: either God's, if we make faith choices, or our own, if we make emotional choices.

I believe born again believers are the only ones who truly have a free choice. Now, surely non-believers have a choice to decide what they want to do, but none of them has the authority or the power to choose to *go against* what they naturally feel, think or want, because they don't have another power source, another spirit, within them to perform anything different.

Christians, on the other hand, have God's *authority and power* to choose something different than what we naturally think and feel, because we <u>do</u> have another power source within us to perform differently. So, we don't have to be carried on by the "tide of emotion," because we have God's Spirit within us, not only enabling us to choose something different than what we think and feel, but also enabling us to perform something different in our lives than what we think and feel.

I call this kind of a choice a *contrary choice.* It's a faith choice, or a non-feeling choice. It's a choice that is often contrary to how we naturally feel, what we think and what we desire, but nevertheless, is valid because God is the One who gives us the authority to make it. 1 Corinthians 7:37 tells us we have "...power [authority] over our own will...."[1]

So, as Christians, we can be honest with God and say, "I don't like this person. I don't want to forgive him. I don't want to love him. He has hurt me too much." But, then we can make a *contrary choice* (contrary to what we are feeling) and say, "Nevertheless, not my will, but Thine" (Matthew 26:39). In other words,

"I'll do what You want, regardless of how I feel." Then we can know that God will honor our choice by changing our feelings in His timing, making us genuine and performing that thing in our lives.

What's so incredible about *contrary choices* is that God does, in His timing and in His Way, not only change our negative thoughts and feelings to align with what we have chosen, but He also gives us the Love we need to go on as if nothing has happened. If we can just be willing to make the right choices, God will do the rest.[2]

An Example: Mother-in-law Troubles

A perfect example: Many years ago, I received a letter from Martha, a dear friend of mine, explaining a very difficult situation she'd had with her mother-in-law. She explained that if she hadn't known how to make "contrary choices," she could have easily "ended up in the pits."

In the letter she wrote:

"My mother-in-law had come for a two-and-a-half week visit at Christmas time. During this time, the Lord had allowed a number of pressure points to surface in our relationship, pressures that can so easily occur, especially during the busy holiday season. The enemy continually sought to divide us.

I had been planning to give my husband a special surprise gift for his 50th birthday coming up shortly after the holidays. In order to give him this gift, I needed to trust the Lord for two things: child care for one week for my seven year old daughter; and $700 which I did not have. Within one day, the Lord provided the child care.

The day before Christmas, my mother-in-law asked what I was going to do for my husband's birthday. When I told her about the surprise, she volunteered to pay for half of it. My first response was to decline her generous offer, knowing that she was on a limited income, but since she was insistent, I believed it was the Lord's way of answering my prayer. I was still a bit uneasy about it, however.

Later that same day, my mother-in-law came to me and said, "Well, when are you going to tell him about his birthday gift?" Now, I had it all planned in my mind how I was going to surprise my husband on his actual birthday. When I told her this, she became very hurt, letting me know that since she was the one who was going to pay for half of it, she should be able to tell her son now, since she would not be here on his birthday.

"Self" screamed inside, "It's not fair! I planned this surprise! I didn't want her money anyway!" But, I knew deep within my spirit, however, that I was to do as she wished.

I relinquished my desires to God and asked Him to give me the grace I needed to genuinely give her permission to do as she wanted. It was so exciting—God not only gave me His Words to tell her this, but He also changed my feelings, softened my voice, and filled me with His Love for her.

I knew God was in this because it was no longer important to me to have "my way." What became preeminent was, "Will I choose to be and do what God wants?"

Well, she did tell my husband, and she did spoil my surprise, but God did deliver me. He took away my hurt and disappointment, and replaced them with His Love in my heart. We ended up having a great birthday week."

Review

Let's review briefly what we have learned so far about the Mind of Christ. In a born again believer, the *Spirit of God* is the power source (the energy source or the life source) that creates the Mind of Christ within us. The *Spirit of Wisdom* is God's supernatural Thoughts in total; the *Spirit of Understanding* is God's supernatural enlightenment of those Thoughts; the *Spirit of Counsel* is God's personal instructions for our particular situations; and the *Spirit of Strength* is His supernatural ability to carry out those instructions in our lives.

Notice here, that the first *four* operations of the Mind of Christ in us are *supernatural* gifts that we receive when we are born again. These are capabilities that are always available to us, providing our hearts are cleansed.

But, there is something very unique and very special about the last two functions of the Mind of Christ in us, the Spirit of *Knowledge* and the *Fear of the Lord*. These two capabilities are our own responsibility to achieve daily. We must not only make faith choices to do God's Will, but we must also make faith choices to lay our lives down, moment by moment, so that God's Will can be performed through us. Both these two choices are necessary to experience the last two functions of the Mind of Christ.[3]

To choose God's Will in the prayer closet is easy, but it's quite another thing to come out and to have to lay our lives down so that His Will can be performed through them. This choice often involves a *death to self*.

"For we who live are always delivered unto death for Jesus' sake, that the life also of Jesus might be made manifest in our mortal flesh. So then death worketh in us, but life in you." (2 Corinthians 4:11-12)

For example, it's relatively easy for the wife of an alcoholic to choose in her prayer closet to obey God and love her husband. However, it's something totally different to lay her life down and love her husband in action when he comes home drunk and intolerable.

Death to self is exactly what these next two functions of the Mind of Christ require. Some Christians, go their entire lives and <u>never</u> truly experience intimate Knowledge of God or walk in the Fear of Him because they're just not willing to relinquish and submit everything—their will and their lives—to God.

This, to me, is what Philippians 2:12 is talking about when it says, "work out your salvation with fear and trembling." Having intimate knowledge of God and walking in the Fear of Him is our own responsibility to *work out* moment-by-moment.

The Spirit of Knowledge

6) THE SPIRIT OF KNOWLEDGE (*Daath - Oida*)

The Spirit of Knowledge does not mean intellectual knowledge, like the secular word means, but it means *experiential* knowledge. It's not *head knowledge*, but something we know through living experience of its working in our life. Some people know the Bible backwards and forwards, and yet, they still do <u>not</u> have this kind of intimate knowledge of God—they don't know His Life as their own.

The Greek word for intimate knowledge is *Oida*. *Oida* means God's Life has come forth from our hearts and is now flooding our souls. It means His *Agape* Love has become our Love, His supernatural Thoughts have become our thoughts and His Power, our power. In other words, we have truly *exchanged* lives with Him. We have given God our own life and, in return, He has given us His. This exchange of life is what intimate knowledge of God is all about.

"I am crucified with Christ: nevertheless I live; yet not I, but Christ liveth in me: and the life which I now live in the flesh I live by the faith of the Son of God, who loved me and gave himself for me." (Galatians 2:20)

Two Ways to *Know* God

See, there are two ways we can *know* God: 1) *Oida* knowledge, which means intimate knowledge of God; or, 2) We can simply know Christ as Savior. And the Greek word for this kind of knowledge is *ginosko,* which means impartial, objective knowledge that we gain from reading books about God or from what we hear others say. I like to call *ginosko* knowledge "beginning knowledge" or knowledge with lots of self effort (or "works"). It's simply knowing Christ after the flesh. *Ginosko* knowledge of God is where many Christians spend most of their spiritual life.

The Hebrew word for *beginning knowledge* is *Yada. Yada* in the Old Testament often refers to marriage or the marriage act. It's interesting because we can be married to someone and even have sex with them for years, and yet, never actually experience that intimacy that God designed for each of us to experience. We are simply "going through the motions." Unfortunately, the physical act alone, is not what gives us intimacy. *Intimacy occurs when our hearts, souls and bodies are one.*

The same can be said of our relationship with Jesus. We can know Him as Savior yet still be totally consumed with ourselves, conformed to this world and living a lie. God says the result of this way of thinking, is captivity, imprisonment, and total bondage to the flesh. "My people are destroyed for lack of [intimate] knowledge;..." (Hosea 4:6)[4]

I believe many Christians never quite progress beyond *beginning knowledge of God* because they can't quite trust God enough to relinquish everything to Him. These precious people see things in their lives going just the opposite direction from what they hoped and wanted; consequently, they become afraid. They pull in, get bitter and blame God, rather than trust more. Fear and doubt then cover our hearts, quench God's Life in us and, as a result, we never go on to experience intimacy with God.

An Example: Her faith just evaporated

Here's an example of a Christian who did this very thing.

Linda's husband finally left her after years of marital struggle. During the entire final year they were together, Linda was convinced that God was going to restore their marriage. When her husband finally left, Linda was devastated and her faith completely evaporated.

After a year and a half, the husband came home again and Linda was thrilled. "See, God is faithful after all and He <u>did</u> hear my prayers."

However, like many other similar stories, not long after they had reconciled, there were again signs that the husband wasn't happy and thinking about leaving.

This time, Linda was determined <u>not</u> to leave it up to God, but to be in complete control herself. She was *afraid* to relinquish everything to God, because she remembered what had happened the last time and she feared losing her husband for good.

As it turned out, Linda *did* stay in control herself, but that only pushed her husband out the door sooner. As a result, Linda lost her faith and, as far as I know, she has not come back to the Lord since.

This is an extremely sad, but fitting example of someone who had only *beginning knowledge* of God. If Linda had truly known God intimately, she would have been familiar with His faithfulness and known that no matter what she could see or understand to be happening, He would be trustworthy to perform His will through it. She would have known that no matter what was occurring in her life and no matter what it looked like to her, God would <u>never</u> leave her or forsake her, even though His ways of doing things is often totally different than our own.

I know trusting God like this is difficult to do, especially in the middle of crushing trials. But, this is what *faith* is all about. I believe God is allowing hard times in all of our lives to teach us to *walk by faith* only—not by sight or our emotions. He wants each of us to be able to say and truly mean, *God though You slay me, yet will I trust You.* (Job 13:15)

I used to read that verse and think that I could easily say it and mean it. Until the truly hard times came. Then, that Scripture took on a whole new meaning to me. He wants us to look to Him for everything, not only the *outward* things like our jobs, our houses, our families, our friends, our possessions, etc., but also the *internal* things like our identity, our reputation, our confidence, our personhood itself.

In the last few years, God seems to be dealing with me internally, by carefully removing or putting a distance between me and every crutch or every "thing" that I have relied upon in my life other than Christ. He wants me to look only to Him for these things. Then, I will be able to say and truly mean, *though You slay me, yet will I trust You.*

"We are troubled on every side, yet not distressed; we are perplexed, but not in despair; Persecuted, but not forsaken; cast down, but not forsaken..." "For we who live are always delivered unto death for Jesus' sake, that the life also of Jesus might be made manifest in our mortal flesh." (2 Corinthians 4:8-9, 11)

Knowing God Loves Us

Much of our lack of faith goes back to the fact that many of us don't really intimately know that God loves us. We know He loves us in our heads, but not in our everyday lives. And because of this, we aren't able to trust Him enough to lay our wills and our lives down moment by moment. As a result, we never will go to experience intimacy with Him.

If, however, we can be willing to yield ourselves completely, no matter what, then we'll begin to realize just how much God loves us, and we'll begin to see His handprint on everything in our lives. Knowing God loves us is the only thing that will give us the confidence to keep on surrendering our lives to Him, thus, assuring us the intimacy with God that we all desire.

Proverbs 3:19-20 teaches, "The Lord by *wisdom* hath founded the earth; by *understanding* hath He established the heavens." And only, "By His *knowledge* [intimate] the depths are broken up and the clouds drop down the dew." (emphasis added)

Knowing God Intimately

As we said, the Greek word for this intimate knowledge of God is *oida. Oida* knowledge is a mingling of two things, like a marriage relationship. We not only have become *one heart* with God as a result of our born again experience, but we also become *one will* and *one life* with Him. This is what Matthew 22:37 means when it says we are to "love God" (*agapao*)—to so bind ourselves with Him that we actually become one. This *oida* knowledge of God is the *union* that consummates our marriage with Him.

Oida comes from the root word *eidon*, which means *to see*. To intimately know Jesus means to see Him in everything. In every circumstance of our lives, good or bad, we see His face, His handprint, and His Love.

Remember, the Old Testament saints, who endured because "they saw Him Who was invisible." (Hebrews 11:27) And Job, who exclaimed, "I have heard of Thee by the hearing of the ear [beginning knowledge]; but now *mine eye seeth Thee* [intimate knowledge]." (Job 42:5)

A Personal Example: "I have heard your cries"

Here's a personal example of how I came to "see Him who is invisible."

We had just been on a wonderful three week trip to Israel and Egypt. Many of us, however, had gotten sick on the trip, probably because of drinking the water in Egypt. Even after I was home, I continued to be very weak and nauseous, so I decided to go in for a routine checkup. After the initial examination, my doctor advised me to get an upper and lower G.I. x-ray.

During the x-rays, it was quite obvious that the doctors had found something, because they kept muttering and whispering to themselves. However, when I asked what they had found, they wouldn't tell me. My personal physician finally called me several days later, and in the typically professional manner told me not to worry, but advised me to go in the next day for a cat-scan. He still would tell me no details.

I became so frustrated during the cat-scan and so upset at not knowing what really was going on, that I finally asked one doctor point blank, "Please, will you tell me what you have found?" He looked me straight in the eye and said, "You have a growth on your liver the size of a baseball and we're not sure if it is malignant or not." Wow! What a blow! First, the x-ray doctors and my own doctor wouldn't tell me a thing, and then this guy bluntly tells me *everything*.

On the way home from the hospital, I began to pray and, again and again, committed my body to God. I began to sing songs of praise and adoration and I kept giving my fears and apprehension over to Him. I seem to be able to handle the big things pretty well. It's those little every day choices, that I fall down in!

Coincidentally, I had been asked to teach my first *Be ye Transformed* class that coming October and I had been earnestly seeking God's Will in this. I was very concerned that it be God's timing for this class and not my own. Obviously, this medical situation would be one way He could let me know His Will.

When I got home from the hospital, there was a phone call for me. It was a woman from the East Coast whom I had never met or talked to before. She had no idea where I had just come from or what had just occurred in my life. She began to share that she had recently moved to California from the East Coast and had heard *The Way of Agape* series. After a few more minutes of general sharing, she told me that God had given her the gift of prophesy and she believed that God had given her something for me. She asked, "Would I mind if she read it to me?" "No, of course not," I said, thinking to myself, "How sweet, I'll just be polite." As she began to read the prophesy, however, it was as if God was standing right there beside me with His arms wrapped tightly around me, speaking directly to me.

Again, bear in mind, I had been earnestly seeking God as to whether or not I should teach this upcoming seminar. At the time, this was even more important to me than the medical problems.

The first part of the prophesy was very general with God telling me not to fear and that He had everything under control and in His hands. Then she read, and I quote: "I have heard your cries. Your prayers have come before Me as a sweet smelling savor. Do not hold back, for I have prepared you for such a time as this... I will bless you with wisdom and knowledge as you teach and minister to My children. I will do exceedingly above all you have asked and thought possible and I will show Myself mighty on your behalf. I will move through you giving you all you need to minister to My children...Now, My beloved, go and feed My sheep...."

I began to cry. This was definitely God's answer, not only about the seminar, but also about the outcome of the cat-scan. Both through that prophesy and the Scriptures that God gave me subsequently, God not only specifically answered my prayer about teaching, but He also let me know the status of the growth on my liver.

Sure enough, the next day my doctor called and told me not to worry, the growth was benign. I responded, "I know, I know! Praise God!" He seemed rather bewildered as to how I could possibly know!

This anecdote is just a little example of what it means to know God intimately, but it's one that is inscribed in my heart and one that I will never forget. Intimate knowledge of God means abandoning ourselves to God and seeing Him orchestrate our circumstances according to His Will. It's knowing that we can't do anything, but simply yield ourselves to Him and then watch as *He works all things together for good.*[5]

The purpose of all of our lives as Christians is to intimately know the Lord of the Universe, not only as our Savior, our Lord, our Master, our Friend, our Counselor, *but as our very Life itself.* Like Paul, we should be able to say, "For me to live is Christ...." (Philippians 1:21)

Intimate knowledge of Christ is the climax of our relationship with Him. We have finally let go of *self-life* and have been filled with His Life. As Philippians 3:8 and 10 says, "...*I count all things but loss for the excellency of the knowledge of Christ Jesus, my Lord:* for whom I have suffered the loss of all things, and do count them but [refuse], that I may win Christ." "That I may *know Him*, and the power of His resurrection, and the fellowship of His sufferings, being made conformable unto His death."

Knowing Christ as our very Life itself—becoming one with Him—is a completely different kind of knowledge than many of us have ever experienced. This is the type of knowledge that the Mind of Christ brings us.

Proverbs 24:3-4 promises, "Through wisdom is an house builded; and by understanding it is established: and by *knowledge* shall the chambers be filled with all precious and pleasant riches."

The Fear of the Lord

7) THE FEAR OF THE LORD (*Yirah - Phobeo*)

Isaiah 11:3 tells us that the culmination of the Mind of Christ in us is the ability to walk in the Fear of the Lord and not in the fear of man.

Fear of God means essentially two things:

1) It means to stand in reverential awe of who God is; and,

2) It means to hate sin.

Well, we can't reverentially stand in awe of who God is until we really *know* Him and have that intimate relationship. And we can't know God unless we *hate sin*—flee anything that quenches and separates us from His Life. So, *knowing God intimately* and *walking in the Fear of Him* must go hand in hand.

"My son, if thou wilt receive my words, and hide my commandments with thee; so that thou incline thine ear unto wisdom, and apply thine heart to understanding; yea, if thou criest after knowledge, and liftest up thy voice for understanding; if thou seekest her as silver, and searchest for her as for hid treasures; then shalt thou understand the Fear of the Lord, and find the Knowledge of God." (Proverbs 2:1-5)

Fear of God does not mean fearfulness of God or being afraid of Him, but it means walking, speaking and acting in such an intimate relationship with Him that you are in continual awe of what He is doing in your life. And because of this intimacy, you are constantly watching for and fleeing anything that would hinder or quench it. *Fear of God is caring more about what God thinks than about what man thinks.*

An Example: "She wanted out"

Here's a beautiful example of someone walking in the Fear of the Lord: John's wife wanted to divorce him because she was tired of being married and, simply wanted out. John did not want the divorce, but his wife proceeded anyway and amazingly, eventually got custody of their eight year old daughter, their only child.

Six years went by, and just as John was getting his life back in order, his ex-wife decided to sue him for more child support. She didn't need the money, her motive was simply to destroy him emotionally and financially.

Two days after he was served papers to appear in court, he received a letter from his daughter, who had just turned 14. The letter, he said, was the most horrible, bitter, resentful and unforgiving letter anyone could receive. In that letter he was called *everything*, but human.

At first he was shocked, then angry, then absolutely devastated. He said the only thing that saved him, was knowing how to take his hurts and fears to the Lord and knowing that He would heal them. He said all he could see was "the cross" and the Scripture that says, "Father, forgive them for they know not what they do." This became his prayer.

After constantly praying and seeking God, John decided to write his daughter a response. Naturally, he wanted to *justify* his own position (his wife was the one who sought the divorce, not he, etc.). But, the Lord wouldn't let him do that. Instead, he wrote a four page letter to his daughter about *how* to take all your hurts to God and *how* to forgive those that have hurt you. He wrote that, "forgiveness is the only thing that will set you free to love."

He asked his daughter's forgiveness for all the things she had named in her letter. He continually re-affirmed his love for her and shared "even if you want to write things that hurt me, it's okay because I will love you anyway."

A few days later, he received a hand written post card from his daughter saying, "I don't understand it all or why, but I love you, Daddy, and I do forgive you."

When the court date arrived, both lawyers commented how much the daughter loved her dad. She had evidently held his arm and hugged him the whole time they were in court. The court ruled in John's favor. The ex-wife was so bitter and resentful as a result that John said he had only compassion for her.

Recently, John wrote me another letter, "You know what's neat, Nancy, is our being *free* to love. The choice to take the hurts captive and give them to God is ours, but then Jesus gives us the Love we need to respond. In other words, I give Jesus the junk, He then gives me His Love. What an incredible exchange! Nan, it seems to me so few people understand this...."

The Genuine and Mature Christian

Someone walking in the Fear of the Lord is someone who is walking in God's Truth and Love. This is the *genuine* Christian whose words and deeds match. There's no hypocrisy here, no masks. These people have allowed Christ to be their very life, and thus, they are free to be themselves and yet, reflect Christ in all they do.

As one lady questioned me last week, "Nancy, why are our churches so filled with hypocrites?" I answered her by saying, "It's not so much that we set out to be phonies. We all really want to reflect Christ and be good witnesses of Him. The problem is simply that many of us just don't know how. We know in our heads what we are supposed to do and we say it with our words, but we just don't know how to implement it in our every day lives or in our actions.

And again, we are convinced that no one else has this problem—we're the only ones. So, we hide our true thoughts and feelings even more and raise our facades and masks a little higher. We can't let others see that it's really not working for us.

So the real problem is, once again, *ignorance*. We can't be transformed unless we understand how to renew our minds. And we can't renew our minds, unless we understand what they are. And also, we can't put on the Mind of Christ, unless we understand what it is. So, ignorance is really the reason many of us have become hypocrites.

The mature Christian is one who *understands* how to put off the junk in his own thinking and how to put on Christ. He still has hurts and he still stumbles, but he knows what to do about it. This is the person who is able to walk genuinely and transparently, reflecting Christ in all he does.

Be Transparent

One of the most common remarks I hear about my books is, "Was it difficult for you to be so open and honest?" I always tell them the reason I can be transparent, is because God has taken away, *and continues to take away*, the root cause of my phoniness and hypocrisy and my having to put up a facade, which is my own sin, my bitterness, my resentment, jealousy, envy, unforgiveness, etc.

See, we're all built alike and we all wear masks to one degree or another. But the more we allow God both to show us our sin and get rid of it for us, the more transparent and real we can become. And the more transparent we are, the more others will be able to identify with us and want what we have. If others can realize that they're not alone, that we all experience the same insecurities, fears and hurts, then that gives them hope. If God can remove our hurts, heal our lives and free us to live the truth, then He can certainly do the same in their lives.

A big part of our being able to live the truth, however is again knowing that our identity and security is in Christ and not in ourselves, in others or in things of the world. When we truly know this, then we'll have the freedom to be transparent, not only to God in the prayer closet, but with others in our lives.

Not Perfect or Sinless

Walking in the Fear of God does not mean that somehow we are perfect or sinless—far from it! Remember, our self-life doesn't improve with age. We can be Christians for 40 years and our self-life will still be just as ugly as it was the first day we believed. We can't tame our self-life; we must kill it. We must constantly set it aside, yield and give it over to God—remember 2 Corinthians 4:11-12.

What does improve with age, however, is the ability to recognize that self and to make the appropriate faith choices to give it over to God. This, to me, is all maturity really is—knowing how, moment by moment, to put off our self and put on Christ. That's all transformation is: taking off the one and putting on the other!

When we walk in the Fear of God, we still will have to deal with our hurts, our wounds, our negative thoughts, etc., and sometimes even more than before, because we have become so much more *finely tuned* to the real motives behind our thoughts and actions. It seems to me, the closer I get to Jesus, the more sin and *self* I see in me. Now, it's not that the sin wasn't there before, it certainly was. It's just that I am able to see it so much more clearly now, than I ever did before. The good news is, however, that we'll be able to catch that sin much more quickly and make the appropriate faith choices to relinquish it to God.

An Example: A book of remembrance

One of the most beautiful examples of someone who knew God intimately and walked in His Love and Truth was a precious, 28 year-old friend of mine named Diana Bantlow.

This beautiful sister was only two years old in the Lord when she was diagnosed with leukemia and given six months to live. But no matter how much pain she was in, or what she thought or felt, Diana continually chose not only to make the appropriate faith choices, but also to give God her life so He might perform His perfect Will through it.

Diana was one of the most incredible witnesses of God's Life manifested that I have ever seen, and she had only been a Christian less than two years. Her story proves to me that *maturity in Christ* has nothing at all to do with the number of years that we have been a believer, but simply how yielded we are to God.

Diana was invited to teach a Bible study those last six months of her life. Now, if it had been you or me, we probably would have spent those months at home with our families. Diana had two precious daughters, two and four, and a husband who adored her. But not Diana. She talked to her husband, prayed about it and felt strongly that God wanted her out sharing exactly what He was doing in her life.

Many times she would come to teach the Bible Study after her chemotherapy sessions. To ease her pain we would prop pillows up behind her so she could sit more comfortably. She would then begin to tell us about God's Love and about His faithfulness and His trustworthiness. She had an intimacy with God that none of us had ever seen.

The Bible Study grew to about 50 people because we all saw in Diana a oneness with God that each of us desired with all of our hearts. I had been a believer, at that point, for about 15 years, and yet, I had never met anyone like Diana. Every one of us wanted what Diana had with Jesus!

More than any other Christian I have ever known, Diana represented one who truly walked in the *Fear of God*, because she didn't allow *anything*—sickness, physical pain, negative thoughts, fear, doubts, her own desires—to quench or block God's Life in her.

Now, you know she must have experienced emotions like fear and doubt. She was human, just as we are. But her love and fear of God, and the knowledge that He loved her, kept her making those *contrary choices*, giving over what she didn't understand, and instead, trusting God in everything. She knew in her heart that God wouldn't allow anything into her life that wasn't for her best or that He wouldn't use for His ultimate purposes.

Malachi 3:16 teaches us that there is a "book of remembrance" written for those that Fear God. And, I know my precious friend Diana will be at the top of that list.

Diana was not miraculously healed, even though she was prayed for many times and had hands laid on her by the elders of her church. Diana had faith "to move mountains," and yet God chose not to heal her physically. God promises us healing, but often that healing is a spiritual, mental or emotional healing. God is concerned with the whole man, not just the physical.

As it came closer to Christmas, Diana, who was now confined permanently to the hospital, told everyone that God was going to allow her to go *home* for Christmas. Now, she believed He meant her physical home. But on Christmas day 1974, God took His precious child *home*—not to her physical, earthly home as she thought, but to the one He had prepared for her from the very beginning.[6]

As I have shared Diana's story over the last 20 years through *The Way of Agape* and *Be Ye Transformed,* people would often come up to me and share how they had known Diana personally or how they had heard of her. What an incredible impression she made on all of our lives. In particular, two nurses came up after one seminar and shared that they had attended Diana in the hospital the last few weeks of her life. They shared how they both had come to know Jesus Christ as their Lord and Savior because of Diana's witness.

They said when they would go into Diana's room to administer her pain medication, she would softly say, "No thank you, my Father is taking care of me and may He bless you." They shared how this is so uncharacteristic of terminally ill cancer patients.

These two nurses told me that they saw in Diana a love and a peace and joy "that passed all human understanding." [7] They said they yearned to have what Diana had. Both came to the Lord as a result of seeing Christ's Life through Diana, even though she was dying.[8]

Joy, Peace and Love don't come from the absence of trials, but simply from the presence of Jesus.

The Transformed Life

Fear of the Lord is the culmination of the Mind of Christ in us. Fear of the Lord is walking in God's Love and Truth, continually in awe of what He is doing in our lives and fleeing anything that would quench His Spirit in us.

In review, this incredible gift, the Mind of Christ, belongs to each of us. It's a part of our new birth and the *key* to our living the truth. However, we'll not be able to use it, unless we first understand what we possess. Remember, a people that don't understand, will fall.

To be *renewed in the Spirit of our minds* simply means putting off any self-centered, corrupt or ungodly thinking and putting on the Mind of Christ: His Wisdom, His Understanding, His Counsel and Strength; having intimate Knowledge of His Life in place of our own; and finally, walking in the Fear of God.

This produces the transformed Life that God desires for every one of us. It's the climax of our relationship with Him and the goal and purpose of our lives as Christians.

"Therefore, my brethren, be not conformed to this world: but *Be Ye Transformed* [how?], by the renewing of your mind, that ye may prove [like Diana did] what is that good, and acceptable, and perfect will of God." (Romans 12:2)

Endnotes:

1. Jesus is our example. He had power (*exousia*) to lay His Life down. (John 10: 18)

2. See Chapter Nine, "Our New Willpower"

3. Romans 12:1

4. Isaiah 5:13

5. Romans 8:28

6. John 14:2

7. Philippians 4:7

8. Read more of Diana's story in *The Way of Agape*, Chapter Seven, "All Your Hairs are Numbered."

Scriptural References:

Chapter Seven

Free Choice (*exousia*)
   A. Our choices are the critical crossroads of our lives (Romans 6:6-7, 13; 7:25; Proverbs 4:13, 22)

      1. Our choice decides whose *life* will be lived in our souls: God's or our own (Deuteronomy 30:19-20; Romans 6:16; Matthew 22:37c; Ephesians 1:16-19; Psalm 119:109; Proverbs 15:32)

      2. Only believers have a *free choice*, because they are the only ones who have God's supernatural Power to perform that choice in their lives (Matthew 26:39—"not my will, but Thine")

         a. This is called a *contrary choice*, a non-feeling choice or a faith choice (Romans 6:16-18; 1 Corinthians 7:37; John 10:18; Philippians 2:12)

         b. Only Christians have the authority to choose to *go against* how they feel and what they think, because only Christians have God's Spirit within them to perform something different in their lives other than what they feel (John 1:12; 1 Corinthians 7:37; 2:5; 2 Corinthians 5: 7; Isaiah 59:19)

         c. Our *choice* to continually follow God's Counsel is the *key* (Romans 6:6-7; 7:18b, 25; Proverbs 4:13, 22). It will lead us to intimate knowledge of God (Proverbs 12:1a; 21:11b)

         d. Only *faith choices* bring us true freedom from *self* (Romans 6:6, 18; 8:12; John 8:32)

      3. Non-believers do not have this choice (Ephesians 2:2-3; 4:17-19)

         a. They have no other power source within them to perform something different than what they want, think and feel

         b. They are still alienated and enemies in their *dianoia* (willpower) (Colossians 1:21)

Not Only Faith Choices, but Laying our Lives Down
   A. Only as we yield our lives to God, will He be able to perform His Will through us (Romans 12:1-2; 2 Corinthians 4:10-12)
   B. This yielding is the "working out of our salvation" (Philippians 2:12; Jude 21). Salvation means freedom from the *power of sin* (2 Thessalonians 2:13)

      1. This is referring to the last two functions of the Mind of Christ: Knowledge of God and Fear of the Lord
      2. The working out of our salvation is our own responsibility to achieve

Spirit of Knowledge (*daath — oida*)
   A. This is not *head* knowledge or intellectual knowledge, but knowing something through *living experience* of it working in your life
   B. This is intimate, first hand knowledge of God's Life as our own
      1. It's a mingling of two things (Galatians 2:20), like a marriage relationship
      2. Without intimacy with God, we will go into *captivity* (Hosea 4:1, 6; Isaiah 5:13; Titus 1:16; Matthew 22:29)
   C. There are two types of knowledge:
      1. *Ginosko* knowledge (*yada* in the Hebrew) is knowledge we gain by lots of self-effort of our part (works of the flesh). It's *beginning knowledge* (John 17:3; Hosea 2:19-20; Hebrews 10:16; 1 John 5:13; 2 Corinthians 1: 22)

        a.   This is knowing Christ is our Savior, but not as our *life*

        b.   *Yada* often refers to the marriage act

    2. *Oida* knowledge (*daath* in the Hebrew) means to know something without effort on our part. This is knowledge that is taught by the Spirit of God (1 Corinthians 2:11-12; Job 33:30; 42:5; Psalm 94:10; 119:66; 139:1-6; Proverbs 2:6)

        a.   This is knowing Christ as our *life* itself (Philippians 3:8-10; 2 Corinthians 4:10-12; Hebrews 11:27; 2 Corinthians 4:10-11)

        b.   *Daath* means *intimacy*, becoming one in every aspect

D. It's critical we go on from *beginning knowledge* to *fulness of knowledge* (Galatians 5:24-25; Colossians 2:6; 1 John 4:16; 2 Peter 1:10-11; Hebrews 6:1; Proverbs 8:12; 1 Corinthians 15:28; Isaiah 5:13)

    1. Jesus had this intimacy with the Father (John 8:55; 7:29; 10:30; 17:11, 21-23)

    2. To know is to *see* (John 12:21; 1 John 3:2; Acts 2:25; 22:14; Job 42:5; Hebrews 11:27c; 12:2a; Isaiah 6:5). We know God because we "see" His handprint in everything (1 John 3:2)

E. *Oida* knowledge is knowing Christ's Life in our souls, in place of our own (Hosea 6:6; 1 John 2:20, 27; 5:20; John 14:21b; 17:21-23; 2 Timothy 1:12; 1 Corinthians 2:2, 12; Colossians 3:4; Matthew 13:15-16; Ephesians 1:16-20; 3:16-19; 4:13; Isaiah 41:17-20; 2 Corinthians 4:6)

    1. We have *put off* self life (Romans 6:6, 11-17; John 3:30; 1 Corinthians 9:27; 15:31b; 2 Corinthians 7:1; James 1:21a; Ephesians 4:22, 32; Romans 13:12, 14; Mark 8:34-35; Matthew 5:8; 16:24-25; Colossians 2:11; Deuteronomy 7:1-8) and,

    2. We have *put on* Christ's Life (Romans 6:18; 7:6; John 15:9; Colossians 3:12-14; 2 Corinthians 4:10-12)

    3. "For me to live is Christ" (Philippians 1:21) — He is my Life! (Proverbs 3:19-26; 24:3-4; 1 Corinthians 2:2)

F. Only intimate knowledge of Christ brings precious riches and freedom (Proverbs 8:10; 11:9; 24:3-4; John 8:31b-32)

The Fear of the Lord (*yirah — phobeo*)

A. The purpose of the Mind of Christ is to *walk in the Fear of the Lord* (Isaiah 11:3-4; Proverbs 2:1-5). Fear of the Lord is the culmination of the Mind of Christ in us (Proverbs 14:27; Ecclesiastes 12:13)

B. The Fear of the Lord means two things:

    1. To stand in awe of who God is (Psalms 4:4a; 33:8) (reverential awe, mingled with joy)

    2. To hate sin (Proverbs 8:13a)

C. Fear of the Lord is walking in intimate knowledge of God, fleeing any outside influence that would quench His Spirit (Isaiah 11:3; John 15:4-10; 1 Peter 2:11; 1 Timothy 6:11; Proverbs 2:2-3; 3:7; 8:13; Ezra 10:11-13)

    1. This is not fearfulness of the Lord (2 Timothy 1:7; 1 John 4:17-18), but

    2. Choosing to walk by His Spirit (Galatians 5:24-25; Ezekiel 36:27)

D. This is the *genuine* Christian—walking in God's Truth and Love (3 John 3; Ephesians 4:15; Isaiah 11:3; Ezekiel 36:27; 2 Corinthians 10:11)

    1. Forgiving others (Luke 23:34)

    2. Caring more about what God thinks, than what man thinks

    3. Glorifying God even in our infirmities (2 Corinthians 11:30)

    4. Our confidence is in God alone (Proverbs 14:26; Philippians 4:13)

E. We are not perfect or sinless

    1. Can't tame self-life, must kill it (1 Corinthians 2:2)

    2.   Then, we will manifest His Life and not our own (2 Corinthians 2:14; Malachi 3:16; 1 Corinthians 2:9)

F.   This is the *transformed life* that God desires for all of us—manifesting and glorifying Him in our bodies (1 Corinthians 6:19-20; Philippians 1:20; 2 Corinthians 4:11)

G.   This is the changed life that God desires in all of us (Romans 12:1-2; Ephesians 5:9-10)

H.   Walking in Intimate Knowledge of God is culmination of Mind of Christ in us (Romans 7:25b; Proverbs 2:2-5)

    1.   This is the beginning of more Wisdom, Understanding, etc. (Proverbs 1: 7; 9:10; 15:33; 28:5; Psalm 111:10)

    2.   After we have the Fear of God, we can begin to worship Him (Psalm 5:7)

I.   Promises to those who *Fear God*

    1.   Names to be written in the book of remembrance (Malachi 3:16)

    2.   His Eye will be upon them (Psalm 33:18) and He will deliver them (Psalm 34:7)

    3.   He will make them "His jewels" (Malachi 3:17)

    4.   They will know His covenants (Psalm 25:14)

    5.   Their prayers will be heard (Psalm 34:6-7, 17)

    6.   Health to their bodies (Proverbs 3:8; Proverbs 22:4)

    7.   No *want* to them (Psalm 34:9; Proverbs 22:4)

    8.   His Love will forever be upon them (Psalm 103:17)

READ: Proverbs 24:3-4

Section Four:
The Temple of God

"Know ye not that *ye are the temple of God,* **and that the Spirit of God dwelleth in you?"**

1 Corinthians 3:16

Chapter Eight
Blueprint of a Believer

Overview

As we proceed in this chapter, try to follow along with me on the charts. Because, if you can *see* what I am explaining and the Lord bears witness to you, then you'll have a much clearer and deeper understanding of all these principles that we have been talking about. Again remember, a people who do not understand will fall.

Someone said recently in one of my seminars, "Nancy, your class is like a college crash course." "Thank you; that's a compliment," I told them. "But, you know, it's more like a life course!" These principles are not something that we'll understand and be able to implement after just one sitting, or even after two or three times through. Remember, it's taken us 20, 30, 40 years to get to where we are now, it will take us a while to turn around and go in the other direction. But if you can just get the basics of what I am saying, eventually all the pieces of the *puzzle* will fit together.

Don't be impatient. Just let God take you where you are walking now and allow Him to give you His Wisdom, His Understanding and His Strength to apply these principles to your life.

If you don't understand what I'm saying, I pray you won't put this book down in frustration. The enemy would love for you to do just that. Remember, he wants you *ignorant*, so he will do everything he can to distract you, confuse you and blind you. He doesn't want you to understand these principles. So, if you find yourself confused or frustrated, simply recognize it; pray about it; bind Satan in the name of Jesus; go get a cup of coffee or some fresh air; and then, come back and keep on reading.

So far, we have learned that in order to be transformed, we must constantly renew our minds—constantly put off all the garbage in our thinking and put on the Mind of Christ. We have also learned what the Mind of Christ is and why it's so very important to understand and implement in our lives. Now, we want to get a *visual* picture of just how the Spirit of God produces His Mind in us.

But, in order to do this, first we need to understand what our spirit, heart and soul are and how they differ. Then, we'll be able to grasp a little more clearly how the Mind of Christ fits into this picture.

Difference between Spirit, Heart and Soul

When I first began studying the *Way of Agape* and the First Commandment years ago, I ran to many of the pastors I knew asking them what the difference was between *heart, soul* and *mind*. Many of them simply told me, "Nancy, there is no difference—all these words essentially mean the very same thing."

My question to them was at that time, and still is: if they are all the very same thing, then why did God use three different Hebrew words and three different Greek words to express them? That doesn't make sense. God is very precise and He doesn't use different words, unless there is something special and unique meant by each of them.

I have since learned a wonderful way to determine the Scriptural definition of any word in the Bible. You let the Scriptures themselves define the word. In other words, you take all the places that that Hebrew or that Greek word appears, write them out and then come up with a composite definition. Those Scriptures will define the word.

So, I did that. I took the over 800 words in the Bible rendered *heart* (*leb* in the Hebrew and *kardia* in the Greek) and found that our heart is consistently said to be: evil, deceitful, hardened and impenetrable, prideful and non-circumcised. When we are born again, though, the Bible tells us that God gives us a *new heart*—a clean heart—a heart to know (*yada*) Him, a heart that His Word is inscribed in and a heart that is filled with His *Agape* Love. Scripture tells us that only God can see, search and truly know our hearts.

Then, I took the over 400 words in the Bible rendered *soul* (*nephesh* in the Hebrew and *psyche* in the Greek) and found that our soul is consistently said to be: troubled, trodden down and weary. It lusts, it sins and the enemy persecutes it. It can be cut off, destroyed and left in hell. But, God is the One who rescues it, delivers it, saves it and redeems it. He is the One who heals our soul and then fills it with intimate knowledge of God (*oida*).

What fascinated me about this study is the consistency of the Scriptures. Whether we are talking Old Testament or New Testament, God never delivers, saves and redeems our heart. *He gives us a totally new heart—a clean one and one that knows Him.* In like manner, He never gives us a new soul, *He delivers, saves and redeems our old one.*

So, there are some *major differences* between the meaning of our *heart* and our *soul*. They are not the same thing at all. For us to understand these differ-ences is critical. First of all, so we can love Him with all our heart and soul as He desires. And, secondly, so we can understand ourselves. Do we have a heart that knows (*yada*) God? Is our soul filled with intimate knowledge (*oida*) of God? Remember, a people who do not understand these things will fall.

I'm convinced that God is a God of detail and precision, and He means something very specific and precise by each of the words He uses in Scripture. If God instructs, "Love Me with all your heart" and He uses the Greek word *kardia*, He means something very specific. If He says, "Love Me with all your willpower" and He uses the Greek word *dianoia*, He means something else. And if He says, "Love Me with all your soul" and He uses the Greek word *psyche*, He again means something different, Otherwise, God would have simply said, "Love Me totally," or "wholly" or "completely," since there are places in the Bible where He does just that.

We are the Temple of God

In my quest 20 years ago to understand what my *heart, will* and *soul* were so I could love Him properly, God lead me to Hosea 12:10. In this Scripture, God tells us that He often uses *similitudes* (word pictures), analogies, or comparisons in order to help us understand His Word better.

In researching the word *similitude,* I ran across a definition that I think is terrific. The reason we need similitudes in order to help us understand God's Word better, is, as the definition says, "because we are dumb." Isn't that great! What a perfect definition. We need *word pictures* to help us understand *because we are dumb.*

One of these "similitudes" or word pictures is 1 Corinthians 3:16 which says, "Know [*oida*] ye not, [do you not have intimate knowledge] that ye are the temple of God, and that the Spirit of God dwelleth in you?" Also, in 2 Corinthians 6: 16, Paul teaches, "...for ye are the temple of the living God; as God hath said, I will dwell in them, and walk in them; and I will be their God, and they shall be My people."

Paul is making an analogy, a comparison, or a word picture here in these Scriptures by saying that, "Our body [itself] is a temple" and this temple [our body] is now the dwelling place of the Holy Spirit. Jesus even refers to His own Body as a temple in Mark 14:58.

Where did the Holy Spirit (or the Shekinah Glory) dwell in the Old Testament? God's Spirit used to dwell in the Holy of Holies of Solomon's Temple in Jerusalem. However, now Scripture tells us that God's Spirit dwells in "...temples [not] made with hands," but in the temple of our bodies! (Acts 17:24)

The statement that we are the Temple of God actually occurs seven times in the New Testament. Seven times is enough to indicate that the Holy Spirit is pointing out something very important here. In fact, 52 chapters in the Old Testament speak about the Temple of God. And this should again indicate that we should take note. Something is important for us to learn here.[1]

The Temple of Solomon

In the above Scriptures, Paul is teaching that there is a correlation between Solomon's Temple, which *used to be* the dwelling place of God's Spirit, and our bodies that *now* are the dwelling place of God. He is declaring that Solomon's Temple, in some mystical way, is a model, a blueprint, or a type of a believer indwelt by the Holy Spirit.

This analogy is interesting, because that's exactly what the Jews believed the whole purpose of the Temple was—to be the place where God dwelt and where He would reveal *His Name*—His Character, His Image.[2] And as we have noted before, our whole purpose for our being called as Christians is to reveal Christ—His Name, His Character.[3]

Now, the reason I refer to Solomon's Temple and not the other temples, is because Solomon's Temple was very *special*. It was the only temple, where all the detailed plans, not only of the construction of the temple, but also all the furniture, were given to David by the Spirit of God (see 1 Chronicles 28:12, 19). It was also the only temple in which God's Spirit dwelt permanently[4] until the temple itself was destroyed. And finally, it was the only temple in which the Ark of the Covenant rested. None of the other temples contained the Ark.[5]

So, in order for us to understand God's Word and ourselves better—what our spirit, heart and soul are—we are going to compare our bodies as the Temple of God now to the actual layout and structure of Solomon's Temple way back in the Old Testament. Then, we'll come back to see how the Mind of Christ fits into this whole picture.

Using the Temple as a model of man is not a new idea. Charles Scofield (of Scofield Bible fame) wrote a book back in 1915 called *New Life in Christ* which he expressed some of the same ideas.

Let's begin our exploration of Solomon's Temple by seeing what it looked like from the front or the elevation view.

See **CHART 8** on facing page.

Chart 8: Elevation View

You can see how the main sanctuary sat up on a raised platform and consisted of the Holy of Holies (A) in the rear; the Holy Place in the middle (B); and the Porch (C), with its two pillars in the front (D), facing the Inner and Outer Courts (F), which were on an even lower level.

Be sure to note the side wings on either side of the main sanctuary (E). These were secret, hidden, wooden chambers that were supposed to be for storing the priest's worship items used in the Holy Place and also for storing the historical records of Israel. We'll see in a moment, however, what was actually stored there.

The Temple of God

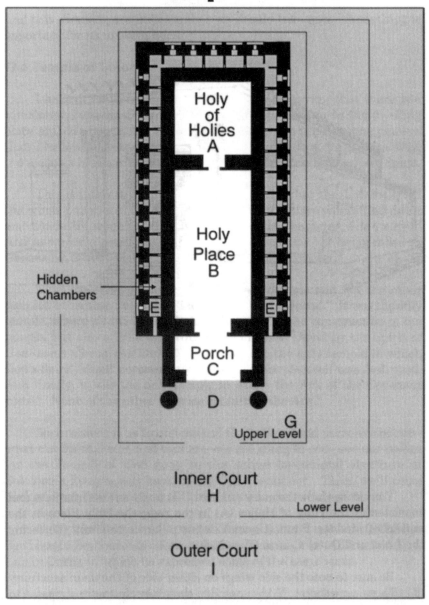

Chart 9

Looking down on **CHART 9** (on facing page), we can see the floor plan of the Temple. The main sanctuary consisted of the Holy of Holies (A) in the rear, the Holy Place (B) in the middle, and the Porch (C) in the front.

It's important to note that the Porch not only included the Golden Vestibule or entryway just inside the main sanctuary (C), but it also included the two Bronze Pillars outside the Porch (D). These two pillars had proper names, Jachin and Boaz. Jachin means "by His Counsel" and Boaz means "in His Strength." Does this remind you of the Mind of Christ? These two architectural structures will become vitally important as we further study the architecture of man and how the Mind of Christ fits into this picture.

The temple sanctuary itself, you can see, rested on a raised platform (G). Surrounding the sanctuary were the secret hidden chambers (E). As noted above, these chambers were supposed to be used for storing the priest's worship items for the Holy Place. However, it was here in these secret recesses that the priests actually stored their own personal idolatrous worship items, thinking that since they were hidden and out of sight, no one would see and no one would know. You might find it interesting to read Ezekiel 8:6-12. It will shock you to see what the priests actually stored there. Read also Ezekiel 14:3-7 and Jeremiah 17:1 about the idols and the sins that were *engraved* upon the hearts of the elders. Maybe you can already guess what these secret, hidden chambers correspond to in our own architectural makeup.[6]

Stepping down seven steps from the Porch, we find the Inner Court (H), and on an even lower lever, the Outer Court (I).

Blueprint of a Believer

Turn to **CHART 10** (on the next page).

Let's study Solomon's Temple as a *model* or a *blueprint* of the New Testament Believer, i.e., one who has the Holy Spirit dwelling within. We will just give a quick *overview* here in this chapter; then we'll come back and explore each area individually in the next two chapters.

The Holy of Holies is analogous to a believer's *new spirit* (*pneuma*) (1) that is now the new *energy* source, the new power source, or life source of our being. This energy source is what will create God's Life in our hearts and also, if we allow Him to, implement that Life out in our souls.

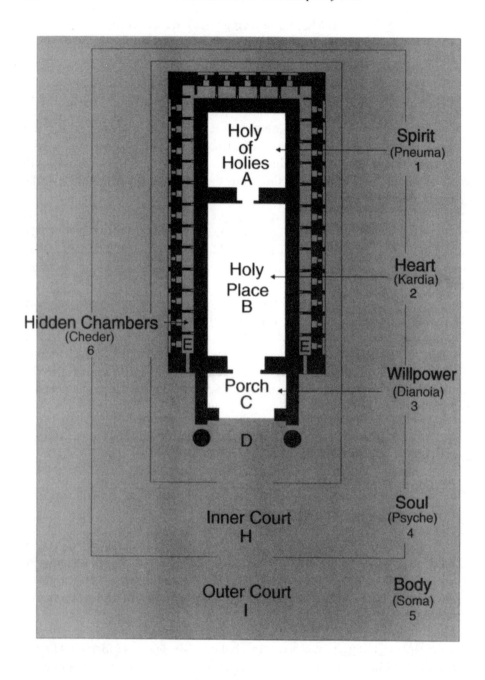

Chart 10

The <u>Holy Place</u> represents a believer's *new heart* (*kardia*) (2), the place where God's Life is actually created, started and brought into new existence by God's Spirit. In other words, when we are born again, God totally removes our old human heart and replaces it with a brand new heart. This, then is not simply our old heart renewed or repaired, but a completely new heart. This is now *Christ in us,* our "hope of glory."[7]

The <u>Porch</u>, including the pillars, is analogous to a believer's *new supernatural willpower* or volition (*dianoia*) (3), which is the most vitally important area of our makeup. Our willpower is the *key* to our Christian walk, because what we choose, moment-by-moment, determines whose life will be lived in our souls—either God's or our own.

Now notice, there are two parts to our willpower: God's supernatural Will and Power (the Golden Vestibule) and then, our own free choice (the Bronze Pillars) (D).

All of this will be explained *in detail* in the next two chapters. This is just an initial *overview*.

The secret, hidden, <u>wooden chambers</u> around the main sanctuary, you probably have already guessed, represent the *hidden part of a believer's soul* which is called in the Hebrew, c*heder* (6). This is the place in our soul where we bury and store our hurts, doubts and fears, etc., (if we don't know how to deal with them) thinking because they are hidden, "no one will see and no one will know." We're going to spend two entire chapters exploring these hidden chambers and how the things we bury and hide there affect everything we think and do.

We noted that one of the purposes for the hidden chambers was to hold Israel's precious historical records and treasures. In like manner, God designed the hidden part of us to hold pleasant and special memories of all of His loving actions towards us.

"By [intimate] knowledge (*daath*) shall the chambers (*cheder*) be filled with all precious and pleasant riches." (Proverbs 24:4)

Just as God wanted the Israelites to continually be reminded of His presence and His provision for them, so too, He wants us to be reminded of His Love and His faithfulness.

The <u>Inner Court</u> represents the *conscious part of a man's soul* (*psyche*) (4)— our own conscious thoughts, emotions and desires that are usually contrary to

God's. This is our self-life that we so often refer to. Our souls are like a *neutral* area that will either be filled with God's Life—His Love, Thoughts and Power from our hearts, if we have made faith choices—or filled with self-life, our own thoughts, emotions and desires, if we have made emotional choices.

The Outer Court represents a *believer's body* (*soma*) (5), which is the vehicle by which we express our life (our soul). We need a soul in order to have life at all; and we need a body in order to express that life. Therefore, we cannot separate our soul and our body, otherwise there is death. Together, our soul and body are known as "*the flesh*."

This is just a quick summary of the internal architecture of man compared to Solomon's Temple. It's a visual illustration to help us understand a little more clearly what our spirit, heart, soul and body really are. In the next two chapters we will examine each of these areas of our makeup in greater detail.

Endnotes:

1.   1 Corinthians 3:16; 6:19; 2 Corinthians 6:16; Ephesians 2:20-21; Hebrew 3:6; 1 Peter 2:5; 4:17

2.   *The Temple*, Joshua Berman, pages 63-64. Also, Deuteronomy 12:9-14.

3.   Malachi 1:11

4.   1 Kings 9:3

5.   For a complete background, see the briefing package, The Mystery of the Lost Ark, from Koinonia House.

6.   We will explore these "hidden chambers" in further detail in Chapter Eleven and Twelve.

7.   Colossians 1:27

Scriptural References:

Chapter Eight

Overview of the Temple of God

A. We must understand the terms *spirit, heart* and *soul* and how they differ
   1. So that we will not be confused (Proverbs 23:7, the Hebrew word is *soul* here and not *heart*)
   2 So we can understand ourselves
   3. So we can love Him with all our heart and soul
   4. So we can manifest "His Name"
B. The purpose of the original temple was to *manifest God's Name* and show forth His character (Deuteronomy 12:9-14; 16:2, 11; 2 Samuel 7:13; 1 Kings 8:16; 9:3). In like manner, we are to reveal His Name (His Character, His Image) through the temple of our bodies—spirit, heart and soul (Malachi 1:11; Romans 9:17)
C. God uses *word pictures* in order to help us understand His Word a little more clearly (Hosea 12:10)

We are the Temple of God (Acts 17:24)

A. Solomon's Temple is a model of the New Testament believer (1 Corinthians 3:9-16; 6:19-20; 2 Corinthians 6:16; Ephesians 2:20-21; Hebrews 3:6; 1 Peter 2:5; 4:17). Jesus even calls His own body a temple (John 2:19-21; Mark 14:58)
   1. Solomon's Temple was special
      a. It was the only Temple that the detailed plans of the construction and the furniture were given to David by the Spirit (1 Chronicles 28:11-12, 19; 22:6-15)
      b. It was the only Temple where God's Spirit dwelt permanently (1 Kings 8:13; 9:3; 2 Kings 21:7; 2 Samuel 7:13; 2 Chronicles 6:2; 7:16) and filled the Temple (1 Kings 8:10-11)
      c. It was the only Temple that housed the Ark of the Covenant
   2. The purpose for Solomon's Temple was to "house" God's *Name* forever (1 Kings 8:29) and, so that His "heart" and "eyes" could be there (2 Chronicles 7:16; 1 Kings 9:3)
B. The Holy Spirit desires not only to permanently indwell us (John 14:17; Romans 8:9; 1 John 2:27), but also to constantly fill and overflow us just like the Shekinah Glory did in Solomon's Temple (1 Kings 8:10-11; Ephesians 5:18; John 4:14; Ezekiel 10:4)
   1. The whole purpose for our being called as Christians is to reveal "Christ in us"—*His Name*, His Character (Malachi 1:11)
   2. By our gaining a better understanding of the structure of the Temple, we will gain a better understanding, not only of God's Word, but of ourselves, our heart, mind and soul (Galatians 1:16a)

Blueprint of a Believer   (CHARTS 8, 9, 10)

A. Holy of Holies = new spirit (*pneuma*) (Ezekiel 11:19; 36:26-27; Psalm 51:10; Jeremiah 31:33; Romans 7:6; Matthew 9:17)
   1. This is the place where God Himself dwells (Psalm 80:1; 99:1; John 14:23; 1 Corinthians 6:17; 1 Kings 9:3; Exodus 25:21-22)
   2. God's Spirit is now united with our human spirit (1 Corinthians 6:17)
   3. God's Spirit is going to create or quicken new life in us (Romans 8:10-11; John 6:63; 1 John 5:11-12)
B. Holy Place = new heart (*kardia*) (Ezekiel 11:19; 18:31; 36:26; Jeremiah 24:7; 31:33; 32:39; Luke 5:37-39)

1. This is the place where God's Life is quickened by God's Spirit (Colossians 1:27; Ephesians 3:17; Proverbs 4:23; Jeremiah 32:39-40; John 17:26; Romans 5:5; Ecclesiastes 3:11b; Ezekiel 11:19; Matthew 9:17)
   a. This is the place where our candle is lit by God's Spirit (Psalm 18:28; 2 Corinthians 4:6) and we receive new *life* (John 10:10)
   b. Jesus' Life is the Light (John 1:4; John 8:12)
2. This is Christ in us, our hope of Glory (Colossians 1:27)
   a. However, we are warned in 1 John 5:12 that if we don't have "the Son," we will not have *life*. The light in us will be dark (Job18:5-6; Luke 11:35)
   b. God's Life is eternal (Jeremiah 31:3; 1 John 5:11-12; Psalm 103:17; Isaiah 54:10; Hebrews 13:5; 1 Corinthians 13:8a)
3. This is the "new creation" (2 Corinthians 5:17)
4. This is the hidden man of the heart (1 Peter 3:4)
5. This "heart" should be the *motivation* for all we do (Matthew 12:34-35; 2 Corinthians 5:14; Proverbs 14:30; 16:23)

C. Porch = new willpower (*dianoia*) (Jeremiah 31:33; Hebrews 8:10; 10:16)
   1. Our willpower has two parts:
      a. *God's supernatural Will and Power* by which He shows us what His Will is and then gives us the Power to perform that Will in our lives (Philippians 2:13)
      b. *Our free choice* to follow what God has shown us or go by our own way (Colossians 1:21)
   2. Our willpower is the *key* to whose life will be lived in our souls, either God's or our own (1 John 5:20, *oida;* Deuteronomy 30:19-20)
   3. Our willpower determines the *direction* of our lives (Eph. 1:17-19)

D. Inner Court = soul (*psyche*) (2 Corinthians 4:16c)
   1. Up to this point, all the rooms have been gold (symbolizing purity and holiness), now the metal changes to bronze (meaning sin is still present)
   2. Our soul is a *neutral area*—filled either with God's Life or self-life
      a. Our soul contains our thoughts, emotions and desires that are usually contrary to Gods
      b. Our soul has two parts: the *conscious* outward expression of our lives showing forth either God's Life (John 17:3) or our own self-life; and, a *hidden, secret* part (our hidden chambers). The priests stored their own idolatrous things in the hidden chambers of the temple (Ezekiel 8:6-12; 14:3-7; Jeremiah 17:1)
   3. In order for us to show forth God's Life, *self* must constantly be yielded, set aside and given over to God (Luke 9:24b; 2 Corinthians 4:11)
   4. Our souls are the outward *expression* of our lives

E. Outer Court = body (*soma*) (2 Corinthians 4:16b)
   1. The Outer Court was on a lower level than the Inner Court, and was open to many outside influences (Matthew 21:12; Mark 11:15; Luke 19:45; John 2:14-16), similar to the external vulnerability we experience in our bodies
   2. Just as the Outer Court was also given over to the gentiles (Revelation 11:2a), so our bodies are also not yet renewed & still in bondage to the flesh
      a. Our body is the place that the "power of sin" dwells (Romans 7:17-24)
      b. Satan uses the power of sin as his tool (John 8:44; Ephesians 6:12) to keep us in bondage
   3. Our soul and body are known as *the flesh*; this is where the battle wages (Romans 7:23)
   4. Our bodies are the *vehicle* for the expression of our lives (Philippians 1:20; 1 Corinthians 6:19-20)

Chapter Nine
New Spirit, Heart and Will

In the next two chapters, we want to explore in more detail what each of the terms—*spirit, heart, willpower, soul* and *body*—really mean, so that we can understand just how the Mind of Christ works in us and what it means to be "renewed in the spirit of our minds."

Turn to **CHART 11** (on the next page).

(1) <u>OUR NEW SPIRIT</u> (Greek, *pneuma*; Hebrew, *ruwach*)

As a born again believer, one who has asked Jesus to take control of his life, the Spirit that now dwells at the core of our being is <u>not</u> our *old* human spirit, but a totally *new spirit*. Now God Himself, the Father, Son and Holy Spirit, dwells in us, which is exactly what being "born again" means.[1]

John 3:3 teaches, "...except a man be born again, he cannot see [know intimately] the kingdom of God." "That which is born of the flesh, is flesh; [but] that which is born of the Spirit is Spirit." (John 3:6)

Being born again means receiving a totally *new power source*—a new life source, light source or energy source. God has united our spirit with His, so we have become *one* spirit with Him. 1 Corinthians 6:17 makes this plain, "...he that is joined unto the Lord is one spirit [with Him]." In other words, God has lit the candle of our spirit.[2]

(2) <u>OUR NEW HEART</u> (Greek, *kardia*; Hebrew, *leb*)

Our *new heart* then, is the actual place where God's Life is created, started, or brought into new existence by God's Spirit. The Hebrew word for *create* is *bara* which means to create something out of nothing, to make alive, or *to bring into new existence something that wasn't there before*. This is why God says we have a *new* heart.

David prays in Psalm 51:10, "Create [*bara*] in me a clean heart, O God..." [i.e., make something brand new, something that wasn't there before]. And in Ezekiel 36:26, God promises, "A *new heart* also will I give you, and a *new spirit* will I put within you: and I will take away the stony heart [old heart] out of your flesh, and I will give you a heart of flesh [a new, living heart]." And finally, in Jeremiah 24:7, God declares, "I will give them a heart to know (*yada*) Me."

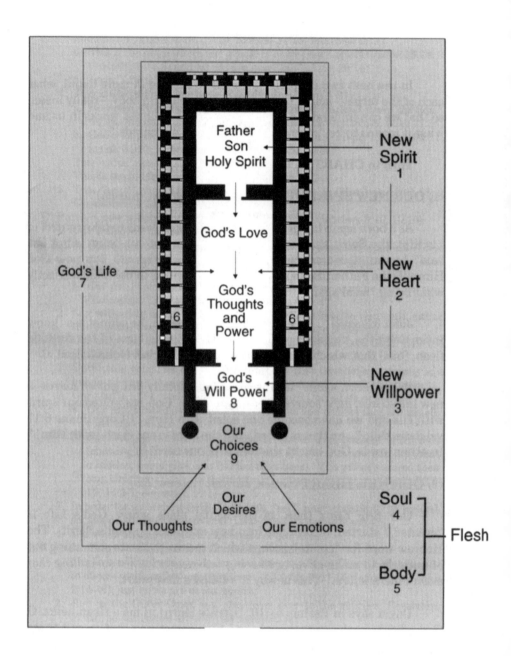

Chart 11

This "new heart of flesh," is not simply our old one changed or somehow renewed, but it's a totally *new* heart, something that wasn't there before. In other words, when we are born again, God replaces our *old* human heart life, our human love, our human thoughts and our human power, with His *brand-new heart life* (7): God's supernatural Love (*Agape*), His supernatural Thoughts (*Logos*)[3] and His supernatural Power (*Dunamis*) to perform in our lives.

This is "*Christ in [us]*, [our] hope of glory." This is the very "nature" of God Himself within us.[4]

Because the Bible speaks of our heart as being the *center core* or the *foundation* of our whole person, this is a very important area for us to really understand. In many commentaries and books about the internal architecture of man, the idea of the *heart* seems to be either overlooked or mentioned in a confusing manner. Many commentators mistakenly theorize that the words *spirit, heart* and *soul* are synonyms, referring to the same concept. Thus, major confusion results. The fact that the Bible refers to the *heart* over 800 times provides evidence that this is a vitally important area and one that we must understand as it is the basis of our spiritual life.

The Bible tells us over and over again that our *heart life* is the center core of our whole being, the essential nature or the true essence of our whole person. Our heart is like the foundation block or the underlying support *upon which everything else is built.* As Proverbs 14:30 declares, "A sound heart [inside] is the life of the flesh [outside]..." In other words, all continuing activity depends upon the "life" that resides in our hearts.[5] (In this light, Leviticus 17:11 is very provocative, "life is in the blood.")

Old Human Heart is Corrupt

In Genesis 8:21 and other Scriptures, we are told that our old, human heart *before* being born again (before receiving the Spirit of God) is evil and corrupt from birth. Thus, our old heart will always be self-centered, proud and bent on going its own way. It's the old man or the old nature and, on its own, will never seek God.

Even in the New Testament, every place that the evilness of the heart is mentioned,[6] it's always before the Spirit of God comes to dwell permanently within the heart [7] (i.e., before God has lit the candle of our spirit). In other words, Scripture is always speaking of the *old, human heart.*

As we said, our old, human heart is the *old man* that Paul tells us in Romans 6:6 "is crucified" when we become born again. "Knowing this, that our old man is crucified with Him, [why?] that the body of sin might be destroyed...." Therefore, once we are born again, that "old man" is ***positionally*** dead. He no longer has any power over us and in his place is a brand-new heart, which is *Christ in us, our hope of glory.*

No One can Understand our Old Human Heart

Jeremiah 17:9 tells us that not only is our old, human heart (the old man) "...deceitful above all things and desperately wicked...," but also that, "no one can even understand it!" This means that without God's Spirit in us giving us light and understanding, we'll never be able to understand the things we think, feel and desire to do. Remember, God is the only One who can see, search and try our hearts.

This might explain why so many people, after spending thousands upon thousands of dollars in psychiatric sessions, are still not finding the answers they so desperately seek. And, in some cases, they're even getting worse in the process, as we mentioned in Chapter Six. The reason is revealed right here in Jeremiah 17:9, "The [old human] heart is deceitful above all things and desperately [incurably] wicked."

No One can Cure our Old Human Heart

This Scripture is telling us that even if we could understand the corruption of our old hearts, no one would know how to cure it. *Desperately wicked* means it's completely incurable, there's no remedy for it. In other words, without God's intervention—without a brand new heart—the hope for any change in our lives is futile.[8]

I received a very interesting letter from a heart surgeon a few months ago. He writes, "...it is an absolutely awesome feeling transplanting a new heart into a dying patient. At least I used to think it was a new heart. Through the study of God's Word I have realized that the best modern medicine has to offer is a used and *incurably wicked heart* (Jeremiah 17:9). I have not figured out how to tell my patients that their transplanted heart is *diseased* and incurable."

He continues, "Everyone today is seeking a healthy heart. They are willing to do almost anything to live longer. They jog, diet and even undergo cardiac surgery. Yet, all their efforts will only get them a few extra years. David had the right answer when he asked God to "Create in me a clean heart, O God, and renew a steadfast spirit within me." (Psalm 51:10)

His letter continues, "God tells us how important our hearts are: 'Blessed are the pure in heart: for they shall see God.' (Matthew 5:8) However, only God can heal us, and only He can write His Laws upon our hearts. It's interesting, however, how our 'hearts of stone' keep us from accepting this new, regenerate and redeemed heart from God...."

An Example: Nothing Ever Changed

We know of one young girl's family who spent thousands upon thousands of dollars trying to cure her of drug abuse. Tracy was in psychiatric hospitals, care units, drug rehab hospitals, etc. Nothing ever seemed to help. Some of these hospitals cost her family as much as $5000 a week. Clearly, they were desperate to make her well. They spared no expense, taking her to every psychiatrist, every therapist, and every counselor who offered hope. Nothing, however, touched or changed Tracy's life—until she met Jesus and received a brand new heart.

When the Spirit of God came inside Tracy's heart, she not only received a *new power source* (a new spirit), but she also received *new life* itself (i.e., a new heart), now giving her God's supernatural power for real and lasting change.

God is telling us in the above Scriptures that before His Spirit intervenes, our nature or our heart is basically corrupt and evil and we are not basically good, as so many people want to think we are. Consequently, we desperately need to be born again—not only receive a new Spirit, but also a new heart.

"Therefore if any man be in Christ, he is a new creature: old things are passed away; behold, all things are become new." (2 Corinthians 5:17) In other words, we now have a brand-new energy source, *a new spirit* and *a new heart* filled with God's supernatural Love, Wisdom and Power.

An Example: Prisoner in Sydney

Let me share a wonderful story about the new nature that God gives us when we're born again.

Many years ago, as I was ministering in Australia, a woman came up and told me this story about some of her friends. The husband, she said, had always been very jealous of his wife. One particular occasion, he lost his temper and beat her up so badly that he almost killed her. He was put in jail, but somehow he escaped. And while his wife was recuperating in the hospital, he broke into the hospital and once again tried to kill her. During this fit of rage, he repeatedly tried to rip her large wedding ring off her finger and in the process, he bent the ring completely out of shape.

Again, he was captured, only this time, he was placed in a maximum security prison. During the years he was incarcerated, someone shared Christ with him. He accepted Jesus into his heart, became born again, and received God's new Life.

At that particular time, someone sent him *The Way of Agape* tapes. (Can you imagine, from a Newport Beach, California housewife to a prisoner in Sydney, Australia! God's Ways certainly are not our ways!) Through the tapes, God revealed to this man that he was "a new creation in Christ," and that he now had God's supernatural Love within him to give out. The man's life became transformed, and he devoted himself to God's Word and showing forth Christ's life.

Some months later, after he was released from prison, he decided to look up his ex-wife. After a period of time in which I'm sure she was very leery of him, he led her to Christ. They were eventually remarried, and she now wears that broken, bent-out-of-shape wedding ring around her neck as a symbol of the miracle that God performed in their lives.

Again, "If any man be in Christ, he is a new creature, old things are passed away; behold *all* things have become new [brand-new Love and brand-new Thoughts]." (2 Corinthians 5:17, emphasis added)

God's Life in Our Hearts

The old heart, then, which Scripture tells us is evil, unknowable and incurable from birth, is totally replaced by a brand-new heart when we are born again by God's Spirit. The Life that is now in our hearts is completely pure, incorruptible, and holy because it's God's Life and not our own.[9] This again describes "...Christ in you [us], the hope of glory." (Colossians 1:27)

1 Peter 3:4 confirms that the Life now in us is pure. "But let it be the hidden man of the heart [God's Life in us], in that which is not corruptible...."

Years ago when I first taught *The Way of Agape*, I thought our hearts were still basically evil even after we were born again and that our hearts were transformed only by making the right faith choices, moment-by-moment. Many Christians still believe this.

God showed me through Scripture, however, that it's our lives, not our hearts, that need to be transformed. Heart transformation occurred at our new birth.[10] Thus, if we are born again, the only life that now exists in our hearts is God's incorruptible Life (His Love, Wisdom and Power). And, all we need to do is to learn how to let it out.

A woman at one of my recent classes told me, "This is the most liberating message I have heard in years." She had heard the first *Way of Agape* Series back in 1982 and confessed that the "divided heart" message that I had spoken of then had always been a stumbling block for her. She said that she felt defeated before she even started, knowing that no matter how hard she tried, her heart would always be evil. This new insight—that when we are born again we receive a brand-new heart (God's heart)—was just what she had been waiting for. "God's Life is already in me," she excitedly said, "I just need to learn how to let it out!"

Fountain of Living Water

God's Spirit in our hearts is often spoken of in the Bible as a "fountain of living water" that wells up within us, gushes forth, and fills us to overflowing. However, when we make self-centered, emotional choices, our hearts become covered over and that fountain of living water is blocked (9). Christ's Life is then unable to come forth and this grieves God. "Doth a fountain send forth at the same place sweet water and bitter?" (James 3:11) And verse 10, "...my brethren, these things ought not so to be." In other words, God's Life (sweet water) and self-life (bitter water) should not be coming forth from the same place. This duality is not at all what God planned.

As noted before, when we make self-centered, emotional choices that quench or block God's Life, our hearts become "...*fat as grease*..." (Psalm 119:70). In other words, when we say "no" to the Holy Spirit's promptings, our hearts become covered over with a layer of grease. This grease not only clogs, chokes out, and quenches any personal leading from God, but it also causes us to become insensitive toward others. This is where the "pure" fountain water gets blocked and comes out bitter.

Our new heart, the "hidden man of the heart" or "Christ in us," is now the center core, the essential incorruptible nature and true essence of our being. Upon this foundation everything else is going to be built, and upon this base all continuing activity will depend. This message will <u>not</u> work unless we have received both a *new spirit*—a new energy source— and a *new heart*—new life itself.

(3) **OUR NEW WILLPOWER** (*dianoia*)

Now, let's go back and review **Chart 11** (on page 174) and learn about the *new willpower* that we receive as a result of being born again. Again, this is the most critically important area of all our internal makeup. This is our volition or our resolve—it's our will and the power to perform it. The Greek word for this area is *dianoia. Dia* means *channel* and *noia* means *of the mind.* As you can see, our willpower is the conduit or the channel for God's Spirit to flow from our hearts out into our lives.

Looking at the chart, you can visualize how this occurs. Our willpower is the passageway, the doorway or the gateway for God's Life in our hearts to flow out into our lives (our souls). Now, this doorway or passageway can be *opened* so God's Life can flow freely; or it can be *closed* and God's Life quenched and blocked.

Notice, just as we said the Porch has two parts, the Golden Vestibule and the Bronze Pillars, so our new willpower also has two distinct parts: First, we have *God's supernatural Will and Power*, given to us as a part of our new Birth (8).[11] This is where God counsels us as to what His Will is[12] (Spirit of Counsel), and then where He gives us His supernatural Strength to perform His Will in our lives. The second part of our willpower is *our own free choice* (9):[13] The free choice to follow what God has counseled us to do and trust in His Power to perform His will in our lives, or the free choice to follow what we think, feel and desire, and then trust in our own ability and power to perform our will in our lives.

Free choice simply means we have the *authority* and *power* of God to either make faith choices—non-feeling choices—to do what He desires; or, to make emotional choices and do what we think, feel and desire. Because of the indwelling Spirit, as Christians we can live in complete obedience to God's Will, if we so desire. And even when we don't *feel* like following what God has asked us to do, we still have *His authority* to choose His Will over our own and *His power* to perform His will in our lives.[14]

Contrary Choices

Our will is the place where we make *contrary choices*—choices that go against what we *naturally* think, feel and desire. This is exactly why I call it a **contrary** choice. It's a faith choice or a non-feeling choice to walk by faith and not by sight.

We are so programmed to *feel* everything we choose. And when we don't feel our choices, we don't really think they're genuine. However, in God's kingdom, this is not the case. Born again believers are the only ones who possess a supernatural ability *to go against* self. And the reason is, *we're the only ones who possess a supernatural power within us to be able to perform something different (in our lives) from what we naturally think, feel and desire.*

Certainly, nonbelievers have a choice to decide what they want to do. But, none of them has the *authority to choose to go against* how they feel, what they think, or what they desire, because they don't possess another power source within them to perform differently. Christians, on the other hand, don't have to be carried on by the "tide of emotion" because we have God's Authority not only to choose His Will (regardless of how we feel), but also God's Power to perform His Will in our lives, again, regardless of how we feel.

"Not My Will, but Thine"

So as Christians, we can be totally honest with God and admit, "I don't want to love this person anymore. I hate him right now. I don't understand what You are doing. I don't feel Your Presence. I am doubtful that You are leading me to do this. But, by faith, I give these negative thoughts and feelings to You, for I know I have Your authority to claim, like Jesus did in Matthew 26:39 "...not my will [not my natural feelings and desires], but Thine." Then I can be assured, by faith, that since I'm a cleansed vessel, God <u>will</u> perform His Will in and through me.

Our new, supernatural willpower is simply God's *authority* to choose His Will over our own thoughts, emotions and desires—our self-life—no matter how we feel, and His *power* to perform that Will in our lives. To me, this is the most incredible gift of all. I don't have to feel my choices. I just have to be *willing* to make them and God will do the rest.

God Changes Our Feelings

What's so exciting about choosing God's Will over our own desires is that *after* we have made the appropriate faith choices, in His perfect timing, God will change our thoughts and feelings to match the faith choices we have made. In other words, in His timing, He will align our feelings with our choices.

So we're not responsible to change our negative thoughts and emotions. There's no way we can do that! We're only responsible to put in charge the Person who <u>can</u> change our thoughts and feelings, and that is God. And, we do that by making the right faith choices. God then changes our emotions to match that choice. Mark 9:24 fits perfectly here: "...Lord, I believe; help Thou mine unbelief."

God's Will or Our Own

Therefore, we are constantly faced with two choices.[15] We can make a *faith choice* and follow what God desires us to do, by praying "Not my will, but Thine," and then, depend upon God's supernatural Power to accomplish His Will in our lives, or we can make an *emotional choice* and follow what we think, feel and desire and trust in our own strength to accomplish our will in our lives.

An Example: It's Worth a Million Dollars

We all have many examples in our own lives of the consequences of these two kinds of choices. Here's a classic situation I was faced with many years ago:

I had been praying that God would make me a more supportive wife for Chuck in his business. Now, that's an easy commitment to make in the prayer closet. It's quite another thing, however, to trust God to do it in my actions. God was going to give me a perfect opportunity to see what I would choose.

At this particular time, I was teaching *The Way of Agape*. Tammy, a friend of mine, volunteered to watch 10-year-old Michelle for me on my teaching days. One time Tammy decided to take all the kids to the beach. My Michelle is very fair, and on that particular day Tammy forgot to bring sunscreen. When I picked Michelle up that night, she was "burnt to a crisp."

The following afternoon she seemed better, so I decided to take a chance and go grocery shopping. Michelle acted fine until my cart was completely filled, and then she began to lean over the front of the grocery cart, moaning and groaning about her sunburn. I needed the groceries desperately, so I decided to gamble and see if I could check out quickly! Well, as you know, whenever you're in a hurry, it always ends up taking forever.

We got up to the check-out stands and there were at least five people in every line. Michelle, by this time, was leaning over the front of the cart, crying softly. People began to stare at us. I'm sure some of them thought I must be beating her because they couldn't see her sunburn. Terribly flustered and embarrassed, I felt like leaving the groceries and running out of the store, but I really needed the milk and butter that were at the bottom of the cart.

Finally getting through the line and out of the store, we flew home. As I was driving, I was thinking to myself, "I can't wait to get home, put Michelle to bed, wash my filthy hair, get comfortable, put my feet up, and read all evening." I was totally bushed!

When we pulled up to our street, a detour sign had been posted because it had been dug up for repairs. Now, that detour was two miles out of my way and poor Michelle was still whining in the back seat. By the time I finally got home, I was absolutely frazzled.

As I was carrying the first grocery bags down the steps with Michelle on my arm, I could hear the phone shrilly ringing. I dropped the bags, fumbled for my keys, and finally reached the phone on the ninth ring. It was Chuck's secretary, and she seemed frantic. "Nancy, where have you been? We almost sent the police after you!"

With that, Chuck got on the phone and said, "Honey, don't say a word, just quickly get dressed in your fanciest outfit. We are being driven by a chauffeur up to Scandia, a fancy restaurant in Los Angeles tonight, and it could be worth a million dollars to the company. *But you need to be here by 5 PM sharp!* With that, he hung up! I looked at the clock. It was now twenty minutes to five!

CHOICE POINT: Emotional choice or a faith choice? Which way am I going to choose? Emotional choice would have me scream, stamp my feet, call him back and declare, "I'm sorry, but there's just no way I can do it: I'm a mess; Michelle's a mess; groceries are still in the car; dinner's not made, etc.!" Or, am I going to make a faith choice and choose what I know to be God's Will by simply trusting Him to get me ready and there on time?

Lisa had come home by that time and had heard all the commotion. I took Michelle and Lisa by the hands and said, "We really need to pray for Mommy." In that prayer, I told God it was impossible to do what Chuck had just asked. It was now a quarter to five. His office was at least 10 minutes away, even without the rush hour traffic. Nevertheless, I told God I was willing to do whatever He wanted me to.

With that, little Michelle said, "Mommy, don't worry about me, I'll just go lie down and rest." Michelle had never before lain down of her own free will! Lisa then chimed in, "Mom, don't worry about the food. I'll bring in the groceries and fix dinner for the two of us." Lisa had never, up until that time, offered to bring in groceries or to make dinner. This was a first! It was a miracle!

That left me free to concentrate on me. I flew upstairs, called Grandma to babysit, took a one-minute shower, did what I could with my wild hair, got dressed, and would you believe I made it to Chuck's office by five past five, rush-hour traffic and all.

We didn't get the contract, but I'll tell you, Chuck sure noticed and appreciated my supportiveness. And again, I experienced God's faithfulness to perform His Life through me, in spite of how I felt.

1 John 5:20 instructs that the purpose of our willpower is to *know* Him. "And we know that the Son of God is come, and hath given us an understanding [*dianoia*], that we may know Him that is true; and we are in Him that is true, even in His Son Jesus Christ. This is the true God, and eternal life."

Our Choices Are Critical

Our new, supernatural willpower is not only God's *authority* to enable us to choose His Will over our own negative thoughts, emotions and desires (our self-life), but also His *power* to carry out and perform His Will in our lives.

"For it is God which worketh in you both *to will* and *to do* of His good pleasure." (Philippians 2:13, emphasis added)

The reason our supernatural willpower is critical is because *what we choose*, moment-by-moment, not only determines the *direction* of our lives, but also, whose life will be lived in our souls...either God's or our own!

In the next chapter, we'll explore in detail the make-up of our soul and body and what function they play in regards to the Mind of Christ.

Endnotes:

1.   1 Peter 1:3, 23

2.   Psalm 18:28

3.   Romans 5:5; Hebrews 8:10 (be sure to check the Greek); and Galatians 4:6. See also Romans 8:39; John 17:26; 1 Corinthians 1:24; 2 Corinthians 4:7. This is the "fulness of God" that John 1:16 talks about.

4.   Colossians 1:27

5. The new nature that God gives us when we are born again is a brand new spiritual transformation (a fresh, new existence) that occurs in the inner man (heart). This is the new man (Romans 6:6; Ephesians 2:15; 4:22-24; Colossians 3:9-10), "...Christ in you [us], the [our] hope of glory." (Colossians 1:27)

   The new man must be "put on," moment-by-moment, just like one would put on a new suit of clothes. (Colossians 3:10) We must not revert to putting on the old suit of the former life; rather, we must continue to grow in this new life. (Ephesians 5:8)

6. For example in Mark 7:21

7. John 20:22

8. Romans 3:11-12

9. Ecclesiastes 3:11 ("world" here can be translated *eternity*)

10. Ezekiel 11:19; 36:36

11. Hebrews 8:10; 10:16 (check Greek)

12. Ephesians 1:18

13. Philippians 2:13

14. See Chapter Seven, "Our Free Choice."

15. Deuteronomy 30:19; Joshua 24:15; Proverbs 1:29; Isaiah 7:15

Scriptural References:

Chapter Nine

The Spiritual View of Solomon's Temple (CHART 11)

A. Our new spirit
1. This is a totally new spirit. This is what being "born again" means (1 Peter 1:3, 23; John 3:3, 6; Ezekiel 11:19; 36:26; 37:14; 1 Corinthians 6: 17)
2. This spirit is the new *power source, life source or energy source* of our lives. This is God in us, the Father, Son and Holy Spirit (John 14:23). We have become one spirit with Him (1 Corinthians 6:17; Galatians 4:6; Romans 8:11, 16, "beareth" means *union*)
3. God's Spirit is what will create *new life* in our hearts (Ezekiel 36:27-28; Job 33:4).
    a. God has lit the candle of our spirit (Psalm 18:28)
    b. Only *one* life source in our hearts now (John 3:6)

B. Our *new heart* (Ezekiel 11:19; 18:31b; Jeremiah 24:7; 32:39; Deuteronomy 30:6; Romans 2:28-29)
1. This new heart is the place that God's Life is created, started or "brought into new existence" (Ezekiel 11:19; 36:26-27; Psalm 51:10)
2. This heart is totally new (Ecclesiastes 3:11b; 2 Corinthians 4:6; 1 John 5: 12; Ezekiel 18:31)
3. This is God's Life in us (1 John 4:8, 16; John 1:1, 14; 1 John 1:1; 5:7). It's "Christ in us, our hope of Glory" (Colossians 1:9, 27; 1 John 5:11; 2 Timothy 1:7; 1 Peter 3:4; 1 Corinthians 2:16; Philippians 2:13)
4. Our new heart consists of God's supernatural Life: His Love (*Agape*), His Thoughts (*Logos*) and His Power (*Dunamis*) (Romans 5:5; 8:39; Luke 4:4, 14; 5:17; 8:12; John 17:26; 4:24; Hebrews 8:10; Galatians 4: 6; 1 Corinthians 1:24; 2 Corinthians 4:7; Acts 1:8; Ephesians 3:16-19; 2 Corinthians 4:6; 1 John 1:5; 4:8)
    a. This is the very nature of God Himself in our hearts (1 Peter 3:4; 2 Corinthians 5:17; 2 Peter 1:4). This is the *new man* that we must put on in our souls everyday (Romans 6:6; Ephesians 2:15; 4:22-24; Colossians 3:9-10)
    b. This Life is God's eternal Life (Jeremiah 31:31; 1 John 5:11-12; Psalm 103:17; Isaiah 54:10; Hebrews 13:5, 8; 1 Corinthians 13:8)
    c. Our heart life is the center core of our whole being (Proverbs 14:30; Leviticus 17:11)
5. Our old heart
    a. The *old heart* is the *old man* which was crucified when we became born again (Colossians 3:9). It no longer has any power over us (Romans 6:7, 14, 18)
        .   Our old heart is corrupt from birth (Genesis 8:21; Mark 7:21)
        .   Our old heart is unknowable (Jeremiah 17:9; Ecclesiastes 9:3; Matthew 15:19-20a; Mark 7:21)
        .   Our old heart is incurable (Romans 3:11-12; Jeremiah 17:9)
    b. The old heart is proud and arrogant (Isaiah 14:13-14; Ezekiel 28:2; Jeremiah 13:9-10; 48:29; 49:16; Deuteronomy 8:14,17)
    c. The old heart will never on its own seek God (Romans 1:21-22; 3: 11-12; Philippians 2:21)
    d. This is why we desperately need to be born again (John 3:3, 5-6; 1 Peter 1:3) and receive a new spirit and a new heart (Jeremiah 24:7; 32:39; Ezekiel 11:19-20; 36:26-27; Galatians 4:6; Hebrews 8:10)

    e.   If we are in Christ, we now have a new heart (1 Corinthians 6:17). The Life that now resides in our hearts is completely pure and holy, because it's God's Life (1 Peter 3:4; 2 Corinthians 5:17; 2 Peter 1:4)

        .   This is the "hidden man of the heart" (1 Peter 3:4)

        .   And the mystery hidden from all ages (Colossians 1:26-27)

    f.   So, it's not our hearts that need to be transformed anymore, but our souls (our lives) (Romans 12:1-2; 1 Corinthians 6:20; Galatians 2:20)

6.   Fountain of living water

    a.   God's Spirit (His Life) in our hearts often spoken of as an *unending* fountain of living water that wells up within us to overflowing (John 4:14; Jeremiah 17:13c; Romans 8:38-39; Psalm 46:4)

    b.   His Life in our hearts is unquenchable (Song of Solomon 8:7; Romans 8:38-39; Psalm 103:17; 139:7-13; Isaiah 43:2-4; 54:10). It will always keep on flowing to our hearts

    c.   However, if we make wrong emotional choices, His Spirit can be blocked from flowing out into our souls (Psalm 119:70; James 3:10-11)

C. Our new willpower

    1.   Our willpower is the *key* to our Christian walk because it determines whose life will be lived in our souls, either God's or our own (Deuteronomy 30:19-20; Jeremiah 21:8; Ephesians 1:18; Psalm 119:109a; Proverbs 15:32; Romans 6:13, 16; 7:18, 25; 8:5-6)

    2.   Our new willpower enables us to put God's Life from our hearts out into our souls

    3.   Our willpower has two parts:

        a.   God's supernatural Will and Power

           .   This is part of our new birth (Hebrews 8:10; 10:16; Jeremiah 31:33)

           .   This is where God counsels us as to what His Will is; and then gives us His Power to perform it in our lives (Philippians 2:13; Romans 9:17; 1 Corinthians 2:4; 2 Corinthians 6:7; Ephesians 1:18)

        b.   Our own free choice (*exousia)*

           .   This is the *free choice* to do as God has counseled us; or, do as we desire

           .   The purpose of our willpower is to *know* Him (1 John 5:20) and to experience His Life through us (Ephesians 1:18-19)

    4.   The two parts of our willpower is demonstrated by the Temple model (Zechariah 4:2-10; Revelation 11:3-4)

        a.   The Golden Vestibule represents the supernatural *authority and power of God* to make faith choices (Philippians 2:13; Zechariah 4:6; Matthew 26:39)

        b.   The Bronze Pillars (Jachin and Boaz) represent *our free choice* to follow God's Will or not (Deuteronomy 30:17-19)

    5.   Contrary choices

        a.   These are choices that *go against* what we feel, think and desire. They are non-feeling choices or faith choices. (Mark 9:24) Jesus made these kind of choices (John 10:18)

        b.   We too, have God's authority and power to make these choices (Matthew 26:39; 1 Peter 4:2)

        c.   God then, will change our feelings to make our faith choice (Mark 9:24)

    d.   Christians are the only ones who can make contrary choices (Philippians 2:13; 1 Corinthians 7:37; Matthew 26:39)

- We have the authority of God and the power of God to override our own will and do what is pleasing to God (Hebrews 13:21; Mark 9:24; John 10:17-18; Matthew 26:39; Romans 8:13; 13:1)

- We don't have to feel like doing this (Psalm 119:101; John 10:17-18; Luke 22:42; 1 Corinthians 7:37; Romans 7:18b), but simply be "willing" to do it (Isaiah 1:19; Matthew 26:39; Philippians 2:13; John 5:30). God will do the rest
- Christians are the only ones who have another *power source* within them to perform something different in their lives than what they feel
- Non-believers have no other choice but to follow their own thoughts, emotions and desires (Ephesians 2:2-3; 4:17-19; Colossians 1:21; Romans 7:18)

6.   We will constantly be faced with two choices: God's way or our own way (Deuteronomy 30:19; Isaiah 7:15; Proverbs 1:29; Joshua 24:15)

    a.   Faith choices (*boulomai*) "Not my will, but Thine" (Matthew 26:39; Luke 5:5; 18:28-30; 22:42; Acts 19:21b; Philippians 2:8; Galatians 2:20; 3:11; Romans 6:6, 16, 18-19; 8:13)

- Faith choices give God control of our lives to *rein in* our own thoughts, emotions and desires (Ephesians 5:2; Galatians 5:16a; Colossians 4:5; Romans 3:22), so that His Life can come forth
- This is single-mindedness because one life is being lived (God's)
- Whatever is "born of God" overcomes the world (1 John 5:4)

    b.   Emotional choices (*thelema*) "I will" (Matthew 23:27; Luke 8:14; James 1:8; 2 Peter 2:10)

- Emotional choices cause the pure fountain water to be blocked off (Jeremiah 2:13; Proverbs 25:26)
- Emotional choices give the flesh full control and God's Life will be quenched (Joel 1:10-12; Romans 7:15, 19, 23)
- Making emotional choices results in double-mindedness because two lives are being lived (God's and my own)
- Power of sin, at that moment, is in control of our lives (Romans 7:17-21, 23; Luke 11:17; John 8:34; Proverbs 5:22)

7.   Our choices are critical because this is where the sin begins. Whatever choice is not of faith is sin (Romans 14:23)

Chapter Ten
Soul and Body

Let's continue our comparison of Solomon's Temple and the internal architecture of man by exploring our soul and body.

Turn back to **CHART 11** (page 174**).**

(4) <u>OUR SOUL</u> (*psyche*)

We said that our souls are made up of our conscious thoughts, emotions and desires. This is the self-life that we have so often referred to. Now, there is a *hidden, secret part* of our soul—our secret hidden chambers (6)—which we will discuss in the next chapter. But, it's important for us to recognize that these hidden chambers are a part of our soul, and thus, a part of our *flesh*. Remember, our soul and our body make up or comprise our flesh—the whole grey area on the charts.

The Greek word for soul (life) is *psyche*. *Psyche* has a very interesting two-fold root meaning. It means *it shall have life* or *it shall wax cold*. This is a perfect definition because our soul is either going to be Spirit-filled and "have life" because of the free flow of God's Life from our hearts to our souls or, our soul will be empty and "waxing cold," because God's Life in our hearts has been quenched (blocked) by wrong, emotional choices.

Our soul is like a neutral area that can either be *filled with God's Life,* if we have made faith choices, or our soul will be *filled with self-life* because we have made wrong emotional choices.

As a friend once said, "Our soul is like a spiritual playground. Either it's filled and controlled by God's Spirit or it's filled and controlled by the flesh." It's either one or the other. Unfortunately, there is no middle ground.

For simplicity, think of our souls as the outward *expression or manifestation* of our lives. In other words, our souls are the *life* that we see, feel and hear coming forth from each other.

An Analogy

What's often confusing is that *life* exists both in our hearts and in our souls. What's the difference? The difference is that life is *originally created, started and brought into new existence (bara) in our hearts,*[1] whereas, that life is *outwardly expressed, manifested, or shown forth* in our souls. So, you could say that "heart-life" is *invisible life* (we can't see it—only God can); whereas, "soul-life" is mainly *visible life* (we can sense it, feel it, see it and hear it).

The best analogy I can think of to show the difference between these two kinds of life, is with plants in a garden. *Heart-life* is like the "root life" of plants. We can't see it—it's underground—nevertheless, it's essential to the health and growth of the plants above.

In contrast, our *soul-life* is like the beautiful flowers that grow above ground. We can visibly see the flowers, smell them, feel them, touch them and enjoy them. Jeremiah 31:12 explains, "...their souls shall be as a watered garden."

Our Soul is a Neutral Area

As we said before, our soul is a neutral area that is either going to be filled with God's Life from our hearts ("flowers"—if we have chosen to be open and cleansed vessels); or filled with self-life ("weeds"—if we have quenched God's Life by making wrong choices).

See **CHART 12** (on facing page).

Let's visually see how this works. This chart is the one that I want *burned into* your memory. Ideally, our souls (4) *should be* the expression or the manifestation or the showing forth of God's Life (7) from our hearts (i.e., the *flowers*). In other words, God's *Agape* Love (11) from our hearts has become *our* love (12) in our souls, His Thoughts (13) from our hearts has become *our* thoughts (14) in our souls, and His supernatural Power (13) in our hearts has become the power and ability of our lives.

This is what it means to be "spirit-filled" (17) or filled with the "fulness of God." Remember, *our purpose for being called as Christians is to be filled with the fulness of God, sharing His genuine Life—His Love and His Thoughts—with others.*[2] *Nothing else will bring us fulfillment like this—it's the whole meaning of our Christian walk.*

Ephesians 3:19 puts it so eloquently: "And to know the Love of Christ, which passeth knowledge, that ye might be filled with all the fulness of God."

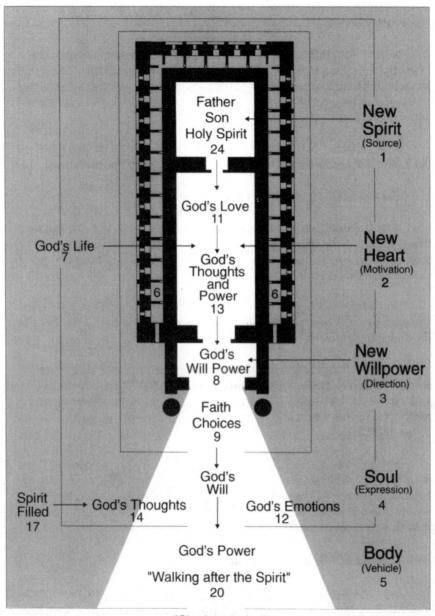

Chart 12

This is also what it means to be "single-minded," or more precisely, *single-souled* because only one life is being lived here—God's Life (7)![3] This person is an open vessel, truly loving (*agapao*) God and walking in His Truth and Love.

Notice the light that is coming from this Temple looks like a *flashlight*. This is illustrated in Luke 11:33 when it says, "No man, when he hath lighted a candle, putteth it in a secret place, neither under a bushel, but *on a candlestick, that they which come in may see the light.*" (emphasis added)

So in a believer, then, our soul can either show forth God's Life or His Light (**Chart 12**), if we have chosen to be open and pure channels, or:

See **CHART 13** (on the facing page).

If we have chosen to make emotional choices (9) by refusing to deal with the things in our life that are not of faith (19), either out of disobedience or ignorance, then our souls will become not full of *flowers* as God desires, but full of *weeds*.

God's Life, His Light (7) will then become quenched (18), blocked or "greased over." Thus, the soul-life that is produced is not God's Life, as He desires, but our own self-life (10).

This, again, is called double-mindedness, or more precisely, *double-souled* because two lives are being lived here—*God's Life* (7) which is still in our hearts and our own *self-life* (10) in our souls.[4] This is a person being conformed to this world and living a lie because his words and his deeds do not match.

Notice how the light in this temple is blocked or quenched from coming forth. The candle of his spirit is lit, but it's unable to shine forth because it's covered over and hidden, bring to mind what Luke 11:33 means when it says, "No man [should], when he hath lighted a candle, *putteth it in a secret place, neither under a bushel....*" (emphasis added)

Where Does *Self-Life* Come From?

Let me ask you a question. If we have God's Life in our new hearts (7) and this is now our "true nature" (Christ in us), where does this "self-life" (10) originate from?

One of the primary ways self-life is triggered is by the hurts, resentments, doubts, pride, bitterness, etc., that we have never properly dealt with because of either ignorance or disobedience, but have stuffed and buried in our secret, hidden

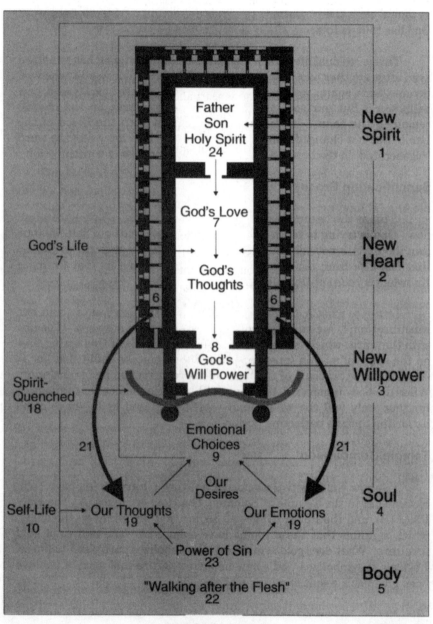

"Double-minded"

Chart 13

chambers (6), thinking no one will see, no one will know. Self-life is triggered when we choose to follow what these buried things are prompting rather than God's voice.

This is *residual life*, which means a part of the original has remained even after another part has been taken away. In other words, when we become born again, we received a new spirit, a new heart and a new willpower. But our soul and body (all the grey area on the charts) remained the same. It was redeemed, bought with the Blood of the Lamb, but not changed, renewed or regenerated. (I am using the word *regenerated* in the broad sense, including the process of sanctification.)

Sanctification Process

This renewal of our soul and body is called *sanctification* and every one of us are at some point in that process. God is trying to teach each of us how to set aside our self-life, our own thoughts, emotions and desires that are usually contrary to His, so that His *Life* from our hearts can come forth giving us that intimate Knowledge (*oida*) of God. (Review **Chart 12**, page 191).

Listen to what A.J. Gordon in *Ministry of the Spirit* says about our sanctifica-tion: "Our sanctification moves from within outward. It begins with the spirit, which is the Holy of Holies; the Spirit of God acting first on the spirit of man in renewing grace, then upon the soul till at last it reaches the outer court of the body at the resurrection and translation. When the body is glorified, then only will sanctification be consummated, for then only will the whole man—spirit, soul and body—have come under the Spirit's perfecting power."

Temple Comparison

To show you how this works, let's review **Chart 10** (on page 168) which is the floorplan of Temple of Solomon. The Holy of Holies (A), the Holy Place (B), and the Porch (C) were rooms or areas in the temple that were gold. Each had solid gold walls and solid gold furniture, which is symbolized on the chart by *white*. What does gold symbolize? It symbolizes purity and holiness. It stands for God's new imparted nature that each of us have been given as a result of our new birth.

Notice, however, that the Pillars (D), the Inner Court (H), and the Outer Court (I) are all gray on the charts—which signifies that these rooms had bronze struc-tures and furnishings. Bronze is symbolic of something that must still be judged. It means that sin is still present in these areas. Bronze indicates something that is *not* yet totally renewed. It's redeemed, but not yet renewed.

Also note, the secret hidden chambers (E) are gray on the charts, but they were actually made of wood, which symbolizes *humanity*. The root of the Hebrew word for wood actually means *something to be burned up*." This is interesting because that's exactly what God would have us do with most of the "junk" that we have stored in this area.

[I would recommend that you color the different rooms and areas on your charts so you can get the full impact of these charts. Use yellow for the *gold* rooms and, perhaps, brown for the *bronze* areas. If you want, color the hidden chambers *black* to remind you that the things there must be burned up.]

The Temple model symbolizes that at our new birth, we are given a *new* supernatural spirit (1), a *new* supernatural heart (2), and a *new* supernatural will-power (3), but the gray area—our soul (4) and our body (5))—is not yet renewed or regenerated (again in the broad sense).

"Off with the Old—On with the New"

We said in Chapter Eight, that our old heart is the "old man" that Paul tells us in Romans 6:6 is "crucified" and destroyed when we become born again.[5] The "old man," then, is our old, unconverted self; it's the "old me," strong in deeds of sin. But, praise God, Paul tells us in Colossians 3:9 that, at our new birth, we *put off* that old man. However, that "putting off" of the old man is twofold: *positionally* at our conversion and *experientially* in the gradual process of sanctification.[6]

The new heart that God gives us as a result of our new birth is *Christ in us, our hope of Glory.*[7] Scripture tells us that if we have been baptized into Christ, if we have been born again, then we have put on" Christ. The *putting on* of Christ is also twofold: positionally it begins in our hearts at our new birth, as you can see in **Chart 11** (page 174), and experientially, by moment by moment, putting on Christ in our lives (our souls) as you can see in **Chart 12** (page 191) and **Chart 13**, page 193). This illustrates the process of sanctification that all believers are going through now.

Ephesians 4:24 exhorts us to "...put on the new man, which after God is created in righteousness and true holiness." And Colossians 3:10 confirms this: "...put on the new man, which is renewed in knowledge after the image of Him that created him." *Paul is referring to Christ's Life in our hearts, which we are to daily, moment-by-moment, "put on" in our lives. This is the "new man," the new me.*[8]

This is exactly what we do when we renew our minds. We put off our old thinking and we put on the Mind of Christ, His Wisdom, Understanding, Counsel,

Strength and Knowledge. This is the "preparation" and the "readiness" that God desires for each of us to do daily.[9] This is the "washing of our feet" (souls) that John 13:8 exhorts us constantly to do.

(5) **OUR BODY** (*soma*)

Let's go back and again review **Chart 13** (page 193).

One last area of the temple that we want to cover briefly is our body. Our body (5) is analogous to the Outer Court of Solomon's Temple, which, as you can see, was on an even lower level than the Inner Court. Scripture tells us that the Outer Court was constantly exposed to many "outside" influences, just as we are through our bodies.

King Solomon's own palace was adjacent to the Outer Court. Here he housed his 700 wives (yes, 700 wives)! Also, in the Outer Court were his harem buildings, where reportedly he kept 300 concubines. Boy, talk about outside influences!

1 Kings 11:1-6 tells us that it was these foreign wives (and playmates) and their ungodly influence that turned Solomon's heart away from following the Lord. He wasn't careful to *love* the Lord with all his heart and soul, as his father, David, had done. And thus, the Bible says his heart "was not perfect with God" anymore.[10]

In Jesus' day, the Outer Court was also the place where the money changers and the dove sellers did business. Even Satan himself tempted Jesus from the pinnacle of the Outer Court. Just think of all the outside influences in our own lives (television, movies, magazines, advertisements, etc.) that continually draw us away from whole-heartedly and single-mindedly following God.

1 John 2:16 tells us, "For all that is in the world, the lust of the flesh, the lust of the eyes, and the pride of life, is <u>not</u> of the Father, but is of the world."

Our Vehicle of Expression

As we said earlier, our bodies are the vehicles or the carriers for the expression of our lives. In other words, we need a soul in order to express life, and we need a body to express life through. Therefore, our souls and our bodies can't be separated; otherwise there is death.

If we are born again, then technically we are always in the Spirit. However, by our continual choice, our willpower (9), we can either "walk after the Spirit" by making faith choices and allowing God's Life to fill our souls and motivate our actions; or, we can "walk after the flesh" by making emotional choices, thus allowing our self-life to fill our souls and prompt our actions. Galatians 5:25 exhorts us, "If we *live in the Spirit*, let us also *walk in the Spirit.*" (emphasis added)

Walking after the Spirit

If we choose to *walk after the Spirit* by making faith choices (see **Chart 12** (20), page 191), then our bodies will be filled with and show forth God's Life (7) from our hearts (i.e., "the new man"). At this point, we are Spirit-filled (17) and it's Christ's Image (God's Character) that we are showing to the world, not our own.

Notice at this moment, we are freed from Satan's oppression, because our self-life has been reined in, set aside and given over to God.[11] Therefore, Satan has no control over us at such times—there are no holes (no openings) for him to get his hands on.[12]

Romans 6:7 makes clear, "For he that is dead [he who has crucified the self-life or forbidden the self] is freed from sin."

This is a Christian who, for the moment, has been transformed. He has presented his body as a "living sacrifice" and he is *living the truth*. His words, *Jesus is my life* match his actions.

Walking after the Flesh

If, however, we choose to *walk after the flesh* by making emotional choices (see **Chart 13** (22), page 193), our bodies will manifest and reflect our own self-life (10) (i.e., our "old man").

In other words, we will have chosen to follow our own thoughts, emotions, and desires (our self-life) (10), over what God has prompted, (8) and thus, God's Spirit has been quenched, (18) and His eternal Life (7) cannot flow into our souls.

Ephesians 4:30 warns, "Grieve not the Holy Spirit of God, whereby ye are sealed unto the day of redemption."

Therefore, we can be Christians all our lives, yet because we continue to make emotional choices, no one will ever see the difference between our life and that of our neighbors' who don't even know God.

God's Life in us will be quenched, so that the life that comes forth from us is self-life and not God's Life at all.

Such duality describes exactly what a *hypocrite* is: one whose words and actions don't match. We say we are Christians, and yet our lives show something totally different. We're living a lie. We know in our heads that "Jesus is the answer," but our lives don't prove it. This is why the Christian body is having such a difficult time these days: many of us are living two lives. We're double-minded. We're *saying* one thing, and yet our lives are *showing* forth something completely different.

Notice on the chart, we still have a new spirit (1), a new heart (2) and a new willpower (3), but because we have emotionally chosen (9) to follow what we think and feel (19) over God's voice, we have quenched His Life within and opened ourselves up to Satan's arrows. We have given him many holes to attack—uncontrolled thoughts, wild emotions and self-centered desires.

Power of Sin

One of the reasons we are so prone to making self-centered, emotional choices, is that our souls (4) and our bodies (5) (i.e., the *flesh*) are still dominated and controlled by the *power of sin* (23). The power of sin is the energy force that Paul tells us in Romans 7:20-21, 23, dwells in our unrenewed bodies. The power of sin's whole intent and purpose is to cause us to "veer off course" and to "miss the mark",[13] the *mark* being, the Image of Christ.

Satan uses the power of sin as his tool to gain access to our flesh (all the gray area on the charts). Now, no one can take us out of the keeping power of God once we have been born again.[14] *We have that eternal security!* But we can, by our continual choice, quench God's power in us and open our souls and bodies up to the power of sin.

Wide-Open Prey for the Enemy

When we are walking after the flesh rather than the Spirit, we'll be pleasing *self* and not God, which, in turn, will open us up for the arrows of the enemy. Our self-centered thoughts and emotions will trigger and prompt reactions from our hidden chambers (6) (things that we haven't yet given over to God), giving Satan a perfect inroad for more of his "cords of sin".[15]

At this time, we walk *saying* we are Christians yet, our *actions* are manifesting our *own* thoughts and emotions and not God's Life at all. This behavior not only grieves God, but also gives a false witness to others. Jesus says in John 5:31, "If I bear witness of myself, my witness is not true." And, I believe, the same can be said of us.

Bearing witness of self and not God is what a *carnal Christian* does continuously. He still has God's Spirit energizing God's new supernatural Life in his heart, but he has chosen to hang onto his own self-centered thoughts, emotions and desires, thereby quenching God's Life and, showing forth the "old man" instead.

The War

In conclusion, the war that goes on within us between the *Power of God* (24) **Chart 12** (page 191) and the *power of sin* (23) **Chart 13** (page 193) is not in our hearts, as I used to believe and teach, but in our souls and bodies, i.e., the flesh. Recognizing this truth and bringing the flesh into captivity by putting off that "old man" so that God's Life can come forth, is what the sanctification process is all about.

Paul tells us in Romans 6:6-7 that since our old, evil heart-life (our old man) has been exterminated and done away with at our new birth, the power of sin's hold on the flesh has *already* been destroyed and we have been freed from sin.

Christ in our hearts, therefore, is the only overcoming power that will give us victory in this war. If we can continually choose to renew our minds, we can, in God's Strength, overcome anything the flesh is urging us to do.

In Galatians 2:20 Paul declares, "I am crucified with Christ; nevertheless I live; yet not I, but Christ liveth in me; and the life which I now live in the flesh I live by the faith of the Son of God, Who loved me and gave Himself for me."

God Wants us to be "Spirit-Filled"

So, just as Solomon's Temple in 1 Kings 8:10-11 and 2 Chronicles 5:13-14 was filled from the inside out with God's Spirit, this is exactly God's purpose for us. Remember the flashlight (review **Chart 12**, page 191).

"For ye are bought with a price: therefore glorify [be filled with, reflect, manifest and shine forth] God in your body...." (1 Corinthians 6:20)

Daily we are to allow God's Spirit to issue forth from the Holy of Holies of our hearts and fill our souls and our bodies with His Life and His Glory. This is not just a one-time event; it's a moment-by-moment choice to be filled with the Spirit.

"...Be ye not unwise, but understanding what the will of the Lord is. [...That ye] be [being] filled with the Spirit [all day long, every day]." (Ephesians 5:17-18)[16]

The only way, however, we are going to be filled with God's Spirit and transformed into Christ's image, is for us to, moment by moment, *put off* the garbage in our own thinking and *put on* the Mind of Christ. Then, God's Spirit can freely issue forth from the Holy of Holies of our hearts and fill our souls as He desires.

"Therefore, I beseech you, my brethren, by the mercies of God, that ye present your bodies a living sacrifice, holy, acceptable unto God, which is your reasonable service. And be not conformed to this world, but *be ye transformed* [how?] *by the renewing of your mind*, so that you may prove what is that good and acceptable and perfect will of God." (Romans 12:1-2, emphasis added)

Endnotes:

1.　　Proverbs 4:23

2.　　Ephesians 5:2; 2 Corinthians 2:14

3.　　John 4:14

4.　　James 3:10-11

5.　　Ephesians 4:22

6.　　See Chapter Nine, "Our New Heart" and "God's Life in our Hearts."

7.　　Colossians 1:27

8.　　2 Corinthians 4:10-11

9.　　Matthew 24:42, 44, 46

10.　1 Kings 11:4

11.　Romans 6:13

12.　John 14:30

13. The power of sin, *hamartia* (266) is an energy force that dwells in our bodies. It produces lusts (strong, self-centered desires) that cause us to "miss the mark" (being conformed into Christ's Image). The Greek words for these lusts are *enthumesis* (1761) and *epithumia* (1939), both come from the root word, *thumos* (2372) which means "for the purpose of revenge" or, *thuo*, to kill.

14. Colossians 1:13-14; John 10:27-29; 1 John 5:18

15. Romans 6:12

16. John 7:38

Scriptural References:

Chapter Ten

Spiritual View of Solomon's Temple   (CHARTS 12 and 13)

A.   Our soul
1.   Our soul is like a *neutral area* that "shall have life" because of free flow of God's Life) or, "shall wax cold" (because God's Life is quenched
2.   For the most part, our souls are the *outward expression* of our lives. It's the life that we see, hear and feel coming forth from each other
3.   There is a *hidden, secret part* of our soul (the hidden chambers)
4.   The whole purpose of our being called as Christians is to be filled with God's Life—the "fulness of God" (Ephesians 3:19; 2 Corinthians 2: 14), walking by His Spirit (Galatians 5:14), conformed into His Image (Romans 8:29) and manifesting His Name (2 Corinthians 4:10-11)
5.   Our souls are made up mostly of our conscious thoughts, emotions and desires
6.   Life exists both in our hearts and souls; what's the difference?
    a.   Life is *originally created* in our hearts. (Proverbs 4:23) It's invisible life —only God can see it (Jeremiah 17:10; 12:3; 1 Chronicles 28:9; 1 Samuel 16:7d; Psalm 17:3; Proverbs 21:2b; Luke 16:15b)
    b.   Life is then *outwardly expressed* in our souls (Isaiah 58:10-11; Proverbs 14:30a; Matthew 12:35). It's visible life, all can see it (Jeremiah 31:12; 1 Samuel 16:7e)
7.   Our souls are a neutral area that can be filled with God's Life or self life
    a.   If we have made the appropriate *faith choices*, God's Life will be showing forth through our souls. His Love will become our love, His Thoughts, our thoughts, His Power, our own (John 4:14)
    .   This demonstrates single-mindedness — one life is being lived (God's)
    .   This symbolizes the light on top of the candlestick (Luke 11:35)—the flashlight
    b.   If we have made *emotional choices* to follow our own thoughts, God's Life becomes blocked or quenched and self life will show forth
    .   This results in double-mindedness—two lives are being lived (God's and our own) (2 Peter 2:17a). This is what a *hypocrite* looks like
    .   This is how the light gets "hidden" under a bushel (Luke 11:33; James 3:10-11)
8.   Where does "self-life" come from?
    a.   Self-life comes from the hurts, doubts, resentments, etc., that we have never dealt with, either out of ignorance or disobedience, but have simply stuffed in our hidden chambers. Self life is triggered when we choose to follow what these things are telling us to do over what God is saying (Proverbs 5:22; John 8:34)
    b.   These hidden things work on our conscious thoughts and emotions to make us choose to follow them
    c.   These hidden things are stored in a secret place is called *cheder*
    .   These chambers are analogous to the secret, hidden chambers of the Temple (1 Kings 6:5-10) where priests stored their own personal idolatrous things (Ezekiel 8:6-12)
    .   They represent the place in our soul where we hide, bury and store our hurts, wounds, guilt and fears (Proverbs 18:8; 26:22; Ezekiel 14:3-5)

9. We must learn to set aside our self-life, so that God's Life can come forth (Romans 6:6-7, 11-13; Colossians 2:11; 1 Corinthians 5:7-8; Acts 20:24)
    a. This is what the sanctification process is all about (2 Corinthians 4: 10-11)
    b. It's putting off the old man (Ephesians 4:22; Romans 6:6) and then, putting on Christ (Colossians 3:10; Ephesians 4:24)
        . The *putting on* of Christ is twofold: positionally at our new birth and experientially in the process of sanctification
        . It's Christ's Life (Colossians 1:27) that we are to, moment by moment, "put on" in our lives
        . This is the new me (2 Corinthians 4:10-11)
10. This is what we do when we "renew our minds' (Romans 12:1-2)
    a. This is the "washing of our feet" (souls) (John 13:8)
    b. This is also the "shodding our feet" (1 Peter 1:13)
B. Our body
    1. Our bodies are the *vehicle* or the carrier for the expression of our lives (Philippians 1:20; 1 Corinthians 6:19-20)
    2. Our soul and body together are known as the *flesh*
    3. Just as the Outer Court of the Temple had many outside influences (1 Kings 11:1-6; 1 John 2:16), so our bodies are "wide open" prey to the wiles of the enemy
    4. The "power of sin" resides in our bodies (Romans 7:20-21, 23)
        a. The power of sin is an energy force whose whole purpose is to cause us to "veer off course" and "miss the mark" (Philippians 3:14; Romans 7:19-23)
            . Satan is author of the power of sin (John 8:44; Ephesians 6:12)
            . "It's no more I" that does these bad things, but the power of sin in me (Romans 7:18, 20)
            . No one can take us out of the keeping power of God, once we are born again (Colossians 1:13-14; John 10:27-29; 1 John 5:18)
            . However, when we quench God's Spirit, we open ourselves up for the arrows of the enemy. We then give him access to all the gray area on the charts (Proverbs 5:22; Romans 7:17; John 8:34; Joel 1:10-12)
        b. This is the reason we are not sinless, even though we have God's Life in our hearts (Matthew 26:41)
    5. We have a constant choice to either "walk by the Spirit" or "walk by the flesh." By "birth" we are always *in the Spirit* (Romans 8:9), but by "choice" we can either:
        a. *Walk after the flesh* (Review CHART 13) (Romans 6:21; 7:5; 8:6a, 13a; Matthew 26:41)
            . We still have God's Life in our hearts, but because we have chosen to follow what we want and desire, we have blocked His Life from coming forth (Matthew 12:25; 26:41; James 3:10; Ephesians 4:30; Titus 1:16; Isaiah 59:2; Luke 9:24a; 18:9, 11; Amos 3:3)
            . We have opened ourselves up to the arrows of the enemy and are in bondage to the power of sin (Galatians 5:19; Romans 6:12, 16, 21; 7:18-20; 8:6-7). We are serving the law of sin (Romans 7:25c)
            . We are "pleasing self" (Ezekiel 33:31; Romans 8:8; Hosea 10:1)
            . His Light in us has been darkened (Luke 11:35; Psalm 38:10 and we are "living a lie" (John 5:31; 12:35; Jeremiah 7:28)
            . We grope for the wall like the blind (Isaiah 59:10)
            . This is where pure water gets blocked up (Jeremiah 2:13; Proverbs 25:26)

. This ought not to be (James 3:10-12; 1 John 3:6-9; 5:18; Ephesians 4:30; Romans 8:9; Matthew 12:34-35; Amos 3:3)
b. Or, we can *walk after the Spirit* (Review CHART 12) (Romans 8:6b, 13b; 6:13, 22; Galatians 5:24-25; 1 Peter 4:6c)
. We are filled with the "fullness of God" (Ephesians 3:19; Luke 9:24b; Ephesians 5:2; Galatians 4:19b)
. We are freed from the power of sin (Galatians 5:1; Romans 6:2,7; 7:25; 8:2; 1 John 3:9; Romans 6:6-7, 18, 22; Colossians 2:11; John 14:30)
. *Salvation* means freedom from power of sin (2 Thessalonians 2:13)
. There is no dark part (Luke 11:36b) and we are "living the truth" (2 John 4; Ephesians 6:5-6)
. We have intimate knowledge of God (Philippians 1:21). We are experiencing His Life in place of our own

The War
A. The war that goes on within us between the Power of God and the power of sin, is waged in our soul and body, not in our hearts (Romans 7:21-23; 6:13, 16; 8:5-6; Galatians 5:17)
1. Since our "old man" no longer exists (Romans 6:6), the power of sin's hold on the flesh has been destroyed and we have been, if we so choose to be, freed from sin (Romans 6:7-14,22; 6:11-13,16; Luke 11:17)
2. Soul and body are the battlefield, not our hearts (Romans 7:23)
3. The battle is spiritual (2 Corinthians 10:3-4)
B. Christ is now the "overcoming power" to free us from this war (Romans 6:2, 6-7; 7:25; 8:9, 13; 1 Corinthians 15:57; 1 John 3:4)
C. As believers we have God's authority and God's power to resist what the "flesh" is urging us to do (Romans 6:6-7; Colossians 2:11)

God Wants Us Spirit Filled
A. Just like Solomon's Temple was filled from the inside (where the Source was) outward (1 Kings 8:10-11; 2 Chronicles 5:13-14; 7:1; Exodus 40:34-35; Ezekiel 10:4), so too, we are filled by God's Spirit from the inside, where the Source is, outward (Ephesians 5:17-18; 1 Corinthians 6:20; John 7:38)
B. The only way this can happen, however, is by the constant "renewing of our minds" (Romans 12:1-2)

Section Five:
Searching the Hidden Chambers

"The spirit of man is the *candle* of the Lord, searching all the inward parts of the belly."

Proverbs 20:27

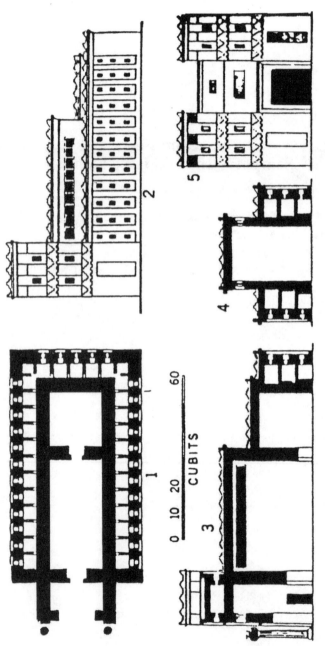

(1) Ground plan; (2) Side view; (3) Longitudinal cross-section; (4) Breadth cross-section; (5) front view.
From Vincent-Steve, *Jerusalem de l'Ancien Testament*, J. Gabalda & Cie., Paris 1956, tome 11.

Chart 14

Chapter Eleven
The Hidden Chambers
(Part 1)

Over the last several chapters, we have been exploring Solomon's Temple as a model or blueprint of the New Testament believer: spirit, heart, will, soul and body. In this chapter, we want to further investigate the secret, hidden chambers of Solomon's Temple to understand how they correspond to the *hidden, secret* place in our own internal design.

This subject is very controversial, as many Christians do not believe that we have a hidden part—a place where we hide and bury our hurts, wounds, painful memories, etc., (our secret faults). So again, be as the Bereans, check everything out.

A very important part of renewing of our minds, is the cleansing, healing and filling of these hidden chambers. Proverbs 24:3-4 tells us, "And by [intimate] knowledge shall the chambers be filled with all precious and pleasant riches." This is why we want to spend some time understanding these secret places, and the importance of putting off these hidden things so that we <u>can</u> put on Christ, even here.

Let's begin by exploring **CHART 14** (on facing page).

Again, this chart is a floor plan of Solomon's Temple. The hidden chambers, as you can see, were built all around the outside of the sanctuary.[1] These chambers belonged to the original floor plan of the Temple that God gave to David in 1 Chronicles 28:11-12.

Notice in illustration #1 that these chambers had no access (no doors) into them, either from the Holy of Holies, the Holy Place or the Porch. This will be important later. The only entrance to and from these secret recesses was by one door in the very front of the sanctuary building. See illustration #5.

1 Kings 6:5-8 tells us that there were three levels of these tiered chambers—31 hidden cubicles on each level.[2] (See illustration #4.) Since the walls around the main sanctuary were three feet thick, these chambers simply rested on ledges or brackets, so they were not actually built or secured into the walls.

As we noted in Chapter Eight, these secret recesses were supposed to be used for storing the priest's items of worship used in the Holy Place[3] and also, for displaying Israel's treasures to remind the people of all that God had done for them. Instead, the priests actually stored their own personal idolatrous worship items here, thinking that since these were secret, hidden places, *no one would see and no one would know.*

One of the arguments made to me recently by someone who does not believe we have a hidden place within us (he believes we are aware of everything we think and feel), was, "Wouldn't these priests know exactly what they had stored in these hidden recesses? Wouldn't they be aware of everything that was in there?" I answered him by saying, "They would probably be aware of *some* of the things they had stored in there. But, like my own attic in my house, I'm certainly not aware of everything that I have put in there over the years." Are you? I think it was the same for these priests. They were aware of some of the things that were hidden there, but certainly not all of the items—*they were secret and hidden, even to them.*

Our Hidden Place

Symbolically, these secret, hidden, storage chambers of Solomon's Temple correspond to our own *innermost part, our own secret place*—the place in our soul where we store, hide and bury our wounds, hurts, guilt and memories, either out of ignorance or disobedience—thinking *no one will see, no one will know.* These are thoughts and emotions that are just too painful to retain in our consciousness, so we push them down and try to forget about them.

In Scripture, these Temple hidden recesses are called in the Hebrew *cheder.* *Cheder* means *innermost part*, the secret place or the hidden chambers. Now, there is no mention of the word *subconscious* in Scripture, so to be completely Scriptural (and not stumble anyone), we must call this area *cheder.*

Here are a few provocative Scriptures that refer to our "*cheder:*"

Proverbs 20:27, "the spirit of man is the candle of the Lord, searching all the inward parts (*cheder*) of the belly." Why would the spirit search our inward parts if not to reveal sin in us, to us?

Proverbs 18:8, "The words of a talebearer are as wounds, and they go down into the innermost parts (*cheder*) of the belly."[4] This picture is very graphic, because we all know what it's like to hear that someone has gossiped about us.

If we don't deal with that hurt right away, it can easily become a "root of bitterness." Now, if there is no secret place or hidden chambers, what is this Scripture talking about? (Note also Proverbs 26:22)

And then, there's Proverbs 24:4 which we read earlier, "by knowledge [intimate] shall the chambers (*cheder*) be filled with all precious and pleasant riches." God wants to empty out the hidden chambers of all the debris, and then fill them back up with His Truth.

Of the 38 Scriptures that use the word *cheder* in the Bible, over half of them refer to a secret, hidden, innermost chamber or parlour. See more of the Scriptures that use the word *cheder* in the Appendix.

Turn now, if you will, to **CHART 15** (on following page).

Just as access to and from these hidden chambers was allowed through only one door at the front of the Temple sanctuary, so, too, the "power of sin" (23) that resides in our bodies (and that we talked about last chapter), has access not only to the conscious part of our soul (our self-life) (19), but also has access to these secret, hidden recesses of our souls (6). Remember, the hidden chambers <u>are</u> a part of our flesh.

Note that neither Satan nor the power of sin have access to our new spirit, our new heart[5] or our new willpower. It's very important to understand that these areas are inviolate. Just as in the Temple of Solomon, there was no outside access to the Holy of Holies, the Holy Place and the Vestibule of the Porch. In like manner, our spirit, heart and willpower are inaccessible to outside influences.

However, just like in Solomon's Temple, there *was* free access to the Inner and Outer Courts, similarly, we give the enemy access to our soul and body (the gray area), when we make emotional choices (review **Chart 13**). This is how the "walls of our souls" give way.

The Walls of our Souls

Nehemiah 4 is an interesting chapter in regards to the *walls of our souls*. It tells us, "The strength of the bearers of burdens is decayed, and there is much rubbish; so that we are *not able to build the wall*."

Wall here, alludes to the *walls of our souls*,[6] which can either become *strong walls* and hold off the enemy (the power of sin), or *untempered walls* that will easily crumble, fall and give way to the enemy's onslaughts.[7]

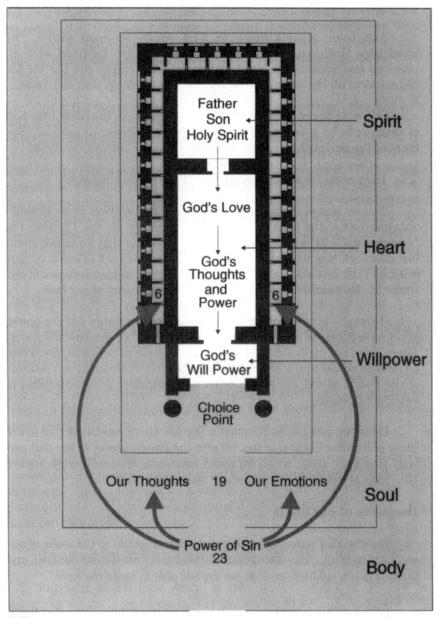

Chart 15

The Power of Sin

Remember, the power of sin's whole intent and purpose is to cause us to "veer off course" and to "miss the mark." The *mark*, we said, refers to Romans 8:29, *being conformed into the image of Christ.*

Because of our ignorance, not only as to how we renew our minds, but also what the Mind of Christ is and the power and authority of God we possess because of it, Satan has been having a "field day" keeping us his prisoners.

Through the power of sin, Satan's goal is to work hand-in-hand with our flesh influencing, persuading and manipulating us to follow our own self-life, rather than obey and trust God to perform His Will in our lives. The enemy wants us to be conformed to the world's image, because then the Gospel will not be passed on. (Again, review **Chart 13**.)

God, on the other hand, wants us to constantly yield our self-life to Him, regardless of how we feel or what we think, and put on the Mind of Christ. Then, we'll be conformed to Christ's Image and the Gospel will have a chance to be passed on. (Again, review **Chart 12**, page 191)

Can Satan Read our Thoughts?

In terms of the symbolism of the temple model, we give Satan access to <u>all</u> the *gray area* on the charts (i.e., our souls and our bodies—the flesh) every time we don't *deal with* our self-centered thoughts, emotions and desires, but simply *go with the flow* by making emotional choices.

One question often asked is, "Can Satan read our thoughts?" Most Christians seem to agree that Satan certainly can *insert* thoughts into our minds, but can he actually know what we're thinking? Many pastors and teachers theorize that he cannot. Others believe he can. One provocative passage on this subject is 2 Corinthians 2:10-11, which says that if we don't forgive, then Satan will have an advantage.

Another interesting Scripture is Ephesians 4:26-27, "Be ye angry, and sin not; let not the sun go down upon your wrath; neither give place to the devil." Again, many of us don't show our anger visibly and yet, somehow, this Scripture says that Satan will know when we are angry.

When we are clean, having given everything we are aware of over to God, then there are no holes and no vulnerabilities for Satan to grab hold of. The contrary, however, is also true. When we hang on to our sin, we give Satan many hideouts and strongholds. If Satan can't read our thoughts, then how is he going to know about our bitterness, our resentment, our unforgiveness, etc., that we have chosen to hold on to? We don't always show these attitudes in our behavior, but somehow Satan seems both to know and to be right there to capture us through them.

Through the power of sin, Satan's goal is to stop God's plans and purposes, anyway he can. One of the root word definitions for the *power of sin* is "for the purpose of revenge." Satan wants to "revenge God" or get back at Him by thwarting His plans and purposes in us.[8]

The Temple and the Question of Demon-Possession

If our spirit, heart and willpower are areas that are inviolate, similar to the sacred areas in Solomon's Temple, then the power of sin has no access there. This truth then, answers the question of whether or not a Christian can be demon-possessed. *A person who has the Spirit of God in his heart cannot be demon-possessed, because a believer's heart cannot be co-inhabited by God and Satan at the same time. Our spirit and our heart will either belong to one or the other.*

The following Scriptures serve as evidence to support this argument: 1 John 5:18 says, ...*he that is born of God...God keeps him, and the wicked one cannot touch him.* Colossians 1:13-14, *God [has, past tense] delivered us from the domain of darkness*[9] and transferred us to the Kingdom of His beloved Son, in whom we have redemption...even forgiveness of sins. And, John 10:27-29, "My sheep hear my voice, and I know them, and they follow me. And I give unto them eternal life; and they shall never perish, *neither shall any man pluck them out of my hand.* My Father, who gave them to me, is greater than all, and *no man is able to pluck them out of my Father's hand.*" (emphasis added)

However, if we give the enemy strongholds in our souls by refusing to deal with some of the buried things as they come up, Satan will use these hidden things as "chains and cords of sin" to keep us his prisoners.[10]

According to the above Scriptures, even though evil spirits cannot co-inhabit the spirit or the heart of a believer, nor touch any believer without the Father's permission, they certainly can harass, deceive and try to paralyze us through our "flesh."

An Example: Tasmania

Several years ago I traveled to Tasmania, a beautiful island off the coast of Australia, to do a *Be Ye Transformed* Seminar. It's a literal paradise with white sandy beaches, aqua blue water, lush green grass and trees, brightly-colored flowers, brilliant yellow fields with horses, sheep and cows grazing everywhere. It's absolutely idyllic.

Much to my amazement, however, it is also a land of many evil spirits. Satan and his hordes seem to always pick the beautiful places for their hideouts and camping grounds. I was shocked as the women who had invited me began to tell me of the drug use, porno businesses, alcoholism, marriage breakups, and child abuse that seemed to be so prevalent on that small island. They also told me of a Satanic cult who knew about our upcoming meeting, and who had been interceding against it.

Now, I expected perhaps 30 to 40 people to show up for the seminar (this was Tasmania, after all), but God surprised us all when almost 400 people crowded into the small auditorium, the largest facility in town.

All weekend the ladies and I had been praying against the evil forces of darkness. However, the very first night as I began to speak, I experienced the most bizarre things. As I would speak, my words seemed to bounce back in my face, as if there was a wall of glass between me and the audience. So that when I spoke, my words would hit that glass and fly back into my face. I had never experienced anything like it in over 15 years of speaking.

I know this all sounds absolutely crazy, but since that experience, I've spoken to several other Christian speakers and missionaries who also have had similar experiences.

When it first happened, I naturally I became "unglued." I stopped speaking. I prayed. Then, I began again. However, the same thing happened. Finally, the Lord brought to my mind the Scriptures He had given me that morning. "I am sending you forth as sheep among the wolves...." "False brethren [will be] spying out our liberty...." "Some will trouble you and [try to] pervert the Gospel of Christ." "I will give you a mouth and wisdom...." (Matthew 10:16; Galatians 1: 7; 2:4; Luke 21:15)

I finally recognized that this seminar was an intense spiritual battle and I just happened to be the "battlefield." I stopped the lecture, gathered the leaders together and all of us began to pray. We pleaded the blood of Christ over the auditorium, the audience and ourselves and we prayed for the enemy to be bound. Three from our team decided to march around the auditorium continually praying.

The result of this intense prayer was a wonderful and miraculous intervention by the Holy Spirit. When I began to speak again, my words just flowed and I was able to deliver a message I knew was anointed from on high (just as He had promised). The enemy's hold truly had been broken.

Five minutes into the lecture, I noticed three people get up from the audience and leave. We found out later that a group of people from the nearby Satanist camp had, indeed, come into the lecture hall and were interceding for confusion, disruption and chaos. They almost succeeded. Satan tried to paralyze and disrupt the whole meeting, but God gave us the discernment and the weapons we needed to overcome. The only way we are transformed into God's image is by the renewing of our minds, and Satan did *not* want those women to hear the *Be Ye Transformed* message that I was presenting.

Definition of Our Hidden, Secret Chambers

Turn in your books to **CHART 16** (on facing page).

One definition for these secret chambers might be: *a hidden reservoir of mostly untrue beliefs and assumptions* (#A on chart), *which strongly influence how we evaluate all that happens to us in the present* (#B on chart) *and upon which we make our choices* (#C on chart). *These choices then determine our actions.*

In other words, painful wounds, hurts, traumatic experiences, evil deeds, etc., that have happened to us in the past, if we don't give these things to God at the time they happen (either because we don't know how to or we don't want to), can end up being buried in our hidden chambers and eventually, affect how we think and act in the present.

An Example: Trudy

Trudy, a dear friend of mine, was in a Nazi Germany concentration camp when she was little. One evening around sunset as she and her parents were standing watching an event, she somehow was separated from them, spending 12 hours lost and alone. Trudy was three years old at the time.

Since that time, whenever Trudy would see a sunset, this cold, clammy, fearful and horrible loneliness would inexplicably come over her. Trudy, obviously, did not remember the incident when she was three, so she didn't understand her fear. A few years ago as Trudy and her older sister were sitting together at a barbecue watching the sun go down, she mentioned to her sister the horrible fear and loneliness that again she was beginning to experience. At first her sister didn't know what to make of it, but then was reminded of the incident when they were children. There was the key. Again, Trudy had no recollection of the incident, but because

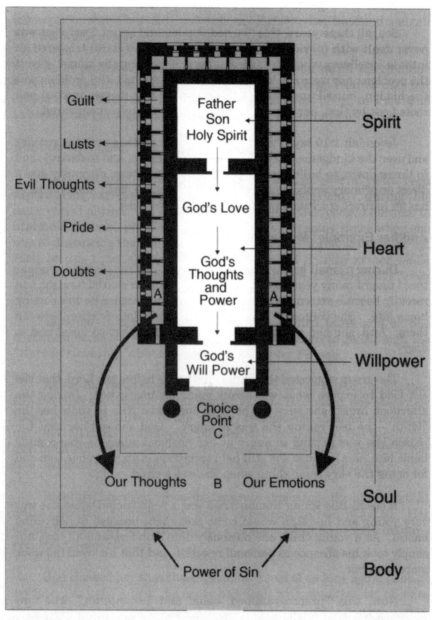

Chart 16

she knew what to do with it and how to give the root of her fear over to God, she was freed. And ever since then, she has she been able to enjoy watching every sunset with no any negative feelings at all.

For fifty years, the buried, hidden and secret fear that was never dealt with, because she was only a child, triggered an intense loneliness when she saw a sunset. Watching the sunset wasn't the problem, nor were the lonely feelings that she had. The problem was the hidden, buried and long-forgotten fear. Once it was exposed and rooted out by God, her loneliness at sunset completely disappeared. Jeremiah 1:10 proclaims, "See, I have this day set thee over the nations and over the kingdoms, to root out, and to pull down, and to destroy, and to throw down, to build, and to plant." This Scripture, obviously, has a direct or primary application for that period of time, but I also believe, it has an indirect spiritual application for our own lives.

Another Example: My Father

During a small group discussion in a *Be Ye Transformed* seminar that I taught many years ago, a sweet, young woman shared how she had recently become extremely angry at her husband because he was coming home late. She confessed it was causing tremendous friction between them. And, she had no idea why his lateness was making her so upset and so angry.

The group suggested that in her quiet time before the Lord, that she ask God to expose what was really going on inside her. During the afternoon break, she went to the Lord and asked Him to show her the truth—the real reason she was so angry. God showed her that the reason she was getting so angry at her husband when he was coming home late was because she still held tremendous anger at her own dad for doing the very same thing when she was a child.

When she was very young, this woman's dad was a family physician who often came home late because of delivering babies. As a young child, she obviously didn't understand why he was late, but simply took his absence as personal rejection, evidence that he loved his work more than her.

In adulthood, her "preprogrammed, belief and assumption," was now determining how she consciously evaluated what was happening to her in the present. Because her husband was now coming home late, he too, loved his work more than her. This, of course, triggered her self-life, her hurt and anger.

In the next discussion group, she excitedly shared what God had shown her and said she could hardly wait to go back to the Lord, get rid of the source (root) of the problem (untrue, preprogrammed beliefs and assumptions about her dad), go home, apologize to her husband and tell him the whole story.

As we proceed in this chapter, we'll realize that we all will continue to act out of our buried negative thoughts and feelings rather than out of God's Love and Truth, if we don't begin at some point to allow God to expose the garbage and deal with it as He would have us to do.

Another Example: "I'm Ugly"

I received a letter from Amanda who had, for several years, been experiencing extreme periods of depression. Coincidently, during this same period of time, she had developed allergies that caused her face to break out in small pimples. She said there were many times when she was so despairing that she just wanted to go to sleep and never wake up. At this time, she also found herself angry and grumpy at her whole family for no apparent reason. Normally, she said, she was fairly even tempered.

Amanda listened to the *Be Ye Transformed* tapes and on one particular occasion, was so desperate, that she chose to go through the "steps of cleansing" that are covered in Chapter Fifteen.

As she did these steps, God brought back to her remembrance that as a teenager she'd had horrible skin problems. Back then, she absolutely hated looking at herself in the mirror, because she thought she was so ugly with all those puss-filled pimples all over her face. Her face didn't stop breaking out until she was 28 years old and married. After that, her face had been fine and she had forgotten about the whole thing.

Recently, however, when she began to experience the allergies that caused her face to break out, bouts of depression had resulted. Her doctor had put her on estrogen, but still she continued to have extreme periods of despondency.

God showed Amanda that those "hidden" roots of so long ago ("Look at my face, I'm ugly"), that she never had dealt with or gotten rid of, were now motivating her present thinking: "Look at my face. I'm ugly. I want to die." And this kind of thinking caused her emotions of anger, grumpiness, depression and despondency.

It's not so much that these buried things in themselves hinder our sanctification—they don't. But they do affect our choices. And it's our choices that hinder our sanctification. Buried hurts and wounds definitely influence us, but they don't need to determine our choices. There is a much "more excellent way."

A sweet girl wrote me recently, "There's a lot that I have swept under the carpet over the years (thinking *no one will see; no one will know*). I can just see myself in a few years tripping over all the huge lumps in the rug and wondering to myself, why on earth can't I walk straight." Great analogy!

How Can These Hidden Chambers Become Cleansed?

Being aware of the dangers of simply burying our negative thoughts and emotions in our hidden chambers makes us examine three essential questions:

1) How can we catch our negative thoughts and emotions *before* they go into our hidden chambers?

2) How can we get rid of the ones that are already in there?

3) How can we reprogram the truth back in? (Psalm 51:6)

In His perfect timing and in His perfect way, God wants these hidden chambers (this innermost part) to be cleansed, healed and then filled with the knowledge of the Truth (i.e., the sixth function of the Mind of Christ).[11] Then we can genuinely walk in the Fear of God and not the fear of man.

One of the Scriptures that indicates that God wants these hidden chambers cleansed is 2 Chronicles 29:16. This verse explains that the priests went into the Temple of the Lord (i.e., the hidden chambers) to bring out into the Court of the House (i.e., the Inner Court) all the uncleanness they found. The Levites looked at the garbage, seeing it for what it was, and then took it out to the Kidron Brook where they disposed of it.

The analogy between Solomon's Temple and the believer is clear. God wants to show us the things in our hidden chambers, so that we can *see* and understand what exactly it is that we need to give over to Him. It's impossible to give things to Him, if we don't understand what they are. Again, we are not to *re-live* the experiences of the past, but simply acknowledge and confess them as God reveals them to us.

In Psalm 32:5 David declares, "I *acknowledge* my sins and I will *confess* my transgressions."

Seeing the Garbage

It's imperative that we allow God to bring up the garbage—*not wade in it, relive it or spend years churning it over and over again*—but simply *acknowledge it, confess it, then, give it to God.* Then, we can truly be cleansed and healed.

Therefore, God purposely allows the power of sin access to our innermost part (*cheder*) as a means of exposing and unearthing the false assumptions, the lies, the insecurities and the fears that we have unknowingly tucked tightly down there. In other words, God uses the power of sin as His tool (His pawn) to accomplish His own purposes. He wants to expose exactly what's down there, so we'll see it and then choose to have Him remove it "as far as the east is from the west." [12]

With this cleansing in mind, listen to Nehemiah 13:7-9: "And I [Nehemiah] came to Jerusalem, and understood the *evil* that Eliashib [a priest] did for Tobiah [an evil man] in preparing him a chamber in the courts of the house of God. And it grieved me sore: *therefore I cast forth* all the household stuff of Tobiah out of the chamber. Then I commanded, and they *cleansed the chambers*: and thither brought I again the vessels of the house of God, with the meat offering and the frankincense."

I think a good case can be made that these storage chambers that Nehemiah is speaking about here were actually the "hidden chambers" of the Temple, because Nehemiah says that he returned to that *chamber* "all the vessels of the house of the Lord." If you recall, one of the purposes for the hidden chambers was to store and house the holy things that were used in the sanctuary.

Why The Hornets?

We mentioned Deuteronomy 7:20 earlier. This Scripture illustrates God's motives in bringing these things up. "Moreover the Lord thy God will send the hornet among them, until they that are left, and hide themselves from thee, be destroyed."

Why does God allow the hornets? I believe God sends the hornets to expose and bring to light what is hidden there. God loves us so very much, that He wants us freed from the power of sin's control in our innermost man. He wants "...truth in the inward parts (the hidden part)..." (Psalm 51:6) Therefore, He sends the hornets to expose the hidden things, so we'll see them for ourselves, choose to deal with them the proper way, and then be rid of them for good.

So, God allows these hornets (the bad things) into our lives, because He knows many of our choices are based upon our hidden beliefs and assumptions. And He knows that many of these are false, because they have been programmed into us by our own warped thoughts and emotions, by things other people have said and done to us, and also by thoughts and feelings that we have never chosen to deal with before—all of which have led to more enemy strongholds.

Numbers 33:55 declares that if we don't drive out the inhabitants of the land, they will be "pricks in our eyes and thorns in our sides."

A Perfect Example: "Nightmares"

Now, God can be very creative in the ways that He chooses to reveal some of these hidden things to us.

Many years ago, Ilene, a dear, committed Christian sister of mine came over for a visit. I began sharing with her some of the incredible things I was learning about the hidden chambers and the secret part of our soul.

As she listened very intently to what I was saying, Ilene felt prompted to tell me about some very scary things that had been happening recently to her. She said she had been having horrible nightmares that had sexual overtones, dreams about her single life before she was married. They had been troubling her terribly because they wouldn't go away.

Ilene said she had prayed and asked God to take them away, because they were so evil. But, again and again they returned. She prayed harder and harder, but still they returned. Finally, she began to feel dirty and guilty, and began to think that something must be very wrong with her. She felt God must not care about her anymore because He hadn't answered her prayers. And so, not knowing what else to do, she began to just "bury" everything: the dreams, her guilt, her doubt, her thoughts of condemnation, everything. See, if we don't know how to *put off* the garbage and give these things to God, what other choice is there?

As Christians, many of us have been taught that we're not supposed to have bad thoughts or feelings. When we do, then we think, "Well, I'm obviously the only one who has these—something must be very wrong with me. I'm sure no one else thinks this way." And since we know of no other option, we begin to bury and hide these things, thinking *no one will see and no one will know*.

And, this is how these hidden chambers get filled in the first place. That, of course, is exactly what the enemy wants, because then we give him more strongholds to build even stronger. As a result, we become his captives and eventually, in total bondage to his schemes and tricks.

Anyway, as I sat there and listened to Ilene, I was grieved for her because it was obviously a very painful and hurtful situation for her. I prayed for her and then began to share some of the things God was doing in me. I showed her the Temple model and the hidden chambers and told her how God had begun to open up some of my own secret places. And, how He was revealing things in me that had been influencing my choices and actions for years.

I hinted to my friend that this might be exactly what God was trying to do in her case even through her horrible dreams (the "hornets"). I explained that often God has to unearth some of our own past experiences that He knows are still motivating our present actions, so that we'll see them and choose to give them over to Him.

A few weeks later, my dear friend called to say, "Oh, Nan, you'll never believe what's happened!" You could hear, even on the phone, how excited she was. She said that she had gone home, confessed to God that she had been burying all her "real" feelings of guilt and unbelief because she didn't know what else to do with them. She gave God full permission to expose everything that He wanted to in her. She told God that she would trust Him to do whatever He needed to do to cleanse her and to heal her.

Sure enough, another dream came, but this time my friend was ready for it. This time she didn't bury it, but she took a long, hard look at it, calling it for what it was. God gave her insight as to how some of the buried things of years ago were still affecting her relationship with her husband in the present. So, she chose to allow God to renew her mind.

Ilene recognized some of the bad things; she cried over them; she confessed them as sin; she repented of them (she changed her mind about holding on to them) and chose, instead, to give everything over to God. After that, she excitedly shared that she had had no more bad dreams, and she knew that God had freed her from some major strongholds of the enemy! Now again, she didn't have to wade in the garbage of the past or again re-live it, she simply recognized it for what it was and gave it to God.

Our God is so wonderful! He promises in Psalm 103:12, that He will remove our transgressions (anything that is not of faith) "as far as the east is from the

west..." when we choose to hand them over to Him. God is a "gentleman" and
He won't force these things from us. *We* must make the faith choices to willingly open ourselves up to Him[13] and give him our sin and self-centeredness.
He then, will cleanse us, heal us and fill us. As 1 John 1:9 states, "If we confess
our sins, He is faithful and just to forgive us our sins, and to cleanse us from *all*
unrighteousness."

Another Example: Twelve Full Years!

Years later, in one of my seminars, there was a young lady who always came
in last, sat in the very back row looking miserable the whole time. Amy hadn't
even wanted to come to the retreat in the first place, but was dragged there by her
sister. After the second session, she wanted to leave, but she had no ride home.
Again, I was teaching the *Be Ye Transformed* message.

When I told the story of Ilene's nightmares, Amy was absolutely spell-bound,
because she too, had been in the exact same place, for 12 full years! She too, had
prayed and prayed for God to take away her bad dreams, but again and again,
they had returned. As a result, her faith had evaporated, and she was convinced
that God didn't love her because He hadn't answered her prayers. In response,
she simply let go of God's hand.

God poured His Love on Amy in a very special way that night, as she began
to see that she had done the exact same thing as Ilene—by burying all her hurts,
doubts, guilt, etc. That night, like Ilene, she chose in the privacy of her heart
to trust God once again. She gave Him permission to search her innermost part
by His Spirit and to expose all that was down there that was not of faith. There
was a prayer meeting after the teaching session and this precious woman went
forward and cried and cried and cried, as she confessed her innermost thoughts
and feelings to God.

The next morning, Amy was sitting right up in the front row looking like a
turned-on lightbulb! She said she felt as if a 1000 pound weight had been lifted
off her shoulders—one she had carried for 12 years!

Now, no psychiatrists, no psychologists and no counselors were there that
night, just the Spirit of God. And as He was given permission to search Amy's
hidden chambers,[14] He exposed and revealed to her the "secret faults" that had
quenched His Life and had kept her in bondage.

Don't Bury Real Feelings

Jesus proclaims in Matthew 16:24 that we are to deny ourselves, pick up our cross and follow Him. But "to deny" in this Scripture does not mean hide, bury, or push down our real thoughts and feelings, even if they are negative, ungodly or evil. As Christians, many of us have been doing this out of ignorance, because we haven't known what else to do with them.

The truth is that God has made us emotional and feeling people. The fact is we have no control over what we initially think. Remember, the sin does not occur until after we have chosen to follow, entertain and keep those negative thoughts and emotions over what God has prompted us to do. This is the point at which God's Spirit gets quenched.

So, the first negative thought is not sin; what we choose to do with the thought is what makes it sin or not.[15] Therefore, real feelings and thoughts need to be examined, they need to be expressed and they need to be brought forth before they lead us to make wrong choices that will quench God's Life.

We said earlier that our wounds—all our hurts, fears, insecurities, rejection, etc.—are incurable. In other words, they won't go away on their own. They will just continue to accumulate, trigger more negative thoughts and emotions, and eventually, produce our actions, unless we allow the Spirit of God to search our hidden chambers and expose them, unearth their hold on us and cleanse us completely from them.

"For thus saith the Lord, Thy bruise is incurable, and thy wound is grievous. There is none to plead thy cause, that thou mayest be bound up; thou hast no healing medicines." (Jeremiah 30:12-13) *But, "...I [the Lord] will restore health unto thee, and I will heal thee of thy wounds...."* (Jeremiah 30:17)[16]

While this Scripture has a primary meaning for that particular time in history, a spiritual application can also be made for our lives today. We need to ask God to expose the real root causes of our wounds so that He can heal us.

A Personal Example: Mental Insecurity

During my almost 40 years with Chuck, often he has emphasized someone's intelligence by saying, "Now, that guy is really bright." Conversely, if he feels a person is not too sharp, he'll say, "Now, that person is really not very bright at all," etc. Over the years, every time

Chuck has made these comments, something deep within me would get very upset, hurt and angry.

Not understanding why I felt or reacted this way, I would just push all these thoughts and feelings down deep and, once again, bury them. However, over the past few years, as I have been trying to "take every thought captive," every time I emotionally overreact to something or lose my peace, I try to stop and ask God, "Why?" Why am I so upset right now? What has caused this reaction? Remember, being aware of what we are thinking is the *first* step to having a renewed mind.

A short while ago, Chuck made a similar comment and I reacted as always. This time, however, I stopped and asked God to expose my soul. "Why am I so angry and upset at what Chuck has just said?"

God is always so faithful to show us our true selves, if we are listening and wanting to know. He showed me that the reason I was so angry every time Chuck talked about someone "not too bright," was because, I was still insecure about my own intellectual abilities. And so, every time Chuck would say, "he's not too bright," deep inside, he was talking about *me*!!

Now, in order for you to understand the whole picture a little more clearly, I must tell you that my precious Chuck has an I.Q. of over 180. He went six years to college. He graduated with honors from the U.S. Naval Academy, and he has a double master's degree. I'm lucky to have an average I.Q. of 100. I went one year to college. And I have a marriage license!

Comparing the two of us seems funny now, but, in reality, this has been a stronghold of the enemy all these years. Satan has used this deep-seated insecurity in me ("I'm not too bright"), buried tightly down in my hidden chambers, so that every time I got around learned people, I felt insecure and unsure of myself. And, of course, you know what happens when we "think" in a certain way, we end up "acting" that way!

Most of my insecurities, I'm sure, come from my 40 years of living with "a brain." Just try having an argument with an encyclopedia! Or, try casually conversing with someone who knows everything there is to know about every subject! Point in hand, this weekend, my Chuck has gone to Rochester, New York, to speak to the Rochester Institute of Technology on physics, the Bible and the theories of the Big Bang. Who in all of America could do that better than my Chuck? But, living with that, day in and day out, can be very intimidating. And, I just hadn't realized how much it had affected me.

Before I learned about the Mind of Christ and renewing my mind, I just bought into the fact that my negative thoughts and feelings were *a part of me* and, certainly not something that I could ever change or be rid of. However, I was wrong! Praise God!

The good news of the Gospel is that because of Jesus in us, we <u>can</u> be freed of our insecurities, fears and doubts forever. Because of the Mind of Christ is us, we have His Authority and His Power <u>not</u> to buy into and follow what these hidden thoughts and emotions are prompting us to do. As we allow God to expose these secret things and we give them to Him, *we <u>can</u> be free from their influence forever!*

"You shall know the truth and the truth shall make you free." (John 8:32) For the Lord is the One that "looseth the prisoners and raises them that are bowed down." (Psalm 146:7-8)

God Takes Them Away

If God takes the *hidden root cause* away, then we can be assured the *conscious* negative thoughts and emotions, the angry reactions, the inhibitions, the intimidations will not occur again over the same issue. In other words, when the hidden chamber is emptied and God's Truth put back in, we'll be a cleansed vessel, acting out of God's Life and not our own.

You should see me now around highly intelligent and educated people! I'm able to carry on a decent conversation without stuttering and stammering. After all, I have the Mind of Christ! Why on earth should I be insecure?

In fact, not too many years ago, I spent an entire evening with a delightful woman from Australia. Dawn was extremely bright, very articulate and seemed to have accomplished so much in her life. She had a Ph.D. owned her own fashion design business, traveled extensively all over the world and was involved politically in several countries.

Now, the old Nan would have been all tongue-tied. What does an average housewife have to share with someone like her? But, as a result of knowing how to *renew my mind*, I couldn't get over the freedom I felt to just "be me." I didn't have to put on airs or pretend I was something that I'm not. Dawn and I talked for three hours. Not only did I enjoy all that she shared, but she seemed to be interested in what I had to say also. I even got a chance to share about God's Love and His Wisdom—and she seemed to hang on every word.

Philippians 3:3 tells us our confidence and our trust must be in who God says we are in His Word, and not in what our deep-seated insecurities, fears and hurts try to tell us.

Now obviously, we are not accountable for thoughts and feelings that are still hidden. However, once God begins to reveal and expose some of these secret things, if we continue, at that point, to hold on to what God has exposed, it will be sin and we will be held accountable. James 4:17 declares, "To him that knoweth to do good (he knows he should make a faith choice and give it over to God), and doeth it not, to him it is sin."

So as Christians, we don't have to work at cleaning up our past as psychology teaches, but simply giving God permission to expose the root causes of our present problems. Once He brings up the root, and we are faithful to deal with it as He would have us to do, then He will remove it "as far as the east is from the west" and we truly will be healed.

An Example: Give Me Your Real Feelings

Several years ago, I spent an entire day with a woman who "naturally" I have a very hard time liking. Now, I couldn't admit the truth to myself, because everyone else absolutely adored her. Whenever I talked with her, however, I could feel the hypocrisy (saying one thing, but feeling another) inside me and I immediately would lose my peace.

Finally, I asked God to show me what was really going on inside. Why am I having such a hard time with this person? God revealed to me, "Nancy, you don't like her. Admit it. It's okay. Because," He said, "*I love her. And if you will just give me your real feelings about her, I will give you Mine.*" So, I did just exactly as He told me. I confessed, repented and gave all my negative thoughts about her to Him, and He faithfully gave me His Love and His compassion for her. Immediately, the freedom to be "me" returned and I was able to love her as God would have me do, with His Love.

In Psalm 34:4 David declares, "I sought the Lord, and He heard me, and delivered (freed) me from **all** my fears!"

Endnotes:

1.   1 Kings 6:5

2.   The Temple blueprint we obtained showed 31 hidden recesses. The Temple
       Institute said there were 38 (but, I believe, this referred to Herod's Temple, not
       Solomon's). Ezekiel Temple will have 30. (Ezekiel 42:4-13)

3.   2 Chronicles 31:11-12; Nehemiah 13:4-5

4.   Proverbs 26:22

5.   Many Christians stumble over Hebrews 3:12 when we say that our heart is inviolate. The way William Welty of the School of Christian Apologetics, Simon Greenleaf University, explained Hebrew 3 to me, was: Verses 1-6 apply to the "holy brethren" (believing Jews, i.e., Christians) because in these verses the writer of Hebrews refers to them as "we." Verses 7-13 refer to "brethren" (i.e. non-believing Jews) because the writer refers to them as "ye" or "you" and not "we." Verse 14 again refers back to the believing Jews, "we." And, the rest of the chapter, verses 15-19, once again to the non-believing Jews, "ye" and "they".

6.   Isaiah 49:16

7.   Ezekiel 13:10-15

8.   The Greek word for lusts (our "strong desires") is *epithumia* which comes from the root word, *thumos*, which means "for the purpose of revenge."

9.   Colossians 2:15

10.   The Lord is the One that "looseth the prisoners." (Psalm 146:7-8)

11.   Proverbs 3:20; 24:4; Psalm 51:6

12.   Psalm 103:12

13.   Psalm 139:23

14.   Proverbs 20:27

15.   James 1:14-15

16.   Isaiah 30:26

Scriptural References:
Chapter Eleven

The Secret Hidden Chambers (*cheder*) (our innermost part)   (CHARTS 14 and 15)

A. These were secret, hidden side wings of the Temple, supposed to be used for the purpose of storing worship items for the priests (2 Chronicles 31:11-12; Nehemiah 13:4-5)

    1. These were part of God's original master plan given to David by the Spirit of God (1 Chronicles 28:11-12) with all the details, not only of the construction, but of the furnishings (1 Kings 6:5-8)

        a. There were three tiers of these hidden chambers — 31 cubicles in total

        b. The priests used these chambers for storing their own idolatrous worship items (Ezekiel 8:6-12) and other abominations (Ezekiel 8: 13-16) thinking that "no one would see, no one would know" (Isaiah 29:15)

    2. These chambers were also supposed to be used to display Israel's treasures to remind them of all God had done for them

B. These secret, hidden chambers represent the hidden, secret part of our soul. The place where we hide, bury and store our hurts, wounds, guilt, fears and memories, thinking because they are hidden "no one will know" (Proverbs 7:27; 18:8; 26:22; Ezekiel 8:12; 14:3-5; Job 37:9 ["south"=cheder]; Deuteronomy 32:25 ["within"=cheder]); Psalm 105:30; Jeremiah 15:18-19) (See full list of Scriptures using the word *cheder* in the Appendix)

    1. *Cheder* is called "chambers of death" (Proverbs 7:27; 26:22, "innermost parts"=*cheder*), "source of evil" (Job 37:9; John 8:44; Deuteronomy 32: 25)

    2. The power of sin resides in our flesh, having full access there (James 1: 14-15; Romans 7:17-24), but our spirit, heart and will are inviolate

        a. "Cords of sin" (Isaiah 5:18; Proverbs 5:22)

        b. "Strongholds of the enemy" (Nehemiah 4:7-8, 10; 2 Corinthians 2: 10-11; Psalm 11:2-3)

        c. The purpose of the power of sin is to cause us to *veer off course* and to miss the mark, which is being "conformed into the image of Christ" (Romans 8:29)

    3. God allows the power of sin access to these recesses (Job 12:22; Judges 2:21-23; James 1:2-4; Revelation 2:10) to expose sin

        a. God uses the power of sin as His tool (Proverbs 20:30; Job 37:13)

        b. God uses "the hornets" to bring to light what's buried there (Deuteronomy 7:20)

          . He causes the "storms" to come (Job 37:13; Leviticus 26:19)

          . So we will learn obedience (Hebrews 5:8)

          . So we will learn to depend only upon Him (Matthew 10:37-39; 16: 24-25; John 12:2)

        c. God wants these areas exposed, cleansed and healed so we will be free of the power of sin's hold on us (Job 12:22; Psalm 19:12-13; 34:4; 44:5; 68:6; 139:23-24; Nehemiah 4:10; 13:4-9; Deuteronomy 7:1-8, 20, 22; John 8:32, 36; 14:30b; Romans 6:6-7, 11-12, 14; 1 Corinthians 4:5; Psalm 103:12; Joshua 7:13; Proverbs 20:27, 30; 2 Corinthians 10:4-5; Numbers 33:55; Jeremiah 1:10)

    4. God wants these hidden recesses cleansed and then filled with His Spirit giving us *intimate knowledge of God* (Proverbs 24:4; Jeremiah 1:10;

2 Chronicles 29:15-16; Psalm 51:6; Proverbs 3:20; Nehemiah 13:4-9; Exodus 23:30; James 1:2-4; 5:16; 2 Corinthians 3:17)

    a.   In order to really *know* God, we must be willing to allow God into our whole man—not only the conscious part, but these hidden chambers (Psalm 19:12-13; 77:6; Proverbs 20:27)

    b.   We need to look at the things God brings up and then give them over to Him (2 Chronicles 29:15-16) just as the priests did in the Inner Court

5.   If evil is allowed to stay in this area, it will vex us for the rest of our lives (Nehemiah 4:10; 6:1-2; 13:4-9; 2 Peter 2:20-21; Numbers 33:55; 2 Corinthians 2:11; Exodus 23:29-30; Joshua 23:11-13; Deuteronomy 7: 1-8)

    a.   By allowing God's Spirit into these areas to cleanse them, we will be delivered for good (2 Corinthians 1:10; 3:17; John 5:14; Proverbs 11: 9)

    b.   The Spirit is the one searching these areas (Proverbs 20:27)

    c.   Only by intimate Knowledge of God, can these depths be broken up (Proverbs 3:19-20) and then filled with pleasant riches (Proverbs 24: 3-4)

6.   Truth needs to be re-established here (Psalm 51:6; Nehemiah 13:9; James 5:16; 1 John 4:18; John 8:32)

    a.   So there will be no further "breach" in the wall (Nehemiah 4:6-7; 6: 1; Psalm 51:18)

    b.   If truth is not replaced, the evil will return (Luke 11:24-26)

7.   God is trying to teach us to "take every thought captive" and renew our minds so that we don't keep on filling these chambers (Titus 3:5)

8.   God wants us to make the "walls of our souls" strong, so they won't crumble (Nehemiah 4:10; Ezekiel 13:14; Proverbs 24:31; Isaiah 49:16; Lamentations 2:8). Strong walls come as a result of our salvation (Isaiah 26:1)

9.   Christ is the only "overcoming power" to free us from the power of sin's hold on us (Romans 7:24-25; 1 John 3:9; Matthew 8:17; Luke 10:19)

Can Satan Read our Thoughts?

A.   If we don't deal with our sin, we open ourselves up for the arrows of the enemy

    1.   If we don't forgive, we give Satan an advantage (2 Corinthians 2: 10-11; Ephesians 4:26-27)

    2.   If we deal with our sin, Satan's power will be broken (John 14:30)

B.   When we renew our minds, we put the "shield of faith" on over our *submitted* thoughts

Can a Christian be Demon-possessed?

A.   A person's *heart* can be inhabited by only one spirit, either God's Spirit or our own human spirit (Colossians 1:13-16; 1 John 5:18; John 10:27-29; Romans 8:8). If our heart belongs to God, then there is no place for demons in our heart

B.   If our spirit is united with God's Spirit, then Jesus has already delivered us from this present evil world and destroyed the works of the devil (Galatians 1:4; 1 John 3:8)

C. If, however, we make emotional choices and don't deal with our sin, we then open our *souls* up for the enemy's strongholds and we will be held by the "cords of our sin" (Proverbs 5:22)

D. Evil spirits can, therefore, harass and deceive us in our souls, but not possess us in our hearts

Definition of our Secret, Hidden Place   (CHART 16)

A. Our hidden chambers are a reservoir of mostly untrue, preprogrammed beliefs which try to determine how we consciously evaluate all that happens to us in the present and upon which we base our choices
  1. This is the buried debris that prompts our *self-life* and prevents us from building strong "walls of our soul" (Ezekiel 13:10-15)
  2. This is why God puts so much emphasis on "taking every thought captive" (2 Corinthians 10:5) and knowing how to deal with it

B. God wants these chambers cleansed, healed and then filled with the Spirit

Strict or Discipline Love?

A. God allows "storms" or hot blasts to come either for correction or for mercy (Job 37:9, 13)
  1. *Chesed,* the Old Testament word for God's Love, can either come *mercifully* to free us from Satan's strongholds or *strictly* to force us to deal with our sin (Proverbs 20:30)
  2. Our wounds are incurable (Jeremiah 30:12), only the Spirit of the Lord can search, expose and cleanse these hidden things from us (Proverbs 20:27)

B. When these hidden things come up, if we confess and repent of them (1 John 1:9) and give them to God, He will remove them "as far as the east is from the west" (Psalm 103:12)

C. Only God can be our healer (Jeremiah 30:12, 17; Luke 4:18-19; Isaiah 61:1; 1 Peter 2:24; Isaiah 53:5). Man cannot see or know our hearts (Isaiah 30:1; 1 Samuel 16:7; Job 34:32)

D. If we don't allow God to search these chambers, we will continue to act out of those thoughts and emotions, and not God's Life. Only the "truth" will set us free (John 8:31-32)
  1. If God takes the *hidden* root cause away, then the *conscious* symptoms will not occur any more
  2. Our confidence must be in God and what His Word says, and <u>not</u> in these deep, hidden things (our own thoughts) are telling us (Philippians 3:3). We have His Mind (Proverbs 3:19)
  3. We are not accountable for the hidden things, but once God reveals them to us, if we don't deal with them, they will quench His Spirit and become sin (James 4:17; Romans 14:23)

E. God wants us to clean up His temple (John 8:32; Psalm 34:4)

Chapter Twelve
The Hidden Chambers
(Part 2)

Deliverance

"Ye shall know the truth, and the truth shall make you *free*." (John 8:32)

Now, the freedom and the deliverance that we have been talking about in the last few chapters, is a process. This process of healing will continue in for the rest of our lives. Made up of our moment-by-moment choices, it's called *sanctification*—experientially separating ourselves from anything that's not of faith,[1] so that God's Life can come forth from our hearts.

Scripture tells us that Jesus has *already* delivered us, past tense, from the power of darkness, so there's no need for deliverance from demons for believers.[2] Read Colossians 1:13; John 10:27-29 and 1 John 5:18. What <u>is</u> necessary, however, and what we are focusing on here, is freedom from our fears, our insecurities, our hurts, our bitterness, our guilt, etc., that the power of sin[3] has used all of our lives to control and cripple us. This freedom comes only from our moment-by-moment choices to go God's way

An Example: What Went Wrong?

A young man whom I have known for years, and one who loved *The Way of Agape*, attended a healing and deliverance service. Afterwards, he boasted of being totally delivered from drug abuse. Three months later, however, he was fully back into a life laced with addiction.

I saw him one day and asked him "Tom, what happened? You said you were totally freed? What went wrong?" "Nan," he said, "we're all looking for the easy way out (to be delivered instantly)." He went on, "There's no easy way out. It's only our constant, moment-to-moment choices that will allow us to remain free.

Greg Laurie, pastor of Harvest Christian Center in Riverside, California points out, "It's the flesh that we need freedom from. We can't cast it out, we need to die to it. It's not the devil that makes us do it or demons." The Bible teaches, "To whom we yield ourselves as servants to obey, his servants we are." So, it's our own decision, our own choice, and our own responsibility to stay free.

Demons, therefore, can do nothing in the life of a believer, unless the Christian himself cooperates. Demons cannot imprison, control or direct us, unless *we* allow them to do so. As Luke 11:21-22 tells us, Jesus has *already* taken away the weapons of Satan; and, has given us power and authority over demons. However, if we don't know how to use this incredible gift that God has given us or if we choose not to use it, then we'll end up making wrong, self-centered, emotional choices and, once again, open ourselves up for more demon strongholds.

I could easily stop choosing God's way today and in a very short time, I could easily *refill* all the hidden chambers that God has so magnificently emptied in my life over the last 10-15 years. And, I'd be right back to where I started from. "For if, after they have escaped the pollution of the world through the knowledge of the Lord and Savior, Jesus Christ, they are again entangled in it, and overcome, the latter end is worse with them than the beginning." (2 Peter 2:20)

An Example: "I Had That Message Once"

I had lunch with a dear friend, Gloria, several years ago, who had done this very thing. She had neglected to make, moment-by-moment faith choices, so she had allowed the enemy to re-build old strongholds that had once been destroyed and cleansed. Gloria had become discouraged, beginning to doubt God's faithfulness, because she was again experiencing problems she thought she had dealt with years ago.

What she didn't realize was that because *she* had stopped taking every thought captive, and *she* had stopped making contrary choices, *she was the one* allowing new, ungodly things to be reprogrammed back into her once cleansed, hidden chambers. So, it wasn't God who was unfaithful. *Gloria* was the one who was responsible for re-filling her hidden chambers.

M & M's

Another friend came up to me and said. "I had hold of this message once." I asked her, "What happened?" She said, "It's too hard and I just let go." I agreed with her. Moment-by-moment choices <u>are</u> hard to make. And, for many, it's just too high a price to pay.

That's why Matthew 7:14 exhorts us, "...strait is the gate, and narrow is the way, which leadeth unto life, *and few there be that find it.*"

Transformation is a process that we will be in for the rest of our lives and, unfortunately, there's just no room for coasting—it's a moment-by-moment faith walk.

Some precious sisters in Northern California call these moment-by-moment choices, their "M & M's." When I spoke there a few years ago, they not only gave me a box of M & M's, but they also made me a beautiful embroidered picture with a large M & M in the center.

James 1:3-4 declares, "Knowing this, that the trying of our faith [these constant M & M choices] worketh patience. But let patience have her perfect work, that ye may be perfect and entire, wanting nothing." That's the transformation that God wants in all our lives.

Begin With Small Steps

So, begin with small steps. Take one area at a time. Don't think you can cleanse all your hidden chambers over a period of days. How many years has it taken you to fill them? Give God time to empty them in His Way and in His timing. You must just be *willing* to deal with the things that God brings up and He will do the rest.

A young girl came running up to me after class one time and said, "I'm so depressed. I've been praying and praying this weekend for God to show me myself and nothing seems to come. I guess it just doesn't work for me."

I told her, "Honey, praise God for the period of rest He is giving you. If you have asked Him to expose what He wants, then don't worry, *He will*! He just knows *how* and *when* to do it perfectly. Remember, it's <u>not</u> in our timing or in our way that this occurs. It's in God's perfect timing and in His way.

So, if you pray and ask God to show you yourself and you don't see anything right away, then praise Him and be thankful for the rest period. Because, believe me, if you have given God permission to show you yourself, *He will*!

Example: Have No Fear

We also needn't be afraid of *how* or *when* God will reveal these hidden things to us. We simply must trust Him completely, knowing that it's His Will for us to be freed.

A precious sister at a seminar a few years ago was so afraid of opening herself up to God because of some extremely painful traumas that had happened to her in the past. Ruth was terrified, but dared to trust God enough to give Him full permission to search her hidden chambers and reveal whatever He wanted to.

That night, in the middle of the night, Ruth's roommate awoke to find her sobbing and crying out in her sleep. The roommate immediately got up out of bed and quietly came over to comfort Ruth. However, when she got to Ruth's bed, she heard her saying, "Jesus, Jesus, Jesus." The roommate was so moved and touched, that she didn't want to wake Ruth, but knelt down beside her and began to pray and intercede for her.

In the morning when the two of them compared notes, Ruth said she knew that God had done a marvelous work within her during the night. She knew in her spirit that God had emptied some of the hurtful things in her hidden chambers, even while she slept.

When she got home from the retreat, her husband noticed that she was changed. He said her countenance was so radiant that he could tell she had let go of some "baggage" she had been carrying around for years.

So, we don't need to be afraid of how or when God will reveal to us some of the painful wounds of the past. We simply must trust Him enough to know that since He has made us, He knows the perfect timing and perfect way to do it. 2 Timothy 1:7 says, "God has not given us the spirit of fear, but of power and love and of a sound mind."

I'm convinced that we *all* desperately need this deep inner cleansing and healing in order to know God intimately (the sixth function of the Mind of Christ). By this, I simply mean we need to allow the Spirit of God the freedom, moment by moment, to search the deep, unchartered recesses of our soul and bring to light all that needs to be dealt with there.

Now, we don't have to be cleansed of *all* the things in our hidden chambers, *before* we can know God intimately. That's not at all what I mean. It's going to take us a lifetime to do that and we still won't have gotten all of the hidden things. What I am referring to here, is being obedient to God's Spirit, and as He reveals something to us, we must immediately deal with it and give it over to Him. With each thing that we hand over to Jesus, and with each hidden chamber that is emptied, we'll experience a closer intimacy with God.

"By His [intimate] knowledge the depths [strongholds of the enemy] are broken up." (Proverbs 3:20)

Take One Day At A Time

A woman at one of the retreats years ago had some great advice for all of us. She had a severely retarded child. She said that when she first found out her child was handicapped, she began to worry about what would happen when he began to walk. Could she handle him? Then, she said she began to worry about what would happen when he began school. And then, what about when he became a teenager? Adulthood, etc.?

She told us a dear friend of hers gave her the best advice ever. *"Take one day at a time. Don't think and worry about how to handle the future. Just allow God to give you strength and power to get through today."*

That's good advice for us also. Jesus even tells us there's enough evil in one day to be concerned about without looking ahead.[4] In other words, take one day at a time and deal with the things it brings. Don't look ahead to the next. God knows the perfect way and the perfect timing to reveal truth. We just need to be willing to hear it and deal with it. God, then, will do the rest.

He will help us be obedient in "Casting down imaginations, and every high thing that exalteth itself against the knowledge of God, and bringing into captivity every thought to the obedience of Christ; *and having in a readiness to revenge* [deal with] *all disobedience....*" (2 Corinthians 10:5-6, emphasis added)

Now, if you have very serious problems in your background (perhaps like the woman in Chapter Six, who had been raped and whose mother had tried to kill her), then you might want help going through the cleansing steps in Chapter Fifteen. Seek out intimate friends like she did, ask them to pray for you and help you go through the Inner Court Ritual. If you recall, this woman was not healed or freed through her psychiatrist, whom she had seen all her life, but through God using her dear Christian sisters, who simply loved her and held her, while *she* made the appropriate faith choices to renew her mind.

Remember, friends and counselors can't make those choices for you. Nor can they renew your mind for you. They can only lead you to Christ, hold you and pray for you *while you make the appropriate choices*. Don't let pride keep you from asking others for their help. God wants all of us cleansed and healed and "filled with all precious and pleasant riches." He wants us conformed into His Image and walking in His Truth and Love.

One suggestion that was made in one of the classes is to form Encourager Groups, groups of maybe two or three of your intimate friends who don't talk, where you can confess your sins and be accountable to each other. Then take a year or so to go through *Be Ye Transformed.* Use the video series or just do a Bible study with your own workbook.

Over time, renewing your mind will become a habit. Read Chapter Fifteen of this book over and over again, play the tapes and write out all the Scriptures that the Lord ministers to you. Every time through, God will always show us new and deeper things from His Word, and the renewing process will become more and more first nature to us.

Psychology Versus God's Way

The word *psychology* means the study of the *psyche* (or soul)—*self-knowledge*. Psychology focuses on the knowing and the building up of self, whereas, the Bible teaches us to do just the opposite. "For we who live are always delivered unto death for Jesus' sake, that *the life also of Jesus might be made manifest* in our mortal flesh. So death worketh in us, but life in you." (2 Corinthians 4:11-12)

Christ wants us to die to our self—to set it aside, to deny it, and surrender it—so that *He* can live His Life through us. If we could really learn to do this, then we wouldn't have to work at *improving ourselves* as psychology teaches, but simply *exchanging lives* with God. This is the *transformation* that God desires for all of us—taking off self and putting on Christ.

Galatians 2:20 says it all, "I am crucified with Christ: nevertheless I live; yet not I, but Christ liveth in me; and the life which I now live in the flesh I live by the faith of the Son of God, who loved me and gave Himself for me."

Psychology attempts to deal with our inner problems through therapy—where we tell our side of the story to someone, and then, have them tell us what we should do. The Bible teaches us, however, that only God can see, cleanse and heal our hearts[5] (our inner problems). So, if Jesus is not in the center of each counseling session, then all we are doing is reprogramming those same negative hurts, fears and insecurities right back into our hidden chambers where they will become even stronger strongholds for the enemy.

Psychology leads us to blame others for not loving us *perfectly*, whereas, the Bible teaches us that only God can love us perfectly. Once we understand His Love, then we can go on, forgive and love others in spite of their behavior towards us. In other words, we won't expect them to love us perfectly. When we really know Jesus loves us and that He is the Only One who can meet <u>all</u> of our needs, then we won't look to others for that security.

Psychology encourages us to visualize and picture in our own minds what has gone on in our past. The Bible, however, teaches us to do just the opposite. "Casting down imaginations, and every high thing that exalteth itself against the knowledge of God, and bringing into captivity every thought to the obedience of Christ." (2 Corinthians 10:5) *God, by His Mind in us, will reveal the hidden causes of our actions today; then it will be up to us to hand these over to God and be rid of them forever.*

Finally, psychology teaches us that in order to make faith choices, all of the garbage of the past must be healed. The Bible teaches, however, that it's just the other way around. In order to be healed of the past, we must make constant faith choices.

Psychology Can Be Dangerous

One of the reasons why I believe psychology can be so dangerous is that it's really another gospel. It leads us to the wrong goal—being conformed to the world's image, and not Christ's.

Psychology can be dangerous because it causes confusion and it really promotes a lie. It promises to heal us, to remove strongholds from us, to help our relationships, and to help us progress in our Christian walk. The truth is, however, psychology doesn't heal us, it doesn't remove strongholds, but often strengthens them, it doesn't improve relationships, and it doesn't help us in our Christian walk. In fact, sometimes we even end up even worse off than when we started.

Here are a couple of letters that seem to validate all of this:

"The problem with Christian therapy today is that it keeps us focused on those dysfunctional systems, our own behaviors and other's responsibilities, not on God, His Love, His Commandments, or dying to self. The result of *dying to self* teaching is that we <u>do</u> become functional, because Jesus' Spirit is living through us, and we are glorifying Him and not ourselves."

"I have seen so many of my close friends as they go through therapy become totally self-absorbed and even deeper in bondage to sin and self."

"Nancy, we're not receiving this message in our churches today. I belong to a church that is getting more and more involved in psychology teaching, especially the "Christians in Recovery" type, where everyone is a *victim* of a dysfunctional family of some sort or another and we all need to get in touch with the child within. I have been slowly sucked into this teaching and am currently involved in a 12-step group and have been in counseling off and on over the past year.

"I am here to tell you that all of that succeeded in getting me more and more in touch with myself, my feelings, my hurts, my resentments and not until I heard your message was I able to turn my heart away from self and back to God.

"I know there are many people out there who need to deal with all those things in order to be able to clean out their hidden chambers, but what actually happened to me is that when I started going through counseling I was instructed to dredge up all the things that I had already given over to the Lord in the past. Through this act I was instructed to try and feel things I had long since forgotten and for-given. This I think was detrimental to my relationship with the Lord because for the entire year that I was in counseling I *never* gave anything over to Him; *never* forgave anyone; nor accepted anyone. I was just told to *feel my feelings.*

"Why", she says, "are we not hearing this *Be Ye Transformed* message to-day?"

Loving Self

Psychology is simply learning to *love self*, whereas, what the Bible teaches, is for us to learn to set our self aside so that we can *love God*. In *The Way of Agape*, we learned that the Greek word for the verb *to love* is *agapao*, which means to totally give ourselves over to something. Now we can either love ourselves, totally give ourselves over to self, and always do those things that are pleasing to us; or, we can learn to love God, totally give ourselves over to Him, and always do those things that are pleasing to Him. This is a choice that we will continually be faced with.

When we try to analyze and figure out our own negative thoughts and emo-tions, we simply end up reprogramming these things right back down into our hidden chambers, where they become even stronger strongholds of the enemy. When we do this, we're not "forgetting those things which are behind" as Philip-pians 3:13 exhorts us to do, but we're dredging up old memories and dwelling on them. We're not "reaching forth unto those things which are before [us]," but we are living in the past trying to figure out our behavior with our own human under-standing. By doing this, we are not "revenging all disobedience" as 2 Corinthians 10:6 exhorts us to do, but simply strengthening the enemy's control.

Psychology is ultimately doomed to frustration since the Bible tells us it cannot penetrate *beyond* the psyche (soul). Hebrews 4:12 declares that God's Word is the only thing that can "divide between the soul and spirit." While psychology recognizes the destructive and corrosive role of guilt in the human psyche, it can only address the symptoms, not the cause: sin. Psychology has no ability to deal with the problem of sin. Only God can—and has. This is the core issue in the entire Biblical drama: Christ's redemption of a fallen race through a love story, written in blood on a wooden cross erected in Judea almost two thousand years ago.

Scripture says that only God can be our true counselor and healer:[6] *because only Jesus can see our hearts; only He can show us the real root causes of our problems; only He can remove them "as far as the east is from the west"; only He can align our feelings with our faith choices and make us genuine; and, only He can give us the Love we need to go on as if nothing has happened.*

As Christians then (with God in us), we don't have to *work at* cleaning up our past, but simply give God permission to expose the real root causes of present problems. Once He brings something up, if we are faithful to deal with it the way He wants us to, He promises us He will remove it "as far as the east is from the west." And we will truly be cleansed and healed.

Someone once told me a suggestive analogy about the priorities God desires: They said, "Think of the *large* front windshield of a car as what God wants us to primarily focus our attention on as we drive. Think of the *little* rear view mirror as the hidden chambers that every once in a while God wants us to glance at to see if there is anything He wants us to deal with."

It's Not A Witch Hunt

Cleansing of the hidden chambers is a process, not a witch hunt. *We* don't prompt the inward search, the Spirit of God does. In other words, we don't make an appointment and then in our own timing, go to try to figure out our past. *That's self trying to figure out self.* The revealing of the hidden causes of our ungodly thinking and acting today will be in God's perfect timing and in His perfect way. God's way of exposing root causes usually occurs as a result of *our* over-reacting to something that has occurred in the present. Remember lack of peace is a barometer that shows us something is blocking or quenching God's Spirit in us.

So God, by His Spirit and in His timing, will initiate the search of our innermost part. "The Spirit of man is the candle of the Lord," and He is the one "searching all the inward parts [cheder] of the belly." (Proverbs 20:27)

Two Examples

In one seminar recently, a lady shared how she hated to read the Bible. So, she decided to put into practice what she was learning. She went to God and asked Him to reveal the hidden cause for this. God's Spirit brought back to her remembrance that as a child, her mom used to punish her by making her sit in the corner and read the Bible.

Another girl shared how much she loved to play the guitar, but was petrified at the thought of getting up in front of an audience. God's Spirit revealed to her that when she was a small child, her dad, who was in the Metropolitan Opera, used to ridicule her whenever she got up on the stage and tried to imitate him.

Who but God the Holy Spirit could reveal these hidden causes? Truly, "The Spirit of man is the candle of the Lord," and *He* is the one "searching all the inward parts [hidden chambers]."

One of the indications that God is trying to reveal something to us is that our peace will be gone. Lack of peace is how we know that something is blocking God's Spirit within us.

Complete Healing Before Faith Choices?

Again, it's important to understand that we don't have to be healed from all the garbage of the past in order to make faith or non-feeling choices. Some Christians believe this. The truth is, it's completely the other way around. *From the moment the Spirit of God enters our hearts, we have His Authority and His Power to make contrary choices. And, it's our contrary choices that will set us free from all the junk of the past.*

Our past hurts do affect us because Satan often uses these buried wounds to try to paralyze us and bring us down into the pits. As Christians, however, we don't need to follow what these buried things are telling us to do. If we can simply recognize what we are thinking and make the appropriate non-feeling choices to give it over to God, then we can know that God will be faithful to set us free.

Remember the story of Joseph (Genesis 50) in Chapter Two? There were no psychologists or psychiatrists in his day, yet Joseph was able to be cleansed and healed and freed from of all the traumatic events of his past.

God's Truth

Our secret, hidden chambers do need to be exposed and cleansed in God's timing and in His way, so that His Spirit can then fill them with intimate Knowledge of God. "...Only by [intimate] knowledge can the depths [the strongholds of the enemy] be broken up..." (Proverbs 3:20) Intimate Knowledge of God means God's Love and Truth has filled our soul—even to the depths of these chambers.

It's imperative that, after we have been cleansed from Satan's lies and our own ungodly thoughts and emotions, we must always replace those lies with God's Truth—His Word.

Luke 11:24-26 teaches about an unclean spirit that had gone out of the man and his house was swept clean. But because that man forgot to put something else back in its place, the evil spirit returned and brought seven more demons with him. This Scripture tells us that the last state of the man was worse than the first.

Truth must be put back in the hidden chambers so that more lies do not return.

Conclusion

Allowing the Spirit of God the freedom to expose all of our *conscious* hurts, negative thoughts, feelings, etc. (i.e., the symptoms) is critical. Equally important, we must ask Him to expose all the hidden *root causes* of these things. Once the root cause can be exposed and dealt with, then the *conscious negative emotions* over that particular issue will not occur again either.

Here's an analogy to make my point: Many years ago, I had a wonderful, old horse named J.D. One time, he got a sliver (splinter) between his hoof and his shoe and he began to limp. I put on my glasses and pulled the splinter out as best I could. I thought I had gotten it all out, so I let J.D. go several more days. However, he continued to limp.

Finally, after two more days had passed and the limp still had not gone away, I called the shoer. He immediately came over and took off J.D.'s shoe. By doing so, he exposed the "real" root cause of my horse's pain which was another one and a half inch sliver that had pierced a hole in the side of his foot underneath his shoe! Now, I *never* could have seen that with my own natural eyes. What I needed was the *master shoer* who was the only one who could expose and remove the real root cause of J.D.'s limp. Once the remaining hidden sliver was gone, J.D. never limped again.

Remember this little story, because it's so applicable to us. We can all see and pull out the external slivers in our lives (*the symptoms*), but we will continue to limp. Therefore, we must allow the Master Builder to pull out the buried, hidden arrows, things we can't see, which are the real *root causes* of our limping.

We already possess Christ's Life in our *hearts*. *We* simply must make sure that that's what's showing forth in our *souls*. And, the only way that this is possible, is by the constant renewing of our minds. Then, God's Spirit can fill those chambers with intimate Knowledge of God

"Through Wisdom a house is built; and by Understanding it is established, but it's [only] by [intimate] *knowledge* shall all the chambers [*cheder*] be filled with all precious and pleasant riches." (Proverbs 24:3-4)

Boxes Of My Mind

A precious sister from Amarillo, Texas wrote the following poem called "Boxes of My Mind." It has ministered to many all across the country and I thought you might enjoy reading it also. Let's make it our prayer as we close this chapter.

"Jesus gave me emotions to feel pleasure and pain.
So why do I lock them in BOXES...given no name?
Boxes......buried so deep that I can't find
Those hidden chambers in the depth of my mind.

Not even I know what's in my innermost part,
Or can discover what lies deep in my heart.
I can't look there.... for if I should see
There would be things I can't accept...about me.

But Jesus accepts me...and to each box holds the key.
With my permission He will empty them, setting me free.
But I protect "self" and to *me* ....tightly hold.
If I yield to Him...I...I will be out of control.

Then came His question 'Who do you love most, Me or your sin?
If I'm your *choice*......then you must let me in.'
Then gently He showed me the names...now so clear,
And the boxes, once hidden, began to appear.

The name on the first box was......*Pride.*
I had kept it hidden so well because of the "junk" inside.
Judging, condemning others...while promoting me.
I just couldn't be like that. How could it be?

The label on the next box was......*Fears.*
The contents are insecurities, rejections and tears.
But I stuffed and packed that one so well
That no one by looking at me...could tell.

Boxes, so many boxes, holding memories from long ago.
Hurt feelings I nurtured and wouldn't let go.
Some boxes I saved just to make me feel good,
When the world treated me unjustly, as I knew it would.

But Jesus You knew me before I was formed.
You chose me and loved me and now I'm reborn.
So please empty the boxes, I'm willing but don't know what to do.
And Lord, when they are empty, please fill them with *You.*

I lay my life down before You as I open the book
And together we face it and You help me look.
As we walk through the pages of disappointments and pain
You cleanse me and bathe me, in Your gentle rain.

Now the pain is gone and in its place comes Your Peace
For You take those things as far away as west is from east.
No longer do I have to feel the guilt and the shame.
All that is left in my boxes are ashes, sweet smelling ashes, in
Your Holy Flame

You have given me knowledge and the tools it will take.
They are called choices, "contrary choices," that I must make.
When negative thoughts creep in, now I know I have the choice
Not to follow them with actions...or give them a voice.

Neither to stuff them in a box entrenched in my soul
But to express them to You, then release them, making me whole.
Emotions aren't sin! Jesus, You must have felt just like we do.
But You chose to be obedient and act as the Father told you to.

I choose too, to be transformed by the Light, not bound to sin.
I don't have to fill my boxes with "junk"........ever again.
Now You can fill the empty space Lord, but each day I must ask.
Please fill me with Your Love, equipping me for the task.

Of helping others see their boxes they have hidden away
Showing them how they may be emptied, Your Perfect Way.
Having Your Mind in place of my own is the Good News!
By submitting to You......we are truly *free to choose*.

Vicki Eaton
Rt. 3 Box 820
Canyon, Texas 79015
November 1987

Endnotes:

1.   Romans 6:11

2.   See Chapter Eleven, "Can a Christian be Demon Possessed?"

3.   Law of sin - Romans 7:23

4.   Matthew 6:34

5.   Jeremiah 17:9

6.   Jeremiah 30:11-15 (and especially verse 17)

Scriptural References:
Chapter Twelve

Deliverance
   A. Deliverance is a process of healing and cleansing that we will be in for the rest of our lives (Romans 6:11)

   B. The deliverance comes through our moment by moment choices. We must continually choose to stay free

   C. Christians need no deliverance from demons (Colossians 1:13-14; 2:15; John 10:27-29; 1 John 5:18). We have already been delivered at our new birth
      1. After salvation, there is only one *Spirit* and one life source (2 Cor. 5:17-18)
      2. Just like a fountain of water has only *one* Source (James 3:11; John 7:38; Revelation 21:6), so, our lives have only one *power source*

   D. What is necessary is freedom from our hidden sins (insecurities, fears and hurts) that the power of sin has used all of our lives to keep us captive (Luke 10:19). The Lord looseth the prisoners and raises them that are bowed down (Psalm 146:7-8)
      1. The first original negative thought is not sin, it's what we choose to do with it that makes it sin or not (James 1:14-15)
      2. Anything that is "not of faith" is sin (Romans 14:23)

   E. Demons cannot control us, unless we give them room in our souls, to do so (Luke 11:17-26)

   F. We need to constantly choose to stay clean, or we will re-fill those empty chambers (2 Peter 2:10; Hebrews 6:6)

We need to make constant faith choices ("M & M's")
   A. Healing is made up of many faith choices on our part

   B. It's a process that we will be in for the rest of our lives (James 1:3; Matt. 7:14)

   C. There is no need to fear how or when God will bring these hidden things up (2 Timothy 1:7). We should take one day at a time (Matthew 6:34)

   D. It's critical to keep on choosing to be cleansed inwardly (Proverbs 3:20)
      1. We must deal with these hidden things (2 Cor. 10:5-6)
      2. Form encourager groups — be accountable to each other

Psychology versus God's Way
   A. Psychology is *self-knowledge*. It focuses on the building up of the self, whereas, the Bible teaches us to "die to ourselves," to put our self aside and let Christ live His Life out through us. (Galatians 2:20)

   B. Psychology deals with our problems through therapy. The Bible tells us that only God can be our healer (Jeremiah 30:12-13, 15 and 17)
      1. Without God taking away our sin (Psalm 103:12), these hidden things will simply be re-programmed back into our hidden chambers, and eventually become strongholds of the enemy
      2. As believers, we don't need to work at cleansing ourselves, but simply giving God permission to search, cleanse and heal these secret things (Prov. 20:27)

   C. Psychology blames others for not loving us perfectly; we are encouraged to *feel our feelings* and mull over all that has happened to us; the Bible says "only God can love us perfectly" and we are encouraged to give *all* to Him
      1. God's Love then frees us to forgive and love others as God would have us do
      2. God's Love allows us to initiate His Love and not look to have it returned

Psychology can be dangerous
   A. Psychology is *another gospel*. It leads us to being "conformed to the world's image" and not God's

    B. When we try to analyze our own feelings and the traumas of the past, we simply re-program these things right back in our secret place
       1. This makes Satan's strongholds even stronger
       2. We are not "forgetting the past" as Scripture exhorts us to do (Philippians 3:13), but dwelling on it and making it worse
       3. We are not dealing with our sin as Scripture tells us to do (2 Corinthians 10: 6), but "adding sin to sin" (Isaiah 30:1)
    C. Psychology cannot penetrate beyond the soul, only the Spirit and Word of God can do that (Hebrew 4:12)

Inner Healing versus God's Way
    A. Inner healing is directed towards self-acceptance, not self-subjection as the Bible teaches
       1. God's wants us to be continually cleansed, not for self-acceptance, but so that God's Life can be manifested in our lives
       2. God wants us conformed into His Image, not self-image (Romans 8:29)
    B. The way we are *transformed* is by the constant renewing of our minds, not by reliving the experiences of the past

Visualization
    A. The Bible never suggests that we visualize or imagine in our own thoughts what went on in our past. In fact, the Bible strongly tells us just the opposite. We are not to use our imagination (2 Corinthians 10:5), but to "cast it down"
    B Our imagination is not a reliable source for truth
    C. God, by His Mind in us, will reveal the secret, hidden causes of our actions today. There's no need to again live through the actual experiences of the past in order to do this

It's not a "witch hunt"
    A. We don't initiate the search for these hidden things, God does in His timing and in His way (Proverbs 20:27)
    B. No one but God knows the *hidden causes* that motivate our actions today
    C. Only He, in His perfect timing and way, knows how to expose these things

Healing of our past before *faith choices*?
    A. We do not need to be healed completely of our past *before* we can make *faith choices*
    B. In fact, it's really the other way around. From the moment the Spirit of God enters our lives, we have His authority and His power to make faith choices. And it's these faith choices that will free us of our past
    C. The buried things in our hidden chambers do not affect our sanctification; but they do affect our constant emotional choices
    D. Only by intimate Knowledge of God can these hidden chambers be cleansed, healed and then filled with the Spirit of God (Proverbs 3:20)

God's Truth
    A. Once the hidden chamber is cleansed, God's truth needs to be re-established there (Luke 11:24-26)
       1. After dealing with our sin, we must read God's Word (Ephesians 5:26)
       2. It's imperative to replace the lies with God's truth
    B. We must allow God not only to expose the symptoms of our sin, but also their root *causes* (not every thing we think and feel has root causes, but much of what makes us angry and resentful does)

Chapter Thirteen
How God's Mind Works In Us

Hidden Treasure

Isaiah 45:3 tells us that God "...will give [us] treasures of darkness and hidden riches of secret places, [so] that [we] may know that [He is] God...." And Daniel 2:21-22 says, "...He giveth wisdom to the wise and knowledge to them that know understanding and to them He reveals the deep and secret things...."

This chapter, I pray, will be full of "hidden treasures" and "deep and secret things" of God's Word. I pray these treasures and secrets will excite you as much as they have me, as you realize the depths of the treasure house that God has given us in His Word. My prayer is that God will open our understanding so we might see that we *already* possess everything we need in order to walk the victorious Christian walk.

In the last three chapters, we spoke about Solomon's Temple being a perfect blueprint or model of the internal architecture of a New Testament believer. Well, if God has given us so many secret riches and treasures in the *physical structure* of the Temple of Solomon, I believe there also must be just as much to be learned from the *furnishings and features* of the temple. These are some of the things we are going to explore in this chapter.

I mentioned earlier that there are over 50 chapters in the Old Testament that have to do with the temple, its rooms, its furniture and its rituals. Those details are not there by accident. They are there for our instruction.

Temple Furnishings

Again, my purpose will not be to dissect the furniture, but rather to understand a little more clearly, how we ourselves operate and *how God's Mind works in us*. We do this so we can use this incredible gift that God has already given us. The information you are about to learn will be the Scriptural basis for the practical application of renewing our minds that we will discuss in the following chapters.

I believe the features and furnishings of Solomon's Temple represent the different facets of the seven-fold Spirit of God that produces the Mind of Christ in us. (Can you name these functions without looking?) Let's study the Temple furnishings and features and see if there are any parallels.

Let's begin by again exploring each room of the Temple. Only this time, let's concentrate on the *furniture* and the *features* of each room. Let's see if we can discover more of the "hidden riches" and "secret treasures" that God promises us in His Word.

Main Sanctuary

Turn, if you will, to **CHART 17** (on the facing page).

HOLY OF HOLIES

The most important room of the Temple is the Holy of Holies. We have seen that the Holy of Holies is analogous to the *new Spirit* that God gives us when we are born again. We said that this is God Himself dwelling in us.

Let's take a look at the features and furnishings of the Holy of Holies and see if any correlations can be made. Inside the Holy of Holies there were three items: the *Ark of the Covenant* with its *Mercy Seat* covering, and the *Shekinah Glory* overshadowing both. These were three separate elements that were always considered to be one whole. (See illustration on page 252.)

The Bible teaches us that God Himself is a Trinity: He is the three in one.[1] Therefore, when we asked God to come into our hearts and we are "born again," God the Father, God the Son and God the Holy Spirit came in as one.

John 14:23 is evidence of this: "Jesus, answered and said unto him, 'If any man love Me, he will keep My words: and My Father will love him, and *We will come unto him, and make Our abode with him.'*" (emphasis added)

I believe these three features of the Holy of Holies (the *Ark of the Covenant*, the *Mercy Seat* and the *Shekinah Glory*) represent the triune God (God the Father, God the Son and God the Holy Spirit) that dwells in the Holy of Holies of our own hearts.[2]

HOLY PLACE

The next room of the Temple is the Holy Place. We have seen that the Holy Place is analogous to the *new Heart* that we receive when we are born again. In the Holy Place, there were also three types of furniture: the *Golden Altar of Incense*, the ten *Golden Tables of Shewbread* and the ten *Golden Lampstands*. Notice these are all gold. Let's explore each one of these items and see if they hold any correlation to the Mind of Christ in us.

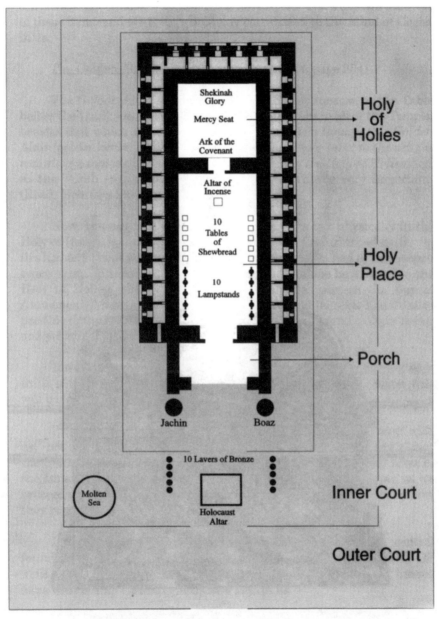

Chart 17

The Ark of the Covenant

The Golden Altar of Incense (see illustration page 254)

The Golden Altar of Incense (Altar of Sweet Incense or the Table before the Lord) was the *most* Holy piece of furniture in all of the Temple, besides that which was in the Holy of Holies. *Even though this Golden Altar (golden censer) physically sat in the Holy Place next to the veil, it was always considered in Scripture to be a part of the Holy of Holies*[3] or, as the Torah says, "aligned with the Ark." This is very important. (Read: Hebrews 9:3-4 and Leviticus 16:12-13)

Now, the only reason the Golden Altar was not physically in the Holy of Holies is that it had to be attended to and refurbished daily. Its fire had to be kept perpetually burning and its incense had to be changed twice a day. Since God had commanded that no one be allowed in the Holy of Holies except the High Priest once a year on the Day of Atonement,[4] it was decided that this Altar would be placed as close as possible to the Holy of Holies so that the priests could tend to their duties and yet not disobey God's commands.

Therefore, when you think of the Golden Altar of Incense, always think of it as an *extension, or a part, of the Holy of Holies*. Again, this will be important later.

Exodus tells us that God promised Moses that He would "meet with us," not only at the Ark of the Covenant in the Holy of Holies, but also at the Golden Altar of Incense in the Holy Place and the Holocaust Altar in the Inner Court.[5] All these details will become important later, as we proceed with our investigation of the furnishings of the Temple and how they relate to the Mind of Christ in us.

Golden Altar of Incense symbolizes the central foundational part of the Mind of Christ in us, which is the SPIRIT OF THE LORD as He first comes forth from the Holy of Holies of our hearts, joins with our spirit and ignites new Life in us.

Remember Proverbs 20:27 told us that "the spirit of man is the *candle of the Lord....*" And, at our new birth God is the One who lights or ignites the candle of our spirit. (Psalm 18:28)

Altar of Incense

Rabbinic Insights

Several years ago while we were in Jerusalem, I spent several afternoons in the Rockefeller Museum Library researching the Temple of Solomon. Many rabbis often study there. One gentleman found out that I was interested in his Jewish Temple and offered to help.

He brought me all the books and articles written in English that he could find on the Temple. One article particularly fascinated me. It said there is an old Rabbinic tradition—not Scripture)—probably based on the incident in 1 Kings 8:10-11 where the Shekinah Glory came forth from the Holy of Holies so that the priests were not able to stand or minister, that this Golden Altar was originally *ignited* and *lit* by the Shekinah Glory as it passed by the Altar to fill the Temple.

This last year when we were in Jerusalem, we went to the Temple Institute where they are actually rebuilding the furnishings and implements for the third temple, and we asked about this incident in 1 Kings. They told me that, yes, the Shekinah Glory <u>did</u> come forth from the Holy of Holies, and He <u>did</u> pass over the Incense Altar and He <u>did</u> fill the Temple from the inside out.

This excited me, because it validates that the temple was, indeed, filled from the *inside*, where the Shekinah Glory dwelt, *outward*. Many people believe the temple was filled from the outside inward.

The Temple Institute people even went on to explain that the Temple windows were built in such a way as to capture the Light from inside and *funnel* it outward, so that all could see it. This will all become important later, as we apply this analogy to our own daily being "filled with the Spirit," from the inside where the Source is, outward.

To me, one of the first spiritual applications of this Golden Altar of Incense is that this is the place where the Spirit of the Lord comes forth from the Holy of Holies of our hearts, joins with our spirit and then creates or begins or quickens new life in us.[6]

Cloud of Incense

This Altar, as we mentioned earlier, is one of the places where God meets with man. It's called the *ana-ha-ketoret* which means *cloud of incense* and echos a term from Moses' encounter with God at Sinai. This altar symbolizes the principle of *intimacy*—where the Divine and the human meet. It reminds us of the intimacy that Moses had with God. He conversed with God, *face to face,* but it was always done amid the shroud of what the Bible calls the *anan* or the cloud.[7]

Also, while we were at the Temple Institute, I asked about the spiritual signifi-cance of this Golden Altar of Incense, and I received a very provocative answer. They said that to the Jews, this Altar has both a physical and a spiritual meaning. The physical meaning, they said, refers to the actual flowers, herbs and incense that are used on this Altar. But, the spiritual meaning fascinated me. They said it is *symbolic of a union or a fusion of two separate things*. This is the place where God's Spirit joins with man's spirit to make one new creation.

"Therefore, if any man be in Christ, he is a new creation; old things are passed away; behold, all things are become new." (2 Corinthians 5:17)

Turn if you will to **CHART 18** (on facing page).

The *new Life,* or the new creation, that the Holy Spirit begins, quickens or ignites in our hearts is God's Eternal Life: God's supernatural Love *(Agape),* His supernatural Thoughts *(Logos),* and His supernatural Power *(Dunamis).*[8] Remember, God's Thoughts and His Power together are often called the Mind of Christ.[9]

Throughout this book, we have emphasized the importance of God's Love and God's Mind (His Wisdom and Power) working together. This is the full character of God and what He desires us to be filled with daily—so we can walk in His Truth and Love. In this particular study we are concentrating on the Mind of Christ, but always remember, right along side of God's Mind, is always God's Agape Love—together they are the Cloud and Fire.[10]

Perpetual Fire

Also significant, is that this Golden Altar needed to be perpetually lit. As we learned in Chapter Two, God's Eternal Life (his Love, Thoughts and Power) will <u>never</u> stop flowing into our hearts once we are born again. God's Love is unconditional and it will keep on coming to our hearts no matter what we do or don't do. If we sin, we will quench His Life, His Love, from flowing out into our souls, but still His Light will remain "lit" in our hearts. His Love never stops flowing to our hearts.[11]

The fire on the Altar was kept perpetually burning by the priests who daily brought hot coals from the Holocaust Altar in the Inner Court and placed them

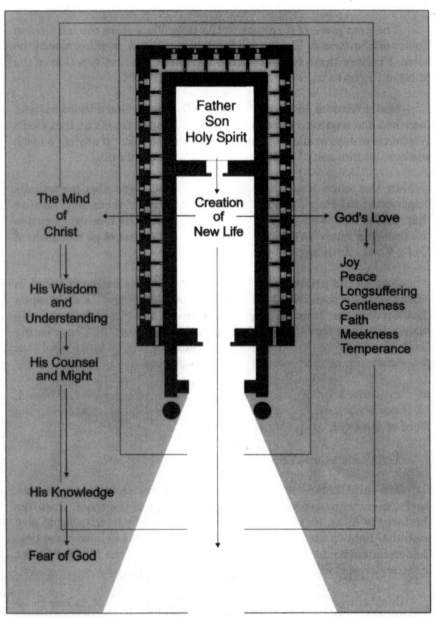

**Father
Son
Holy Spirit**

**Creation
of
New Life**

**The Mind
of
Christ**

**His Wisdom
and
Understanding**

**His Counsel
and Might**

His Knowledge

Fear of God

God's Love

Joy
Peace
Longsuffering
Gentleness
Faith
Meekness
Temperance

God's New Life

Chart 18

on this altar. Jesus' one time sacrifice for all sins[12] is what keeps the fire in our own hearts continuously burning.[13]

Now, let's go back and review **Chart 17** (page 251) and look at the second piece of furniture.

The Ten Golden Tables of Shewbread (see illustration on facing page).

The next piece of furniture in the Holy Place was the ten Golden Tables of Shewbread. There were five tables of bread on either side of the room. I believe these tables of bread represent the first function of the Mind of Christ in us, which is the Spirit of WISDOM.

God's Wisdom, as we said in Chapter Five, is God's Word burned, inscribed and engraved upon our hearts.[14] James 1:5 tells us that God's Wisdom is always available to us; we have only to ask. "If any of you lack wisdom, let him ask of God that giveth to all men liberally...."

In the same way, these loaves of bread were also perpetually displayed in the Holy Place with incense alongside of them, to symbolize that God's Word is always available to us. Again, the incense alongside the bread, is symbolic of *God's Spirit* that must always go alongside of *God's Word.* Together, they are the *truth.*

Just as the priests were told to *eat* of these loaves of bread in order to sustain their lives, so we are told in Scripture that God's Wisdom, His Word, is our "bread of Life" and we are to eat of it daily in order to sustain our lives. In other words, our very lives depend upon our eating God's Word. "...Man shall not live by bread alone, but by every word that proceedeth out of the mouth of God."[15] (Matthew 4:4)

Proverbs 3:13-19 and Proverbs 8:1-5, 11 are also wonderful to read. All these Scriptures declare that our very lives depend upon eating the Word of the Lord.

Ten Golden Lampstands (see illustration page 260).

The third feature of the Holy Place was the ten Golden Lampstands, five lampstands on either side of the room. Just like the Incense Altar, these lamps had to be perpetually lit in order to give continual light to the Golden Tables of Shewbread. I believe these ten Golden Lampstands represent the second function of the Mind of Christ in us, which is God's supernatural UNDERSTANDING.

Just as we said in Chapter Six, God's Wisdom is of no use to us without God's Understanding or His illumination alongside. So, too, the purpose of these ten

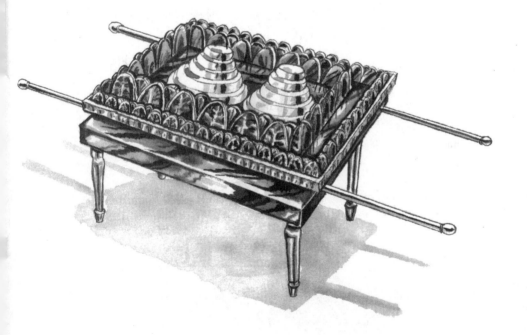

Table of Shewbread

One of ten Lampstands

Golden Lampstands was to give continual *light* to the Shewbread Table.[16] These lampstands, by the way, were the only source of light in the Temple, other than the flames from the Golden Altar.

"For God, who commanded the light to shine out of darkness, hath shined in our hearts, to give the light of the knowledge of the glory of God in the face of Jesus Christ." (2 Corinthians 4:6)

PORCH

Continuing on in **Chart 17** (page 251).

The next room of the Temple is the Porch. As we have shared before, for our purposes, this is the most fascinating and also the most important room of all. We have seen that the Porch represents the *new willpower* that we receive as a result of being born again. This is the place where God *counsels* us about His Will and then, gives us His *Strength* to perform that Will in our lives.

Just as we saw there are two separate areas to our willpower, God's supernatural Will and Power and our own free choice, so, too, there were two separate areas to the Porch of the Temple:

1) The first area of the Temple Porch, the Golden Vestibule, was really a part of the main sanctuary of the Temple, so it was gold.

2) The second part of the Temple Porch was the two huge free-standing *Bronze Pillars*, named Jachin and Boaz. Until we reach the porch, all of the furniture in the temple has been solid gold. At this point, a drastic change of metal occurs and all the furniture becomes bronze in the Inner and Outer Courts. Bronze, representing judgment because sin is present, is a metal that's always associated with fire.

Even though these Pillars actually stood in the Upper Level of the Inner Court, they were always considered to be a part of, or extensions of the Porch.

When I discovered the names of these two Pillars, and the meaning of those names, it intrigued me so much that I began to compare the features and furniture of Solomon's Temple with the Mind of Christ. I had already come to the conclusion that Solomon's Temple was a blueprint of the internal architecture of man. But when I found the passages in Isaiah 11:2-3 which talks about the Spirit of Counsel and the Spirit of Strength, and I found that the right Pillar means *in His Counsel* and the left Pillar means *in His Strength,* that tied the temple features to the Mind of Christ. That coincidence so piqued my interest, that I began to

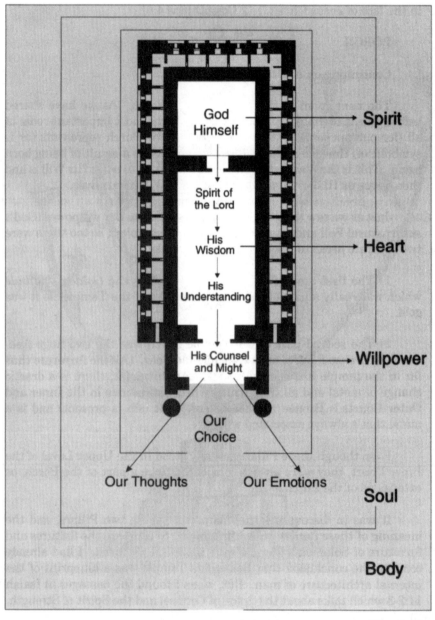

Chart 19

pray and study to see if the rest of the seven-fold Spirit of God of Isaiah 11 fit the Temple model. And, of course, it did!

See **CHART 19** (on the facing page) and let's summarize what we have learned so far.

The three features in the Holy of Holies, the Ark of the Covenant, the Mercy Seat covering and the Shekinah Glory, represent the triune God in us, God the Father, God the Son and God the Holy Spirit. The Altar of Incense represents the Spirit of God as He first comes forth from our hearts, unites with our spirit and ignites new Life in us. The table of Shewbread represents God's supernatural Wisdom or His Word that He has inscribed on our hearts. The Lampstands represent God's supernatural Understanding or His illumination of His Wisdom (His Word).

And, the Golden Vestibule represents the fourth and fifth functions of the Mind of Christ in us, which is *God's supernatural Counsel and Might* (or Strength). This is God's supernatural Will and Power in us, the place where He shows us what His Will is and then gives us the supernatural strength to perform that Will in our lives.

The Bronze Pillars represent our own *free choice*: the free choice to either follow God's Counsel and rely upon His Strength; or, the free choice to follow our "own" will and rely upon our own ability to perform it in our lives.

Notice that even though these pillars were considered to be a part of the Porch, they physically sat in the upper level of the Inner Court. I think this is significant, because it means that we have the Authority and Power of God to choose His Will over our own thoughts and emotions.

Two Olive Trees

As you recall, our willpower is called in the Greek, *dianoia*. *Dia* means channel or passageway and *noia* means of the mind. Just as the Vestibule's main purpose was to act as a passageway to and from the Holy Place, so too our willpower is the channel or the passageway for God's Life in our hearts to flow out into our souls.

In light of this symbolism, Zechariah 4:11-12 is a very interesting passage. "What are these two olive trees upon the right side of the candlestick and upon the left side thereof? And I answered again, and said unto him, What be these *two olive branches through which the two golden pipes empty the golden oil out of themselves?*"

To me, this Scripture describes the exact purpose of our willpower: to allow the "golden oil" (God's Life) to be emptied out of our hearts into our souls. God has already given us all that we need in order for this to occur.[17] He has given us His *supernatural Counsel* in order to let His Life flow, and He has given us His *supernatural Strength* in order to produce His Life in our souls.

To be *willing* is our only responsibility, willing, not only to choose what He counsels us, but also willing to allow Him to perform His Will in our lives by His Strength.

INNER COURT

Let's continue our comparison of the furnishings and features of Solomon's Temple to the functions of the Mind of Christ in us. Turn back to **Chart 17** (page 251) and let's explore the Inner Court. The Inner Court represents *our soul* or our self-life—all our thoughts, emotions and desires that are contrary to God's.

As we said, the Inner Court had two levels: an *upper level* which contained the multiple secret hidden storage chambers and the Pillars, Jachin and Boaz; and, the *lower level*, which contained three pieces of furniture—the *Brass Lavers,* the *Bronze Holocaust Altar*, and the *Molten Sea.*

Both the upper and lower levels of the Inner Court represent *our soul*, where the sixth function of the Mind of Christ, intimate knowledge of God, is desperately needed.

Intimate (*oida*) Knowledge of God, we said, is experiencing Christ's Life in place of our own and our souls are the place where this *exchange of life* takes place. This is where we need to learn *how* to set aside our own thoughts and emotions that are contrary to God's, so that His Life from our hearts can come forth.

Let's see if this is be demonstrated by our Temple model.

See **CHART 20** (on the facing page).

This is a close up picture of lower portion of Inner Court. The Lower Level of the Temple Courtyard had three pieces of bronze furniture: *Ten Bronze Lavers*, the *Bronze Holocaust Altar* and the *Molten Sea*, sometimes called the Brazen Sea. These three pieces of furniture were in the Inner Court expressly for the purpose of cleansing and atoning for sin.

The order of service for the priests as they came from the Holy Place to the Inner Court to minister was as follows: Initially, they entered the Courts with

Holy
Place

Porch

Jachin
"In His Counsel"

Boaz
"In His Strength"

10 Lavers of Bronze

Washing of hands and feet
of the Priests

Molten
Sea

Complete emersion
of Priests

Holocaust
Altar

Sacrifices

Inner Court

Chart 20

Thanksgiving and Praise.[18] Then, they went to the *Lavers of Bronze* where they washed their hands and feet. *A*fter that, they went to the *Holocaust Altar*, where they sacrificed the animals, in order to purge the sins of the people. Next, they went to the *Molten Sea* where they bathed completely by bodily immersion. And finally, they took hot coals from the *Holocaust Altar*, went back into the Holy Place where they changed their clothes, and then sprinkled incense over the hot coals at the *Golden Altar*.

The order of service is important: Ten Bronze Lavers; Holocaust Altar; Molten Sea and then back into the *Holy Place where they changed their clothes*, and to the Golden Altar. This all will become significant later as we make personal application of these steps in our own lives.

Three Cleansing Agents in Our Soul

God tells us that there are three cleansing agents at work in our own souls continually cleansing and washing away our sins. They are the *Spirit*, the *Blood* and the *Word of God,* sometimes called "the water of the Word." (1 John 5:8) All three of these divine agents work hand-in-hand to cleanse, purify and heal our souls so that God's Life can come forth from our hearts.

I believe the three pieces of furniture in the Lower Courtyard, the Bronze Lavers, the Holocaust Altar and the Molten Sea, represent these same three cleansing agents, the Spirit, the Blood and the Word that God has given us in order to deal with our sins.

These are the three steps that we must take daily in order to have intimate Knowledge of God and experience His Life in our souls in place of our own. What we will be sharing now is the Scriptural basis for the practical application (the Inner Court Ritual) that we will be discussing next chapter.

Inner Court Furniture

Let's explore these three pieces of furniture in the Inner Court and see what personal application can be made.

Ten Bronze Lavers (review **Chart 20**, on previous page).

The first piece of furniture in the Inner Court was the *Ten Bronze Lavers*. (See illustration on the facing page.) There were five lavers on each side of the court yard. These were movable wash basins, each sitting on four wheels and each large enough to hold water for 40 washings. These lavers were used for the continual

3 cubits
(4.5 feet)

wheels
1.5 cubits
(2.25 feet)

Brazen Laver

washing of the priests' hands and feet *before* they went on to do their worship service. This washing was mandatory, because all things used in worship had to be cleansed and washed first, "lest they die" as Exodus 30:18-21 tells us.

I believe these ten lavers represent the *Spirit,* which is the first spiritual agent that God has given us, in order that we might deal with our sins, so we can know Him intimately.

Remember, God's Spirit continually reveals and exposes our sins, so that we will see them for ourselves, and choose to wash ourselves from them by confessing and repenting. "And when He [the Holy Spirit] is come, He will reprove the world of sin, and of righteousness, and of judgment." (John 16:8)

Isaiah 1:16 tells us, this washing is our *own* responsibility, "Wash ye, make yourselves clean; put away the evil of your doings from before Mine eyes and cease to do evil."[19] In other words, as we recognize sin in our lives, God wants us to admit that we have quenched and blocked His Spirit in our hearts, and admit that there is a breach in our fellowship. We need to confess this and choose to turn around (repent) from following that sin.[20]

Reflection of Our Souls

The Lavers of Bronze were made of "looking glasses" or mirrors. As the priests looked in the basin to wash themselves, what they saw was a true reflection of themselves. And that's just what the Spirit does with us. He exposes truth, so that we'll see it for ourselves and then, make the appropriate faith choices to get rid of the sin. The way we get rid of sin, is by confessing it, repenting of it and giving it to God.

Joel, Chapters 1 and 2, reveals that precisely at these lavers "between the Porch and the Holocaust Altar," the priests confessed and repented of their own sins and the sins of the people. It says that they "mourned, wept and howled because they recognized that the Holy Spirit had been *cut off.*" In Joel 2:12-13, the Lord exhorts them to "...turn ye even unto Me, with all your heart, and with fasting and with weeping and with mourning; and rend your heart...and turn unto the Lord...."

In like manner, Christians need to allow the Spirit of God to search our souls and expose any unbelief, doubt, pride, etc., *before* we go on to worship. Scripture tells us that God won't hear our prayers[21] if there is unconfessed sin in our lives. "Thou hast covered thyself with a cloud, that our prayer should not pass through." (Lamentations 3:44)

"If I Wash Thee Not"

Jesus tells us in John 13:7-10 that we need to cleanse our souls constantly or else we "will have no part of Him." God is *always* in our hearts. He never leaves us or forsakes us, but because of unconfessed sin we have quenched His Spirit from coming forth out into our lives—our souls.

Peter says to the Lord, "Lord, doest thou wash my feet?" (verse 6) And Jesus answers: "What I do thou knowest not now, but thou shalt know hereafter. Peter saith unto him, Thou shalt never wash my feet. Jesus answered him, *If I wash* [Greek word *nipto*, which means partially wash] *thee not, thou hast no part with me.* Simon Peter saith unto him, [then] Lord, not my feet only, but also my hands and my head. Jesus saith to him, *He that is washed* [Greek word *louo*, which means completely washed] *needeth not* [to wash totally again, except] *to wash [nipto] his feet....*"

Now, there are two Greek words here for the word *wash*. *Louo* which means to *completely wash* as we are when we are born again, and *nipto* which means to *partially wash*.

What Jesus is saying here, is that he that is washed—completely washed, i.e., born again—needeth not to be completely washed again, except to continually wash his feet.

Our souls can be compared to our feet. When we make wrong, emotional choices, our *souls/soles* get dirty, as if we'd stepped in mud. At this point, we need not completely bathe again (be saved again), but only cleanse our feet—our souls. We become clean by *confessing our sins, repenting of them and then giving them to God.* This cleansing is what Jesus refers to when He asserts that if we don't constantly wash our feet, we will have no part of Him.

Christian's "Bar of Soap"

Without this step of confession and repentance, God's Life in us will be quenched from being manifested in our souls no matter how many prayers we say, Bible Studies we go to or churches we attend.

This step of confession and repentance is one that is so very often left out of our *quick fix* Christian self-help books. Scripture tells us, until we confess and repent of our own sin, the situation that we find ourselves in will remain our own responsibility. But once we confess and repent, however, the problem then becomes God's responsibility.

Forgiveness

Along with our confessing and repenting of our own sins, we also need to choose to *unconditionally forgive others* of their sins through the power of the Holy Spirit.[22]

In John 13:14, Jesus continues, "If I, then, your Lord and Master, have *washed your feet* (i.e., cleansed your soul and forgiven your sins), ye also ought to go and wash one another's feet." In other words, we need to extend that same unconditional forgiveness to others that God has extended to us.

An Example: "As Far As the East is From the West"

A beautiful example of unconditional forgiveness is my friend Sara whom we spoke about in Chapter Three. Remember, Sara had two children who were kidnapped by her former husband and missing for three years. Obviously, Sarah was devastated by what happened. But rather than let the bitterness and hatred overwhelm her, she turned her life completely towards God in total surrender.

Constantly, she not only confessed and repented of her own hurts and resentments toward her ex-husband, but over and over again, she made those difficult faith choices to *unconditionally forgive him.* Because of her contrary choices, Sara stayed released from the bondage of her own emotions. Now, I didn't say she felt no negative emotions. I'm sure she was tormented at times. But she wasn't captured and imprisoned by those feelings because she kept making faith choices to give them over to God. And He, then, was faithful to take them "as far as the east is from the west."

Also, by unconditionally choosing to forgive her ex-husband, she was released from the enemy strongholds and God was enabled to work freely in the situation. John 20:23 tells us that there is a "supernatural binding" that occurs if we don't forgive others. Only our unconditional forgiveness releases that bondage.

God not only gave Sara His Love and forgiveness for her ex-husband, but He also gave her His supernatural Wisdom, Understanding, Counsel and Knowledge. Through a series of events that I know God directed, my friend Sara was able to locate her children and, as you recall, was eventually happily reunited with them.

To me, Sara's story offers an incredible example of how we can unconditionally forgive others through the power of the Holy Spirit. Because of Sara's faithfulness, not only in confessing and repenting of her own sins, but also in unconditionally forgiving her ex-husband of his sins, God was able to become her defender and her avenger.

The Lavers of Bronze represent God's *Spirit* that continually exposes our own sins, so we'll be able to see them, confess them, repent of them and unconditionally forgive others of theirs. This is the first step towards having that daily *intimate Knowledge of God.*

The Holocaust Altar

Continuing on with **Chart 20** (page 265).

The next piece of furniture in the lower portion of the Inner Court is the *Holocaust Altar.* A very large altar, 15 feet high and 30 feet square, it was called "the mountain of God." (See illustration on the following page.)

This altar is where the blood of the animals was shed to purge the offender's sins and restore him to fellowship with God. Symbolically, this altar represents the *Blood of Christ*, the second spiritual element that God has given us so we can know Him intimately. Only by Christ's blood can all our sins—past, present and future—be purged and wiped away, so we <u>can</u> be reconciled to God. 1 John 1:7 confirms this: "...the blood of Jesus Christ cleanseth us from ALL sins."

God wants us to willingly sacrifice and give over to Him everything that is not of faith. He wants us to hand over—whether we feel like it or not—all of our *justified* hurts, negative thoughts and emotions, doubts, fears, pride, insecurities, memories—everything that God shows us.

Luke 11:39-41 corroborates this: "The Lord said unto him, 'Now do ye Pharisees make clean the outside of the cup and the platter; but your inward part is full of ravening and wickedness...But rather give alms [love gifts with no strings attached] of such things as ye have; and behold all things are clean unto you.'"

A wonderful book to read that brings all of this subject into proper perspective is *The Calvary Road,* by Roy Hession. In this little book there is a list of all the subtle things that quench God's Life in us just as much as the *big sins* of Galatians 5. Let me list just a few:

Self-pity, self-defensiveness, over sensitivity, criticalness, resentfulness, worry, grumbling, bossiness, self-complacency, self-energy, self-seeking, self-indulgence, self-consciousness.

Holocaust Altar

As I joke with my seminar audiences, if you don't experience any of these feelings, you have <u>no</u> need of this teaching!

So, to me, the Holocaust Altar symbolizes the place where we sacrifice ourselves to God. The place where we totally give ourselves over to Him—relinquishing and yielding everything that is not of faith. This is where we offer ourselves as a "living sacrifice," so He can fill us and use us. We are to "...walk in Love, as Christ has loved us and has given Himself for us, an offering and a sacrifice to God...." (Ephesians 5:2)

A Beautiful Example: I Always Wondered Why

A dear friend, Hannah, wrote me a number of years ago how all her life she has been rejected by everyone she has ever loved. First of all she felt rejection from her father, whom she adored, when he ran off with another woman. Then, she felt rejection from her mom who became bed-ridden for two years after her father left. Recently, she has experienced rejection from her husband of 35 years because of marital difficulties. And finally, because she is Jewish, she has felt rejection from her whole family, including all her children, because she has become a Christian and has invited Jesus Christ into her life. [23]

Hannah writes that for years she hung on to all these *justified* hurts and rejection, and continued to act out of her all-consuming fear of more rejection. Listen to what she wrote me recently, as she is beginning to learn to use the Mind of Christ. She is the Messianic Jew I spoke of in Chapter Two.

"The thing that staggers me the most is that the Church doesn't really know that they must choose to give up every scrap of self-protective, justified hurt, and that we cannot feel anything [negative] for anyone, but Christ's Love. *It seems to me that most of the Church is living half a Christian life. I always wondered why Christians were not more noticeable in the world.*"

Hannah is right. Most of the church *is* living half a Christian life. Because we have not been taught that "all these things within" quench God's Life in us just as much as any of the big "outward" sins. And by our hanging on to them—justified or not—we will not have God's Love or His Mind working in or through us.

Hanging on to all that's within not only will keep us "half a Christian," but will also guarantee our not being noticed in the world. And, the reason is—we're being "conformed to the world's image," and not being "transformed out of it."

Listen, if Hannah with that horrible background of rejection, can hand over and sacrifice to God "all that's within,"[24] be healed and set free; then any of us can.

Showing Our Love To God

God desires for us to offer ourselves [25] *as living sacrifices*, so He can fill us and use us. "I beseech you therefore, brethren, by the mercies of God, that ye present your bodies a living sacrifice, holy, acceptable unto God, which is your reasonable service." (Romans 12:1)

Now, there are really two steps to being a "living sacrifice" and surrendering everything to God: 1) *We* are the ones who must climb up on that altar and choose to give ourselves as "offerings in righteousness." This is our own responsibility. 2) *God*, then, is the One who purges our sins by His Blood, takes them as far as the east is from the west[26] and reconciles us to Himself.

"And He shall sit like a refiner and purifier of silver; and He shall purify the sons of Levi, and purge them as gold and silver, that they may offer unto the Lord an offering in righteousness. Then shall the offering of Judah and Jerusalem be pleasant unto the Lord, as in the days of old, and as in former years. And *I will come near to you....*" (Malachi 3:3-5)

When we sacrifice ourselves to God, we not only receive intimate Knowledge of Him, His Life in place of our own, but we also become a "sweet smelling savor" unto Him. 2 Corinthians 2:14 tells us that "God...makes manifest [through us] the savor of *His knowledge* [His Life]... in every place."

So, to me, the Holocaust Altar represents the Blood of Christ (the second spiritual agent that God has given us in order to deal with our sin). It's the *cross* where we are to lay down anything that is not of faith.[27] This surrendering is the second step towards intimate Knowledge of God in our souls.

The Molten Sea

Again, on **Chart 20** (page 265).

The last piece of furniture in the Lower Portion of the Inner Court was the *Molten Sea* or the Brazen Sea,[28] a huge basin of water that sat on 12 oxen and contained enough water for 2000 washings.[29] (See illustration on the facing page.) This huge bath was used for the complete immersion of the priests *after* they had offered their sacrifices on the Holocaust Altar.

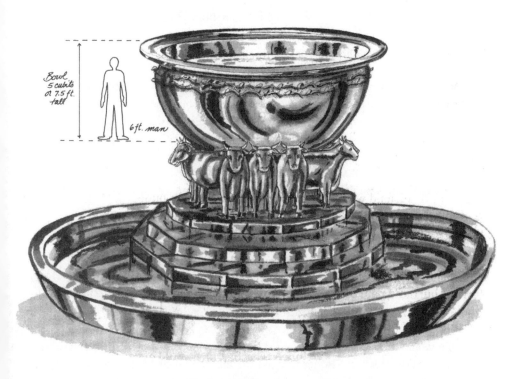

Bowl
5 cubits
or 7.5 ft.
tall

6 ft. man

Molten Sea

This Molten Sea represents the written *Word of God*, the third spiritual element that God has given us in order to know Him intimately. Only the Word of God will cleanse, sanctify and heal us completely from our sins.

Ephesians 5:26 says it so well, "That He [God] might sanctify and cleanse it [meaning us, the Church] with the washing of water by the Word."

After they had sacrificed their offerings at the Holocaust Altar, the priests needed to immerse themselves entirely in the Molten Sea to completely rid themselves of the blood-splattered stains. Similarly, we need to immerse ourselves in the Word of God to remove the stains of our own sins.

After we have sacrificed all our hurts, bitternesses, rejections, memories, fears, etc. and given everything over to God, we too are blood-stained, just like the priests were. Our lives have been wrenched and torn apart by the exposure of these things, so we are in desperate need of the Word's healing and renewing power. Only the Word of God can heal us.

Psalm 107:20 states, "He sent His Word and healed them, and delivered them from their destructions."

An Example: She Ate the Word

I have a friend, Joyce, who never could read her Bible in public. For some reason, whenever she was asked to read at a Bible Study, she would get overly emotional, begin to cry and ask someone else to read for her.

One year, God allowed a very hard trial concerning her husband and another woman into Joyce's life. Rather than let the terrible hurt and pain overcome her, Joyce became glued to her Bible. She was never separated from it. In fact, she even slept with it. The Word became her *life-line*!

When we went out to lunch together, she would always plop her huge Bible down on the table and literally have her finger pointing to one promise after another while we ate. I was totally amazed at the transformation that occurred in this dear sister's life because she allowed the crisis to push her into God's Word. Joyce knew her life depended upon her "eating the Word" and she knew her cleansing and healing would only come from it.

"Unless Thy law had been my delights, I should then have perished in mine affliction." (Psalm 119:92)

Don't wait for a crisis to learn this lesson. It's vitally important to read God's Word—bathe in His Word—daily, especially after we have given something over to God. If we don't put *truth* back in where the lies have been, then we leave a hole for the enemy to come back in and re-fill those chambers with more of his lies. (Luke 11:24-26)

"I Just Stopped Choosing"

Many years ago, I had a dear friend, Marge, who loved the *Way of Agape*. God had done some incredible things in her life and had set her *free* in so many areas. Running into Marge recently, I asked her how she was doing. She confided in me that she was really having a hard time, so she was seeing a counselor and going through a 12-step program.

Shocked, I asked, "Dear one, what happened?" Beginning to cry, she confessed, "I just stopped making *faith choices*" (choosing to confess, repent, give over to God and read His Word). Thus, one by one, all the things that God had so magnificently taken "as far as the east is from the west" she had allowed to come back into her life.

Unfortunately, this message is not one you can put on the shelf and simply stop practicing. God's way allows no room for coasting. Otherwise, the enemy will come in like a flood, re-polluting all that God has previously cleansed. Truly, *straight is the gate and narrow is the way that leads to Life and there are only a few that are willing to stay on that path.* (Matthew 7:14)

To me, the Molten Sea represents *God's written Word* to which we must run daily, in order to have our souls cleansed, sanctified and completely healed. Then, we can have that intimate Knowledge of God and experience His Life in place of our own.

Now, turn if you will, to **CHART 21** (on following page) and let's summarize what we have learned so far.

God's three cleansing agents, *God's Spirit, God's Blood* and *God's Word* work together daily in our souls, helping to cleanse and wash away our sins: by our *confessing and repenting* of our own sins and *forgiving others* of their sins (ten Lavers of Bronze); by our *giving our sins and our self over to God* and allowing Him to purge us by His blood (Holocaust Altar); and finally, *by God healing and sanctifying us through His Word* (Molten Sea).

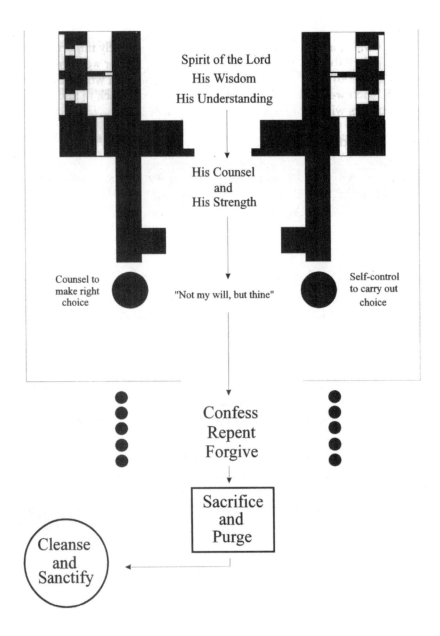

Chart 21

In order to have *intimate Knowledge of God*, the sixth function of the Mind of Christ, we must choose to do these three steps daily. This is the "...working out of our own salvation with fear and trembling" that Philippians 2:12 talks about.[30] In other words, it's our <u>own</u> responsibility to daily ask God to cleanse our souls (wash our feet), so that we <u>can</u> be transformed into His Image and we <u>can</u> have victory over the enemy.

"And they overcame him [the devil] by the *blood of the Lamb*, and by the *word of their testimony*; and *they loved not their lives* unto the death." (Revelation 12:11, emphasis added)

OUTER COURT

Let's turn back and review, one last time, **Chart 17** (page 251).

The final area of the Temple that we want to briefly explore is the Outer Court. We mentioned before that the Temple Outer Court, on an even lower level from the Inner Court, was exposed to many outside influences. Solomon had his palace and harem buildings adjacent to and accessible to the Temple Outer Courtyard, with his 700 wives and 300 concubines.

1 Kings 11:1-6 tells us that it was these foreign wives and their ungodly influence that turned Solomon's heart away from the Lord. Because Solomon was not careful to walk in the fear of the Lord, his heart was *no longer perfect with God.*

In Jesus' day, the Outer Court was the place where the common people, the money changers and the dove sellers, all the outside influences, were allowed to enter. Even Satan himself tempted Jesus from the pinnacle of the Outer Court.

Just think in our own lives all of the outside influences that continually draw us away from whole-heartedly and single-mindedly following God—other people, sex, money, power, movies, T.V., videos, books, music, education, politics, etc. 1 John 2:16 tells us, "For all that is in the world, the lust of the flesh, the lust of the eyes, and the pride of life, is *not* of the Father, but is of the world."

The Outer Court is analogous to *our body*, which is the vehicle or the carrier for the expression of our lives (our souls). Remember, we need a soul to express life and we need a body to express life through. So, we will either "walk in the fear of man" and manifest our own self life (review **Chart 13**, page 193) or: we will "walk in the Fear of God" (the seventh function of the Mind of Christ) and manifest His Life (review **Chart 12**, page 191).

Now, more than ever before, we must constantly walk in the Fear of God, not in the fear of man. We must seek only to obey God and flee all outside influences that would seek to quench our intimacy with Him.

An Example: "Why Did I Come?"

Several years ago, I was invited to do a seminar on the East Coast at a mainline denominational church. I sensed such tremendous resistance to this message, for I could tell visibly that many of the ladies were rejecting what I had to say. Their faces were like stone. They didn't smile or laugh at my jokes or funny stories. It was horrible. I kept thinking to myself, "God, why on earth did You send me here? I must have misunderstood You. They don't want to hear what I have to say. They all seem so preoccupied with their own worldly comforts."

God was quick to point out to me later that I was walking in the fear of man more than the Fear of God. I had become more concerned about what the audience was thinking and feeling about me than what God wanted of me. He lovingly and gently told me, "It's none of your business *why* I sent you here; you just do what I have called you to do and I'll do the rest."   He then gave me Jeremiah 1:17: "Thou, therefore, gird up thy loins and arise and speak unto them all that I command you; *be not dismayed at their faces, lest I confound thee before them.*"

Well, He certainly got my attention. I quit belly-aching, pulled myself up short, confessed and repented of my attitude and determined to do His Will, no matter what. After the next session, the audience seemed to warm as God's Spirit began to touch their hearts and move upon them. Many not only received the message, but allowed God to begin to change and transform their lives.

Now, more than ever before, we must walk in the fear of God, not caring what others think, seeking only to obey God and fleeing any outside influence that would quench that intimacy.

Summary

So, in summary, turn to **CHART 22** (on the facing page).

The furniture and features of Solomon's Temple represent the different facets of the seven-fold Spirit of God that equips us with the Mind of Christ.

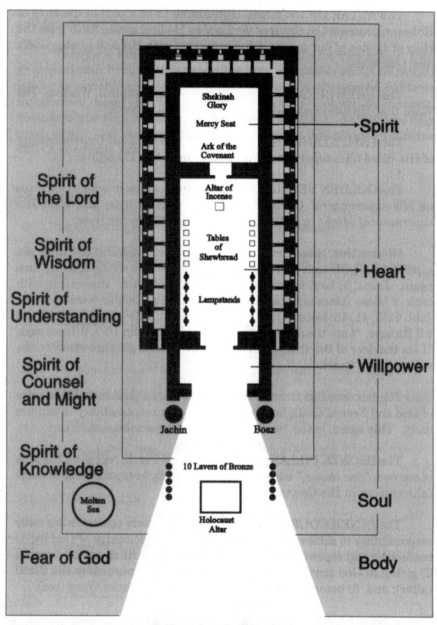

Mind of Christ

Chart 22

The ALTAR OF INCENSE (considered to be a part of the Holy of Holies) represents the *Spirit of the Lord* as He first comes forth from the Holy of Holies of our hearts, joins our spirit with His and ignites God's new Life in us.

The SHEWBREAD represents *God's supernatural Wisdom*—His Word that He has inscribed and burned into our hearts.

The LAMPSTANDS represent *God's supernatural Understanding* of His Word—His supernatural illumination of His Thoughts.

The GOLDEN VESTIBULE represents the area in which God gives us *His supernatural Counsel* as to what His Will is; and then *His supernatural Might* in order to perform that Will in our lives.

Notice that these first five capabilities of the Mind of Christ are *supernatural gifts* that God has already given us as a result of being born again. Jesus, in fact, identifies Himself in His "I AM" statements with each of these features of the Holy Place and the Golden Vestibule. In John 6:35, 41, 48 Jesus declares, "I am the *bread* of Life"; In John 8:12 and 9:5 He states, "I am the *light* of the world"; and in John 10:7, 9 Jesus says, "I am the *door* of the sheep." In other words, these gifts are always ours, we have only to ask.

The last two functions of the Mind of Christ, Intimate Knowledge of God and Fear of God, however, are our *own* responsibility to achieve daily. This again, is the "working out of our own salvation."[31]

The BRONZE PILLARS, still a part of the Porch, represent the area of our own *free choice*, where it's our own "daily" responsibility to make faith choices in His Counsel and by His Might.

The INNER COURT represents our soul, where again it's our daily responsibility to achieve *intimate, experiential Knowledge of God* by: 1) confessing and repenting of anything the Holy Spirit shows us (lavers); 2) giving to God anything that is not of faith to be purged by His Blood (altar); and, 3) being cleansed and healed by His written Word (sea).

And lastly, the OUTER COURT represents our body, where it's our daily responsibility to walk in the *Fear of the Lord*, fleeing anything that would quench His Spirit in us.

This, to me, is how the Mind of Christ works in us and how we are daily to be "renewed in the spirit of our minds." [32] *This is the Scriptural basis for the Practical Application Section that we will explore in the next two chapters.*

"Therefore, I beseech you, my brethren, by the mercies of God, that ye present your bodies a living sacrifice, holy, acceptable unto God, which is your reasonable service. And *be not conformed to this world, but be ye transformed [**how?**] by the renewing of your mind* [moment by moment, putting off the junk and putting on the Mind of Christ], so that you may prove what is that good and acceptable and perfect Will of God." (Romans 12:1-2, emphasis added)

Endnotes:

1.   See the briefing pack called, *The Trinity*, by Chuck Missler.

2.   In the Old Testament God's Name was often spoken of as "dwelling in the Holy of Holies" (1 Kings 8:29). God's Name means His Person, His Presence, and His Glory.

3.   Leviticus 16:12-13, ("cloud of incense covers the Mercy Seat").

4.   Leviticus 16:11-13

5.   Exodus 25:22; 29:42; 30:6, 36

6.   Our human spirit and God's Spirit form "one new spirit." (1 Corinthians 6:17)

7.   *The Temple,* by Joshua Berman, Jason Aronson Inc., Northvale, New Jersey, 1995

8.   See Chapter Nine, "Our New Heart."

9.   See Chapter Five, "What Is The Mind Of Christ."

10. Psalm 105:39; 25:10; 40:11; 100:5; Nehemiah 9:12.

11. 1 Corinthians 13:8

12. Hebrews 10:12

13. Hebrews 10:10, 14

14. Hebrews 8:10

15. Jeremiah 15:16

16. Psalm 119:105, "Thy Word is a lamp unto my feet..."

17. 2 Peter 1:3

18. Psalm 100:4

19.   Hebrews 10:22

20.   James 4:9-10

21.   Psalm 66:18

22.   2 Corinthians 2:10; Matthew 6:14-15

23.   I have been told, in some Jewish families, if you accept Christ as the true Messiah, you are as "dead."

24.   Hosea 6:6; 2 Timothy 2:21

25.   Hosea 6:6

26.   Psalm 103:11-12

27.   Colossians 1:20

28.   1 Kings 7:39; 2 Chronicles 4:6, 10

29.   1 Kings 7:25-26

30.   2 Thessalonians 2:13

31.   Philippians 2:12

32.   Ephesians 4:22-24

Scriptural References:
Chapter Thirteen

Hidden Treasure
    A. God's Word reveals "hidden riches of secret places" (Isaiah 45:3)
    B. God's Word reveals "deep and secret things: (Daniel 2:21-22)

Correlation of the furniture and features of Solomon's Temple to the Seven-fold Spirit of God
(Isaiah 11:1-3) Understanding the Temple will help us understand how the Mind of Christ works in us (Ephesians 5:18; 1 Corinthians 6:20; 2 Corinthians 6:16) (CHARTS 17, 18, 19)

    A. <u>Holy of Holies</u> represents our *new Spirit* (1 Kings 6:19-35; 8:6-9, 12; 2 Chronicles 3:8-14; 2 Kings 19:15; Exodus 25:22; Numbers 7:89)

        1. This is the dwelling place of God (Psalm 99:1; 80:1)

        2. The Holy of Holies had three features (The Ark of the Covenant with its Mercy Seat covering, and the Shekinah Glory over-shadowing it)

            a. These three features represent the triune God (John 14:23; Mark 9: 37), God the Father, God the Son and God the Holy Spirit dwelling in the Holy of Holies of our hearts (John 1:1-4; 4:24; 1 John 4:8; Psalm 119:130; Leviticus 16:2)

            b. God's *Name* dwelt in the Holy of Holies (1 Kings 8:29)

              . This means His Person, His Presence, His Glory

              . His Divine Voice was heard here (Exodus 25:21-22)

              . This is the *place God will "meet with us"* (Exodus 25:22)

    B. <u>The Holy Place</u> represents our *new heart* (1 Kings 7:48-50; 2 Chronicles 3:8; 4:19-21)

        1. These were three pieces of *gold* furniture in the Holy Place: the Golden Altar of Incense, the ten Tables of Shewbread and the Golden Lampstands

            a. The Golden Altar of Incense represents the *Spirit of God* as He comes forth from the Holy of Holies of our hearts and ignites or brings into new existence God's Life in us (1 Corinthians 15:45; 2 Corinthians 3:6; John 6:63; Romans 8:11; 1 Peter 3:18; Isaiah 32:15; 42:1; Joel 2:28; Psalm 80:1c). This Altar represents our *union with Christ* (Colossians 1:27; 1 Corinthians 6:17)

              . This is the place that God's eternal Life is created, started and brought into new existence (Psalm 48:9; John 1:1, 12, 14; 5:7; Romans 5:5; Luke 8:12; Hebrews 8:10; 1 John 4:8, 16; Isaiah 11: 2)

              . This Altar of Incense was the most Holy piece of furniture in all the Temple, except for the furniture in the Holy of Holies (Leviticus 16:11-13; Hebrews 9:3-4)

              . It was considered to be *a part of the Holy of Holies* (Hebrews 9: 3-4; Leviticus 16:12-13; Exodus 30:1-10, 36; Revelation 8:3; 9: 13; Ezekiel 10:1-2)

              . This is the second place that God said He would *meet with them* (Exodus 30:6, 34-38; 29:42-46; 40:34-35; Leviticus 16:12-13)

              . Rabbinic tradition says that this altar was originally lit when the Spirit of God came forth from Holy of Holies and filled the temple (1 Kings 8:10-11; 2 Chronicles 5:13)

              . Just as the *candle of our spirit* is lit by God's Spirit when He fills the temple of our bodies (Psalm 18:28; 2 Corinthians 3:9-16; 4: 6).

. Just as this Altar was kept continuously burning (Exodus 30:8) by coals from the Holocaust Altar (Leviticus 16:12), so the light is kept burning in our hearts by Christ's one-time sacrifice (Colossians 1: 20; 2:14)

. The priests burned only sweet incense on this altar (Exodus 30:8-9, 34-38; Isaiah 3:24; Leviticus 10:1-3; Malachi 1:10). It was called the "cloud of Incense" (Leviticus 16:13)

b. The ten Golden Tables of Shewbread represents God's Word (His *Wisdom*) that He has inscribed in our hearts (1 Kings 7:48; 2 Chronicles 4:8; Exodus 25:30; 40:22-23; Leviticus 24:5-9; Hebrews 8:10; James 1:5)

. Just as the priests were told to eat of the shewbread in order to live, so we too, are told to "eat of God's Word" in order to sustain our lives (Matthew 4:4; Jeremiah 15:16; John 1:14; 6:32, 35, 48-51; Exodus 16:15; Proverbs 9:5; Ezekiel 3:1-3; Joshua 1:8)

. Our lives depend upon daily "eating His Word" (Proverbs 3:13-18; 8:1-5, 11; Joshua 1:8)

. Jesus says, "I am the *bread* of life" (John 6:35, 41, 48)

. These shewbread loaves were called "the place of His Presence"

. The loaves were perpetually displayed with incense along side (Leviticus 24:7-8)

c. The ten Golden Lampstands represent God's supernatural *Understanding* that illuminates God's Wisdom in our hearts (2 Corinthians 4:6; Revelation 3:18; Proverbs 9:5-6)

. These were portable light stands that were fed by pure oil

. They furnished light for the Table of Shewbread (Exodus 40:24-25)

. God's Wisdom is of no use, unless God's Understanding gives us light (Psalm 119:105; 2 Corinthians 4; 6)

. These lampstands had to be perpetually lit (Leviticus 24:2)

. Jesus says, "I am the *light* of the world" (John 8:12; 9:5)

C. <u>The Porch</u> represents our *new willpower* (1 Kings 6:3; 7:15-22, 41; 2 Chronicles 3:4, 15-17)

1. There were two separate areas to the Porch:

a. The Golden Vestibule represents God's supernatural Spirit of *Counsel* and Spirit of *Might* or strength, where God counsels us as to what His Will is and then gives us the might to perform it in our lives (Philippians 2:13; 1 John 5:20; Hebrews 10:16; Ephesians 1:17-18)

. The vestibule is a passageway or a doorway to and from the Holy Place. It acts as a channel for God's Life to flow from our hearts out into our lives (Ephesians 5:17-19; Zechariah 4:12)

. Jesus says, "I am the *door* of the sheep" (John 10:7, 9)

b. The two Bronze Pillars, Jachin and Boaz, represents our own *free choice* to follow what God has counseled us and depend upon His power to perform in our life; or, the free choice to do as we desire and depend upon our own abilities (Zechariah 4:6)

. These pillars were bronze, free-standing and hollow (Jeremiah 52; 21)

. They had no structural value and were crowned with oil basins (1 Kings 7:41-42)

. Each pillar had a name. Jachin means "by His *counsel*" and Boaz means "in His *strength*" (1 Kings 7:15-22; 2 Chronicles 3:15-17; Jeremiah 52:17; Psalm 89:21; 2 Kings 25:16-17; Ezekiel 40:49)

- These pillars technically stood in the upper level of the Inner Court, but were always considered to be a part of the porch (Ezekiel 40: 49)
- The purpose of the pillars was to allow God's Life (the "golden oil") out of our hearts into our lives (souls) (Zechariah 4:11-12; Philippians 2:13; 2 Peter 1:3)
- *Pillar* means witness (Revelation 3:12; 11:4; 2 Samuel 18:18; Genesis 31:52)

D. The Inner Court represents *our soul* where intimate *Knowledge of God* is desperately needed (1 Kings 7:23-40; 2 Chronicles 4:1-6, 14-19; 2 Kings 25: 16; 2 Corinthians 7:1)

1. The Inner Court had three *bronze* features: twelve Bronze Lavers, the Holocaust Altar and the Molten Sea which were all there for the purpose of cleansing and atoning for sin (CHARTS 20 and 21)

   a. The order of service for the priests were as follows: they entered the Courts with praise (Psalm 100:4); then they washed their hands in the *Lavers of Bronze*; offered their sacrifices for sin on the *Holocaust Altar*; bathed bodily in the *Molten Sea*; took hot embers from the Holocaust Altar and returned to the Holy Place, where they changed their clothes and put the hot coals and incense on the Golden Altar

   b. The three pieces of furniture in the Inner Court represent what we must do daily with our own self life, in order to have true intimate knowledge of God (2 Corinthians 7:1; Hosea 6:6)

      - Then we can be true witnesses of God (2 Corinthians 4:10-11; Acts 22:14-15)
      - It's our own responsibility to achieve this kind of knowledge (Philippians 2:12)

   c. The three specific cleansing agents that God has given us in order to help us daily cleanse our souls are: the Holy Spirit, the Blood of Jesus, and the Word of God (1 John 5:8; Revelation 12:11; John 15:3; Hebrews 10:22; 9:14)

2. The three pieces of furniture in the Inner Court represent these three cleansing agents

Ten Bronze Lavers (2 Chronicles 4:6a; 1 Kings 7:27-39a; Exodus 30:18-19)

A. Represent the *Spirit of God* that continually exposes our sins, so that we will *confess and repent* of them and unconditionally *forgive* anyone who has wronged us (1 John 1:9; Isaiah 1:16 James 4:9-10; Joel 2:12-13, 17; Hebrews 10:22; John 13:8-15; 16:8; 2 Corinthians 7:1, 10; Psalm 19:12; 141:8; Job 36:8-12; 1 Chronicles 28:9; Matthew 6:14-15; 18:32-35; Colossians 3:13; Jeremiah 3:13-14; Ephesians 4:32) so we might have "intimate knowledge of God"

1. God wants us to *see* our sins so we will confess them and repent of them (Isaiah 1:16; James 4:9-10)

2. These lavers were made of women's looking glasses (Exodus 38:8), so as the priests bent over to look in the lavers they would see their own reflection (Joel 2:12)

3. This was a mandatory washing before the priests went on to worship (Exodus 30:18-21), just as it's critical for us to confess and repent of our own sins before approaching God (Isaiah 1:12-20; 59:2, 7-15; James 4:7-10; Matthew 3:2; Jeremiah 31:19a; 1 Corinthians 11:30-31; Lamentations 3:40-41)

   a. If we don't confess and repent, we'll quench God's Spirit and won't have intimate knowledge of Him (Luke 11:34b-35; Revelation 2:5; Lamentations 3:40; Hosea 5:15; Joel 2:12-17)

      b.   Jesus says, "If I wash thee not, you will have no part of Me" (John
13:7-10). We don't need to "wash completely" each time we sin, but
only to "partially wash" our hands and feet (Titus 3:5)

      c.   This washing is the Christians "bar of soap" (1 John 1:9)

         .   If we continually confess and repent, the situation becomes God's
responsibility

         .   If we don't do this, the situation remains our responsibility

B.   Along with confession and repentance of our sins, we must also *forgive others*
of their sins (2 Corinthians 2:7-11; Matthew 6:14-15; 7:5; John 13:8-15). If
we don't forgive, then a supernatural binding will occur (John 20:23; Matthew
18:35)

    1.   Jesus says if He has washed our feet, we must go and wash one another's
feet (i.e., forgive them) (John 13:14; 2 Corinthians 2:10)

    2.   Why forgive?

      a.   If we don't forgive, the Father will not forgive us (Matthew 6:14-15).
We forgive because we are commanded to in Scripture (2 Corinthians
2:7-11; Matthew 6:14-15; 18:32-35)

      b.   The more we confess and repent and forgive others, the more of
God's Love we will experience, not only in our own lives, but also
through us to others (Luke 7:47)

C.   If we humble ourselves by confessing, repenting and forgiving, the Lord will
then raise us up (James 4:9-10; Joel 2:12-13; 1 Thessalonians 4:6; Luke 14:11)

The Holocaust Altar (2 Chronicles 4:1; 8:12; 1 Kings 8:22-54; Ezekiel 43:13-21)

A.   Represents the *Blood of Christ* that continually *cleanses and purges our
sins* (1 John 1:7-9; Hebrews 1:3; 9:14, 22; 10:14, 22; 13:10; Colossians 1:
20; Psalm 65:3; 103:12; Isaiah 4:4; 6:1-7; 2 Corinthians 5:21; Romans 3:
25; Revelation 1:5d; 7:14; Titus 2:14; Ephesians 2:13), so we might have
"intimate knowledge of God"

    1.   Blood, in the Old Testament, purged the offender's sin (Leviticus 1:4-5;
17:11; 1 John 1:7; Hebrews 9:22). Blood was a symbol of life (Leviticus
17:14; Deuteronomy 12:23)

    2.   We are to choose to sacrifice *and give over to God* "all that's within"—
anything that is not of faith (Luke 9:23; 11:39-41; 12:33; 14:33; 18:22;
Hosea 6:6; 2 Timothy 2:21; James 1:21; Colossians 1:20; Psalms 51:17;
65:4; 76:11; 118:27-29; Isaiah 55:7; 1 John 5:3)

      a.   Our responsibility is to choose to hand over these things to Him.
He then, will purge our souls by His Blood (2 Timothy 2:21; 2
Corinthians 7:1; 10:5-6; Hebrews 9:4; 12:1; John 15:2; 1 Corinthians
5:7; Romans 8:13b; Proverbs 25:4; Ecclesiastes 3:11; John 15:2)

         .   Our responsibility is to give to Him anything that is not of faith as
a love-offering (Romans 12:1)

         .   God's responsibility is to cleanse, forgive and heal us (1 John 1:
9; Psalm 103:11-12)

      b.   The Holocaust Altar is the place that we show our love for God—this
is where we give our love offerings to Him (Luke 11:41). Totally
giving ourselves over to Him

         .   Whole burnt offerings symbolize an entire life given to God (Romans 6:13; 12:1)

         .   Scripture tells us God desires *mercy and knowledge* of Him more
than "burnt offerings" (Hosea 6:6; Micah 6:6-8; Amos 5:21-24)

   c.   This is the third place *He will meet with them* (Exodus 29:42). The
        Ark, Altar of Incense and the Holocaust Altar all imply the same term
        to meet (cloud and fire) (Exodus 19:9, 18; 30:6; 25:22)
3.   When we give God our "love offerings," we make a sweet smelling savor
     unto Him (Ephesians 5:2; 2 Corinthians 2:14-15; Hosea 6:6; Leviticus 2:
     1-2). This is where our *scent* is changed (Jeremiah 48:11; 2 Corinthians
     2:14-15)

The Molten Sea (2 Chronicles 4:2-5, 10; 1 Kings 7:23-26, 39b)

A.   Represents the *written Word of God* that is the only thing that can *cleanse,
     sanctify and heal* our souls (John 15:3; 17:17; Ephesians 5:26; Psalm 19:7-11;
     119:92), so we can have intimate knowledge of God
1.   Just as the priests had to bathe themselves in the Molten Sea after
     sacrificing because they were all blood splattered, we, too, have to bathe
     ourselves in the Word of God for total cleansing and healing of our
     souls (Psalm 103:12; 107:20; 2 Peter 1:4; 2 Timothy 3:15; James 1:21;
     Ephesians 5:26; John 15:3)
     a.   It's critical that we put truth back in where the lies have been (Luke
          11:24-26)
     b.   Our faith in God's Word and His Promises are what give us victory
          over the enemy (Revelation 15:2; Psalm 119:92)
     c.   It's critical we have faith in God's Word to heal us (1 Peter 1:9;
          Hebrews 4:2; 10:23, 35-38; 11:6; James 1:6; Psalms 37:3-7; 105:19;
          141:8; Luke 8:48; John 17:17, 19; Romans 15:4)
2.   Our lives literally depend upon God's Word (2 Peter 1:4; John 15:3;
     Psalm 19:7-8; 107:20; 119:25; James 1:21; Hebrews 4:2)

Summary

A.   These three cleansing agents in our souls, God's Spirit, His Blood and His
     Word, work hand in hand to daily cleanse and wash our souls, so that we
     might have "intimate knowledge of God"
1.   Our responsibility is to continually *confess and repent* of our own sins,
     forgive others of theirs, *give our sins over to God,* and then *read His
     Word.* "Loving not our own lives" (Revelation 12:11)
2.   This is the "working out of our salvation" (Philippians 2:12; 2
     Thessalonians 2:13; 1 Peter 1:9; 2 Peter 1:10; 3:14)
B.   Just as the priests, after they had washed their hands in the Lavers, sacrificed
     at the Holocaust Altar and bathed in the Molten Sea, went back into the Holy
     Place *to change their old clothes and put on new ones*, this is the point where
     we change our clothing
1.   It's at this point that we have "put off" our old clothes and "put on" Christ
     (Ephesians 4:22-24; Colossians 3:12-14; Isaiah 52:1; Zechariah 3:1-5;
     Psalm 132:7-9; Song of Solomon 5:3; Ezekiel 16:8-14)
2.   We have exchanged "our ashes" for "His beauty" (Isaiah 61:3)
3.   We can now worship the Lord in "the beauty of His Holiness" (Psalms
     29:2; 90:17)
C.   Going through the "Inner Court Ritual" daily is what will bring us that sixth
     function of the Mind of Christ, "intimate knowledge of God" (John 12:21-26;
     2 Corinthians 4:10-11)
1.   Salvation of our soul means freedom from the power of sin (Psalm 142:7;
     118:14)
2.   This comes through sanctification (2 Thessalonians 2:13c)

3. Only "fulness of knowledge" brings this about (Proverbs 11:9; 24:3-4; Isaiah 5:13a)
4. "Salvation is a lamp that burneth" (Isaiah 62:1) It's that "light on top of a lampstand" (Luke 11:33b)
5. Remember, however, our light can be "hidden and covered," if it's put under a bushel (Luke 11:33a)

Outer Court (1 Kings 7:9-12)

A. Represents *our bodies* where we will either walk in the *Fear of the Lord* (Isaiah 11:3; Romans 6:13; 12:1-2; 1 Corinthians 6:15-20) or in the fear of man.
   1. Just as the Outer court was open and exposed to many "outside" influences (1 Kings 11:1-10; John 2:14-16; Matthew 21:12; Mark 11:15; Luke 19:45), so we too, must flee anything that would quench God's Life in us (John 15:4-10; I John 2:16; 2 Timothy 2:21-22; Romans 8:13)
   2. We are to glorify, reflect and magnify God in our bodies (1 Corinthians 6: 19-20)
   3. If we do this, we'll be walking in the truth (3 John 4)
   4. Jesus says, "I am the Way, *the Truth*, and the Life" (John 14:6)
B. We are to continually praise God with our mouths (Psalm 34:1-3; 50:23a; 51: 15; 63:5; 71:8,15; 89;1; 100:4; 135:1-2)

Summary (CHART 22)

This is *how* the Mind of Christ works in us and *how* we are renewed in the spirit of our minds (Isaiah 11:2-3; 1 Corinthians 2:16; Romans 12:1-2; Ephesians 4:22-24)

Section Six:
Setting the Prisoners Free

"The Spirit of the Lord is upon Me, because He hath anointed Me to preach the gospel to the poor; He hath sent Me *to heal the brokenhearted*; *to preach deliverance to the captives, recovering of sight to the blind* [and] *to set at liberty them that are bruised...*"

Luke 4:18

Chapter Fourteen
How Do We Renew Our Minds?
(Attitudes)

David Needham, author of the book *Birthright,* states, "The big task is not the finding of the truth, but the living of it." I agree with him completely. What good are God's principles if they really don't change our lives? With this in mind, let's put all we have learned so far into practical application. What are the moment-by-moment steps to renewing our minds?[1]

Now, it was important that we laid out the Scriptural basis for these steps last chapter; otherwise, we are using man's wisdom rather than God's Wisdom. So, the steps that we will learn in this chapter are not just things that I have "made up" or found in a psychology book or a self-help book. These are the actual steps that the priests took in the Inner Court of Solomon's Temple in order to deal with their sin and be reconciled to God.

The first four steps are simply *attitudes* that we need to form daily. These are *not* steps we have to do each time we quench God's Spirit, but simply attitudes we need to have *on* daily in order to be transformed. We might go over each of these attitudes prayerfully every morning to remind ourselves of the need to be cleansed vessels—just like getting dressed.

Romans 8:6 tells us we can be "spiritually minded"—having an attitude (*phronema*) which results in life and peace; or, we can be "carnally minded"—having an attitude that results in death or separation from the source of life.

The final four steps that we will cover next chapter are *essential steps*. These are ones we *must* do each time we quench God's Spirit and find ourselves separated from Him. I call these last four steps the *Inner Court Ritual*, because they are the actual steps that the priests took in the Inner Court in order to deal with their sin.

My Survival Kit

I call all of these eight steps my *Survival Kit* because I literally go through these steps at least once a day—and, the last four, the Inner Court Ritual, sometimes as many as two and three times—if I am dealing with something very difficult or extremely painful. I chose the term *Survival Kit* because the word *survival* means *"keeping alive against all odds."* And, that's exactly what these steps allow me to do in the middle of hard circumstances—keep alive against all odds.

So, let's first explore the four *attitudes* that we must have on in order to renew our minds. These are simply *predispositions* or ways of thinking that will keep us "willing" and "open" to putting off the garbage of our thinking and putting on Christ. These attitudes help us to form a *mental state of openness* and readiness.

"Let this mind [attitude] be in you, which was also in Christ Jesus..." (Philippians 2:5)

Living Sacrifices

First of all, we need to have an attitude of being continually willing to present our bodies [to God] as living sacrifices. (Romans 12:1) Daily, we need to willingly give God permission to walk through us and to expose anything that's not of faith.[2] Notice, by the way, Romans 12:1 says we are to be "living sacrifices" which means, because we are living, we can get off that altar at any time. And, it's only by our choice that we choose to remain there.[3]

We need to be willing, on a moment-by-moment basis, to offer ourselves to God and to allow His Holy Spirit to expose what *He* wants in each of us. Again, we don't have to *feel* this first step. In fact, most of these steps we will not *feel* at all, they'll simply be *faith choices* or contrary choices.

Genesis 15:17 teaches that God literally *walked through* the parts of the sacrifice, "a smoking furnace and a burning lamp" exposing all that is there.

A good prayer to pray is Psalm 19:12-13: "...Cleanse Thou me from [hidden or] secret faults...Let them not have dominion over me...." Also, Psalm 139:23-24, "Search me, O God, and know my heart: Try me, and know my thoughts: And see if there be any wicked way in me, And lead me in the way everlasting."

God Loves Us

As we open ourselves up to God for inspection, we must always remember just how much He loves us and that He will not allow anything to happen to us that is not "Father filtered."

So, we can trust Him and rely upon Him no matter what we see or what we understand to be happening. I know this is so hard to do in practice, but this is what faith is all about. Read Hebrews 11:11 about Sara, "...*she judged Him faithful who promised.*"

"For I know that my redeemer liveth, and that He shall stand at the latter day upon the earth; And though after my skin worms destroy this body, yet in my flesh shall I see God. Whom I shall see for myself, and mine eyes shall behold, and not another; though my heart be consumed within me." (Job 19:25-27)

We must know in our hearts that no matter what it looks like to us, He is working out His purposes in our lives in His perfect Way. If you have trouble believing that God loves you and will be faithful to perform what He has promised, I strongly suggest getting *The Way of Agape* book and specifically reading Chapter Seven, "How Do I Know God Loves Me?" You might also go over the *Knowing God Loves* Me Scriptures in the Appendix of this book and, by faith, choose to believe what God says in those Scriptures.

(Remember also, as the charts illustrate, if we choose not to renew our minds, we not only won't experience God's Love to pass on to others, but we also will not experience it for ourselves. His Love will be quenched in our hearts and unable to flow out into our souls.)

Denying Ourselves (on the inside)

The second crucially important attitude we need to have "on" each day is that of being willing to continually deny ourselves—setting aside our own *justified* feelings, our own rights, our own frustrations, offenses, and anything that is not of faith. This is something that we do internally. This internal denying of ourselves is often much harder to do than denying ourselves outwardly (like our careers, positions, material things—houses, cars, clothes, etc.), because it affects who we really are—it's our *personhood* and our emotions are so involved. It hurts to set ourselves aside, especially when we are justified (by the world's standards) in thinking and feeling the way we do.

Each time we struggle with this, I would suggest reading Philippians 3:8-15, where Paul says, "I count all things but loss for the excellency of the knowledge of Christ Jesus, my Lord...." Note specifically verse 10, which says that the reason we are to "count all things but loss" is so that we may "know [*intimately experience*] Him and be made conformable to His death."[4]

We must continually ask ourselves, "Am I really more concerned with doing God's Will in my life then I am my own happiness?"   There will be many times when we must choose to do God's Will, knowing that temporarily it will <u>not</u> bring us happiness. Of course, the long-lasting joy and peace that will come from being in the center of God's Will is something that nothing else can ever compare with.

An Example: A Miracle

I met a woman, Charlotte, several years ago who was convinced that God wanted her to stay in her marriage, regardless of the horrible circumstances. Her husband, a "professing" Christian, no longer loved her, and he had bluntly told her so. He had tired of her and wanted her out of his life.   Therefore, he was doing everything he could to make her life miserable so that she would file for the divorce.

Certainly, she would have been much happier out of the marriage and away from this abuser, and yet, she knew in her heart that God had not given her permission to leave. And she was more concerned about doing His Will, than her own happiness.

I happened to see this Charlotte at a party not too long ago, and she had absolutely incredible news. Something major had happened in her husband's life and God had totally changed his heart. He had privately and publicly repented about the abuse of his wife, and was now doing everything he could to love her and make things up to her. God eventually did restore their marriage and they not only began to experience *Agape* Love for each other, but also enjoyed a restoration of all the human loves.

I believe the miracle of this story is due to the fact that Charlotte was more concerned about doing God's Will than she was about what would bring her temporary happiness.

Be Willing

Luke 14:26 reminds us that we really cannot be God's disciples unless we are "willing to" (not wanting to or feeling like it, but simply <u>willing to</u>) lay everything down (father, mother, wife, children, brothers, sisters). "Yea," He says, "even our very own lives" (all of our justified hurts). Again, we don't have to "feel" like doing this; we simply must "be willing" to do this![5]

Several years ago, while having lunch with some dear old friends, we began to talk about how very important it is for us to be willing to deny ourselves and to follow God. One friend, Suzy, said, "Nancy, I don't agree with you. I think some people don't have the ability or the capability to lay everything down and do it God's way." She then gave various reasons why she was convinced they couldn't do this: dysfunctional families, codependency, poor marriages, physical abuse, emotional problems, and other environmental circumstances.

I thought for a moment and then replied, "Suzy, if these people are Christians, then God is in them. And *He* is the One who will make them capable and give them the ability to deny themselves. I think *all Christians are capable of laying themselves aside* because God is in them, *but not all Christians are willing to do so*! That, to me, is the bottom line!"

The people Suzy was talking about, simply weren't willing to lay themselves aside. Their excuses ranged from "dysfunctional families," to "my husband is not trying." But, I don't believe these things were the *real* problem, because God has all the Love, Wisdom and Power they need. The real problem was they just weren't willing to set themselves aside so that God could pour these things through them.

Perhaps this example helps us to understand Matthew 24:12 a little more clearly. It says here, that in the end times "...because iniquity shall abound, the *Agape* of many will grow cold." This is simply saying that many Christians (the only ones who possess *Agape)* in the end times, will not be willing to deny themselves, but rather they will want to hold on to their "justified" hurts, unforgiveness, etc. Therefore, the *Agape* Love of God in their hearts *will grow cold.* It will be covered over and quenched and unable to flow forth.

So again, all Christians have God's Love in them, but not all Christians are willing to set themselves aside to let it flow.

God promises us in Luke 18:30, as well as many other Scriptures, that if we are willing to deny ourselves, He will return a hundredfold "in this life" as well as in the world to come, all that we have chosen to surrender. In my own life, it seems the more I'm willing to lay at God's feet, the more He returns a hundredfold! My book *Why Should I Be the First to Change?* shares how God has restored a hundredfold my marriage, my family, my kids, etc. because I learned how to surrender and deny myself first. The more I give to God, the more of Him I get. Now, I'm certainly not any more capable than anybody else, but one thing *is* for certain. I am willing. And that seems to be all that's necessary!

1 Corinthians 2:9 promises, "But as it is written, Eye hath not seen, nor ear heard, neither have entered into the heart of man, the things which God hath prepared for them that love [*agapao*—totally give themselves over to] Him."[6]

Get Up and Do What God Says

Another crucial attitude we must have "on" in order to have our lives trans-formed, is that of being willing to <u>obey God's Will, no matter what He tells us to do</u>. No matter how we feel, what we think or what we want, we are to be willing to get up and <u>do</u> exactly what God has asked us to do. 2 Corinthians 8:11 says, "...As there was a readiness to will, so there may be a performance also...."

The attitude we spoke about in step #2 (denying ourselves) really concerns our *inner man*, setting aside our own thoughts, emotions and desires—our self-life—so that God can come forth. This third step of "obeying God's Will" is different. It concerns our *outer man*—our outward actions. It's now getting up and *doing in action* what God has called us to do, saying, "...not as I will, but as Thou wilt..." (Matthew 26:39) or, like Peter said, "...at Thy word I will...." (Luke 5:5) Again, we're simply trusting that God will perform His Will and His Life through us no matter how we feel.

If this is a difficult step, I would suggest reading Philippians 2:5-9. This is where God talks about being *"obedient unto death,"* getting up and actually doing in action whatever God has called us to do.

Example: "Obedient Unto Death"

Here is a wonderful example of how one of my dearest friends overcame her pride, humbled herself, and became "obedient unto death." Sarah is only five feet tall and weighs about 100 pounds soaking wet. Many years ago, her husband had an affair with a woman who worked in his office. Sarah found out about it and was violently angry. The next day she marched down to her husband's office and literally beat the woman up.

A year or so later, after their separation and divorce, God got hold of Sarah and began to transform her life. One of the things God began to speak to her about was her behavior to the other woman. He convinced Sarah that it was His Will for her to go back to the office and ask her forgiveness.

My precious friend not only chose to deny herself by setting aside her own *justified* feelings and emotions, but she also was willing to get up and *do* what God had asked her to do by going to her husband's office and asking forgiveness of this woman. Could you have done that?

When the other woman at the office saw Sarah coming, understandably, she ran. Sarah pursued her, however, and they finally began to talk. Sarah asked the lady's forgiveness for beating her up, and then she told the lady that she forgave her for "taking her husband away." The woman was so amazed at what was happening, that Sarah sensed an opportunity to talk more and asked if she would like to go to lunch. The woman agreed.

At lunch, Sarah had a chance to share what God was doing in her own life and the woman sought to know more. They became friends and, to this day, I believe, they are still friends. Only in God's Kingdom could something like this occur! Sarah is a real, true and precious friend of mine. And, I believe, much of the miracle happened because she was willing, in action, to "be obedient unto death."

Do you love God that much? Are you willing, not only to deny what you think, what you feel and what you desire, but also willing to get up and *do* what God has called you to do? This is what God is asking each of us daily.

Take Every Thought Captive

A final critical attitude that goes right along with the others, is that of being willing to "take every thought captive" and "revenge all disobedience" that occurs. In other words, we must constantly be willing to simply *deal with* our sins. 2 Corinthians 10:5-6 teaches us that we are to, "[Cast] down imaginations and every high thing that exalteth itself against the knowledge of God, and *bringing into captivity every thought* to the obedience of Christ; and having in a *readiness to revenge all disobedience*, when your obedience is fulfilled."

(Note: The next four *essential* steps (the Inner Court Ritual) are the actual steps to "revenging all disobedience" and are covered in the next chapter.)

We have shared before that we are not responsible for the original, self-centered negative thought when it first comes in. It's what we choose to do with that thought that produces the sin or not.[7] If we can simply recognize that ungodly thought and choose to give it over to God, then we have not sinned. However, if we do nothing with that thought but mull it over and think about it, it will eventually stir up our self-centered feelings and become sin in us.

As we mentioned before, our thoughts are crucial because they are the first to be triggered in the *chain reaction* of our souls. Remember, our thoughts stir up our emotions; our emotions then influence our desires; and our desires produce our actions. This is why it's so very important to take every thought captive. Then, we'll be able to prevent that chain reaction before it even begins.

To recognize our negative thoughts and to renew our minds takes constant discipline, however. And sometimes, it seems like it would just be easier to give in and let our wild emotions rule. But, you know what happens if we do this? *Our emotions then take us captive.*

Personal Example: Move Again?

Here's an example of what I mean: Chuck and I have just been through several horrendous years of stretching, testing and trials. In 1991 we lost our ultimate dream home in California that we had just moved into six months earlier, our cars, our insurance, etc., through bankruptcy.

In this same period of time, many of our old Christian "friends" turned their backs on us when Chuck's company went under. Many spread libel and slander about us. In contrast, several of our largest financial investors stood by us and continue in their support, even to this day. For me, the loss of my close Christian friends has probably been the hardest part of these last few years.

As a result of the bankruptcy, we were forced to move to a smaller rented home. In June 1992, that rented home turned out to be on the epicenter of a 6.8 earthquake that destroyed most of our personal belongings. Actually, we were the fortunate ones—the house we were renting was left standing. Houses on both sides of us twisted off their foundations.

In September of that same year, the Lord moved us to Idaho, and we were so excited and so looked forward to having our own home again. When we got to Idaho, however, we found out that the property we thought had been purchased for us (and into which we had moved all our belongings) had fallen out of escrow. Once again, we had to move.

Thus, we ended up living in a motel room and at a friend's house for five weeks until the Lord provided a wonderful house for us to rent.

But, this made five moves in two and a half years, besides the three total clean-up jobs after the 7.2 earthquake (15 miles away in Landers, California), the 6.8 earthquake under our home, and a 5.5 aftershock.

None of these moves were my choice! They were forced moves. Now, moving is never easy for anyone. But moving for us was particularly difficult because we had 35-odd years of collectibles (really old and broken now because of extensive earthquake damage), in addition to all of the ministry's furniture, computers, files and office equipment.

In the middle of those two and a half years, every time I would look at my circumstances, I became overwhelmed and paralyzed in my emotions. ("Why, God?") But, when I would be obedient and "take my thoughts captive" (whether I felt like it or not), God would always be faithful to remove my confusion, doubt, fears and anger and fill me with His peace and strength. And, once again I could go on. Taking my thoughts captive was the only thing that kept me sane.

So, yes, to catch our negative thoughts and deal with them does take constant discipline and effort and it is hard. But, you quickly find out that *there is no other* choice!

God's Thoughts

Since we are exploring the importance of "taking every thought captive," I thought we might also explore where our thoughts come from. How can we tell the difference between God's Thoughts, our own thoughts, and the thoughts that Satan inserts into our souls?

God's promptings come in that still, small voice that bears witness with our spirit that it is, indeed, *God's* voice. We usually will have an immediate peace. God's Voice encourages us and always draws us closer to Him. Now often, the Holy Spirit will need to reprove us and convict us of sin, but still, His voice will always *push us towards Jesus*—and towards being more loving—rather than away from Him. Always be leery of anything that pushes you away from God, away from being loving or removes your peace. That result is probably not from the Holy Spirit.

God's voice is always going to be in perfect agreement with His written Word. Any voice that does not correlate with what God's Word teaches should be immediately rejected. God's voice *always* confirms His Word. The way I weed out a lot of spurious thoughts is by asking myself, "If Jesus were bodily standing here beside me now, is this what He would be whispering in my ear?"

Thoughts "Not From God"

Thoughts that are not from God have two other sources: the flesh and the devil. Thoughts that are from our flesh are sometimes harder to distinguish, because Satan often uses the things of the flesh (our self-life) to cause us to sin. Think of the temple model. Things that occur in the grey area, representing our soul and body, would be *things of the flesh*. These are things that need to be immediately confessed if we have held on to them, repented of, and given over to God, so that Satan won't be able to get a hold in us.

It seems to me that sins of the flesh do go away pretty quickly if I'm faithful to acknowledge them, confess them, repent of them and give them over to God.

Satan's Voice

While most of the things that God will show us that are of the flesh, and will go away pretty quickly if we are faithful to go through the cleansing steps. Some of the things God will expose are long-standing strongholds of the enemy and he (Satan) won't let these go easily. So don't be dismayed or discouraged if these kinds of negative thoughts seem to reappear.

In fact, God takes our negative thoughts and emotions the moment we give them to Him, but often our *feelings* don't align with that choice for a while. And this is where Satan tries to make us think that God isn't faithful and that He hasn't taken these thoughts and feelings from us. Satan wants to use these in-between times to destroy us; God often lets us go a while to test us and to strengthen us. Will we keep on believing Him even though we see no evidence of change?[8]

Again, God is teaching us to walk by faith, not sight or feelings.

Satan, of course, wants to use our negative feelings to destroy us. What God means for good, Satan obviously wants to kill us with. It's important for us to understand this. As we mentioned earlier in Chapter Eleven,[9] God often uses Satan as His own tool to help bring up some of the ungodly and self-centered thoughts and emotions that we have erroneously programmed into our hidden chambers. Remember the Scripture "The Lord thy God will send the hornet among them, until they who are left and hide themselves from thee, be destroyed." (Deuteronomy 7:20)

Once these negative things surface—even though through Satan's promptings—we have a choice: God wants us to give Him these buried things and be rid of them forever; Satan, of course, wants us to crumble in confusion and discouragement over them. Satan's motive is to get us to push these things back down in the secret part of our soul, which will again motivate ungodly actions.

Therefore, if you have confessed, repented and given your negative thoughts and emotions over to God and they don't immediately go away (i.e., you still feel them), don't give up, saying, "Oh, this just doesn't work for me!" That's exactly what Satan is hoping you'll do. Recognize that you are in a battle. Know that you'll win if you will just persevere.

God is the One, in His timing and in His way, who will align your feelings to match the choices you have made. Something to keep in mind, the deeper the wound, the longer it will take for our feelings to align with our choices. Use your *weapons of warfare*: God's Word, His Blood, and His Name.[10] Fast, pray and have others pray for you. God promises us that if we do our part, He will do His![11]

"For though we walk in the flesh, we do not war after the flesh: (For the weapons of our warfare are not carnal, but mighty through God to the pulling down of strong holds)...." (2 Corinthians 10:3-4)

Satan's voice is very different from God's. He speaks to us in a loud, shrill and demanding voice, planting an urgent, "do it now" kind of a thought, often prompting unrest and doubt.

Satan uses all sorts of tactics to condemn us, make us feel guilty and like failures as Christians. These kinds of thoughts will always push us away from God, not towards Him. So, recognize thoughts like, "Oh, it doesn't work for me," "God doesn't care," "His Word is not true," "He doesn't love me," "He isn't faithful." Know where these kinds of thoughts come from.

Satan's three main tactics that we talked about in Chapter Four, are illustrated in Genesis 3 and also from Matthew 4:[12]

1) *"Don't obey* God's Word; follow your own feelings and thoughts."
2) *"Don't trust* God to perform it; trust in your own abilities."
3) "Don't give God your will and life; *follow what you want.* You're Number One."

Watch out for these temptations and constantly be alert to them. Spotting Satan's tactics will help in knowing how to fight.

Satan's Subtle Tactics

Elsa from the East Coast wrote to me cautioning, "Nancy, warn the girls. When I take any kind of P.M.S. medication or any kind of anti-depressants, my spiritual discernment is totally wiped out." She said "At these times I hear Satan's voice *much* louder than at other times in my life."[13]

Another thing Satan revels in doing is causing us to dwell in our past by imagining and fantasizing. Satan loves to prompt thoughts of "how wonderful it used to be," in contrast to, "how horrible it is today." The enemy will do anything he can to produce dissatisfaction with today and he's a master at doing this.

Brenda, recently separated from her husband, shared a few weeks ago, "The thing that draws me down faster than anything else is remembering what we used to be like." She and her husband had a "storybook" marriage. They met in grammar school, went out in high school—he was the football star and she was the head cheerleader—and married in college. They even had two adorable children and that pretty little house with a while picket fence in the country.

Thoughts of "how it used to be" and "how it could have been" pulled this woman down into the pits faster than anything else. That's our imagination working. Watch out for it! Catch those negative thoughts and choose to deal with them rather than entertain them.

2 Corinthians 10:5 tells us what we are to do with these kinds of thoughts. "*Casting down imaginations* and every high thing that exalts itself against the knowledge of God." And, then we are to "...[Forget] those things which are behind, and [reach] forth unto those things which are before." (Philippians 3:13)

Imagining and fantasizing can also simply be our entertaining negative thoughts. This is <u>not</u> forgetting the past, but dwelling on it and trying to figure out for ourselves what went wrong.

God's answer is, "Submit yourselves, therefore, to God. Resist the devil ("have a readiness to revenge all disobedience"), and he will flee from you. Draw nigh to God, and He will draw nigh to you...." (James 4:7-8)

In the next chapter, we will learn the four specific steps needed to "resist the devil." (the Inner Court Ritual)

Spirit-Controlled Thinking

Therefore, to be aware of, recognize, and catch the ungodly thoughts as they come in is critical. We are to refuse them, crucify them and annihilate them. And we do this by giving them to God.[14]

We must recognize that we are in a mind battle and we <u>will</u> win, if we just persevere. So, in review, the *four critical attitudes* we must have "on" daily are:

1) <u>Presenting our bodies [to God] as living sacrifices</u>.
2) <u>Denying ourselves</u> (our own thoughts, emotions and desires that are contrary to His).
3) <u>Obeying God's Will</u> (being willing to get up and *do* exactly what He has asked us to do).
4) <u>"Taking every thought captive"</u> and revenging all disobedience.

Endnotes:

1. Note: For those of you who have read and studied *The Way of Agape*, loving (*agapao*) God with all our heart, will and soul is essentially the same thing as "renewing our minds." Truly, as we love (*agapao*) God, our minds (our whole conceptual process) will be renewed. Remember, when we renew our minds, we not only receive the Love of God (the subject of *The Way of Agape*), but we also receive the Mind of Christ (the subject of this book).

2. Genesis 15:17-18

3. Hosea 6:6

4. John 3:30, 2 Corinthians 4:10-11

5. 2 Corinthians 8:11-12

6. Job 42:10b

7. James 1:14-15

8. Deuteronomy 13:3

9. See Chapter Eleven, "Why the Hornets?"

10. Luke 10:19

11. 1 John 5:4

12. Review Chapter Four.

13. Another woman wrote that when she uses drugs (even "over the counter" types), "they kill people spiritually in a way that can't be explained. They distort reality, vandalize and put people in darkness."

14. Philippians 4:8

Scriptural References:
Chapter Fourteen

Survival Kit — Attitudes (*phronema*) (Romans 8:6; Philippians 2:5)
- A.   We need to *present our bodies as a living sacrifice* (Romans 12:1-2; Hosea 6: 6; 2 Corinthians 7:2; 2 Timothy 2:21)
  - 1.   We must open ourselves up for God's inspection (Gen. 15:17; Psalm 19: 12)
  - 2.   We don't have to *feel* this step. We must simply make a faith choice (Psalm 19:12-13; 139:23-24)
  - 3.   We must remember how much God loves us (Psalm 118:6) (See "Knowing God Loves Me" Chart in the Appendix)
    - a.   We can trust Him in everything (Job 13:15; 19:25-27)
    - b.   Everything is "Father filtered" (Romans 8:28)
- B.   (Inside) We need to *deny (relinquish) ourselves* by choosing to set aside our own thoughts, emotions and desires, even if they are *justified* by the world's standards (Luke 9:23; 14:26-33; 18:28; Ephesians 4:31; Matthew 10:39; 16: 24; Mark 8:31-35; John 12:24-25; Matthew 16:24; Acts 20:24; 1 Peter 4:19; 5:7; Hebrews 12:1; Romans 6:11-14, 17-18; Colossians 3:5, 8-10; Galatians 5: 24), because "the way of man is not in himself" (Jeremiah 10:23)
  - 1.   We must choose to give "everything that is not of faith" over to Him (Romans 14:23)
  - 2.   We must count "all things but loss" (Philippians 3:8-15; 2 Corinthians 4: 10-11; John 3:30)
  - 3.   We don't have to *feel willing*, but simply *be willing* (Luke 14:26-33; 2 Corinthians 8:11-12)
    - a.   All Christians are *capable* of laying everything down because God is in us (Galatians 2:20; Philippians 4:13)
    - b.   But, many Christians are *not willing* to lay things down (Matthew 24: 12)
  - 4.   If we love (*agapao*) Him first, He will "drive out the inhabitants of the land" (Deuteronomy 11:22-23)
  - 5.   Then He will give us back a hundredfold all we have chosen to surrender (Luke 18:29-30; 1 Corinthians 2:9; Job 42:10-12; Mark 10:29-30; Matthew 19:29)
- C.   (Outside) We need to get up and *do what God has asked.* We are to choose to obey God's Will no matter how we feel or what we think (2 Corinthians 8:11; Ephesians 4:31-32; 6:6; Isaiah 1:19; 1 Corinthians 2:2; Psalm 40:8; Proverbs 3:5-6; Job13:15; 1 Peter 4:2)
  - 1.   Saying, "not my will, but Thine" (Matthew 26:39; Luke 5:5; 1 Peter 4:2)
  - 2.   Being "obedient unto death" (Philippians 2:5-9; Galatians 5:20)
  - 3.   Not *feeling* willing, just *being* willing (2 Corinthians 8:11)
- D.   We need to take every thought captive to the obedience of Christ (2 Corinthians 10:5-6)
  - 1.   Find out where the thoughts are coming from: from God, the flesh or the devil
    - a.   *God's Voice* is always in agreement with His Word. It will always push us closer to Him. God often reproves and convicts us of sin, but still He pulls us towards Himself (gives us peace) (1 Kings 19:12; Psalm 46:10; John 10:4)
    - b.   *Things of the flesh* Satan often uses to cause us to sin. These things usually go away quickly if we confess and repent of them and give them to God (James 1:13-15)

    c.   *Satan's voice* is urgent, loud and shrill. It's a "do it now" kind of a voice (Genesis 3:1, 4-5; 1 Chronicles 21:1-8). It causes us to look to men rather than to God (Mark 8:33-34; 2 Corinthians 11:3)

- These kinds of thoughts are often hard to get rid of because they have become "strongholds" and Satan won't let them go easily
- It seems the deeper the wound, the longer it takes for our feelings to align with our faith choice
- If our emotions don't align with our faith choices for a while, Satan wants us to think that God is not faithful and that he doesn't love us. He wants to use our feelings to destroy us (Proverbs 5:22)
- Use your "weapons of warfare" (2 Corinthians 10:3-6; Luke 10:19)
- Cast down anything that exalts itself against knowledge of God (2 Corinthians 10:5)

2.   God is using Satan as His tool, to bring up some of the hidden things so we'll see them and get rid of them (Deuteronomy 7:20). He is testing us to see if we will keep on choosing to believe *by faith,* even if we don't see or feel anything (Deuteronomy 13:3)

3.   God wants us to "forget the things that are behind" and press forward (Philippians 3:13). We do this by "submitting ourselves to God" (James 4:7-8)

- We are not responsible for the original bad thought—it's what we choose to do with it that makes it sin or not
- When we don't take our thoughts captive, they take us captive

4.   Sharing negative thoughts with others will not only contaminate them, but also reprogram those thoughts back into our minds (Ephesians 4:29-32)

5.   God wants us to have "Spirit-controlled" thinking—filling our minds with only good things (Philippians 4:8; Isaiah 43:18)

Chapter Fifteen
How Do We Renew Our Minds?
(Inner Court Ritual)

My Survival Kit: "Essential Steps"

In the previous chapter we focused on the *four attitudes* that are necessary to have in order to continually "be renewed in the Spirit of our minds": 1) presenting our bodies as living sacrifices; 2) denying ourselves (our self-life); 3) obeying God's Will in action, no matter what; and, 4) "taking every thought captive" and dealing with those things that are "not of faith."

In this chapter we want to discuss the *four essential steps* that we need to take in order to deal with our sins. This is our "readiness to revenge all disobedience," as 2 Corinthians 10:6 exhorts us. We must:

1) Recognize, acknowledge and experience our ungodly thoughts and emotions as they come in.
2) Confess our sins and choose to "turn around" from following them.
3) Give over to God all that He shows us is "not of faith."
4) Read God's Word and replace the lies with the truth.

The Inner Court Ritual

These four steps are critical to do each time we recognize we have quenched God's Spirit and have blocked His Life in our hearts. *I call these steps the* **Inner Court Ritual** *because they are the actual steps that the priests of Solomon's Temple went through in the Inner Court in order to deal with sin.*

The ritual went like this: First, the priests went to the ten <u>Bronze Lavers</u> to *wash their hands and feet* before worshiping. Then, they went to the <u>Holocaust Altar</u> where they *offered their sacrifices.* And finally, they *bathed totally* in the <u>Molten Sea</u>.

These steps, then, are not just something that I have made up or something that I found in a psychology book. This is the actual process (the Inner Court Ritual) that the Lord has laid out in Scripture for us to deal with our sin.

I recommend putting each of these *essential* steps on 3x5 cards and keeping them with you at all times because things will happen when you are out on the road and away from your Bible and notes. So, you'll want to keep these cards handy—in your purse, briefcase or in your car, until they become first nature to you. God is always faithful. When we do our part, He assuredly will do His.

Going through these four necessary steps every time we are confronted with a hurtful remark, a painful situation, pride, fear, resentment, bitterness, and so on, is the *only* way we can stay cleansed and prepared vessels for what God might call us to do next. These steps are our responsibility. If we don't *cleanse our feet*, we'll *not have any part of Him* (like we read in John 13) and also, we'll end up contaminating everyone we come in contact with (i.e., "making a stink" as Isaiah 3:24a says).

Something important to remember: unless we have asked Jesus into our hearts to be our Savior and have been *born again* as John 3 tells us, these steps will not work. We must have a brand *new power source* or life source within us (i.e., the Holy Spirit) and also a brand, *new heart* (God's Life), in order to produce some-thing different from what we ourselves naturally think, feel and desire.

See **CHART 23** (on facing page). If something has just occurred, and we already are feeling hurt, angry, bitter, resentful, fearful and so on, this chart is what we look like. But, say we catch ourselves and desire to *turn around* and go God's way. What are the steps we must take in order to "revenge all disobedience"?

(Note: the first and second steps of the Inner Court Ritual are really only one step (it all happens at the Lavers of Bronze). But, since there is so much that occurs in this first step, I've made it into two separate steps to make it easier to remember.)

Recognize Self-Centered Thoughts (Lavers of Bronze)

The first thing we must do is to <u>recognize and acknowledge the negative thoughts, emotions and desires</u> (self-life) that have just occurred. We must not vent how we feel or push our real feelings down, but simply ask God to expose what's *really* going on inside of us. We have lost our peace. We know we have done something that has quenched His Spirit, but at this point, we're not exactly sure what.

Remember, asking God to expose the truth is what the priests did at the Lavers of Bronze. As the priests bent over the lavers to wash their hands, they actually saw "their own reflection" in the mirrored lavers.[1]

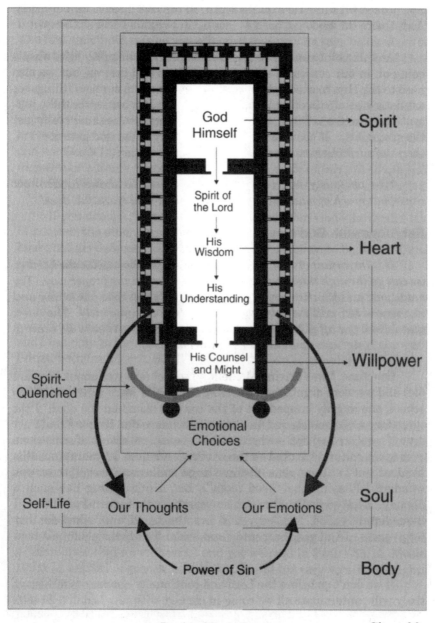

Double-Mindedness Chart 23

And this is just what the Spirit does with us. He exposes the truth, so that we'll see it for ourselves. And, that's the *key*!

At this point, we are to ask God not only to bring to light what's going on in our *conscious* thoughts, emotions and desires, but we also need to ask Him to shed light on the *hidden things* in our soul (things we are unaware of). In other words, are there any *root causes* for these self-centered reactions. Often, the conscious, surface emotions are really just the *symptoms*. If the real *root cause* can be exposed and gotten rid of, then the surface emotions will not occur again either.

Now *obviously, not everything we think and feel has a hidden root cause, but much of what makes us angry, bitter and resentful does!*

Get Alone with God

If at all possible, it's important at this point to get alone with the Lord so we can go through these steps and deal with our sin the proper way. Do not to put this off. Remember, Jesus is the only One who can expose and cleanse our sin, and the only One who can heal us completely. The times that I have put off going through these steps, are the times I do seem to "contaminate" everyone I come in contact with.[2]

One time, I was driving ten-year-old Michelle to school. We were arguing and fighting the entire way. When we got to school, she angrily jumped out of the car and slammed the door. I sat there for a while and stewed, not knowing what to do. Before I could get myself together and deal with my own sin, an acquaintance of mine came over to my car and knocked on the window. It's been 12 years since this incident, but I still can remember putting a smile on, like everything was wonderful, playing the "good mom", but inside feeling like such a phony. I felt so bad after our conversation that when I got home, I immediately called this lady, told her the truth and asked for her forgiveness. (And yes, I repented and asked for Michelle's forgiveness also!)

If we don't go before the Lord and continually cleanse ourselves, we truly will contaminate all we come in contact with. As Isaiah 3:24 tells us, "...Instead of [a] sweet smell there shall be [a] stink...."

So now, whenever I find myself hurt, angry, resentful, critical, self-centered, prideful, ungrateful, anxious, afraid, confused, bitter, judgmental, or filled with any negative emotion, and I try to stop, get alone with God and go through these steps.

Even in the middle of an argument with Chuck, if I find myself getting emotional and over-reacting to something, I stop the conversation, and I simply tell Chuck, "I need to go and be with Jesus." The first time I did this he was offended, but now he says he likes me so much better after I come out from "being with Jesus," that he freely lets me go.

It's so critical to be cleansed in order to respond the way God would have us to do. Don't ever take a stand with someone, unless you are a cleansed vessel! If you're not clean, then it will be self-life out there and not God's Life at all. The other person will immediately sense your judgmental attitude, react from his defenses—not his heart—the truth will be hidden, and you will sink even further into the pit than you were before.

If you can get *clean* first and respond from God's Love and His Mind, then the other person will sense your acceptance, respond from his heart not his defenses. The truth will have a chance to be exposed and the situation righted.

Even if I can only go through these steps *mentally* at the time, I do so. By *mentally*, I mean that if I am busy and I'm not able to pull away from the situation to be alone with the Lord to let my feelings out, then I can only go through these steps in my mind. Even if that's the case, I do it, because it's critical that I not let the sin accumulate in me.

Acknowledge Real Thoughts and Emotions

It's not only important to be honest with ourselves and acknowledge our pride, fears, insecurities and doubts that we are experiencing, but it's also important to be honest and truthful with God. He knows it all anyway. *He just wants us to see it and acknowledge it.*

One woman, not too long ago, asked me if we're supposed to let our *real* emotions out. "Does God want us to do that?" she asked. I told her that God has given us a perfect example in Scripture. David was called a "man after God's own heart," and yet we read in Psalm 55:15, Psalm 109:6-20 and other places, how he expressed his very volatile thoughts and feelings to God.

(As an aside here.) It's important when you are ministering to someone, to make sure you have compassion and empathy for what they are going through. Be sure to let them express how they feel, *before* you admonish, exhort and give them Scriptures as to what to do. Often times, when we are hurting so badly, we really don't want someone telling us *what to do* right away, but simply someone to say, "I understand what you are going through. I hurt with you. I've been there." Then, our hearts will be open to hearing what else they have to say.

This is one of the reasons I love the book of Psalms so much. David makes me feel like he has been there! He seems to know exactly what I'm feeling and thinking, when I have been hurt. When I've identified with him and cried with him, then my heart is open to receive what God wants to say to me next. If I were given all of God's commands first without His empathy and compassion, His principles would probably be hard to accept. This is just another example of the importance of God's Love going right along side of the Mind of Christ.[3] Together, they are that perfect *balance* that God designed.

Remember, we can't give something over to God if we don't know what it is. This is why describing and naming what we're feeling is important. Call your feelings for what they are: "I am angry; I am resentful; I feel betrayed; I am fearful." *Experience your thoughts and feelings.* Cry, scream, or yell if you want to. (Remember, we're doing this only to God alone.) This will not only help us understand what we are really feeling, but it will also help us recognize exactly what we're to give over to God.

Experiencing our emotions, I believe, is part of dealing with our sin and part of the healing process. We're all human, and we all experience negative, self-centered thoughts and emotions. Now, I don't mean going back and reliving the actual experiences of the past, or putting Jesus in the middle of them or visualizing them, I just mean crying about what God has just revealed as the root causes that are affecting our choices today.

Often times, I will go through these Inner Court steps, but either because of time pressures or a lack of opportunity forget to really release my true emotions. After a day or so, I wonder why my peace has not returned. More often than not, it's because I have forgotten to really experience my negative feelings. They are still bottled up within me. Therefore, I have to go back and once again go through these steps, only this time, I cry and acknowledge how I feel. Now again, *I am not choosing to follow these emotional feelings, but simply recognizing what they are, so I can give them to God.*

An Example: "This Message is Impossible"

A dear friend of mine, Arlene, shared with me that she knew she had "years of emotional walls" that she had never released and given over to God. Everything was coming to the surface now because her husband had just recently left her after 35 years of marriage.

Arlene had always known there was *something* preventing her from intimately knowing Jesus, but she could never figure out exactly what it was. She received the *Be Ye Transformed* tapes and immediately gave God permission to expose whatever He wanted to in her.

Two days later, she called me up and said, "Nan, this message is absolutely impossible. Ever since I listened to these tapes, I've been an emotional basket case! I started two days ago to try to live this message, and today I feel I am worse off than when I started. I am consumed with jealousy, bitterness and anger! I feel horrible and I know I'm such a failure as a Christian!" Of course the enemy was right there on her shoulder, whispering she was right.

I asked Arlene if she had given God permission to expose what He wanted in her. She said, "Certainly, that's the first thing I did." Then I said, "Praise Him and thank Him. He is just answering your prayer! God is showing you your real self—your true thoughts and emotions. Don't worry, you are right on course."

We Must "See" Our Sin

I told her simply to recognize what God was bringing up. *Name* the emotions and the thoughts as they came up; then go through the steps we are now learning and get rid of them for good.

What Arlene forgot was that God must expose our negative, ungodly thoughts and emotions *before* we're able to hand them over to Him. *We can't give things over to God if we don't really know what they are!*

Scripture never promises we won't have negative, bad and self-centered thoughts, emotions and desires.[4] We all are still human and we all will have negative thoughts and feelings until the day we see Jesus. However, we can have victory over the "desires of the flesh," if we constantly make faith choices to give these things over to God, not allowing them to motivate our actions any more.

Galatians 5:16 declares that if we choose to "walk in the Spirit," then we won't carry out the desires of the flesh.

Three Choices

As Christians, we have three choices as to what to do with our negative thoughts and emotions:

- We can vent them to others

- We can stuff them down in our hidden chambers, <u>or</u>

- We can give them to God and be rid of them forever
  (This last choice is what we do through the Inner Court Ritual.)

It's important to understand that we can't hold on to negative thoughts and feelings without eventually acting out of them. In other words, undealt with thoughts and emotions <u>do</u> influence our actions and our behavior.

Examples in the Bible include: Esau with Jacob; David with Bathsheba; Rueben and his brothers with Joseph in Genesis; and John and Peter in the New Testament.

Even if we try to keep our real thoughts and emotions buried, they still will become the *motivation* for all our actions, whether we are aware of it or not. Burying our hurts, memories, fears and so on does not get rid of them. Only allowing God to expose them and giving them over to Him, does.

Example: Twenty Years of Buried Hurt

Francie wrote to me several years ago after she had attended a retreat where I had spoken. She shared how much she hated the "Inner Court Ritual" part of the *Be Ye Transformed* message. She told she had such a hard time with these principles, but she wasn't really sure why. Even after she left the retreat, she just couldn't get the study off her mind. Finally, she decided to ask God to expose why she was so upset. "Let's see if this really works," she sarcastically thought to herself. Then she went through these steps.

God answered Francie's prayer, exposing exactly why she was so upset. He showed her that she still had tremendous resentment and bitterness towards her first husband, who had left her some 20 years before. God showed her that she was reacting to these Inner Court Ritual principles out of those past hurts—she never wanted to think about that man again.

Francie thought she had dealt with all her hurt feelings years ago. In reality, all she had done was bury those negative emotions, and for twenty years she had carried them around with her. After wrestling with God for some time, she decided to go through these steps all over again. Only this time, she wanted to deal with her hurts the proper way. So she asked God to expose her soul.

After sincerely going through the Inner Court Ritual, she said she experienced such a freedom that even her new husband commented that evening, "What's going on! You look so happy!" Even our physical countenance will be changed when we learn to renew our minds and become freed from things we have carried around for years. She sat right down and wrote me a sixteen-page letter about what the Lord had shown her.

A few weeks later, after I had responded to her, I got another ten-page letter from Francie, telling me of the most exciting miracle of all. Five years previously, she had suffered a major heart attack during an operation. Since then she had been in constant pain and on a heavy dosage of heart medication. When she made the choice to let go of the horrible feelings of hate for her first husband, God supernaturally healed her heart condition. She wrote me that she has had no more pain and has not taken any more heart medication since. The doctor has confirmed her healing and he is totally baffled. I don't believe we realize how closely tied our spiritual and our psychological well-being is with our physical bodies. Healing in one often does affect the other.

So in order to be truly free of our past and be able to act out of God's Life, we must get rid of our ungodly thoughts and feelings the proper way by allowing God to expose them, by looking squarely at them and calling them for what they are, and then by choosing to give these things back over to God and be rid of them forever. (Psalm 103:12)

Confess and Repent (Lavers of Bronze)

The second step of the Inner Court Ritual is to <u>confess and repent of all that the Holy Spirit has shown us</u>. And, in addition we must, by faith, <u>unconditionally forgive anyone who has wronged us</u>, just as God has unconditionally forgiven us.

If we have caught the negative, ungodly thought and we have <u>not</u> entertained it or mulled it over, then we can skip this step of confession and repentance because no sin or disobedience is involved. Once we give that negative thought to God, we can once again walk by faith.

If, however, we know that we have held on to self-centered thoughts and emotions for a while, mulled them over and entertained them, then we <u>do</u> need to confess them as sin. They have already quenched God's Spirit in us and separated us from Him and we need to repent of them, i.e., change our mind about holding onto them, and choose to go give them to God.

This step of confession and repentance is our own responsibility. As 1 John 1:9 teaches, "If *we confess* our sins, [then] *He is faithful and just to forgive* us our sins...." (emphasis added)

We must acknowledge that what we have done, ignorantly or knowingly, has quenched God's Spirit in us. We need to confess "ownership" of our negative thoughts and emotions and then simply choose to *turn around* from following them.

An Example: "I Confess I Am Depressed"

For example, if we are depressed, and I am assuming that this depression is emotional and mental, and not physiologically caused, and we have been following this emotional way of thinking for some time, we can't simply say to God, "Help me with my depression," and expect Him to automatically take our sad thoughts away.

We must say, "Father, I *confess* that I am depressed (I "own" these thoughts and emotions). I confess that I have chosen to entertain these morose feelings over what You would have me do, i.e., give them to You, and it has quenched Your Spirit in me. I've sinned. I now choose to turn around; I *repent* from following what these thoughts are telling me, and I choose instead to follow what You want."

There have been many times in the past that I have given my feelings of depression to God and asked Him to please take them away. But nothing ever happened. This made feel even more depressed, because I assumed that God didn't care. Now, I realize I was omitting the most important step of all, *confessing my own responsibility and choosing to turn around from following that way of thinking*.

Remember, we are <u>not</u> responsible for changing our own feelings. We can't do that. We're only responsible to put in charge the Person who *can* change our feelings, and that is God. And, we do that by confessing we *own* the negative feelings and then, by repenting of them. After that, it's God's responsibility to change our feelings by aligning them with our faith choices.

Listen to what a young woman wrote me last week. "I was never taught how to handle conflict in Christ. I was taught to fall apart and cry myself to sleep, etc. I was always missing step #2, confessing and repenting of my own sin. I would take every thought captive and then put on the Mind of Christ. But, I would forget the most important step of all, putting off all the junk. And," she says, "there was a lot of junk in there!"

Most of us often <u>do</u> forget this critically important step of confessing and repenting, which is our own responsibility.

Forgive Others

A part of this second step of confessing and repenting of our own sins is that we must also unconditionally *forgive others* of theirs. God is often hindered from working in us and in the other person involved until we have released him.[5] And we release him by unconditionally forgiving him, whether he has asked for it or not![6]

So there are two parts to forgiveness: First, our relationship to God; and second, our relationship to the other person.

The first reason we must unconditionally forgive is because God commands it in Scripture. Mark 11:25-26 teaches, "And when ye stand praying, forgive, if ye have anything against any: that your Father also, Who is in heaven, may forgive you your trespasses. But if ye do not forgive, neither will your Father, Who is in heaven, forgive your trespasses."[7]

The second reason we are to forgive is to reconcile with that other person. When we choose to unconditionally forgive that person who has sinned against us, we will be *clean* before the Lord. Our relationship with Him will be reconciled, and we will experience His Love and forgiveness. Now if that other person comes to us and asks forgiveness, then our relationship with him will also be healed. If, however, that other person never repents or asks forgiveness, then there will be a *breach* in our relationship and only God's wise Love can operate. *We still must love him, but it will be wisely.*

Jesus gave us His own example: In Luke 23:34, as He was being crucified, He said, "Father, forgive them; for they know not what they do....."

Sometimes, to forgive what others have done to us, seems almost impossible in our own strength and ability. But, this is just another place where we can trust God for His *unconditional* Love. Scripture tells us that we can extend that unconditional forgiveness through Jesus. In other words, if we truly love God and totally give ourselves over to Him, He will strengthen us, enable us and give us the grace to genuinely forgive others. 2 Corinthians 2:10 validates that the way we forgive is "...in the person of Jesus Christ."

The process of forgiveness is like a *triangle*. We forgive others because God tells us to. He then gives us the Love and the forgiveness we need for that other person. Remember, our hurt feelings will only heal *after* we have made the faith choice to unconditionally forgive that other person, whether or not they ever come to us.[8]

An Example: Wounds From Our "Friends"

Recently someone who is very dear and very precious to me believed an *evil report* about me and angrily told many others. When I found out it was my beloved friend, I was crushed.

As Christian brothers and sisters (*friends*), Scripture says we are "...to love at all times." (Proverbs 17:17) Now, this doesn't mean sticking our heads in the sand and never taking a stand if someone we love is doing something out of line. But, if we do hear something bad about someone we love, or something that makes us angry at them, Scripture tells us clearly that we are to go to that person and ask them directly about it, "...speaking the truth in love...." (Ephesians 4:15).

My beloved friend never did that, however, nor did she confess and repent of her own error when she found out the truth. Therefore, I was left with a choice. I could choose by faith, not feelings, because I still hurt terribly over the issue, to unconditionally forgive her, thereby reconciling myself to God and opening a way for Him to work upon her, or I could hold on to my justified unforgiveness, create a breach between God and me and end up giving the enemy another handle or another hide-out in me.[9]

The Lord showed me that one of the reasons this recent incident was so very painful for me is that I still had a lot of buried debris (unforgiveness) over other Christian friends who gossiped and slandered us over our bankruptcy experience, several years ago. This latest incident was just a catalyst that triggered much deeper, hidden roots of bitterness within me.

Again, I thought I had dealt with these hurts more than seven years ago, but God showed me that deep wounds like these often take a longer period of time to heal. This recent incident just brought up more debris in the corners of my hidden chambers that God wanted swept clean. I suppose if He brought up all our deep-seated hurts at once, we probably wouldn't be able to take it. But, our God is gentle and kind and His timing is always perfect. I know in His perfect timing, He will align my feelings with the faith choices that I have made and give me His Love for this woman who wounded me.

Our Lord's Example

What does the Lord say true friendship is? He says that it's a relationship that doesn't require any explanations, and the assurance of always receiving the benefit of doubt. The Bible says a friend is one who is loyal and shuns any form of betrayal. (1 Corinthians 13)

If we are at fault in a situation, sometimes God will have us go back to the person we offended and ask forgiveness. Remember, however, each situation is different. Sometimes seeking and receiving God's forgiveness in our own hearts and minds will be enough. At other times, God will have us physically go and ask the other person's forgiveness. In each instance, we must always pray, seeking God's Will. Remember, the Lord not only promises to tell us what to do, but He also promises us to give us the strength to implement His Will.

That we must always be wise, goes without saying. A woman from one of my seminars went a friend who had hurt her terribly, telling him that she forgave him for the sin he had committed against her. Unaware that there was a problem or that he had sinned, the man was very offended. Needless to say, her forgiveness did more harm than good.

Receive God's Forgiveness

As we learn how God wants us to forgive others, it's also imperative that we learn to receive (by faith) God's forgiveness for whatever sins we may have committed. 1 John 1:9 confirms that, "If we confess our sins, *He is faithful and just to forgive us [all] our sins....*" (emphasis added)

If you have trouble believing and receiving God's forgiveness, make a list of all the Scriptures you can find on forgiveness and read them over and over again. By faith, make those contrary choices to believe what those Scriptures are saying. Remember, we walk not by *feelings*, but by *faith*. *God, in His perfect timing, will align your feelings to match what you have chosen to believe by faith.*[10]

Give All to God (Holocaust Altar)

The next essential step of the Inner Court Ritual is to give everything that God has shown us that is not of faith over to Him. God will not violate our free will by forcibly taking these things from us; we must willingly choose to hand them over to Him.

God wants us to give Him—to sacrifice to Him—everything that is not of faith, so it can be purged and cleansed by His Blood.[11] As we willingly give these things over to Him, He promises that He will take them from us, "As far as the east is from the west...." (Psalm 103:12)

I just read a fascinating verse in 2 Chronicles 7:1, "Now when Solomon had ccascd praying, thc fire came down from heaven, and consumed the burnt offering and the sacrifices, and the glory of the Lord filled the house." This reminds me of how God reaches down from heaven and removes our sin—consumes our offerings—"as far as the east is from the west."

A Miracle

So often we take for granted the incredible miracle that God really does take away both the symptoms and the root causes of our sins "as far as the east is from the west...." Do we really understand what this means?

It means that we are allowed to begin each day with a clean slate—a new, fresh start. Chuck and I were sharing last night about what a truly phenomenal gift this is. It allows us to "blow it badly" with each other, yet if we confess and repent of those things and choose to forgive each other. God really will wash us, cleanse us and heal us—even with the memory of that sin wiped away. What a miracle!

Just think, if we didn't have Christ in our lives, all our fights with loved ones, all our guilt, our failures, mistakes, ungodliness, errors, wrongs, immorality, and every sin we have ever committed would always be with us. We would try to bury them in our "hidden chambers" but they would always be there to motivate our actions. We could never get away from them or have a fresh, new start. No wonder so many relationships without Christ fail. I weep at the thought, because that miracle, that answer, that cure, that Love is there, just for the asking.[12]

Give as *Love Gifts*

Luke 11:39-41 says: "And the Lord said unto him, 'Now do ye Pharisees make clean the outside of the cup and the platter; but your inward part is full of ravening and wickedness. Ye fools, did not He that made that which is without make that which is within also? But rather give alms [give as *love gifts*] of such things as ye have [within]; and, behold [then] all things are clean unto you [without].'"

Alms in the New Testament were *love gifts* "with no strings attached." I think of giving our sins over to God just like giving Him alms. As we sacrifice or offer up to God our alms—everything that is not of faith—He, then, makes all things clean for us from the inside out.

Here's a letter I received from a precious sister in Australia who is learning to use the Mind of Christ.

"It's really interesting and exciting. If I feel terrified and I keep giving it over and over, and it won't quite go, then I pick at the past hurts as much as I understand them (and give them over to God) and inevitably I get a relief from the terrible fear and a definite move to a new and more real understanding of life. And, I'm able to see that God has moved me further out into the life I once hid from, and I can feel that yet another piece of my pride and my aloneness and fear has gone. And the real me, (that is actually not self, but God filling my emptiness—creator filling creature) is alive as never before and I have died a little more to myself and thereby, been filled with God."

Do Something Physical

In order to truly experience getting rid of the things that we give over to God, it's sometimes helpful to do something physical. A dear friend of mine writes down on a scrap of paper all her hurts, wounds—memories, whatever God has shown her is not of faith. Then she literally wraps these pieces of paper up in packages and presents them to God as love gifts.

Personally, I like to burn these scraps of paper! I write down everything I give to God and then burn that scrap of paper. I like to watch the paper being consumed, because to me it's a graphic picture of how our sins are really gone forever.

Most of the sins that God shows us are "of the flesh," and will usually go away immediately, or at least within a few days, if we are faithful to go through these cleansing steps.

Recognize the Battles

But some of the things that God will expose are long-standing strongholds of the enemy and Satan won't let go of these kinds of things easily. So don't be dismayed if certain thoughts and feelings reappear. Don't fall into the trap of thinking, "Oh, this just doesn't work for me!" Because, that's exactly what the enemy wants you to do. Recognize you are in a battle. Know you will win if you will just persevere. Luke 10:19 promises that we have authority over all the power of the enemy.

(You may want to review Chapter Fourteen, "Satan's Voice" about the critical importance of recognizing whose "voice" (whose thoughts) you are hearing. More details of this spiritual battle are covered there.)

Read God's Word (Molten Sea)

The final step in dealing with our sin is that we must <u>read God's Word.</u> God is the only One who, by His Word, can *cleanse, sanctify and heal our souls* completely. He is the only One who can replace Satan's lies with the truth.

Remember, it was at the Molten Sea that the priests actually immersed themselves bodily, in order to receive a total cleansing. They had gotten all "blood splattered" at the Holocaust altar where they sacrificed, and now, they needed a complete bathing in order to be cleansed.

In like manner, after we have confessed, repented and sacrificed all to God, we too are "bloody" and "torn apart" and in desperate need of God's complete healing power. Only God's Word can totally restore us. God is the One who washes us "...with the washing of water by the Word." (Ephesians 5:26)[13]

As I read God's Word, I literally picture myself being bathed in God's Love. One of my favorite Scriptures to read at these times is Psalm 18: "...In my distress I called upon the Lord...He heard my voice out of His temple...He bowed the heavens also, and came down...." (ver. 6 & 9)

Another suggestion: Memorize appropriate Scriptures. Often, we must go through these steps when we are away from home and we don't have our Bibles at hand. If we have memorized Scriptures, then we can bathe in His Word any where, any time.[14]

Many people ask me what Scriptures I recite or read at this point. My answer is always, "Check the outlines at the end of each chapter or see the Survival Kit Prayer at the end of this chapter. See which Scriptures minister to you and use those." Most importantly, *truth must be put back in where the lies have been removed, so that more lies don't return.* Read Luke 11:24-26.

Now we can step out in faith, knowing that God will be faithful to align our feelings with our choices, give us the Love and the Wisdom we need, and perform His Will through us.

Example: Putting It All Together

Julie came up to me after a recent seminar and said: "Okay, Nan, this is great material. I love the class. But I need one last simple example of how all these steps work together. Can you please tell me an example that points out all the steps?"

Here, then, is a hypothetical story which shows all these steps in action:

Your unsaved mother-in-law comes over for dinner. You are sitting across from her at the table when all of a sudden, in front of everyone, she makes some very derogatory comments about your dinner, your house, your kids and so on.

At first you get very flustered, then humiliated, then hurt, and then just plain angry. At this point what should you do? Do you continue to sit there and hypocritically smile at her when you would really like to sock her and tell her off?

Remember, we are not responsible for the original ungodly thoughts when they first come in. *What we choose to do with those thoughts produces the sin or not.* Now, if we do nothing with our negative thoughts, they will automatically stir up bitterness and resentment, which will definitely affect our choices and, eventually, our actions.

If I were in this sensitive situation, I'd deal with my angry thoughts right then. I'd excuse myself from the table, then I would go to wherever I could be alone with the Lord (my bedroom, the bathroom, my car). I'd want to catch those hurts and negative thoughts before they are programmed in and before I act out of them!

The first step, then, is to <u>recognize and acknowledge the negative thoughts and feelings</u> I am experiencing, so I can deal with them. Remember, I can't deal with them unless I know what they are.

In the "prayer closet" then (wherever that might be), I'd tell God that my mother-in-law's remark really hurt. "It is humiliating and embarrassing every time she puts me down in front of everyone." I'd go on and express and name all my genuine feelings about her. I'd even cry if I needed to. In other words, I would <u>experience my real emotions</u>.

At the same time, I would also ask God if there are any *root causes* as to why I'm reacting this way. Perhaps my mother-in-law has done this same thing numerous times before, but I have never really dealt with it. Perhaps, I have simply buried my real feelings. I'd ask God to expose everything He wanted to from my hidden chambers regarding this situation.

If God shows me that I have felt this way for years over my mother-in-law's insults but have never properly dealt with my sin, either out of disobedience or ignorance, I would obviously need to <u>confess</u> that my thoughts and feelings were sin.

At this point, I would need to change my mind—turn around—and <u>repent</u> from following these self-centered thoughts and emotions even if they might be *justified* by the world's standards.

At this same time, I would need to <u>unconditionally forgive</u> my mother-in-law so that I could be reconciled to God and that He could be released to work in her life as well as my own.

Then, I would <u>give all the hurts</u>, bitterness, resentment, anger, justified or not, and anything else that God has shown me over to God, asking Him to purge these things from me "as far as the east is from the west."

Finally, I would <u>get into His Word</u>, reading a few of my favorite passages, so that His soothing truth could go back into the hidden chambers where the lies have been.

Now, even though I might not *feel* any different at that moment, I would know by faith that I am now a cleansed vessel and God's Life has been freed to flow through me once again. At this time, I would go back to the table, expecting God to love my mother-in-law through me.

Hebrews 10:22 states, "Let us draw near with a true heart in full assurance of faith, having our hearts sprinkled from an evil conscience, and our bodies washed with pure water."

Praise Him (Golden Altar)

After we have finished the Inner Court Ritual, something very important we should do is now fill our thoughts with praise. This is exactly what the Levites did after the priests finished their Inner Court Ritual. When the priests returned to the Holy Place, *they changed their clothes*, put incense on the Golden Altar, and then they joined the Levites with singing and praising God.

We, too, after we have read God's Word, can change our clothes—we have *put off* the old man and *put on* Christ. We have exchanged lives with Him—we have given Him our life, and He has given us His! Now, we can go on and praise and worship Him in the "beauty of His Holiness." We can praise Him for who He is and know that He "will work all things together" for our best.[15]

(Romans 8:28, by the way, doesn't speak to those who only emotionally love God, but only to those who totally give themselves over to Him. God will maneuver and orchestrate circumstances for those who completely surrender themselves to Him.)[16]

Summary

So, in summary, the four *essential* steps of the Inner Court Ritual are:

1) **Recognizing and acknowledging** the negative thoughts, emotions and desires that have just occurred in our lives. We are not to vent these thoughts and feelings, nor bury them. We are to get alone with God and acknowledge our emotions. We should name how we are feeling and ask Him to expose the real root causes of our ungodly thoughts and feelings.

2) **Confessing and repenting** of any negative thoughts and feelings that are "not of faith" or that we have held onto for awhile. We must choose to "turn around" from following what these things are telling us and choose instead to follow what God is saying. We should then **unconditionally forgive** anyone else involved in the situation. God then will forgive our sins.

3) **Giving over to God** all that He has shown us, not only our conscious negative thoughts and emotions, but also their root causes. He, then, will purge our sin and reconcile us to Himself.

4) **Reading God's Word**. We must make sure to replace the lies in our hidden chambers with the Truth—the truth of His Word. God then, will cleanse and heal our soul with "the washing of the water of His Word."

This is how the Inner Court Ritual works. These steps might seem like a lot to remember now because they are all so new. But, I promise you, if you are faithful to continue to confess, repent and give all to God, these steps will become first nature to you because you will soon see there really is no other way!

This Inner Court Ritual is again "that readiness to revenge all disobedience" that 2 Corinthians 10:6 talks about. Following these steps is also how we "resist the devil" as James 4:7 exhorts us.

"Just Give It to God"

For years, whenever I had a problem, people would tell me, "Well, just give it to God." But I had never understood exactly what that meant...*until now*! I go through these steps daily and sometimes two or three times a day if I am dealing with a particularly difficult situation. This is how I survive and this is how I *"keep alive against all odds."*

In the back of this chapter I have enclosed my own daily prayer, my *"Survival Kit Prayer."* I wrote this when I first started to practice these steps years ago. I found I really needed something to lead me to the feet of Jesus and to help me go through the Inner Court Ritual.

Some have taken the basic content of my prayer, shortened it, made it personal and then written it on 3x5 cards. This is a great idea! So, if this prayer doesn't suit your needs, write your own. Keep it with you at all times, because, believe me, you'll need it. (Others have suggested making a "word game" out of these four Inner Court Ritual steps. One person named them 1) **See it**; 2) **Say it**; 3) **Send it**; and, 4) **Supplant it**. Another called them 1) **Recognize it**; 2) **Repent of it**; 3) **Rocket it up**; and, 4) **Replace it**. If these help, use them.)

At those moments when we are dealing with doubt, hurt, fear, pride, bitterness, resentment, anger, and any other negative feelings, we often are too emotional "to take every thought captive to the obedience of Christ." And we need something to help us along.[17] Having the Inner Court Ritual or this "Survival Kit Prayer" handy will help you through many tough times.

Be an Example

Be open and frank with your children when you use these steps. Give them an example and a model to follow. They, too, have hurts and fears and insecurities just as we do. And if they see that you use this prayer and that it works for you, then they'll want it too.

Keep a notebook or journal of your adventure with God. Date the entries, especially when you give something over to Him. That way when Satan comes along and tries to counterfeit old feelings and thoughts, you can point to the entry and say, "That has already been handled!" "I might not feel it yet, but by faith I believe it."

In Conclusion: "For Me to Live is Christ"

See **CHART 24** (on the facing page).

When we have honestly followed these steps, God promises us that our minds have been renewed, whether we feel like it or not. We have put off the garbage of our own thinking and we have put on the Mind of Christ. *The Spirit of the Lord* has come forth from the Holy of Holies of our hearts and has given us not only His *Agape* Love, but also *His Wisdom, His Understanding, His Counsel and Might*. We're experiencing *intimate Knowledge of God's Life* as our own and we're *walking in the Fear of God*.

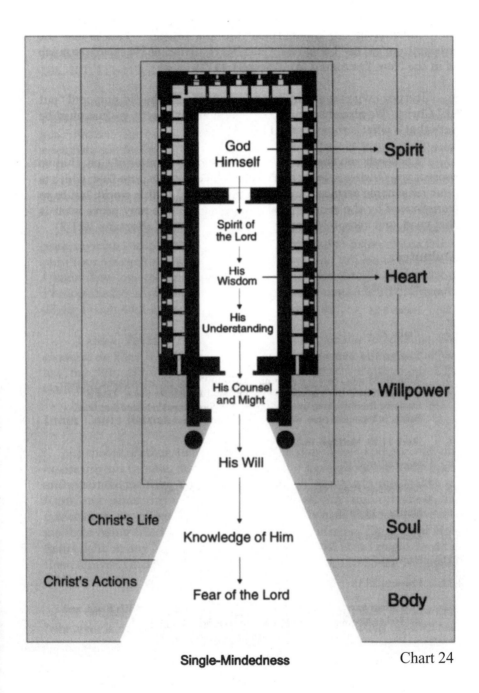

Chart 24

This is the renewing, the equipping and the girding that we must do daily in order to be "transformed into His Image." This is also the preparation or the "being ready" for His return that He speaks so much about in the New Testament (Matthew 24:44)[18].

It's our own responsibility to daily *put off* the old man and *put on* Christ. We already possess God's Life in our hearts, we just must be sure that is what shows forth in our souls.

"I beseech you therefore, brethren, by the mercies of God, that ye present your bodies a living sacrifice, holy, acceptable unto God, which is your reasonable service. And be not conformed to this world, but *be ye transformed* by the renewing of your mind, that ye may prove what is that good, and acceptable, and perfect, will of God." (Romans 12:1-2)

Endnotes:

1.   Exodus 38:8

2.   Isaiah 3:24

3.   Psalm 25:10

4.   Romans 7:15, 19

5.   John 20:23 says there is a supernatural "bond" that occurs between the one who committed the trespass and the one who will not forgive it. God is hindered from working until unconditional forgiveness releases that bond. Satan, in the mean time, works havoc (2 Corinthians 2:10-11).

6.   Mark 11:26; Matthew 18:35

7.   Matthew 6:14-15

8.   See Chapter Four, "Only When They Come to Me First."

9.   Matthew 18:28-35

10.   Ecclesiastes 3:11a

11.   Hebrews 9:14

12.   Proverbs 28:13

13.   Two things have happened: our hearts have been cleansed by His Blood; and our bodies have been washed by His Word. (Hebrews 10:22)

14.   See Chapter Five, "Hiding God's Word in our Hearts."

15.   Romans 8:28

16.   Isaiah 26:3

17.   Psalm 40:12b

18.   Matthew 25:10

SURVIVAL KIT PRAYER

PRAISE HIM: Psalms 8, 9, 19, 33, 34, 47, 48, 66, 89, 93, 96, 98, 100, 101-105, 107, 111-113, 115, 118, 134-136, 138, 144-150.

I love you, Lord God, with all my heart, all my will, and all my soul. I pray my actions today will show and prove my love for You. *I praise you, Father,* for who You are and thank You for this (situation, circumstance, feeling, opportunity, etc.) because I know You have allowed it for my learning and my growth, so I might come to intimately know You better and be more conformed into Your image. (Matthew 22:37; Hebrews 13:15; 1 Thessalonians 5:18; Deuteronomy 8:16c)

I choose to "*present [my body] as a living sacrifice.*" I choose to set aside my own thoughts, emotions, and desires and to listen to and follow only Your Voice (Your Word), no matter what You tell me to do because I know You love me and I am precious in your sight. (Romans 12:1-2; Philippians 3:8-15; Psalm 91; Psalm 18; 2 Corinthians 3:5; 10:5; Proverbs 23:4b; Isaiah 43:2-5; 54:10; 55: 8-9; Jeremiah 31:3)

I know, Father, that You will never leave me nor forsake me. So *I choose to do Your Will,* Your pleasure, above my own at all costs, for You are my life. (Philippians 2:5-9; Matthew 26:39; Philippians 1:21; Galatians 2.20; Deuteronomy 30:19-20; Hebrews 13:5)

Inner Court Ritual

I choose, Father, to allow You to search my heart and my soul, and *expose any sin* (grease, fat), any barriers that have quenched Your Spirit and separated me from You. Show me my *self* (my hurts, my doubts, my fears, my pride, my anger, my insecurities, my unforgiveness, my criticalness, my bitternesses), any self-centeredness that has prevented me from being filled with Your Life to give to others. Shine your Holy Spirit light on any *root causes* for these things, so that I might be rid of them forever. (Isaiah 1:15; 59:2; Psalm 26:2; 51:10; 139: 23-24; Nehemiah 4:10)

I *confess*, Father, that I am separated from You. I know that "whatever is not of faith is sin," and I have sinned by letting my own self-centered thoughts and uncontrolled feelings consume me and motivate me. I have chosen to hang on to these things and follow them rather than follow what You want. I confess also that I have tried in my own ability and strength to work things out. I have not relied upon You. I have not obeyed and trusted You, and that is sin. (Romans 14: 23; Psalm 51:1-4; Proverbs 28:13; Isaiah 1:16; Psalm 141:8)

I *repent* of these sins. I desire to turn around from following my own thoughts and feelings. I know if I don't release them to You, I will continue to act out of them. And I don't want to do that. I ask You, dearest Father, to forgive me for my sin, as I choose to *forgive* those who have hurt me and let me down. (1 John 1:9; Matthew 6:14-15; 18:21-22, 35; Isaiah 1:18b) **(Ten Bronze Lavers)**

Father, I choose to sacrifice and *give all these things* that You have shown me over to You and I ask you to purge them from me "as far as the east is from the west." (Psalm 103:12; Philippians 3:8; 2 Timothy 2:21; Isaiah 1:25) **(Holocaust Altar)**

I trust You, by faith, to *cleanse, sanctify, and heal* me by the "washing of the water of Your Word." I receive, by faith, Your forgiveness of my sins, Your renewing of my mind and Your healing of my soul. I trust You, Father, to now change my feelings and my emotions to align with the choices I have made and to make me genuine. (Romans 12:2; Ephesians 5:26; Hebrews 10:22; Psalm 103: 2-5; Psalm 119) **(Molten Sea)**

* * * * *

By faith, I know that Your Life has now been freed to come forth from my heart and fill my soul. (Colossians 3:8, 10; Ephesians 3:17-19; 4:22-24; 5:1-2; Romans 6:13; 13:14; John 4:14; Philippians 1:21; Zechariah 3:4; Isaiah 52:1)

Also, by faith, I believe You will now openly hear and answer my prayers, because they are "according to Your Will" and not my own. (1 John 5:14-15)

By faith, I have done all that You have asked, so I can now stand firm against the enemy. Even if my feelings and my circumstances seem like nothing at all has changed, I will keep on choosing to walk by faith knowing that *You will do what You promise.* (Romans 4:21; Ephesians 6:10-18; Isaiah 40:29-31; James 1: 12; 2 Corinthians 10:3-6)

My faith is in Your faithfulness, Father. I love You. (Isaiah 26:3-4; 1 John 5:4b; 3:22)

Scriptural References:

Chapter Fifteen

Survival Kit — Essential Steps (*The Inner Court Ritual*) (CHART 23)
A. These are the critical steps that we need to take each time we make a choice that is "not of faith" (Psalm 40:12). This how we "revenge all disobedience" (2 Corinthians 10:5-6); how we "resist the devil" (James 4:7; 1 Peter 5:8-9); and how we "renew our minds" (Romans 12:2)
B. These are the exact steps that the Priests took in the Inner Court of the Temple in order to deal with their sin (See Chapter Thirteen)
C. If something has just occurred that has caused us to make a "wrong response" ("a stink") (Isaiah 3:24), then these are the steps we must take in order to "put off" the garbage in our thinking and "put on" Christ (Ephesians 4:22-24; Colossians 3:9-10)
   1. We are to recognize and experience the negative thoughts and emotions that are coming in
      a. Ask God to expose our soul (the symptoms, as well as the root causes) (Proverbs 20:27; Isaiah 1:16, 18-19)
      b. Get alone with God. Read: Psalms 18; 19:12; 23; 40:8; 91; 119;2; 139:23-24; 142:7; Job 12:22; 1 Corinthians 4:5)
      c. Acknowledge the negative thoughts and feelings that are coming in (2 Corinthians 13:5)
         . Be truthful like David was (Psalms 55:15; 109:6-20)
         . Describe what you are feeling—it's part of the healing process; David did (Psalm 51:3-4) and he still was "a man after God's own heart" (Acts 13:22)
         . Ask God to expose the *root causes* of our thoughts and emotions (Proverbs 20:27: Psalms 119:9-11; 139:23-24; Job 12:22; 1 Corinthians 4:5)
      d. We must *see* our own sin, so we know what to give over to God (Psalm 139:23-24). We can't give something over, if we don't know what it is
      e. We <u>all</u> have negative thoughts and feelings. The sin occurs with what we choose to do with those thoughts (Romans 7:15, 19; James 1:12-15, 21: Galatians 5:16)
         . Entertaining and mulling over a negative thought is sin (Matt. 5: 28)
         . When we know what we are supposed to do (give that thought to God) and we refuse to do it, we sin (James 4:17)
      f. The only way we will have victory over these sins, is by making faith choices (Romans 7:25; Galatians 5:16; 1 John 5:4)
         . We have three choices as to what to do with our ungodly thoughts and emotions (vent them, bury them or give them to God)
         . We can't hold on to these thoughts, without their eventually becoming the motivation for all our actions
      g. The Spirit of God is the One who searches out all the hidden chambers (Proverbs 20:27). We are not to become overly preoccupied with our *inner self.*
   2. We are to *confess and repent* of all that God shows us (Proverbs 1:23; 28: 13; Isaiah 1:16; Ezekiel 18:30b; James 4:8-10; 1 John 1:9; Acts 8:22a; Colossians 3:13; John 20:23; Jeremiah 3:13; Hebrews 12:1; Ezekiel 20: 43; Psalm 32:5; 38: 5-9); and *unconditionally forgive* anyone who has

wronged us (Matthew 6:14-15; 18:32-35; Colossians 3:13; 2 Corinthians 2:10-11; Luke 23:34; Mark 11:25-26; John 13:14-15; Ephesians 4:32) (**Lavers of Bronze**)

    a. It's our own responsibility to confess (1 John 1:9); God then forgives

    b. We need to confess ownership of our negative thoughts and emotions

    c. We are <u>not</u> responsible to change our feelings, but simply give them to God and allow Him to change them for us (Psalm 103:12)

    d. We need to unconditionally forgive others

       . God is hindered from working in us and in the other parties, until we release them (and we do that by unconditionally forgiving them) (John 20:23)

       . Then Satan won't have a "handle" in us any longer (Matthew 18:28-35)

    e. There are two steps to forgiveness:

       . Our relationship to God (Matthew 18:35; Mark 11:25-26). If we don't forgive others of their sins, He won't forgive us of our sin (Ephesians 4:32; Colossians 3:13)

       . Our relationship to others (2 Corinthians 2:10) and the reconciliation of that relationship

    f. Jesus gave us His example of forgiveness (Luke 23:34)

       . We are to love at all times (Proverbs 17:17)

       . We are to speak the truth in love (Ephesians 4:15)

    g. Most painful sin is *gossip* (Exodus 20:16)

       . Gossip is a form of betrayal (Leviticus 19:16; Proverbs 11:13; 18:8; 20:19; 26:20-22)

       . The Lord gave us His example to follow (John 8:7)

    h. We are to receive God's forgiveness (1 John 1:9; Proverbs 28:13; Ecclesiastes 3:11)

3. We are to sacrifice or *give over to God* all that He has shown us is "not of faith" (Luke 11:39-41; Colossians 3:5-9; 1 Peter 5:7; Galatians 5:24; Romans 6:11-13; 2 Timothy 2:21; Ephesians 5:2; 1 John 1:7) (**Holocaust Altar**)

    a. We are to give Him, not only our surface sins, but also their root causes to be purged by His Blood (Hebrews 9:24)

    b. He will take away our sins "as far as the east is from the west" (Psalm 103:12)

    c. We are to give them to Him as "love gifts" (alms) with no strings attached (Luke 11:39-41)

    d. Then, He will make all things clean for us and will align our feelings to match our choices (1 John 3:21)

4. Next, we are to bathe in and *read God's Word* and replace the lies with the truth (Luke 11:24-26; Ephesians 5:26; John 15:3; 17:17; James 1:21; 2 Peter 1:4; Psalm 19:7-8; 107:20; 119:9) (**Molten Sea**)

    a. Only God's Word can cleanse, sanctify and heal our souls (Psalm 18; 51:7; 107:20; 119:9; Philippians 3:13)

    b. Two things happen when we read God's Word: our hearts are cleansed and our bodies are washed (Hebrews 10:22)

    c. We should memorize Scriptures (Proverbs 24:4) to make retaining His Word easier

D. After the priests bathed in the Molten Sea, they took hot coals from the Holocaust Altar, went back into the Holy Place, changed their clothes, put incense on the Golden Altar and began to *praise God*

    1. We know at this point, He <u>will</u> work all things together for good (Romans 8:28)

2. We know that our prayers will be according to His Will (Isaiah 26:3) because they are "in His Name" (in His Character, Image) (John 16:23)

Conclusion: "For me to live is Christ" (Philippians 1:21)   (CHART 24)

A. At this point, our minds have been totally renewed; we have *put off* the garbage in our thinking and *put on* the Mind of Christ (Ephesians 4:22-24; 5: 18; 2 Corinthians 8:11-12,19; 10:5-6; Mark 10:21; Matthew 19:21)
   1. We are able to prove in our actions "what is the good, acceptable and perfect will of God" (Romans 12:2; Ephesians 5:10)
   2. We are experiencing all the fruit of the Spirit (Ephesians 5:9; 1 John 4:17; Philippians 4:7)
   3. We are "single-minded"—experiencing intimate Knowledge of God and walking in Fear of Him (Isaiah 11:2-3)
   4. Our lights are burning (Isaiah 62:1; Luke 12:35; Matthew 5:14)
   5. This is the *preparation, the being ready* (the equipping, the girding) that we must do daily in order to be transformed (Luke 11:36; Matthew 24: 42-47; 25:10; 2 Peter 3:14, 17)
B. We can now walk by faith (1 Corinthians 2:5; 2 Corinthians 5:7) knowing that God has cleansed us and transformed us into His Image (Hosea 2:19-20; Philippians 1:21; Romans 8:1; Hebrews 8:12; 10:22; 1 Peter 1:22a)

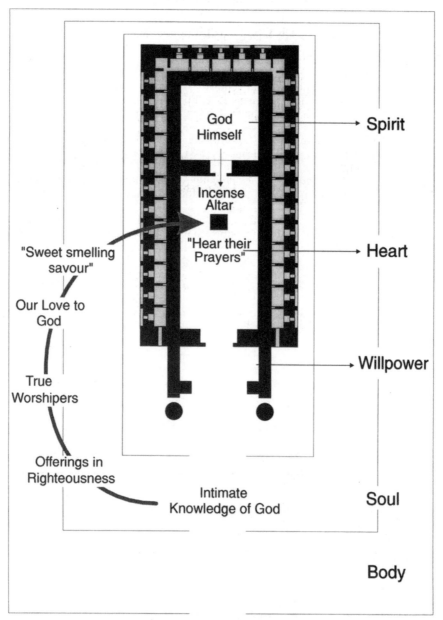

Results of the Renewed Mind   Chart 25

Chapter Sixteen
Results of a Renewed Mind

A renewed mind produces many results and it would take another complete book to cover all of them. However, there are just a few important highlights that I would like to mention before we close.

Please look at **CHART 25** (on the facing page), and visually note some of the blessings that occur as a result of a renewed mind.

Offerings in Righteousness

Just as the priests in Solomon's Temple after they had washed their hands in the Lavers, sacrificed at the Holocaust Altar, bathed bodily in the Molten Sea and changed to new clothes in the Holy Place, could come boldly up to the Golden Altar of Incense to present their offerings and prayers, we, too, after we have renewed our minds and put on our new clothes—Christ's Life, can come boldly in, worship and adore God at the altar of our hearts and present our offerings and prayers.

As Isaiah 61:3 describes it, we have exchanged "the ashes of our lives" for the "beauty of His."

Our offerings are now acceptable to God because they are "offerings in *[His] righteousness.*" "And He shall sit like a refiner and purifier of silver; and He shall purify the sons of Levi, and purge them as gold and silver, that they may offer unto the Lord an offering in righteousness. Then shall the offering of Judah and Jerusalem be pleasant unto the Lord, as in the days of old, and as in former years. And *I will come near to you...*" (Malachi 3:3-5) When we "...count all things but loss, for the excellency of the knowledge of Christ Jesus..."[1] we display not our own righteousness, but the righteousness which is of God by faith.

True Worshipers and Lovers of God

Another result of a renewed mind is that, in God's eyes and according to His Word, we are true worshipers and lovers of God. True worshipers of God worship Him in spirit and in truth. "The hour cometh, and now is, when the true worshipers shall worship the Father in spirit and in truth: for the Father seeketh such to worship Him. God is a Spirit, and they that worship Him must worship Him in spirit and in truth." (John 4:23-24)

These are the ones who are the true "lovers of God" because they bring the Love that was originally placed in their hearts by God when they were first born again, now full circle back to Him as *love offerings*.[2] This, to me, is what Psalm 29:2 means when it says, "...worship the Lord in the beauty of holiness." It's beautiful, because it's God's Holiness, His Love and His Life.

Sweet Smelling Savor

The aroma from these offerings come before the Lord as a sweet-smelling fragrance and are pleasant and acceptable to Him because they are of <u>His</u> Savor and <u>His</u> Scent and not of our own. Remember Jeremiah 48:11, which says, if our "taste" (our thinking) is renewed, then our "scent" (our lives) will also be changed. The "stink" of self-life will have been put off and the sweet-smelling savor of Christ's Life will be manifested.

Listen to 2 Corinthians 2:14: "Now thanks be unto God, who always causeth us to triumph in Christ, and maketh manifest the savor of His knowledge by us in every place."

An Example: "Where's it From?"

There's a strange yet very beautiful story that happened to a dear friend of mine about 20 years ago, as she presented her offerings and prayers for our dear friend, Diana Bantlow, who was dying. (See Diana's full story in Chapter Seven, "A Book of Remembrance.")

The week before Diana's death, many of us took turns staying up all night, praying and interceding for her. My friend, Karen, had been faithful to do this as often as she possibly could.

One night, in the middle of the night, as Karen was kneeling before the fireplace praying for Diana, she began to smell a sweet-smelling savor, very much like perfume. At first, she thought it might be her own imagination so she put it out of her mind and just kept on praying. But when the sweet smell became so strong that she couldn't keep focused on her prayers, she stopped to search her house for its source. However, when she found nothing to explain the overpowering aroma, she woke up her husband to see if he, too, smelled it.

He told her she was crazy and he rolled back over to sleep. But when he, too, began to smell the perfume that Karen was talking about, he immediately got out of bed and began to search the house. He spent about an hour trying to discover where the sweet smell was coming from, but to no avail. Finally, he was so moved by what he was experiencing that he joined Karen in prayer for Diana.

When the two of them finished praying, the husband went directly back to bed. Karen, however, needed to spend a few minutes in the bathroom getting ready for bed. After not more than ten minutes, Karen noticed, as she passed by the living room on her way to bed, the fire was still burning, but the perfume smell had gone. She walked around the house to see if she might be mistaken, but no, the sweet smelling savor was gone.

"For from the rising of the sun even unto the going down of the same, My Name shall be great among the [nations], and *in every place incense shall be offered unto My Name*, and a pure offering; for My Name shall be great among the [nations]...." (Malachi 1:11, emphasis added)

Acts 10:4 tells us that "...Our alms [our love offerings] come up [before the Lord] [as a sweet-smelling savor and] as a memorial before God."

Prayers Heard

Just as the priests burst into prayer after they had put incense on the Golden Altar, we too, after we have changed our clothes—put on Christ, can be confident that God will now hear our prayers. We have exchanged lives with God so our prayers will now be according to His Will and in His Name—in His Image, His Character.

1 John 5:14-15 says that, "This is the confidence that we have in Him, that, if we ask anything *according to His Will*, He heareth us: and if we know that He hears us, whatsoever we ask, we know that we have the petitions that we desired of Him."

"...Verily, verily, I say unto you, whatsoever ye shall ask the Father *in my Name*, He will give it to you" (John 16:23, emphasis added), "...and in every place incense shall be offered unto My Name, and a pure offering: for My Name shall be great among the [nations]...." (Malachi 1:11)

Walking in Truth and Love

A couple of other results of mind renewal are: not only experiencing the *Agape* Love of God[3], but also experiencing all the facets of the Mind of Christ. By faith, we now have God's Wisdom, His Understanding, His Counsel and Strength helping us to make godly choices. We'll be experiencing intimate Knowledge of God and walking in Fear of Him. (Isaiah 11:1-2)

We will be experiencing the "fulness of God," which is the goal and purpose of our being called as Christians. What is the "fulness of God"? (Ephesians 3:19) It's experiencing God's Life, His supernatural Love and His Mind, in place of our own. It's a complete exchange of life. We have given God ours—He has given us *His*! It's His Character, His Image and His Fulness that we will be experiencing and passing on. God is not just *in* our lives anymore, **He is our Life**.[4]

In like manner, remember what the original purpose for Solomon's Temple was? It was to manifest and show forth His Name.[5]

"I am crucified with Christ; nevertheless I live; yet not I, but Christ liveth in me: and the life which I now live in the flesh I live by the faith [faithfulness] of the Son of God, Who loved me, and gave Himself for me." (Galatians 2:20)

Seeing From God's Perspective

Another result of a renewed mind is that we'll be able to see all things that happen to us from God's perspective (His viewpoint), and not get buried in our own emotional outlook.

Remember the eagle that we also spoke of in Chapter Two? We said that it's only after the eagle has shed his old feathers that he actually receives new strength to soar above his enemies. In like manner, only after we have renewed our minds by putting off all the garbage in our thinking and putting on the Mind of Christ, do we receive God's strength both to soar above our enemies and to see our circumstances from His perspective.

These are the true overcomers. *Overcoming* simply means freedom from self, freedom from our circumstances, freedom from other's responses, and freedom from Satan's deceptions.

The Full Armor of God (Keep in mind **Chart 12**, page 191.)

One of the most important results of a renewed mind is that we will have on the *full* Armor of God. *God* is the One who furnishes us with the armor; however *we* are the ones who must constantly choose to put it on. Romans 13:12 tells us that we are to *cast off the works of darkness* and continually *put on the Armor of Light, with no dark part.*

It's exciting because each piece of armor listed in Ephesians 6 lines up perfectly with our own internal architecture—spirit, heart, willpower, soul and body. Let's read Ephesians 6:13-19 and see God's Armor of Light perhaps in a different perspective than we have before.

Ephesians 6:13: "WHEREFORE TAKE UNTO YOU THE WHOLE ARMOR OF GOD, THAT YE MAY BE ABLE TO WITHSTAND IN THE EVIL DAY, AND HAVING DONE *ALL*, TO STAND."

This verse teaches that the only way we can *stand* in the battle against the enemy of our souls, is by having on the *whole* armor of God (i.e., the complete Armor of Light, with "no dark part"). There's no way we can put on just a *few* pieces of armor and be protected. This Scripture exhorts us to put on the *whole armor*—every piece.

Verse 14: "STAND THEREFORE, HAVING YOUR LOINS GIRT ABOUT WITH TRUTH...."

This speaks of the *new Spirit* (or new power source, life source or energy source) that we receive when we are born again. Remember, God's Holy Spirit and His Word together are spoken of as the *truth*. Truth is what we must have securely "fastened" about our loins. *Loins* in Scripture are spoken of as the source of our procreation—the energizing source that brings *new life* into being. And, it is God's Spirit and His Word throughout Scripture that quickens new life in us. "It is *the Spirit that giveth life*; the flesh profiteth nothing. *The words that I speak unto you* [God's Words, His Truth], *they are spirit*, and they are life." (John 6:63)[6]

"AND HAVING ON THE BREASTPLATE OF RIGHTEOUSNESS,"

In 1 Thessalonians 5:8, Paul amplifies the above verse by saying, "...putting on the breastplate of faith and Love...." This breastplate refers to the righteousness and the Holiness that we receive by faith in Him—God's Righteousness, not our own. (Romans 10:10)[7] This also symbolizes the *new Heart* that we receive as a result of our new birth—God's eternal Life in us,[8] His Love and His Thoughts and His Power.

Verse 15: "AND YOUR FEET SHOD WITH THE PREPARATION OF THE GOSPEL OF PEACE,"

The new *willpower* that God gives us at our new birth prepares and equips our souls (our feet) with the gospel of peace. Our supernatural willpower is God's Authority and His Power to "put off" the debris, dirt and filth of our own lives, and to put on Christ.

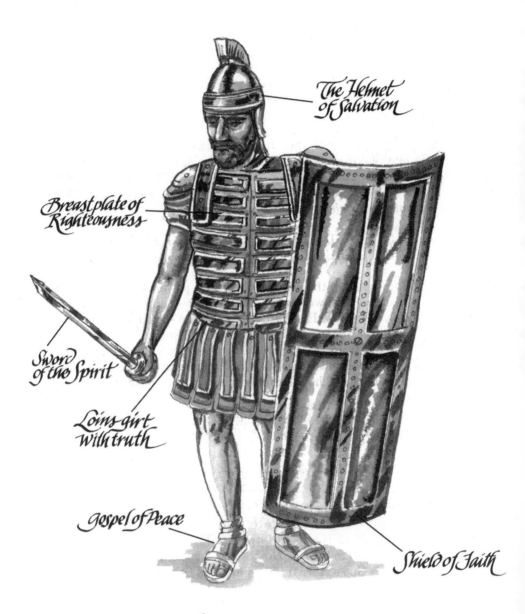

The Helmet of Salvation

Breastplate of Righteousness

Sword of the Spirit

Loins girt with truth

Gospel of Peace

Shield of Faith

The Armor of God

In other words, our willpower "shods" our feet (our souls), for walking. Remember in John 13:8-10 when Peter says to Jesus, "Thou shalt never wash my feet." Jesus answers him, "If I wash thee not [your feet], thou hast no part with me." Jesus is saying that unless we allow Him to daily *wash our feet* (our souls), we won't know Him intimately and we'll have no part of His Life.

Verse 16: "*ABOVE ALL*, TAKE THE SHIELD OF FAITH, WHEREWITH YE SHALL BE ABLE TO QUENCH ALL THE FIERY DARTS OF THE WICKED."

This verse speaks of our *free choice*. Remember, there are two parts to our willpower: our new, supernatural willpower (God's Will and His Power) and our free choice. It's possible, however, to possess God's supernatural Authority and Power and yet, never choose to use it. This Scripture tells us that "above all," only our constant *faith choices* will shield, cover and protect us from the attacks of the enemy.

Did you know that the shields that the Roman soldiers used were almost the size of a door? This shield was so effective and so strong, protecting the warrior so completely, that the enemy's arrows were not able to penetrate it.

So it is with our choices. The only way we can protect ourselves from the enemy's arrows is by choosing to trust God and what He has promised, regardless of what we think or feel. If we don't make these *faith choices*, but simply go along with the tide of our emotions, then our shield will be down and we'll open ourselves up for the devil's schemes.

Only our faith choices that will allow us to be *overcomers*. "For whatsoever is born of God overcometh the world; and this is the victory that overcometh the world, even our faith."[9] (1 John 5:4)

Verse 17: "AND TAKE THE HELMET OF SALVATION..."

Salvation occurs in *our souls* and it means *to deliver, to bring into safety, to save or to heal*. In the long-term spiritual sense, salvation means *freedom from the penalty of sin*, which is death. In the short-term spiritual sense, salvation means *freedom from the power of sin* that continually wants to control our lives. As we put on that helmet of salvation over our "reined in" self-life, we'll be freed from the power of sin's attacks and God's Life will be freed to come forth.[10]

"...AND THE SWORD OF THE SPIRIT, WHICH IS THE WORD OF GOD"

Ephesians 6 is now referring to outward things that we must do in order to walk in the Spirit—things that we do in *our bodies*. One thing that's imperative, is to always remember to carry *God's two-edged Sword* (His written Word in our hands and His Holy Spirit in our hearts). Jeremiah 51:20 talks about God and His Word being like our "battle ax."

As we have said many times, God's Word and His Spirit always work along- side each other, confirming and validating one another. Ezekiel 12:25 says, *God will always perform His Word by His Spirit.*[11]

Verse 18: "PRAYING ALWAYS, WITH ALL PRAYER AND SUPPLICATION IN THE SPIRIT AND WATCHING THEREUNTO WITH ALL PERSEVERANCE AND SUPPLICATION FOR ALL THE SAINTS."

Another thing we must do through our bodies is *prayer*. It's critical that we constantly *pray* and beseech God on behalf of our brothers and sisters in the Lord. "Wherefore I also, after I heard of your faith in the Lord Jesus, and love unto all the saints, cease not to give thanks for you, making mention of you in my prayers...." (Ephesians 1:15-16)

Prayer is our *communication line to God*, not only for ourselves, but also for those we love, even for those who have despitefully used us.

And finally, verse 19: "AND FOR ME, THAT UTTERANCE MAY BE GIVEN UNTO ME, THAT I MAY OPEN MY MOUTH BOLDLY, TO MAKE KNOWN THE MYSTERY OF THE GOSPEL."

This is always my prayer when I speak. That "the words of my mouth and the meditation of my heart would be acceptable" to Him. And that my words and my deeds would match and would only come forth from His presence. And, that He would give me the boldness and the power to show forth His "good, ac- ceptable and perfect will."

And this, of course, takes us back to our pivotal Scripture, *"...Be Ye Trans- formed* by the renewing of your mind, that ye may *prove* [by your words and actions] what is that good, and acceptable, and perfect, will of God." (Romans 12:2, emphasis added)

That we would, indeed, walk in God's Love and Truth...

Conclusion

As long as we have done the above steps, God promises us "we <u>will</u> be able to stand in the evil day."[12] Interestingly enough, in the Old Testament, one of the words we said *mind* was translated into was *reins*. The root word for the Hebrew *kilyah* (reins) is *keliy* which means *armor*. When our minds are renewed, we <u>will</u> have on the Armor of God.

"Putting on" the whole Armor of God (Ephesians 6) is a visual picture of what it means to "*put on*" Christ and to be "full of His Light," with "no dark part." Scripture tells us that Jesus' Life is the Light of Men. And this is the Life and the Light that God wants shining and beaming through each of us. (Romans 13:12b)

Again, the spirit of a man is the candle of the Lord. But once the Lord lights that candle, He doesn't want that Light (that Life) hidden away in our hearts, but set on a lampstand (in our souls) where *all* can see it.

"No man when he hath lighted a candle, putteth it in a secret place, neither under a bushel, but on a candlestick, that they who come in may see the light." (Luke 11:33)

God wants "our loins [to be] girded about [with truth] and **our lights burning**." (Luke 12:35)   These are the lights and the marks of the Spirit that Jesus will be looking for when He returns.

WILL HE SEE YOUR LIGHT? WILL HE KNOW YOU INTIMATELY? WILL YOU BE READY AND PREPARED TO GO WITH HIM?

"I beseech you therefore, brethren, by the mercies of God, that ye present your bodies a living sacrifice, holy, acceptable unto God, which is your reasonable service. And be not conformed to this world; but *be ye transformed* [how?] *by the renewing of your mind*, that ye may prove [in your actions] what is that good, and acceptable, and perfect will of God." (Romans 12:1-2, emphasis added) In other words, *live the truth*.

Jesus' promise to us is that if we will renew our minds, He will transform our lives!

Endnotes:

1.   Philippians 3:8

2.   Leviticus 16:12-13

3.   Galatians 5:22

4.   Philippians 1:21

5.   1 Kings 9:3

6.   Psalm 119:25, 50, 107, 154; 1 Peter 3:18

7.   Philippians 3:9

8.   Colossians 1:27; Romans 5:5; Hebrews 8:10

9.   See Chapter Four, "Shield of Faith."

10.   Romans 6:18 and 22; 1 Peter 4:1

11.   2 Corinthians 6:7; 1 Corinthians 2:4

12.   Ephesians 6:13

Scriptural References:
Chapter Sixteen

Results of a Renewed Mind (CHART 25)
A. We can now present our *offerings in righteousness* (Deuteronomy 33:19; Malachi 3:3; Psalm 4:5; 51:19; Romans 6:13, 16, 19; Psalm 51:18-19) and come boldly into the Holy Place
  1. We now have *free access* to God (Exodus 30:34-36; Hebrews 4:16; Isaiah 33:14-17; Psalms 5:7a; 24:4) and boldness to enter because of Christ's blood (Hebrews 10:19, 22)
    a. We are welcomed in the Holy Place because we are spotless and pure (Psalm 24:3-4; 32:6; 65:4; Hebrews 4:16; 10:19; Ephesians 1:4; 1 Corinthians 3:17; Deuteronomy 23:14)
    b. This is the only way to *see* God (Hebrews 12:14; Psalm 24:3-4)
  2. Our offerings are now acceptable to God and pleasing to Him, because they are in His righteousness and not our own (Philippians 3:9; 4:18; Malachi 3:3-5; Hosea 6:6; Psalm 4:4-5; 24:3-4; Ezekiel 20:41a; Ephesians 1:4).
    a. Self life has been *put off* and Christ's Life *put on* (Malachi 1:11; Ephesians 5:2; 2 Corinthians 2:14-15; 4:10-11). We have "exchanged lives" (Philippians 1:21; 3:8; Galatians 2:20; Romans 6:4c; 2 Corinthians 4:10)
    b. "[His] Beauty for [our] ashes" (Isaiah 61:3; 1 Peter 1:7)
    c. God is now our righteousness (Isaiah 54:17; Jeremiah 23:6, 16; Hosea 2:19; Micah 6:5; Romans 3:22)
    d. We have on the "breastplate of righteousness" (Ephesians 6:14)
  3. The aroma from these offerings are a sweet smelling savor to God (a "cloud of incense," Leviticus 16:13). We can't offer "strange incense" (Exodus 30:9; 2 Chronicles 26:16-22; Leviticus 10:1-2) or it will be a "stink" unto God (Isaiah 3:24). These are things we do in the flesh, out of our *own* power and ability (John 3:6; 4:23-24; 6:63)
  4. Our offerings of righteousness are of God's savor, not our own (Acts 10:4, 31; Malachi 1:11). Our scent has finally been changed (Jeremiah 48:11; 1 Samuel 10:6)
  5. God's Name shall be great among the gentiles and in "every place incense shall be offered" (Malachi 1:11)
B. These are the *true worshipers of God*, who worship Him in spirit and truth (John 4:23-25; Psalm 96:9; 1 Kings 3:6; Ephesians 1:4; Philippians 3:3)
  1. These are the true lovers of God (Hosea 6:6; Numbers 16:5-7; John 14:15) who have brought His *Agape* Love full circle back to God at the Incense Altar (Ephesians 5:2; John 15:9; Acts 10:4,31)
  2. We have become *one* (Matthew 22:37) and are worshiping Him in the "beauty of His Holiness" (Psalms 29:2; 90:17; 96:9; Isaiah 33:17; Ephesians 1:4)
C. God will now *hear our prayers*, because they are according to His Will (1 John 3:22; 5:14-15; John 9:31; 14:14; 15:7; 16:23; Revelation 5:8; 8:4; 2 Chronicles 7:14; Psalms 69:13; 141:2; 1 Thessalonians 5:17)
  1. Our prayers are "in His Name" (in His Character, in His Image) (John 16:23)
  2. He will now answer our prayers (Acts 10:4; Psalm 145:19; Romans 8:27)
  3. And, He will "heal" our land (2 Chronicles 7:14)
D. We will be able *to see all things from God's perspective* (Genesis 50:20; Isaiah 26:3; Job 13:15; 1 Corinthians 2:14-16; Hebrews 11:13; Deuteronomy 32:11-12; Romans 8:28; John 11:28)

1. We will soar above our enemies, like the Eagle (Psalm 18:33; Isaiah 59: 19)
2. We will have total peace and joy in the midst of our trials (Philippians 4: 7; John 16:33; Acts 2:28; Job 13:15; Romans 14:17; Luke 1:79)
3. These are the true *overcomers* (1 John 5:4-5; Romans 12:21; Revelation 2:7, 11, 17, 26; 3:5, 12, 21). "He that overcometh shall inherit all things" (Revelation 21:7)

E. We will be *experiencing all the functions of the Mind of Christ* (1 Corinthians 2:12, 16; Isaiah 11:2-3)
1. Our minds will be totally renewed (Romans 12:1-2; Ephesians 4:23)
    a. We have *put off* the habits of the flesh (Ephesians 4:22)
    b. And we have *put on* Christ (Ephesians 4:24)
2. We are walking in *intimate knowledge of God,* fearing Him only
3. We are able to discern the true from the false (Isaiah 11:3-4)
4. Our body is reined in (James 3:2) and Christ's actions are showing forth (Galatians 6:17)
    a. We are *single-minded* (Luke 11:34a; Ephesians 4:23-24)
    b. Our light is "on the top of a candlestick" (Luke 11:33). We are ready and waiting for Him (Matthew 25:1-10)
5. We will be serving the law of God (Romans 7:25b; 12:2)

F. We have been *transformed into Christ's Image* (Philippians 1:21; John 10:10; 1 John 4:12, 17; Ephesians 1:4; 3:19; 1 Peter 1:22; 1 Timothy 1:5)
1. This is our goal and our purpose for being called a Christian (Romans 8: 29; Ephesians 3:19)
2. We are experiencing Christ's Life in place of our own (1 John 1:2; 4: 12c; 2 Corinthians 4:11). He has become our Life itself (Philippians 1:21; Galatians 2:20)
3. We are proving in our actions, what is the "good, acceptable and perfect Will of God" (Romans 12:2; Ephesians 5:10; 1 Corinthians 13:11)
4. We are walking in Love and Truth (3 John 3-4; 2 John 4, 6; Psalms 26:3; 86:11)—the Pillar of Cloud and Fire (Isaiah 4:5; Proverbs 16:6; Zechariah 2:5, 10) (See Appendix)
5. As God's Spirit fills and overflows us, we'll experience "springs," "fountains," "pools" and "rivers" of water (Isaiah 41:18; Proverbs 5:15)
6. Our Light is on "the top of a candlestick" (Luke 11:33-34)

G. We are equipped for battle because we now have on *the full armor of God* (Ephesians 6:13-19; 1 Peter 1:13; 5:8-9; Matthew 24:42-22; Psalms 18:32-35, 39; 140:7; 149:6; 1 Thessalonians 5:8; Isaiah 11:5; 59:19). We are prepared for battle (2 Samuel 22:33-40; 2 Corinthians 6:7; Nehemiah 4:18; Psalm 18: 32)
1. "Armor of Light" (Romans 13:12-14), "with no dark part" (Luke 11:34-35; 12:35; Ephesians 5:8; Isaiah 62:1; 61:10; Psalm104:2a; James 1:17)
2. We have *armed* ourselves with the same thoughts as Jesus (1 Peter 4:1b)
3. We don't war against "flesh and blood" (2 Corinthians 10:3-6; 11:3; 1 Peter 5:8), but against principalities and powers (Ephesians 6:12)
4. We have "done all to stand" (Ephesians 6:13; Luke 1:79; 1 John 1:7)
5. We are prepared, equipped and watching (Matthew 26:38-41; Deuteronomy 6:12; 1 Peter 5:8-9; Mark 14:35; Luke 22:40)
6. The whole Armor of God is: (Ephesians 6:13-19):
    a. Our "loins girt about with truth" (our *new spirit*) (John 6:63; Psalm 119:25, 50, 107, 154; 1 Peter 3:18; Hosea 2:20) and faithfulness
    b. Having on the "Breastplate of Righteousness, faith and Love" (our *new heart*) (1 Thessalonians 5:8; Isaiah 59:17; 2 Corinthians 6:7)

c. Our feet "shod with the preparation of the Gospel" (our *new willpower*) Our willpower is what equips our souls (our feet) with the gospel of peace. It's God's authority and His power to put *off* the garbage and to *put on* Christ (John 13:8-10)

d. "Taking the shield of faith to quench the fiery darts" (our *free choice*). "Faith is the victory that overcomes" (1 John 5:4; Psalms 5: 12; 91:4; Revelation 12:11)

e. Taking the "helmet of salvation" (our *soul*) (Isaiah 59:17; 61:10; 62: 1; 1 Thessalonians 5:8)

. Jesus's Life is the light of men and this is what He wants shining and beaming through us (Luke 12:35-36; John 8:12; Matthew 5: 14; Philippians 2:15c-16; Psalm 96; 2-3; Proverbs 4:18)

. Salvation is a lamp that burneth (Isaiah 62:1; Psalm 96:2; Matthew 5:14)

. These are the signs and the marks of the Spirit that Jesus will be looking for when He returns (Isaiah 62:1; Ephesians 5:8; Matthew 25:10; 2 Corinthians 4:11; Galatians 6:17; Philippians 3:14; Daniel 12:3)

f. The "sword of the Spirit," which is the Word of God (in *our body*)— a "two-edged" sword (Jeremiah 51:20; Ezekiel 12:25; Isaiah 11:4b; Luke 2:35)

g. "Praying always" (again, in *our body*) (Ephesians 1:15-16)...that utterance may be given that I might "speak boldly" (Psalm 17:2; Romans 12:1-2)

Therefore, "Let your loins be girded about [with truth], and your lights burning." (Luke 12:35)

Will Jesus see your light? (Matthew 25:1-12) **Will you be ready to go with Him?** (Matthew 25:10; Luke 12:35-36, 40; 2 Corinthians 4:11; Galatians 6:17; Daniel 12:3; Revelation 19:7c; 2 Peter 3:14)

His sheep know (*oida*) **His voice**. (John 10:4) **Will He know** (*oida*) **you?** (Matthew 7:22-23; 25:12; Luke 13:25, 27; Revelation 3:1, 8, 15-16)

Section Seven:
Appendices

"I have no greater joy than to hear that my children walk in *Love* and *Truth*..."

3 John 4

A History of the Subconscious

In the early 1700's, two hundred years before Freud, William Law, the English classic writer, wrote a book titled *The Power of the Spirit*, recently re-edited by Dave Hunt. Law states, "*Memory* is the faithful repository ["a place where things are deposited and stored"] [1] of all the fine things that self has ever done, and lest any of them should be lost or forgotten, memory is continually setting them before self's eyes. ...*Imagination*, as the last and truest support of self, lays unseen worlds at his feet, and crowns him with secret revenges and fancied honors. This is that natural self that must be denied and crucified, or there can be no disciple of Christ."[2]

Law's statements are particularly interesting, because *memory* and *imagination* are precisely the two words philosophers have used for centuries to describe the subconscious or the unconscious. [3] "Memory is knowledge of past particulars."[4] Its primary function is *retention*. Recollection occurs through activating connections which have been formed and retaining them. This can happen by chance recall or by purposeful pursuit of the past."[5]

The following is a summary of the secular history of the subconscious. While we do not adhere to some of the philosophies of these earlier investigators, this survey demonstrates that the idea of the subconscious far predates Freud.

Since the early 1600's, the Western world has rediscovered the idea of the unconscious "that had long been taken for granted in Greek and Christian writings."[6] In fact, the idea of an unconscious goes back to Augustine (A.D. 354-430), who believed memory extended *beyond* the grasp of the conscious mind.[7] "Nothing can be utterly forgotten if, as Augustine suggests, what seems to be forgotten remains in the memory."[8] "The ancients speak of the memory as a *storehouse of images*. Every variety of thing which can be perceived can be stored up in the memory."[9] Augustine lived 1500 years before Freud.

Then came Aquinas (1225-1274 A.D.) who developed a theory of the mind covering "processes in the soul of which we are not aware."[10] Most mystics of that time assumed that insights are gained by a process of inner reception during which the conscious mind is passive.[11] This was about 600 years before Freud.

Around the 1600's, the West recognized these unconscious mental processes and began seeking to scientifically validate the unconscious and the separation of the conscious mind from material processes. The purpose of this was to link conscious awareness and behavior with a system of processes of which one is not immediately aware and to establish this connection without losing the benefits of scientific precision.[12] This was around the time of Descartes who lived 300 years before Freud.

After Descartes (1637), acceptance of the validity of the subconscious became widespread and by the close of the 19th century, this view was popular in Germany and Britain and, to a lesser extent, in France. "The existence of the unconscious had become a common assumption of educated and psychological discussions."[13] Ralph Cudworth (1678) wrote: "There may be some vital energy without clear consciousness or express attention—Our human souls are not always conscious of whatever they have in them...There is also a more interior kind of plastic power in the soul...whereby it is formative of its own cogitations, which it itself is not always conscious of...."[14]

Among the 17th and 18th century figures exploring the subconscious were Leibnitz who thought that "ordinary perceptions were the summation of countless small ones, each of which we are not aware of, because they lie below the threshold"[15]; Rousseau (18th century) who tried to explore the subconscious of his own temperament; and J.G. Hamann, a German religious philosopher, who also studied the deeper levels of his own mind as evidenced in his experiences of conversion, in the emotional life and in imaginative thinking. "How much more the formation of our own ideas remain secret." [16]

Between 1750 and 1830, a number of German philosophers and poets increasingly emphasized the emotional and dynamic aspects of the subconscious. Among them were: Herder, Goethe, Fichte, Hegel and Schelling.[17] Other German thinkers in the 1880's who made the idea of an unconscious a "commonplace thing" were: Schopenhauer, C.G. Carus, Gustav Fechner, Eduard von Hartmann and Nietzsche.[18] Hartmann (1869), anticipating Freud, wrote, "consciousness only touches the surface...."[19] Even many of the romantic writers and poets in Germany and England echoed a sense of the powerful, dark and yet creative aspects of the unconscious mind. Thus, J.P.T. Richler wrote, "The unconscious is really the largest realm in our minds...."[20]

This same theme is also alluded to in Francis Schaeffer's writings in more recent decades: "We are constantly brought face-to-face with the concept of the subconscious, which is the realization that man is more than that which is on the surface. All too often the evangelical Christian acts as though there is nothing to man except that which is above the surface.... "[21]

Others who preceded Freud in the study of the subconscious were William Hamilton, student of medicine; psychiatrist, H. Maudsley; and naturalist, W.B.

Carpenter (1879). During the 1870's several theories of unconscious organic memory were developed. And between 1880 and 1910, many physicians and philosophers in different countries were concerned with the various aspects of the unconscious.[22]

This brief review of the history of the unconscious clearly demonstrates that *"Freud was not the first to develop a systematic theory of conflicts in the unconscious."*[23] Consequently, believing that we do indeed have a subconscious (memory or unconscious) *does not make one Freudian or a psycho-heretic!*

Endnotes:

1. *The American College Dictionary,* Clarence L. Barnhart, Random House, New York, N.Y., pages 1028-1029.

2. *The Power of the Spirit,* William Law, Christian Literature Crusade, Fort Washington, Penn., page 142.

3. *Great Books of the Western World,* The Great Ideas II, Robert Maynard Hutchins, University of Chicago, Encyclopedia Britannica Inc., 1952, Vol. 3, Chapter 56, pages 133-157.

4. *Ibid.*

5. *Ibid.*

6. *The Encyclopedia of Philosophy,* Paul Edwards, Macmillan Publishing Co., New York, N.Y., 1967, Vol.1, page 185.

7. *Ibid.*

8. *Great Books of the Western World,* The Great Ideas II, Robert Maynard Hutchins, University of Chicago, Encyclopedia Britannica Inc., 1952, Vol. 3, Chapter 56, page 135.

9. *Ibid,* page 136.

10. *The Encyclopedia of Philosophy,* Paul Edwards, Macmillan Publishing Co., New York, N.Y., 1967, Vol.1, page 185.

11. *Ibid.*

12. *Ibid.*

13. *Ibid,* pages 185-186.

14. *True Intellectual System of the Universe,* Book 1, Chapter 3.

15. *The Encyclopedia of Philosophy,* Paul Edwards, Macmillan Publishing Co., New York, N.Y., 1967, Vol.1, page 186.

16. *Ibid.*

17.   *Ibid.*

18.   *Ibid.*

19.   *Ibid.*

20.   *Ibid.*

21.   *True Spirituality*, Francis A. Schaeffer, Tyndale House Publishers, Wheaton, Illinois, 1971, pages 132-133.

22.   *The Encyclopedia of Philosophy*, Paul Edwards, Macmillan Publishing Co., New York, N.Y., 1967, Vol.1, page 186-187.

23.   *Ibid*, page 186.

Greek Words for *Mind*

NOUS

In the Old Testament, *mind* is referred to as *spirit*; there is no equivalent term

In the New Testament, *mind* and *spirit* are two separate things (mind is the channel or the instrument through which the spirit flows)

Total conceptual process-which begins with the spirit and ends with the life actions—total inner man, real self, ego

Made up of many parts, all associated with the will (*mind* includes will and actions)

Only by a "renewed mind," can we prove what the Will of God is

Mind is referred to as *reins* (which must be prepared); our minds hold the *reins* of our lives

Mind is referred to as *kidneys* (which filter out debris and regulates blood supply (life)

Mind referred to as *eyes*

Our mind is the connection between the flesh and inner self; it's either controlled by Christ or alienated from life of God

Our mind is earthy and can attain to truth only as divinely instructed. God is the One who opens our minds

Mind is *root* of our "scent": either spirit of the world or Spirit of God

Mind is what receives Power of God and then His Image is set up in it; our mind is the embodiment of the Divine

Before the Spirit of God comes in us, our minds are *empty* (Ephesians 4:17-18) because of a "darkened" *dianoia* and they are alienated from life of God

After becoming a Christian, the Spirit of God fills our minds (a gift from God)

Mind is the instrument through which we come to know God, which is the purpose of the Mind of Christ in us

Nous is a term parallel to *faith*

RENEWED MIND (*NOUS*)

A mind of "quick understanding," a mind "made new," "back to youth again," "made young again"

A changed life; a new scent; a new beginning

Purpose of a renewed mind: to walk in the "fear of God" so that God's Will can be shown forth and proven

Renewal of Spiritual powers; causes a transformed life (transfigured)

Preparedness; make ready; put off garbage in thinking, put on Mind of Christ; put on the new man; equip, strengthen; establish; set in order; make oneself ready; bring something into existence

Arm oneself (put on the armor of God)

To cleanse away *grease*; to "shod feet" with equipment; to be groomed

Free of woundedness

MIND OF CHRIST (*NOUS*)

Helps to purge us of sinful thinking and "prepares us for every good work"

Purpose: to know the things given to us by God; and to do His Will

"Eyes of the Lord"; a supernatural conceptual process

The Spirit of God gives us His Wisdom, His Understanding, His Counsel and Strength,
   His Knowledge and helps us walk in the Fear of the Lord
Results in a spiritual attitude (spiritually minded) (*phroneo*)

DIANOIA

A part of our mind; *dia* means a "channel," *noia* means "of the mind"
Always associated with our will, our volition
Power of disposition; concerns acts of our will; power to carry out our will
Power to choose; power of relinquishing oneself or doing as one wants; includes
   our free choice
Discretionary control; resolve
Advisement—purpose; deliberate; impulse of the will
Our will and the power to perform it, our volition, power to carry out our will
Before we are believers, our *dianoia* is "darkened" (power of sin controls it); we
   were "enemies" in our *dianoia*
Becomes illuminated by God's Wisdom
Spiritual consciousness—power of perception; key to our spiritual life
Faculty of spiritual discernment, spiritual counsel and strength from God; He helps
   us to make critical choices and gives us strength to carry them out
Understanding comes from God's counsel; we take His advice
Place we prepare, make ready, "gird up the loins of our *dianoia*"; readiness
The Mind of Christ is in our heart until we appropriate it with our *dianoia*

BOULE (O.T., *esa*)

Counsel of God ; divine counsel and purpose
Gift of God
Whole purpose of God; complete content of apostolic message
Secret intentions; establishes; supports; assists; nurtures
Irrefragable determination; intention after deliberation
Foreknowledge of God
Pre-determined plan; pre-consideration
Volition; advice

KRATOS (O.T., *gibbor*)

God's Strength comes only when we *rein in* ourselves (*krateria*)
Power of God; always refers to God's Strength and His control
Right to put forth power; dominion that God gives us; power to put off and put on
Mastery over self; self-control; management-control; Spirit-control
Take possession of; right of possession
Old Testament word is *gibbor* which means *overcoming*; mastery over self

EXOUSIA

Free choice; denotes freedom; freedom of action
Right to put forth power; delegated power; right to act and exercise authority
Divinely given power; delegated to us by God; linked with God's Will
Comes from God's Spirit
Authority to make choices we don't feel; power to lay down life
Freedom to choose another direction; stand in contradiction to existing power struc-
   ture; freedom from emotions

BOULEMA

Part of our willpower (*dianoia*); choice free of emotion
Result of our free choice (*exousia);* decision of our will
Counsel to make critical choices
Purpose; determined resolve; faith choices; non-feeling choices
Result of God's Counsel (*boule*); every purpose is established by counsel; carrying
    out God's counsel
Deliberate determination; steerage; management of ropes
Mental act; contrary to original impulse
Choosing to follow God's Will by faith, not feelings

THELEMA

Instinctive desire; desires of the flesh; emotional desires
Desires motivated by the flesh
Devil has *thelema* also
We have authority (*exousia*) over our emotional desires
Emotion of being desirous; emotional element
Natural impulse; stronger than our resolve

IXCHUS

Physical strength; our own ability; has to do with physical body
We receive God's strength, when we are "weak"
To be capable; power we ourselves possess
Can be God's ability or our own

Other Words for *mind*:

ENNOIA

Thoughts of Christ
What takes place in our *nous*
Purpose—Christ's Mind

NOEMA

The thoughts themselves (closely related to wisdom and understanding)
Organ of the heart; takes place in the heart (before we are born again)
Human thoughts from "unrenewed" *nous*; corrupt human thoughts
Before we are born again, Satan has access to *noema*
After we are born again, we are to "bring these *noema* into captivity" (now in our
    soul)
Noeo are God's Thoughts in our hearts; we receive these through faith

SOPHIA (O.T., *chockmah*)

Wisdom of God's Will; to make wise; *ear* to hear; to show the Will of God
Secrets; spiritual truths; blueprint
Attribute, not activity
Given and revealed by the Spirit; tree of *life*; gift from God
Mediator of revelation; teacher
God's Word is true wisdom; Jesus is our Wisdom; He is our life

SUNESIS (O.T., *binah*)

> To set together; to understand; to comprehend; to discern or distinguish
> Uniting perception with what is perceived; judging; separate morally
> *Eyes* have been opened; none of us have this naturally
> Consideration precedes actions
> Understanding of heart (God's Wisdom)
> Gift of God

LOGISMOS

> Imagination (comes from *logos*; can be God's or our own)
> Calculation; computation; judgment; reason
> We are to "cast down" our own reasonings, our own imaginations

PHRONEMA

> Result of *nous*
> Attitude; mind set; overview
> Understanding what the Will of God is
> We can be "spiritually minded" or "carnally minded"
> Maturity is "setting aside childish things"
> Becoming "wise" is the result of a renewed mind
> Those who are prepared, ready and wise are ones who do God's Will
> Attitude of obedience; set your mind
> Becoming one Mind with God; attaining God's viewpoint
> Attitude of humbleness
> Opposite attitude is *foolish* (those without understanding)
> Means to lose savour

Hidden Chambers
Scriptures using the Hebrew word *"cheder"*
(The innermost part, the hidden—inner—chambers or the secret place)

Proverbs 20:27, "The spirit of man is the candle of the Lord, searching all the *inward parts* (*cheder*) of the belly." (Why would the spirit search our inward parts, if not to reveal hidden sin in us, to us?)

Proverbs 18:8, "The words of a talebearer are as wounds, and they go down into the *innermost parts* (cheder) of the belly." (If there is no "secret place" or "hidden chambers," where is this "innermost part"? This idea is also presented in Proverbs 26:22)

Proverbs 20:30, "The blueness of a wound cleanseth away evil: so do stripes the *inward parts (cheder)* of the belly." (Again, what does God mean that *stripes* cleanses away evil in the inward parts of the belly, if we don't really have an innermost part or hidden chambers where evil can hide?)

Ezekiel 8:12, "Then said He unto me, Son of man, hast thou seen what the ancients of the house of Israel do in the dark, every man in the *chambers (cheder) of his imagery*? For they say, the Lord seeth us not..." (What could the "chambers of his imagery" mean, if not some secret, hidden internal place?)

Deuteronomy 32:25 tells us that "The sword without, and terror *within* (*cheder*)..." (The reference for this verse in the Companion Bible says that "terror comes from the inner chambers.")[1]

Proverbs 7:27 speaks about "...going down to the chambers *(cheder)* of death."

Proverbs 24:4, "And by [intimate] knowledge *(daath)* shall the chambers (*cheder*) be filled with all precious and pleasant riches." (Intimate knowledge of God happens internally. How can these chambers be filled with "all precious and pleasant riches," if there really isn't an *innermost part*?) (Psalm 51:6, follows this same line of thinking. David says "...in the *hidden part* Thou shalt make me to know wisdom." (God wants this hidden part cleansed of the secret faults and then filled with all precious and pleasant riches, i.e., God's wisdom.)

2 Chronicles 18:24 instructs about going "...into an inner chamber (*cheder*) to hide thyself." (Of the 38 Scriptures that use the word *cheder*, over half refer to a secret, hidden, innermost chamber or parlour.)

Other Scriptural references to the "hidden chambers":

Psalm 19:12-13, "Who can understand his errors? Cleanse Thou me from *secret* faults." Who are these faults secret from? God? I think not. Ourselves? Yes, this is what David is imploring God to do; to show him and cleanse him from secret faults.)

2 Corinthians 10:4-5, ("for the weapons of our warfare are not carnal, but mighty through God to the pulling down of *strongholds;)* casting down imaginations, and every high thing that exalteth itself against the knowledge of God..." (What are the strongholds? Where do they exist, if not in our innermost part? Are these *strongholds* simply conscious attitudes and physical behaviors? Or, could they be the secret hidden faults that David asks God to cleanse him from in Psalm 19:12?)

Deuteronomy 7:20, "Moreover the Lord thy God will send the hornet among them, until they that are left, and *hide themselves* from thee, be destroyed." (Where is it that the "hornets" hide themselves from us? Why does God send them, if not to expose what's hidden there, so we'll see it ourselves and deal with it?)

Psalm 51:6, God wants "...truth in the *inward parts:* and in the *hidden part* Thou shalt make me know wisdom." (What does this refer to, if there is no *innermost part* or *secret place*?)

Hebrews 12:15 and Acts 8:21-23, Paul refers to a "root of bitterness." (What does he mean by "root" if not something hidden or covered up?)

Jeremiah 17:9 tells us that "The heart is deceitful above all things, and desperately wicked: who can know it?" (This means that no one but God, can understand the wickedness of our hearts. In other words, there are things in our hearts that are hidden and secret, even to us!) Daniel 2:30, Psalm 44:21 and 1 Corinthians 14:25 follow this same line of thinking. God is the only One who "knows the secrets of our hearts" because He is the only One who can see, search and try our hearts. (Luke 9:47; Proverbs 21:1-2; Hebrews 4:12; 1 Chronicles 29:17; Jeremiah 11:20; 17:10; 20:12 and many more).

Other Scriptures that hint at covered up, closed up and hidden things that we are not even aware of, are Psalms 139:23-24; Acts 8:21-23; Psalm 16:7; Ezekiel 14:1-6; 1 Corinthians 4:5; 2 Corinthians 4:2 and more.

Endnotes:

1.   *The Companion Bible*, Kregel Publishers, P.O. Box 2607, Grand Rapids, Michigan, page 284.

Knowing God Loves Me

(The following Scriptures are paraphrased with emphasis added)

Herein is Love, not that we loved God, but that HE LOVED US and sent His Son to be the propitiation (substitute offering) for our sins. (1 John 4:10)

He bowed the heavens also, and came down. (Psalm 18:9)

He sent from above, He took me, He drew me out of many waters. (Psalm 18:16)

The Lord appeared unto me saying, `Yea, I have loved thee with an everlasting Love.' (Jeremiah 31:3)

I have engraved thee upon the palms of my hand. (Isaiah 49:16)

I will never leave thee or forsake thee. (Hebrews 13:5)

For the mountains shall depart and the hills be removed; but my Lovingkindness (hesed) shall not depart from thee, neither shall my covenant of peace (rest) be removed, saith the Lord that hath mercy on thee. (Isaiah 54:10)

As the heaven is high above the earth, so great is His Mercy (lovingkindness) towards them that fear Him. (Psalm 103:11)

Many are the afflictions of the righteous. But the Lord delivers them out of them all. He keepeth all his bones; not a one of them is broken. (Psalm 34:19-20)

When you pass through the waters (trouble) I will be with you; and through the rivers, they won't overflow you; when you walk through the fire, you won't be burned; neither shall the flame kindle upon thee. For I am the Lord...You are precious in My sight and I LOVE YOU. (Isaiah 43:2-4)

God commendeth His Love toward us in that, while we were yet sinners, Christ died for us. (Romans 5:8)

For God so loved the world, that He gave His only begotten Son. (John 3:16)

Greater Love hath no man than this, that a man lay down his life for his friends. (John 15:13)

Behold, what manner of Love the Father hath bestowed upon us, that we should be called the sons of God. (1 John 3:1)

...having loved His own which were in the world, He loved them unto the end. (John 13:1)

What shall separate us from the Love of Christ? Shall tribulation, or distress, or persecution, or famine, or nakedness, or peril, or sword?...I am persuaded that neither death, nor life, nor angels, nor principalities, nor powers, nor things present, nor things to come, nor height, nor depth, nor any other creature shall be able to separate us from the Love of God which is in Christ Jesus, our Lord. (Romans 8:35, 38-39)

Bibliography

Bibles:

The Companion Bible, King James Version, Kregel Publications, Grand Rapids, Michigan, 1990.

The New Scofield Reference Bible, King James Version, C.I. Scofield, Oxford University Press, New York, New York, 1969.

The Thompson Chain-Reference Bible, King James Version, B.B. Kirkbride Bible Co., Inc., Indianapolis, Indiana, 1988.

The Interlinear Bible, Hebrew, Greek, English, Associated Publishers and Authors, Wilmington, Delaware, 1976.

The Septuagint Version: Greek and English, Sir Lancelot C.L. Brenton, Zondervan, Grand Rapids, Michigan, 1970.

The Zondervan Parallel New Testament, Greek and English, Zondervan Publishing Co., Grand Rapids, Michigan.

Technical:

Ancient Israel—Religious Institutions, McGraw Hill, New York, New York.

Berman, Joshua, *The Temple*, Jason Aronson Inc., Northvale, New Jersey, London, 1995.

Botterweck, G. Joannes & Helmer Ringgren, *Theological Dictionary of the Old Testament,* Vol.1-3, Eerdmans, Grand Rapids, Michigan, 1974.

Breese, David, *Seven Men Who Rule the World from the Grave*, Moody Press, Chicago, Illinois, 1990.

Bromiley, Geoffrey, *Theological Dictionary of the New Testament* (abridged), Eerdmans, Grand Rapids, Michigan, 1978.

Brown, Colin, *New International Dictionary of New Testament Theology*, Vol.1-3, Zondervan, Grand Rapids, Michigan, 1978.

Chafer, Lewis Sperry, *Systematic Theology,* 'Pneumatology,' Vol. 4 of 8, Dallas Seminary Press, Dallas, Texas, 1947.

Cutman, J., *The Temple of Solomon,* Scholars Press, Missoula, Montana, 1976.

Edershem, Alfred, *The Temple: It's Ministry and Services*, Hendrickson Publishers, Peabody, Massachusetts, 1994.

Encyclopedian Judaica, 16 Vols., Keter Publishing House, Jerusalem, Israel.

Encyclopaedia Britannica, 30 Vols., University of Chicago, Chicago, Illinois, 1985, 12: 125; 19; 582-587.

Hutchins, Robert Maynard, *The Major Works of Sigmund Freud*, Vol.54, Great Books of the Western World, Encyclopedia Britannica, University of Chicago, 1952.

Jamieson, Fausset and Brown, *Critical and Experimental Commentary,* 6 Vols., Eerdmans, Grand Rapids, Michigan, 1948.

Johnson, Paul, *Modern Times,* Harper and Row, New York, New York, 1983.

Josephus, Flavius, *The Complete Works of Josephus*, Kregel Publications, Grand Rapids, Michigan, 1981.

Keil, C.F. and Delitzsch, F., *Commentary of the Old Testament,* Eerdmans, Grand Rapids, Michigan, 1977.

Lauzun, Girard, *Sigmund Freud: The Man and His Theories*, Fawcett, Greenwich, Connecticut, 1962.

Murray, John, *The New International Commentary on the New Testament,* The Epistle to the Romans, Eerdmans, Grand Rapids, Michigan.

Peletzsch, Keil, *Commentary on the Old Testament*, Eerdmans, Grand Rapids, Michigan.

Reznick, Rabbi Leibel, *The Holy Temple Revisited*, Jason Aronson Inc., Northvale, New Jersey, and London, England, 1990.

Soltau, Henry W., *The Holy Vessels and Furniture of the Tabernacle*, Kregel Publications, Grand Rapids, Michigan.

Strong, James H., *Strong's Exhaustive Concordance,* Baker Book House, Grand Rapids, Michigan, 1985.

The International Standard Bible Encyclopedia (old and new), Vol. 1-4, Eerdmans, Grand Rapids, Michigan, 1939, 1979.

The Pulpit Commentary, Eerdmans, Grand Rapids, Michigan, 1963.

Theological Dictionary of the New Testament, Vol. 1-10, Eerdmans, Grand Rapids, Michigan, 1976.

Theological Wordbook of the Old Testament, Vol. 1 and II, Moody Press, Chicago, Illinois.

The Zondervan Pictorial Encyclopedia of the Bible, Zondervan, Grand Rapids, Michigan, 1975.

Unger, Merrill F., *Archaeology and the Old Testament*, Moody Press, Chicago, Illinois.

Unger, Merrill F., *The New Unger's Bible Dictionary*, Moody Press, Chicago, Illinois, 1988.

Vine, W. E., *An Expository Dictionary,* Revell Company, Old Tappan, New Jersey, 1966.

Vine, W. E., *The Expanded Vines,* Bethany House, Minneapolis, Minnesota, 1984.

Wilson, William, *Old Testament Word Studies,* Kregel Publications, Grand Rapids, Michigan, 1978.

Zodhiates, Spiros, *Lexicon to the Old and New Testaments,* AMG Publishers.

General:

Anderson, Ray S., *On Being Human*, Eerdmans, Grand Rapids, Michigan.

Bellheimer, Paul, *Don't Waste Your Sorrows,* Christian Literature Crusade, Fort Washington, Pennsylvania, 1977.

Bobgan, Martin and Deidre, *The Psychological Way—The Spiritual Way*, Bethany House, Minneapolis, Minnesota.

Bonhoffer, Dietrich, *The Cost of Discipleship,* Macmillan Publishing Company, New York, New York, 1963.

Brownback, Paul, *The Danger of Self Love,* Moody Press, Chicago, 1982.

Christenson, Larry, *Renewed Mind,* Bethany House, Minneapolis, Minnesota, 1993.

Collins, Gary, *The Magnificent Mind*, Word Inc., Irvine, Texas, 1984.

Dawson, Joy, *Intimate Fellowship with God by Fear of God*, Baker Book House, Grand Rapids, Michigan.

Edman, Raymond, *They Found the Secret*, Clarion Classics, Zondervan, Grand Rapids, Michigan, 1984.

Greene, Oliver B., *The Mind,* The Gospel House, Greenville, South Carolina.

Harper, *The Love Affair*, Eerdmans, Grand Rapids, Michigan, 1982.

Hession, Roy, *The Calvary Road,* Christian Literature Crusade, Fort Washington, Pennsylvania, 1977.

Hession, Roy, *Be Filled Now,* Christian literature Crusade, Fort Washington, Pennsylvania.

Hoekema, Anthony A., *Created in God's Image*, Eerdmans, Grand Rapids, Michigan.

Hunt, Dave, *Beyond Seduction*, Harvest House, Harvest House, Eugene, Oregon, 1987.

LaHaye, *The Battle for the Mind,* Revell Books, Grand Rapids, Michigan, 1980.

Law, William, *Wholly for God*, Andrew Murray, Bethany Fellowship, Minneapolis, Minnesota, 1976.

Lawless, Agnes*, A Place for God to Live*, Aglow Bible Study #11.

Lindsey, Hal, *Combat Faith,* Bantam Books, New York, New York, 1986.

Maloney, *Wholeness and Holiness,* Baker Book House, Grand Rapids, Michigan.

Nee, Watchman, *The Normal Christian Life*, Christian Literature Crusade, Fort Washington, Pennsylvania, 1970.

Pink, Arthur W., *The Holy Spirit,* Baker Book House, Grand Rapids, Michigan.

Pink, Arthur W., *The Divine Covenants*, Baker Book House, Grand Rapids, Michigan.

Scofield, C. I., *The New Life in Christ Jesus*, The Gospel House, Greenville, South Carolina, 1915.

Sparks, Arthur, *What is Man?*, Pratt Printing Company, Indianapolis, Indiana.

The Institute of Basic Youth, *The Eagle Story*, Rand McNally, Oak Brook, Illinois,

Articles:

Hierowitz, Victor, "Inside Solomon's Temple," *Bible Review*, April, 1994.

Man, H.G., "The Two Pillars Before the Temple of Solomon," *Basor*, 88, 1942, Pages 19-27.

Schmidt, E., *Solomon's Temple in Light of Other Oriental Temples*, 1902.

Scott, R.P.Y., "The Pillars Jachin and Boaz," *JBL* LVIII, 1939, Page 143.

"Solomon's Temple Resurrected," *Biblical Archaeologist* IV, 1941, pages 20-24.

"The Temple of Solomon," *Biblical Archaeologist* VII, 1944, Page 73.

Waterman, L., "The Damaged Blueprints of the Temple of Solomon," *JNES* II, 1943, Page 284.

Wylie, C.C., "On King Solomon's Molten Sea," *Biblical Archaeologist* XII, 1949, Pages 86-90.

Glossary

The purpose of this glossary is to briefly present the thoughts that lie behind important words found in this book. Many people use these same words and phrases differently. This glossary is to help clarify how I have used these words in this text. No attempt is made to be exhaustive. More information may be gathered by consulting the Outlines at the end of each chapter and the Index.

ABUNDANT LIFE. Intimately experiencing God's Life flowing through us to others. First-hand knowledge of God's Love, Wisdom, and Power.

AGAPAO. To totally give ourselves over to something. To become one with it. To yield our wills and our lives to something.

AGAPE. God's supernatural Love that is *not* dependent upon how we feel, what we think, or what we want; upon others' reactions; or upon our circumstances. God's Love is an unconditional, one-sided, freeing, and other-centered Love. It's always a *gift of Love,* i.e. a present with no strings attached.

ALIGNING OUR FEELINGS. God is the one who brings our feelings in line with our choices. He is the one who makes us "feel" *genuine* after we have made a faith choice or a contrary choice.

BLOCKING GOD'S LIFE. God's Spirit is quenched because of emotional choices we have made which prevents His Life from coming forth from our hearts.

BODY. The *vehicle* or the carrier for the expression (showing forth) of our life.

BROKENNESS. To be broken means to have our true *self-life* uncovered, exposed, brought into captivity, and weeded out.

CARNAL CHRISTIAN. A Christian living two lives. One who has Christ's Life in his heart and yet, because of sin, is showing forth self-life in his soul. Double-mindedness.

CHAIN REACTION OF OUR SOUL. Our thoughts stir up our emotions; our emotions create our desires; and our desires produce our actions.

CHESED **LOVE**. Old Testament word for God's merciful (longsuffering) and yet, strict (disciplinary) Love. Only God knows the perfect balance between these two aspects of His Love.

CHRIST IN US. This is God's Life in our hearts (His Love, Wisdom, and Power), our hope of glory. This is the hidden man of the heart.

CLEANSED HEART. A heart that is cleansed of sin. Christ's Life in this person's heart is now free to flow out into his life (soul), because there is nothing blocking or quenching it. This person has made faith choices to follow what God desires over his own will.

CLEANSED VESSEL. An open channel through which God can pour His Life to others.

CONFESS. To admit our own responsibility for sin and for being separated from God.

CONFORMED TO THE WORLD. Depending upon our own thoughts, emotions, and abilities (not God's) just like the world does.

CONTRARY CHOICES. A choice that goes against what we think, feel, and want to do. A choice to walk by faith and not feelings. By our supernatural willpower, we have God's authority and power to make this kind of a choice. God then *aligns our feelings* with that choice.

CORDS OF LOVE. God wants to control, lead, and guide our lives through His reins of Love, i.e. the Mind of Christ.

CORDS OF SIN. Things from our hidden chambers (subconscious) that Satan uses to bind us, hold us in his power, and direct our lives.

COVERED HEART (grease). A sin-laden heart. God's Life is quenched in this person's heart because of his emotional choices to follow his own will over God's. Thus, his heart is covered and God's Life is unable to come forth to his soul.

DELIVERANCE. A process of *freeing and healing* from our thoughts, emotions, and desires that are contrary to God's. This comes from our moment-to-moment choices.

DENY SELF. Choosing to *set aside* what we want, feel, and desire and choosing instead, to do what God wants. Setting aside our own thoughts, emotions, and desires that are contrary to God's so that God's Life can come forth from our hearts. Barring *ourselves* from following our self-life.

DIE TO SELF. Choosing to set aside and relinquish ourselves to God (becoming a cleansed vessel), so that His Life can come forth from our hearts.

DISOBEDIENCE. Not doing what God's Word says, but instead following our own thoughts and feelings.

DOUBLE-MINDED. A believer living two lives (twice souled). God's Life is in this person's heart, but it's quenched and blocked because of *emotional choices*. Therefore, self-life is being shown forth in his soul.

DOUBT. Not believing what God says and not trusting Him to perform His Will in our lives.

EMOTIONAL CHOICES. Choices to follow our own will over God's, prompted by our own self-centered thoughts and desires.

EXCHANGED LIFE. We are <u>not</u> to copy Jesus' Life, we are to literally *exchange* lives with Him. We are to surrender, yield, and give Him our self-life, He then gives us His supernatural Life. And we can say, like Paul, "for me to live is Christ."

EXPERIENTIAL KNOWLEDGE OF GOD. First-hand experience of God's Life flowing through us. Intimacy with His Love, Wisdom, and Power.

EXPERIENCING OUR REAL THOUGHTS AND EMOTIONS. Honestly talking to God about what we are thinking and feeling so we will know exactly what to confess and give over to Him.

FAITH. The choice to obey and trust God no matter how we feel, what we see, or what we think. Being fully persuaded that God is real and that He will do what His Word says.

FAITH CHOICES. Non-feeling choices to obey God's Will, regardless of our own thoughts, emotions, and desires.

FEAR OF THE LORD. To stand in reverential awe of who God is and what He is doing in our life; and because of this, fleeing anything that would quench that intimacy.

FLESH. The part of our old human nature (soul and body) that has not been regenerated yet. The residue (remainder, left-over garbage, dross) that still remains in our soul from the "old man."

FOLLOWING GOD. Worshipping and serving God only. Becoming *one* with Him—one heart, one will, and one soul. Not only being willing to suffer and be rejected as He was, but also willing to die (to self) as He did.

FORGIVENESS. Unconditionally releasing anyone who has wronged us.

FREE CHOICE. (*exousia*) The freedom to either choose to follow what God has counseled us and trust in His ability to perform it; or the freedom to choose to follow what we think and feel. Born-again believers are the only ones who truly have a free choice, because they are the only ones who have another power source within them to perform something different than what they naturally think, feel, and want to do.

FULNESS OF GOD. Filled with God's Life. God's Love and Wisdom flowing through our souls to others by God's Power.

GIVE OVER TO GOD. Relinquish or *sacrifice* to God anything that is not of faith. (Inner Court Ritual).

GOAL OF A CHRISTIAN. To be *conformed into the Image of Christ* and to live His Life (His Love) instead of our own.

GOD'S IMAGE. God's supernatural Life (His Love and His Wisdom) coming forth through us—the Image we were created to bear from the very beginning.

GOD'S LIFE. His supernatural Love (*Agape*), His Thoughts (*Logos*) and His Power (D*unamis*).

GOD'S LOVE NEVER FAILS. God's Agape Love never stops flowing to our hearts.

GOD'S WILL. God has two types of will. They are *thelo* (His instinctive, emotional desires), things that please Him, and *boule* (His planned purposes), the resolve of His Mind.

GREASE OVER OUR HEARTS. Psalm 119:70 speaks of the *fat* that will cover our hearts and quench His Life, when we make emotional choices.

HEART. (*kardia*) The origin of life. The place where life is started, created, or begun. The inward *motivation* of our lives.

HEART LIFE. As Christians, the life that now resides in our hearts is Christ's Life: His Love, His Thoughts, and His Power. An analogy would be the *root life* of plants. No one can see this life—it's hidden. (Just as God is the only One who knows our hearts.)

HIDDEN CHAMBERS. (*Cheder*) Innermost part. The hidden part of our soul where we hide and bury all of our painful experiences, hurts, and fears, thinking no one will see; no one will know. If not cleansed, these buried things can eventually become the motivation of our lives, rather than God's Life in us.

HUMAN LOVE. Affection love (*storge*), sexual love (*eros*), and friendship love (*phileo*) are three natural loves that we are born with. All are dependent upon what we think, feel and want to do, upon others' reactions, and upon our own circumstances. Human loves are always going to be conditional, two-sided (reciprocal), bondage, and self-centered loves. They will always be *need loves*.

HUMBLE OURSELVES. Willingness to set aside what we want, think, and feel and become *obedient unto death* (of self) doing what God wants.

HYPOCRITE. A person whose words and deeds *do not* match. They profess to know God, but in deeds they deny Him. They are not living the truth.

IDENTITY AND SECURITY. Knowing that we are loved by the Father brings us true identity and security. This assurance comes only from knowing that His Love will never leave us or forsake us, no matter what we do. Love and identity have become synonymous.

IMAGE. An exact likeness of something or somebody.

IN THE SPIRIT. If we are believers, then we are always "in the Spirit" (God's Spirit is in us); however, it's our continual choice to *walk by the Spirit* and allow His Life in us to motivate all our actions.

IN THE FLESH. Because we have chosen to follow what we feel, think, and desire over God's Will, God's Life in our hearts has been quenched and our self-life is thus, motivating all our actions. (The "flesh" is a combination of our souls and bodies.)

INTELLECTUAL KNOWLEDGE OF GOD. Knowing *about* God from books we read and from what we hear others say, but not knowing Him intimately. Knowing Him only in our heads, not in our lives. Not experiencing His Life through us.

INNER COURT RITUAL. These are the four steps we must do each time we sin and find ourselves separated from God. They are: recognizing our self-life, confessing and repenting of it, giving it over to God, and then, reading God's Word. Doing these four steps daily is what it means *to renew our minds*—to totally give ourselves over to Him. This is called the Inner Court Ritual because it's what the Priests did daily in the Inner Court of the Temple in order to deal with sin.

JESUS IS MY LIFE. God's Life is freely flowing from this person's heart out into his soul. He has yielded and relinquished his self-life to God and God has given him His own Life in exchange.

KNOWING GOD LOVES ME. Experiencing first-hand in our daily walk God's Love filling us, His Wisdom guiding us, and His power strengthening us.

LAY OUR LIFE DOWN. Choosing to yield, surrender, and relinquish our self-life to God (becoming a cleansed vessel), so His Life can flow from our hearts.

LIGHT. God's Life in us. God Himself (the Holy Spirit) is the Source of all Light (Life).

LIVING A LIE. The *words* of this person's mouth do not match what he does in *action*.

LIVING THE TRUTH. The *words* of this person's mouth ("Jesus is the answer to everything") match the *actions* of his life.

LOVE (*agapao*) GOD. To totally give ourselves over to God. To confess, repent of and give over to God anything that has separated us from Him. To deny ourselves, pick up our cross, and follow Him (Matthew 16:24). To obey His Word, trust His Spirit to perform His Word, and worship and serve Him only. To become an open and cleansed vessel where He can pour His Life to others through us. To become *one* with Him—one heart, one will, and one life. *To love God is to lose self.*

LOVE (*agapao*) OTHERS. To totally give ourselves over to others (before or instead of ourselves). To put their will and desires before our own.

MATURE CHRISTIAN. This is a person who continually recognizes his self-life and makes the appropriate choices to give that self over to God. One who is walking God's Way of Agape.

MEANING AND PURPOSE. This fulfillment in our lives can only come from loving the way God intended—first loving Him and then loving others.

MIND. (*nous*) Mind is a whole conceptual process that begins with the *spirit* that resides at the core of our being and ends with the *life actions* that are produced. The Old Testament defines our minds like "reins," "kidneys," or "spirit." Two other words used to describe our minds are "eyes" and "fountain." Our minds are not the *Light* or the *Source* of water, but only the instrument through which that Light and that water flow.

MIND BATTLE. Whoever directs and controls our thinking, controls our lives. That is why the battle rages in our minds, not our lives.

MIND OF CHRIST. A divine seven-fold conceptual process. It's God's Holy Spirit that creates God's supernatural thoughts in our hearts and through a process (again by His Spirit) produces them as Godly actions in our lives.

MIND RENEWAL. A renewed mind is one that has done two things: it has *put off* any sin (anything that is not of faith) and has *put on* the Mind of Christ.

NEW HEART. This is the brand-new heart (totally new nature) that God gives us when we are born again. This is Christ in us, the Hope of Glory. This new heart is filled with God's supernatural Love, Wisdom, and Power.

NEW MAN. This is Christ's Life from our hearts that we are to, moment by moment, *put on* in our lives—thus making us a "new man."

NEW SPIRIT. God the Holy Spirit has *lit* the candle of our spirit and we have become one with Him. He is now the *Power Source* and the *Light Source* of our lives.

NEW WILLPOWER. God's supernatural *authority* to choose His Will over our own and then His supernatural *power* to perform His Will in our lives.

OBEYING GOD. Choosing to obey God's Word (His Will) in our lives, rather than what we think, feel or want to do. This is the response that shows God we love Him.

OLD HEART. This is our old human heart, filled with our old human thoughts, emotions, and desires. It's the *old man* (evil and corrupt from birth) that is crucified and done away with at our new birth.

OLD MAN. This is the old, unconverted self (the old human heart), strong in deeds of sin. This is the part of our old human nature that was destroyed at our new birth and replaced with a totally new heart (Christ in us, our hope of glory).

OPEN VESSEL. A cleansed channel through which God can pour His Love to others.

OUR WILL. Like God, we have two types of will. However, they are not "perfect" like God's are. In the Greek, they are *thelema*—our own natural and emotional desires (things we take pleasure in) and *boulomai*—our disciplined willing (choices we make free of emotion).

OVERCOMER. A Christian who continues to make *faith* choices that prevail over his own self-centered thoughts, emotions, and desires (self-life). Thus, he enjoys freedom from self, circumstances, and other's responses.

PICKING UP OUR CROSS. Getting up and doing in action what God has asked, re-gardless of how we feel or what we think.

PILLAR OF CLOUD AND FIRE. Symbolic of God's presence. His *Love* shielding, guiding and protecting us, and His *Truth* exposing the way for us.

POWER OF SIN. An energy force that dwells in our unrenewed bodies, whose whole intent and purpose is to cause us to *veer off course* and *miss the mark*. The *mark* is to "be conformed into the Image of Christ." Satan uses the power of sin as his tool to stop this process and to revenge (or get back at) God.

PREPAREDNESS. We must constantly choose to "put of" the old and "put on" the new so that Christ's Life will be showing forth from us and not our own. Then, we will be *prepared and ready* for the battle ahead.

PRIDE. Choosing to follow what we think and feel over what God is prompting us to do. Pride is choosing our own way over God's. It's "I" before God.

PSYCHOLOGY. Self-knowledge. The study of knowing and building up our own thoughts, emotions, and desires.

PUTTING OFF THE OLD MAN. This is the old heart life that we "put off" when we are born again. Putting off the old man is two-fold: positionally (in our hearts) at our conversion and experientially (in our souls) in the gradual process of sanctification.

PUTTING ON THE NEW MAN. This is the "putting on" of Christ in our lives (souls). This new man is Christ's Life in our hearts that we are to daily "put on" in our souls.

RENEWING OUR MINDS. Putting off the garbage in our thinking and putting on the Mind of Christ. Specifically, it's the four steps of the Inner Court Ritual.

REPENT. *Changing our minds* about holding on to whatever has quenched God's Spirit in us and choosing, once again, to turn around and follow God.

SALVATION. This occurs when God lights the candle of our spirit and gives us His Life (His Light).

SANCTIFICATION. The process by which we learn how to "set aside" our own thoughts, emotions, and desires so that God's Life can come forth from our hearts.

SELF-CONTROL. Mastery over self. Power to *rein in* our souls. (Spirit-control)

SELF-IMAGE. Our total mental self-portrait, based on what we feel about ourselves, what others tell us about ourselves, and on our circumstances.

SELF-LIFE. Our own human thoughts, emotions, and desires that are contrary to God's and performed in our lives by our own human abilities.

SET FREE. Set free from our own thoughts, emotions, and desires; set free from other's responses; set free from our circumstances; and, set free from Satan's deceptions.

SIMPLICITY IN CHRIST. Having our thinking *folded together* (intertwined with) Christ. It's single-mindedness. Having on the Mind of Christ.

SINGLE-MINDED. Living one life (one soul). God's Life in our hearts is flowing freely into our souls. It's God's Life that others see in our souls. Living the truth.

SIN. Any choice that is not of faith quenches God's Spirit and covers our hearts with a layer of grease (Psalm 119:70). This then puts a barrier between God and ourselves—thus causing us to be temporarily separated from Him. His Love is not able to flow from our hearts out into our lives. The concordance defines sin as "missing the mark" ("mark" being conformed into the image of Christ).

SOUL (*psyche*). The *expression*, the outflowing, or the manifestation of our life. Our soul is a neutral area that is either going to be filled with God's Life (if we have made faith choices), or self-life (if we have made emotional choices).

SOUL-LIFE. The life others see, hear, and feel coming forth from us. This life can be God's Life, if we have made the appropriate choices, or our self-life, if we have quenched God's Spirit in us.

SPIRIT. (*pneuma*) Our spirit is the energy source, power source, or light source of our lives. It's the generator or engine of our souls. As Christians, that Light Source is God Himself in us.

SPIRIT-CONTROLLED THINKING. The ability to catch the negative thoughts before they stir up our emotions, desires, and actions.

SPIRIT-FILLED. Our soul is filled with God's Life from our hearts. We have chosen to set aside our own self-life and God's Life has freely come forth. It is a moment-by-moment decision to be filled with God's Spirit.

SPIRIT GRIEVED OR QUENCHED. God's Life in our hearts is blocked from coming forth into our lives (our souls) by sin. This is a sin-laden (or grease covered) heart.

SPIRIT OF THE LORD. God Himself. If we have asked God into our lives, He then is the Light and Power source of our lives.

SPIRIT OF WISDOM. All of God's supernatural *Thoughts* that He has already placed in our hearts at our new birth. His Word in total.

SPIRIT OF UNDERSTANDING. God's supernatural revelations. His secret insights to His Word. This gift is what "turns the lights on for us."

SPIRIT OF COUNSEL. Supernatural knowledge of God's Will for our lives. God's personal instructions to make godly choices.

SPIRIT OF STRENGTH. God's supernatural power to perform His Will in our lives. It's critical that God does both the counseling and the implementing so that He is the only One to get the glory.

SPIRIT OF KNOWLEDGE. This kind of knowledge is not "head knowledge," but knowing something through living experience of it working in your life. It's intimate, first-hand knowledge of God's Life as your own.

STRONGHOLDS. Things (hurts, memories, guilt, fears, bitterness, etc.) we have pushed down and stuffed in our *hidden chambers* (subconscious) that Satan uses as his "cords of sin" to bind us and hold us.

SUBCONSCIOUS. A reservoir of mostly untrue preprogrammed beliefs and assumptions; which tries to determine how we consciously evaluate all that happens to us in the present; and subsequently, what we often base our conscious choices on which then determines our actions.

SUFFERING. To suffer means to "bar ourselves from sin." We do suffer when we surrender, yield, and give over to God "anything that is not of faith" and that would eventually become sin if we held on to it.

SURVIVAL KIT. Eight steps back to freedom of Spirit, including the four Inner Court Ritual steps. A process by which we watch out for, are aware of, and deal with our sin, so we can stay open and cleansed vessels—loving God.

TAKE EVERY THOUGHT CAPTIVE. This means stopping and recognizing the hurts, anxieties, fears, and insecurities as they first come into our thinking. It means dealing with them then and not letting them go down into our hidden chambers to eventually motivate our actions.

TEMPLE OF GOD. God gives us "word pictures" in Scripture to help us understand the Gospel even more clearly. One word picture is that we are the "temple of God"— meaning that His Holy Spirit resides at the core of our being, just like the Shekinah Glory did in the Holy of Holies of Solomon's Temple. Solomon's Temple is an exact blueprint of the internal architecture of man.

TRANSFORMATION. *Taking off* the old self and *putting on* God. It's truly showing forth Christ's Life in place of our own.

TRUSTING GOD. Relying upon God's Spirit to perform His Word in our lives, rather than our own ability and power. Cleaving to God with unreserved confidence and being fully persuaded that He will do what He says.

TRUTH. Where the *word* and the *deed* match and become one. What we say with our words matches what we do in our actions. God's Word and His Spirit together are called *the Truth*, because God always performs His Word by His Spirit.

WALKING AFTER THE FLESH. This is emotionally choosing to follow what we think and feel over what God is prompting us to do, so that our bodies reflect and show forth self-life rather than God's Life. The flesh is a combination of our unregenerate souls and bodies.

WALKING AFTER THE SPIRIT. This is choosing by faith to follow God's leading no matter what. It's following His Will over our own desires so that our bodies will reflect and shine forth God's Life (His Light).

WEAPONS OF WARFARE. Scripture tells us that our spiritual instruments for fighting are God's Word, His Blood, and His Name. Ephesians 6 tells us the only way we can stand against the wiles of the enemy is to put on the whole armor of God and to use these weapons.

WILLING HEART. This is a believer who, like David, is willing to do all that God wills. This is a person who has an open and pure heart, allowing God's Life to flow freely.

WILLPOWER. (*dianoia*) Willpower is our will and the power to perform it. As Christians, we have God's supernatural authority to choose His Will over our own and then, the supernatural power to perform it in our lives. Our willpower is the *key* to our Christian walk because it determines whose life will be lived in our souls, God's or our own.

WORKING OUT OUR SALVATION. Intimate knowledge of God and walking in the Fear of Him is something we must "choose" daily. These capabilities of the Holy Spirit do not happen automatically.

WORSHIPPING GOD. Something that we do *on the inside*. Laying aside our self life, so God's Life can come forth. Prostrating ourselves before God. Praising Him for who He is.

YIELDING OUR MEMBERS. This is a person who has chosen to lay down his life and *his body*, so that God might use his body to perform His Will.

YIELD SELF. Surrender, relinquish and give over to God our self-life (our selves), so that God's Life can pour forth from our hearts.

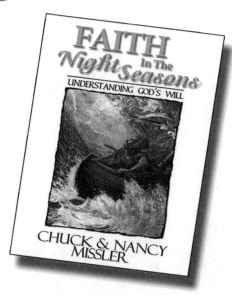

Plain & Simple Series

The Key
HOW TO LET GO AND LET GOD

This book teaches us the moment-by-moment steps to letting go of ourselves, our circumstances and others and *putting on Christ*. It gives us a practical guide to giving our problems to God and leaving them there. One of our most popular books.

Why Should I be the First to Change?
THE KEY TO A LOVING MARRIAGE

This is the story of the amazing "turnaround" of Chuck and Nancy's 20-year Christian marriage which reveals the dynamic secret that releases the power of God's Love already resident in every believer. Riveting, yet easy reading.

Tomorrow May Be Too Late
DISCOVERING OUR DESTINY

A simple, non-threatening and easy to read book that chronicles God's whole plan for mankind. In just a little over a hundred pages, it relates man's spiritual journey from the beginning of time to the very end, showing how God has been personally and intimately involved all along. Perfect for non-believers.

The Choice
HYPOCRISY OR REAL CHRISTIANITY

As Christians, we are faced with a constant choice: either to live our Christian life in our own power and ability, or to set ourselves aside and let Christ live His Life out through us. Written especially for youth.

Against the Tide
GETTING BEYOND OURSELVES

This little book gives the practical tools we need to implement "faith choices" in our lives. These are choices that set aside our natural thoughts and emotions, and allow us to love and be loved as God desires. Great for understanding emotions.

KHW

What is
The King's High Way?

The King's *High* Way is a ministry dedicated to encouraging and teaching Christians how to walk out their faith, i.e., focusing on the practical application of Biblical principles. Our passion is to help believers learn how to love as Jesus loved; how to renew their minds so their lives can be transformed; and, how to have unshakeable faith in their night seasons. Isaiah 62:10 is our commission: helping believers walk on the King's *High* Way by gathering out the stumbling blocks and lifting up the banner of Jesus.

For more information, please write to:

The King's *High* Way
P.O. Box 3111
Coeur d' Alene, Idaho 83816

or call:

1-866-775-KING

On the Internet:
http://www.kingshighway.org